COPING
AND HEALTH

NATO CONFERENCE SERIES

I   Ecology
II   Systems Science
III   Human Factors
IV   Marine Sciences
V   Air—Sea Interactions
VI   Materials Science

III HUMAN FACTORS

Volume 1   Monitoring Behavior and Supervisory Control
            Edited by Thomas B. Sheridan and Gunnar Johannsen

Volume 2   Biofeedback and Behavior
            Edited by Jackson Beatty and Heiner Legewie

Volume 3   Vigilance: Theory, Operational Performance, and Physiological Correlates
            Edited by Robert R. Mackie

Volume 4a   Recent Advances in the Psychology of Language: Language Development
            and Mother—Child Interaction
            Edited by Robin N. Campbell and Philip T. Smith

Volume 4b   Recent Advances in the Psychology of Language: Formal and Experimental
            Approaches
            Edited by Robin N. Campbell and Philip T. Smith

Volume 5   Cognitive Psychology and Instruction
            Edited by Alan M. Lesgold, James W. Pellegrino, Sipke D. Fokkema, and
            Robert Glaser

Volume 6   Language Interpretation and Communication
            Edited by David Gerver and H. Wallace Sinaiko

Volume 7   Alcoholism: New Directions in Behavioral Research and Treatment
            Edited by Peter E. Nathan, G. Alan Marlatt, and Tor Løberg

Volume 8   Mental Workload: Its Theory and Measurement
            Edited by Neville Moray

Volume 9   Human Evoked Potentials: Applications and Problems
            Edited by Dietrich Lehmann and Enoch Callaway

Volume 10   Human Consequences of Crowding
            Edited by Mehmet R. Gürkaynak and W. Ayhan LeCompte

Volume 11   The Analysis of Social Skill
            Edited by W. T. Singleton, P. Spurgeon, and R. B. Stammers

Volume 12   Coping and Health
            Edited by Seymour Levine and Holger Ursin

COPING
AND HEALTH

Edited by
Seymour Levine
Stanford University Medical School
Stanford, California

and
Holger Ursin
University of Bergen
Bergen, Norway

Published in cooperation with NATO Scientific Affairs Division

PLENUM PRESS · NEW YORK AND LONDON

Library of Congress Cataloging in Publication Data

Nato Internation Workshop on Coping and Health, Bellagio Study and Conference
    Center, 1979.
    Coping and health.

    (NATO conference series: III, Human factors; v. 12)
    Includes index.
    1. Adjustment (Psychology)—Congresses. 2. Stress (Psychology)—Congresses. 3.
Stress (Physiology)—Congresses. 4. Medicine, Psychosomatic—Congresses. I. Levine,
Seymour. II. Ursin, Holger. III. Title. IV. Series. [DNLM: 1. Adaptation, Psycholog-
ical—Congresses. 2. Attitude to health—Congresses. 3. Stress, Psychological—Congress-
es. W3 N138 v. 12 1979/WM172 N106c 1979]
BF335.N37 1979   616.07′1′019   79-28833
ISBN 0-306-40422-2

Proceedings of the NATO International Workshop on Coping and Health,
held at the Rockefeller Foundation's Bellagio Study and Conference
Center, Bellagio, Italy, March 26—30, 1979.

© 1980 Plenum Press, New York
A Division of Plenum Publishing Corporation
227 West 17th Street, New York, N.Y. 10011

PREFACE

This volume contains fifteen papers by invited participants
delivered at the NATO International Workshop on Coping and Health
held March 26 through March 30, 1979, at the Rockefeller Foundation's
Bellagio Study and Conference Center, Bellagio, Italy. The editors
of the book were co-directors of the workshop as well as
participants. The conference was a small conference consisting of
only 20 scientists and was designed to be an intensive period of
exchange of ideas dealing with a range of topics varying from
experimental models of coping through coping and its psychosomatic
implications. The exceptional beauty of the Bellagio Study and
Conference Center, the hospitality of the staff at the Conference
Center as well as the support of the administrative staff of the
Rockefeller Foundation, combined with the intensity and enthusiasm
of the participants made the conference a most memorable one for
those who attended it.

A special thanks is in order for the help and assistance of
Dr. B. A. Bayraktar, Executive Officer of Human Factors Program,
Scientific Affairs Division, NATO, and Miss Susan Garfield, Program
Director of the Rockefeller Foundation. Needless to say, without
their participation and help at all points in the organization and
planning of this conference, the conference would not have occurred.
However, the ultimate success of any conference is based on the
activity of the participants and in particular they deserve our
very special thanks not only for the excellent presentations and
ultimate manuscripts which were prepared, but in their devotion to
the task of interchanging ideas on a topic which has both important
implications for human function and ultimately profound consequences
for a number of pathophysiological states.

The ultimate success of any conference can not be determined
only by the quality of the volume, but on the impact on future
research in a new and important emerging area of behavioral medicine.

Seymour Levine, Ph.D.
November, 1979   Holger Ursin, Ph.D.

CONTENTS

Environmental Contingencies as Sources of
    Stress in Animals   1
  J. Bruce Overmier, Jeff Patterson,
  and Richard M. Wielkiewicz

Psychobiology of Coping in Animals:
    The Effects of Predictability   39
  Joanne Weinberg and Seymour Levine

Associative and Non-Associative Mechanisms
    in the Development of Tolerance for Stress   61
  Jeffrey Gray, Susan Owen, Nicola Davis,
  and Joram Feldon

Associative and Non-Associative Mechanisms in the
    Development of Tolerance for Stress: The
    Problem of State-Dependent Learning   83
  J.N.P. Rawlins

A Coping Model of Mother-Infant Relationships   87
  Seymour Levine

Contingent Stimulation: A Review of its Role
    in Early Development   101
  Megan R. Gunnar

Early Adolescence as a Life Stress   121
  Beatrix A. Hamburg

When is a Little Information a Dangerous Thing?
    Coping with Stressful Events by
    Monitoring vs. Blunting   145
  Suzanne M. Miller

Managing the Stress of Aging: The Role of
    Control and Coping   171
  Judith Rodin

Psychobiological Aspects of Life Stress   203
    Marianne Frankenhaeuser

Adrenocortical Responses of Humans to
        Group Hierarchy, Confinement and
        Social Interaction   225
    Joan Vernikos-Daniellis

Coping with Mental Work Load   233
    G. Mulder and L.J.M. Mulder

⨯ Personality, Activation and Somatic Health:
        A New Psychosomatic Theory   259
    Holger Ursin

Gastric Ulceration in the Rat: An Experi-
        mental Approach to Psychosomatics   281
    Robert Murison

Coping and Health - A Clinician's
        Perspective   295
    John Cullen

⨯ A Perspective on the Effects of Stress and
        Coping on Disease and Health   323
    Neal E. Miller

Contributors   355

Index   359

ENVIRONMENTAL CONTINGENCIES AS

SOURCES OF STRESS IN ANIMALS*

J. Bruce Overmier, Jeff Patterson
and Richard M. Wielkiewicz

Dept. of Psychology
University of Minnesota

Control over one's destiny, knowledge of the "laws of nature", privilege of choice, and freedom from conflict are among the higher values and goals espoused by individuals. Are these values cultur- ally determined and uniquely human, or are they rooted in the evol- utionary biology of the organism? The latter belief is fostered by continued recognition that learning is an evolutionarily derived adaptive mechanism (e.g., Spencer, 1855) the raison d'être of which is to engage behavioral dependencies (control), environmental contingencies (prediction), and behavioral-environmental alterna- tives (choices). Averill (1973) and White (1959), recognizing the general adaptive significance of control over the environment, have argued that need for control is a "deep seated" motivational variable of phylogenetic as well as ontogenetic origin. If striving for control, prediction, and choice are emergent properties of basic biological processes, we might well inquire about the pathological consequences for the organism--psychological or physiological--of not having control, of inability to predict, or of the absence of choice. These might be potent sources of stress for man in modern societies which tend toward ever more minute regulation. But how do we assess this within ethical bounds?

One tack is to assess these potential sources of stress by means of animal models. The consequences for animals placed in circum- stances which deprive them of control, prediction, or choice would be informative to the extent that analogous processes are operative

* Thanks are due to Dan Linwick and Marty Wurthman for their
  assistance in the preparation of this manuscript.

1

in humans. While animal models of behavioral dysfunction have hardly
been ignored (e.g., Fox, 1971, Hanin and Usdin, 1977; Keehn, 1979b;
Kimmel, 1971; Liddel, 1956; Maser and Seligman, 1977; Masserman,
1943; Serban and Kling, 1976; Zubin and Hunt, 1967), relative to
other topics psychologists as a group have neglected the effects of
stress on animal behavior, seeking instead to establish the functional laws relating "normal" behaviors to "normal" variations in
environmental conditions.

The behaviors we propose to discuss appear maladaptive and
dysfunctional and are no doubt statistically deviant and in this
sense "abnormal". However, this statistical deviance may often
arise from the infrequency with which the necessary environmental
conditions are encountered (contra Broadhurst, 1960). They need
not be the product of morbid or disordered learning mechanisms, and
thus are not "abnormal" in this latter sense (see Kimmel, 1971;
Ullman and Krasner, 1969). Both Keehn (1979a) and Davis (1979) have
sought to show analytically how the lawful mechanisms of behavior
control can trap the organism into bizarre, maladaptive response
patterns. The thesis is that such unprofitable behaviors are but
the end product of normal processes in special circumstances. The
problem is to identify these circumstances.

What we seek then are etiological principles governing
behavioral and somatic responses in stressful environments. Whereas
many searches for animal models of psychopathology focus instead upon
congruences of symptoms between animal and man in hopes that such
will provide a basis for empirically discovering effective
therapeutic techniques, our alternative is to identify causal
factors of behavioral dysfunction. Recognition of these not only
might allow us to avoid pathogenic circumstances, but may give
insight into the operative underlying mechanisms and hence to
therapeutic principles. Some have argued against the approach
endorsed here (e.g., Sandler, 1972). However, a schema identifying
critical characteristics and consequences of psychological stressors
would be a powerful heuristic, since even axiomatically incorrect
models can be productive (Lehman, 1972).

In seeking to identify environmental circumstances stressful
to organisms it is necessary to acknowledge the critical role of
biological factors as well. Not every instance of the critical
environmental circumstances will trap every individual into behavioral or somatic dysfunction. Just as species constrains the
symptoms that can be manifest, so too is the individual's biological
state a factor in what symptom, if any, will emerge. Constitutional
types have long been recognized in this context (e.g., Corson, 1971;
Pavlov, see Gray, 1964).

An experiment by Friedman, Ader, and Glasgow (1965) illustrates
how environmental circumstances and biological state can interact.

Four groups of mice were inoculated with a virus (Coxsackie B) and four groups with vehicle only. On the three days prior to the inoculation the groups had been given one of four treatments: pairings of a signal and a noxious event, presentations of unsignaled noxious events, presentations of the signal only, or simple placement in the experimental chamber. Four days after the injections, susceptibility to the virus as indexed by weight loss was determined. Only one group showed significant weight loss, the virus-inoculated group which had received signaled noxious events; it differed from all others. Thus, neither the environmental treatment nor the pathological agent acting independently was sufficient to cause "disease"; disease only resulted from an interaction between the biological condition (exposure to virus) and environmental circumstances (exposure to signaled noxious event).

Further analysis of biological factors involved in responses to stressful circumstances suggests that they can not only affect the consequences of such circumstances but they may serve as one index of their effects as well. That is, the effects of stressful environmental circumstances can be indexed by both somatic and behavioral consequences. One might then inquire as to the relationship between somatic and behavioral effects. Although one might intuitively expect behavioral management of stressors to be reflected in lowered physiological strain (e.g., Ursin, Coover, Kohler, Deryck, Sagvolden and Levine, 1975) and failure of behavioral management to be reflected in greater physiological strain, this need not be so. Indeed, in the "executive monkey" experiments (Brady, Porter, Conrad and Mason, 1958), all flaws recognized, subjects that showed behavioral management of the imposed shock schedule also suffered severe physiological symptoms even eventuating in death; their yoked partners which failed behaviorally in the initial sessions showed few physiological symptoms.

TABLE 1

FOUR POSSIBLE PATTERNS OF ADJUSTMENT TO STRESSORS

Behavioral Responses

		Successful Management	Abnormal Behavior
Physiologic Responses	Normal	A. Coping	B. Behavioral Strain
	Somatic Dysfunction	C. Physiological Strain	D. Adaptive Failure

The suggestion here is that if we look at a 2 x 2 matrix of absence or presence of physiological management versus absence or presence of behavioral management (Table 1), we see that four possible patterns of organismic adjustment to stressors exist. We clearly identify pattern A as coping and pattern D as adaptive failure. What, then, do the other two patterns (cells B and C) represent? Are they successful, and possibly alternative, adaptive strategies for the organism? The answer, in part, lies with the alternatives to a particular coping pattern. For example, with pattern C, we must ask what would have occurred had somatic dysfunction not. Is there a trade-off between behavioral dysfunction and somatic dysfunction; will one substitute for the other? And, what laws describe the final pattern of adjustment?

Answers to such questions may eventually be provided by a consideration of selected environmental circumstances which result in other than full coping (B, C, and D). We shall focus upon one circumstance--absence of control--which has been identified with behavioral strain. (Weinberg and Levine, Chapter II, this volume, discuss pathogenic implications of predictable versus unpredictable experience; see Murison, Chapter XII, this volume for a review of the somatic effects of psychological trauma.) As indices of behavioral strain we shall consider not only aberrant behaviors generated by a given set of circumstances but the effect of such experiences upon later performance and learning as well. We cannot explore all of the possibilities and shall restrict ourselves to environmental circumstances which prohibit behavioral control of events by the organism. Our general thesis is that absence or loss of control has negative consequences for the organism, resulting in one or more kinds of coping failures.

If control is of fundamental value to the organism, then we ought to be able to detect this in various ways. For example, animals should prefer to exercise control, while absence of control should have negative sequelae. We shall seek evidence on preferences for and consequences of control in this review.

PREFERENCE FOR CONTROL

We all have some intuitive idea of what is meant by "control", but precise statements are necessary for systematic analysis. For example, given that situations rarely allow complete control, a metric for comparing degree of control across situations is needed. Efforts to metricize degree of control have been made (Catania, 1971; Jenkins and Ward, 1965; Seligman, Maier and Solomon, 1971) with that by Gibbon, Berryman and Thompson (1974) being the most sophisticated. All focus upon the scheduled relationship between (a) the conditional probability of reinforcement per unit of time given that the organism responds ($p[rft/R]$), and (b) the conditional probability

of reinforcement per unit of time given that the organism does not respond (p[rft/no R]). When the former does not equal the latter (i.e., p[rft/R]) ≠ p[rft/no R]) control is said to be possible, the degree of which is some increasing function of the magnitude of this inequality. Of course, the degree of control is also partially determined by the animal's behavior. When the two conditional probabilities are equal, events are independent of the organism's behavior and the situation is said to be uncontrollable.

The data bearing upon whether or not organisms have a preference for control are limited and generally indirect but clearly suggest such a preference. There is a substantial body of data showing that animals given a choice between performing some operant response to earn food or accepting identical food freely available will choose to work for and earn the food (see Osborne, 1977, for review). This surprising preference for response dependent rewards might be dubbed "learned industriousness," but it is as likely a reflection of preference for control. This preference for earning rewards certainly is at variance with the "principle of least effort" (Hull, 1943; Tolman, 1955). However, the effects of effort are varied (Lewis, 1965) with some experiments even showing that effort expended in earning a reward enhances the value of that reward (e.g., Lewis, 1964).

Singh (1970) provided an excellent demonstration of the preference for response dependent food. In his experiments, rats were first trained to press a lever to earn food in one of two adjacent chambers according to some schedule (e.g., CRF); on alternate days the rats were exposed to the second distinctive chamber and there received free food deliveries in a temporal pattern and density matching that which they had produced in the work chamber (i.e., self-yoked). Then the rats were given a series of test days during which they could choose to be in either the work chamber and receive response dependent food or be in the free-food chamber and receive response independent food. Ninety-seven percent of the rats preferred the work chamber and some 89 percent of all food received was response dependent. The preference for response dependent food was maintained by 95 percent of the animals even when the density of reinforcement in the no-work chamber was 25 percent greater than that being earned in the work chamber.

The preference for response dependent reinforcement is so great that animals will even learn de novo to work for food in the presence of concurrently available free food (Neuringer, 1969). In addition, Stolz and Lott (1964) showed that hungry rats trained to run down an alleyway to earn a pellet of food would continue to run all the way down the alley to earn the pellet even if they had to wade through thousands of pellets identical to the reward in order to get to the goalbox! Since the rats were allowed unlimited access

to this mid-alley pile of food, continuing to run to the goalbox for a single pellet resulted in a net loss of food; nevertheless some rats persisted in this behavior for hundreds of trials. The authors could not explain these data but we take them as adding to the evidence that rats prefer to earn food rather than accept free food.

The preference for response dependent reinforcer deliveries over response independent ones may obtain even when the outcome event is a noxious electric shock. This is quite surprising given that the shock presentations would be expected to punish the immediately antecedent response. Nonetheless, Knapp, Kause, and Perkins (1959) showed that rats in a T-maze reliably (i.e., > 90%) chose immediate, response contingent shock over shock delayed 30 seconds. To the extent that delay degrades the response-shock contingency and hence control, this preference for immediate, response contingent shock also implies a preference for greater controllability with respect to aversive events.*

Some evidence suggests that the source of the preference for controllable events is modulation of the affective value of the reinforcer. In the appetitive case, Faircloth (1974) demonstrated that rats worked more vigorously in the first component of a chain schedule when this component was succeeded by a component of response dependent electrical brain stimulation (EBS) than when it was succeeded by a component of response independent EBS of equal density. Thus, response dependent EBS is apparently more reinforcing. Similarly, in the aversive case, Brennan and Riccio (1975) showed that shocks over which the animal has some control are less fear inducing than shocks which are uncontrollable. Apparently, control enhances positive affective value and decrements negative affective value. Taken together, the experiments cited in this section are consistent with the idea that organisms prefer to control events in their lives and do so because control modulates the affective value of the event.

ABSENCE OF CONTROL: BEHAVIORAL EFFECTS

If control is biologically important to organisms, its absence may be deleterious. Here we will review the consequences of exposure to uncontrollable events. The consequences are of two types: (a) effects upon subsequent learning and behavior (proactive effects) which have been pursued by Maier, Seligman, Overmier and associates, and (b) effects upon physiology which have been pursued by Miller, Weiss and associates. The behavioral effects will be examined first.

---

* It is difficult to interpret results such as these with certainty since controllability may imply predictability (Averill, 1973).

Basic Phenomena

In the classic proactive interference experiment, Overmier and Seligman (1967) explored the effects of exposure to inescapable shocks upon subsequent avoidance learning. They began by placing naive dogs in a restraining hammock enclosed in a sound-attenuating cubicle. These dogs received 64 five-second electric shocks of moderately high intensity for a dog (6 mA) delivered on an average of once a minute through electrodes fixed to their hind feet. At the end of this session, the dogs were returned to their home cages--they commonly walked there on a leash--for a rest. Then 24 hours later, the dogs were placed in a standard two-way shuttlebox and given signaled avoidance training by the method of emergence in which a failure to avoid is immediately followed by escapable shock (see Solomon and Brush, 1956).

The basic observation was that dogs pretrained with inescapable shocks in the hammock later failed dramatically in the avoidance task. Three features were prominent in this failure to learn avoidance: (1) in addition to not learning to avoid, they also did not learn to escape the moderate intensity (4.5 mA) grid shock; (2) even when occasional escape or avoidance responses did occur, they did not lead to increased probabilities of future escape/ avoidance behavior, contrary to the normal pattern; and (3) the dogs appeared "passive," showing much less persistence of strug- gling and vocalization in the continued presence of the shocks than naive dogs.*

Overmier and Seligman (1967) provided evidence against several initially plausible accounts of the phenomenon (learning of a motor response incompatible with the required avoidance response, habit- uation to shock, and sensitization induced overarousal) competing with the notion that the uncontrollable nature of the pretreatment shocks caused the proactive interference. Curarization (which blocks voluntary motor responses) during the pretreatment did not prevent the proactive interference. Nor did dogs show changes in sensitivity to the shock across the inescapable shock series as indexed by comparisons of the unconditioned cardiac responses to the inescapable shocks themselves. Heart rate (as indexed by

---

* The basic finding of proactive interference with subsequent
  escape behavior after exposure to inescapable shocks has since
  been confirmed in a variety of species (e.g., fish, Padilla,
  Padilla, Ketterer, and Giacolone, 1970; mice, Braud, Wepmann and
  Russo, 1969; rats, Looney and Cohen, 1972; humans, Hiroto, 1974;
  see Maier and Seligman, 1976 for review).

rate during shock minus the rate post shock, after Church, LoLordo,
Overmier, Solomon, and Turner, 1966) in response to shocks administered early and late in the inescapable series did not differ.
This result, presented in Figure 1, mitigates against accounts of
the interference on the basis of sensitization, habituation, or
even, in more contemporary analyses, stress induced analgesia, and
leaves intact the suggestion that the effects are the result of the
uncontrollability of the prior aversive events.

Overmier and Seligman also explored the strength of the
interference effect over variations in the inescapable shock
parameters. In addition to testing after 64 5-sec shocks, they also
tested after 640 0.5-sec shocks--a condition which reduced each shock

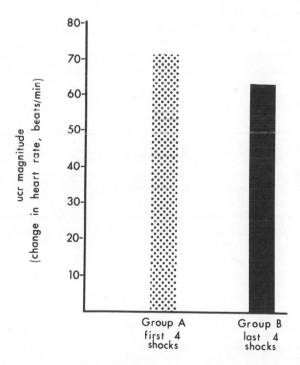

Figure 1

Cardiac responses of dogs to initial (Group A) and final
(Group B) shocks. Both groups had been immobilized for 75 minutes
by curare. Group B had been exposed to 60 5-sec shocks while Group
A received no shocks. The difference was not statistically
significant.

duration but held total shock exposure constant, and they tested
after 64 0.5 sec shocks--a condition which held number of shock
onsets constant but reduced total shock exposure. All shocked
groups were impaired but only the 64 5-sec and the 640 0.5-sec shock
groups significantly so in terms of escape/avoidance failures.*
Note specifically that when total shock exposure was held constant,
a series of inescapable 0.5-sec shocks still produced dramatic
interference with subsequent escape/avoidance learning. This
observation, often overlooked, presents a problem for those (e.g.,
Anisman, Decatanzaro, and Remington, 1978; Glazer and Weiss, 1976a)
who seek to explain the interference effect by reference to the
duration of the inescapable shocks (see discussion below).

The final observation of Overmier and Seligman (1967) was that
if one waited 48 or more hours rather than 24 to begin the avoidance
test trials, interference seemed to disappear. We would like to note
that this disappearance of interference may be attributable in part
to the choice of an insensitive index, one focusing upon failures to
respond during shock stimulation. This is suggested by a somewhat
different look at Overmier and Seligman's data from curarized dogs
(plus a heretofore unpublished point) on the time course of the interference in curarized dogs (Figure 2). The dotted bars, which combine
escapes and avoidances, confirm Overmier and Seligman's initial report.
The solid bars which are based only upon avoidance responses tell
another story. They indicate that avoidance learning is impaired
and that impairment persists for longer than six days (144 hours)
even though some responding has returned to normal. The increasing
trend in avoidance over the five time intervals is significant
(Whitney's test for trend, p < .05).

Overmier and Seligman's original report of the relatively short
time course of proactive interference stimulated Miller and Weiss
(1969) to suggest that the impaired escape/avoidance performance was
the product of some physiological after-effect, a suggestion Weiss
has vigorously pursued via an elegant series of experiments with rats,
which will be discussed later. The present observation, however, on
the long term trend in avoidance interference suggests, we think,
two things. First, Overmier and Seligman erred in implying that the
interference effect lasted only 24 hours. Recent experiments
(Seligman and Groves, 1970; Seligman, Rosellini and Kozak, 1975)
confirm this as an error. Second, it seems that Overmier and Seligman initiated an unfortunate trend toward a narrow focus on escape
learning in most subsequent experiments on the interference phenomenon (e.g., Anisman et al., 1978; Maier, Albin and Testa, 1973;

---

* However, Overmier and Seligman reported that latencies of the three
  shock groups did not differ among themselves and all differed from
  the naive control.

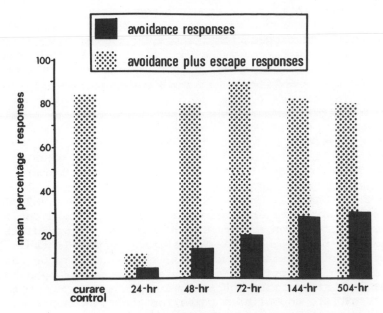

Figure 2

Time course of proactive interference with avoidance responding
(solid bars) and avoidance plus escape responding (dotted bars). Prior
experience with uncontrollable shock while curarized causes significant interference with avoidance learning several days after exposure to uncontrollable shocks (data from Overmier and Seligman, 1967).
Maier and Seligman, 1976; Maier and Testa, 1975; Seligman and Beagley,
1975). The focus upon escape behavior as a test response has
directed attention away from other--perhaps less dramatic but
possibly more important--consequences of exposures to uncontrollable
events. Overmier (1968) tried to counter this focus upon shock
escape behavior by demonstrating that prior exposure to 64 5-sec
inescapable shocks impaired dogs' learning in a pure avoidance task.
The results of this procedure make clear that proactive interference
is not dependent upon exposure to some minimum shock duration during
test, as some have recently implied in their attempts to explain
this phenomenon (e.g., Anisman et al., 1978).

Although the dogs in the initial experiments were exposed to
unsignaled, uncontrollable electric shocks in the pretreatment phase,
the experiments failed to provide definitive evidence that
uncontrollability was the critical causal factor. Seligman and
Maier (1967) quickly corrected this. They provided evidence that

<u>uncontrollability</u> of the pretreatment shocks caused the interference effect by comparing two groups: one group received a series of escapable shocks; a second group received inescapable shocks, the durations of which were determined by the first group, i.e., this group was "yoked" to escape subjects. The addition of a third group, naive with respect to shock in the pretreatment phase, constituted the now popular "triadic design."

Generality

So far the discussion has been restricted to instances of exposure to inescapable shocks in one situation disrupting shock-produced performance in another, i.e., shock-shock interactions. One might well wonder how general such a phenomenon might be with respect to other combinations of hedonic events. Cast this way, we see immediately that four classes of interaction exist. The shock-shock instantiation is a special case of one of these, in particular of the interaction between experience with one aversive event and learning based upon a second aversive event. If we substitute events of different hedonic qualities for either event one or event two, we obtain four classes of interaction in which the experience of uncontrollability might modulate subsequent adaptive behavior. These are shown in Table 2. Furthermore, within the aversive-aversive cell, similar effects of uncontrollability can be found when stimuli other than electric shock are utilized.

TABLE 2

CLASSES OF PROACTIVE INTERACTION EXPERIMENTS, INCLUDING EXEMPLARS

		Controllable Event in Learning Test	
		Aversive	Appetitive
Uncon-trollable Event in Pretreat-ment	Aversive	Porsolt, Le Pichon and Jalfre (1977) Altenor, Kay and Richter (1977) Payne, Anderson and Mercurio (1970)	Rosellini (1978)
	Appetitive	Wight and Katzev (1977) Rosellini and Bazerman (1976) Goodkin (1976)	Rhue and Brown (1978) Walker (1976)

In this regard, Altenor, Kay and Richter (1977) provided a
trenchant demonstration. In a 2 X 2 X 2 factorial experiment,
groups of rats were initially exposed to either footshocks or
submersion in 15°-C water; for half the rats exposed to each aversive
event the event was escapable (via nose-key or swimming through a
door, respectively) while for the other half the exposure was
inescapable and duration was yoked to an escape animal. Finally,
one half of each of these four groups was tested in a shuttlebox
for shock escape learning while the other half was tested in an
underwater U-maze for water escape learning. The subjects from
each of the inescapable pretreatment conditions were significantly
slower in performance on the test tasks than the corresponding
escapable pretreatment group. More importantly, the magnitude of
the proactive interference effect appeared no smaller when the
aversive stimuli were different in pretreatment and test than when
they were the same.

Payne, Anderson and Mercurio (1970) found that prior treatment
with inescapable shock proactively suppressed a different coping
response, shock-evoked aggression (see also Maier, Anderson and
Lieberman, 1972; Rapaport and Maier, 1978). Interestingly, Payne,
et al. (1970) showed that initial fighting experiences (which
were themselves generated by a series of inescapable shocks) prior
to the uncontrollable shock treatment partially blocked (immunized
against) the proactive suppression. This protective effect of
fighting in this behavioral test is of special interest because
Weiss, Pohorecky, Salman and Gruenthal (1976) have shown that the
opportunity to fight during exposure to uncontrollable shocks
reduced significantly the amount of gastric ulceration that
typically results from such shock exposures. Further, Stolk, Conner,
Levine and Barchas (1974) found that animals shocked inescapably
when alone suffered systemic norepinephrine depletion while those
shocked in pairs, thus allowing fights, did not. These results
identify fighting as an effective coping response, indexed both
behaviorally and somatically, which is also subject to proactive
interference effects.

The data derived from the other three classes shown in
Table 2 are markedly limited, in part because researchers are just
now becoming aware of the considerable importance of systematic
demonstrations of these interactions. Sufficient examples do exist
to suggest that further work in each class will be fruitful and will
lend insight into the mechanisms that underly proactive interference
effects.

Rosellini (1978) has demonstrated aversive-appetitive interference. In two experiments, prior exposure of rats to inescapable
shocks in one chamber (durations determined via yoking to escape
trained rats) interfered with subsequent learning to press a lever

to earn food in a second chamber, with greater interference under
delay of reinforcement conditions.

With respect to the appetitive-appetitive class of interactions,
Welker (1976) and Wheatley, Welker and Miles (1977) have provided
two exemplars, the first with pigeons and the second with rats. In
both, three groups differing in their initial treatments were used:
(1) a response dependent reinforcement group, (2) a matched group
which received reinforcers independently of behavior, and (3) a
naive control group. After several sessions of the initial treatments, all groups were required to press a treadle or lever to earn
food reinforcers. In both experiments, the group initially exposed
to response independent, uncontrollable food presentations was very
much slower to learn the required response. For example, while the
naive control and response contingent control rats in Wheatley et
al.'s experiment required 122 minutes and 47 minutes, respectively,
to achieve their 50th instrumental response, the group that received
response independent reinforcers required nearly 10 hours. Tomie
(1976) has obtained related results but argued that the interference
is context specific. This argument does not apply to Wheatley
et al.'s experiment which involved a change of context across
phases.

Even recognizing the powerful effects that flow from exposure
to uncontrollable events, the class of interaction which has produced perhaps the most surprising results is the appetitive-aversive
one. For example, Rosellini and Bazerman (1976) found that rats
exposed to 17 days of noncontingent food deliveries were significantly impaired relative to control groups in FR-2 shock-escape
responding in a shuttlebox. They also replicated this interference
effect when the test task was bar-pressing on an FR-3 schedule to
escape shock. Others have obtained results congruent with these
(Goodkin, 1976; Wight and Katzev, 1977). The effects of experiencing uncontrollability must be powerful indeed for initial appetitive
treatments to result in interference with escape from life-
threatening stimuli.

In this section, we have reviewed four classes of experiments
in which experiences with uncontrollable hedonic stimuli result
in the impairment of later response learning and performance. That
the effect is obtainable in all classes speaks to the broad
generality and biological significance of uncontrollability as a
behaviorally and associatively debilitating experience. Furthermore, the variety of induction and test operations by which the
phenomenon may be demonstrated argues against explanation in terms
of such specific mechanisms as incompatible motor responses (see
below) or yoking bias.*

---
* Church (1964) has argued that individual differences in stimulus
  (continued, page 14)

Boundary Conditions

Only the shock-shock interaction experiment has been studied
sufficiently to begin to identify boundary conditions. With
respect to shock parameters, the degree of interference is a
function of the interaction between number and duration of the
inescapable shocks (Glazer and Weiss, 1976a; Looney and Cohen, 1972;
Overmier and Seligman, 1967), the interaction between the intensities
of the inescapable shocks and the escapable test shocks (Jackson,
Maier, and Rapaport, 1978; Rosellini and Seligman, 1978), and the
qualitative properties of the shocks (Lawry, Lupo, Overmier,
Kochevar, Hollis and Anderson, 1978).

A second set of boundary conditions involves the nature of the
test task. In the experiments with dogs, escape/avoidance testing
was usually contingent upon emission of a single response (i.e., CRF
or FR-1). Interference with rat escape behavior, however, is
neither reliable, marked, nor persistent under FR-1 conditions
(e.g., Lawry et al., 1978; Weiss, Kriekhaus and Conte, 1968). Rather,
it is necessary to make escape/avoidance contingent upon two (FR-2)
or three (FR-3) responses in order to observe the interference effect
(e.g., Kelsey, 1977; Maier, Albin and Testa, 1973; Seligman and
Beagley, 1975).

While technically not boundary conditions, note should be taken
of operations which can eliminate an established proactive interference effect. Treatment with selected antidepressant drugs prior to
testing seems to reduce or eliminate it (e.g., Porsolt, Bertin and
Jalfre, 1977; Porsolt, LePichon and Jalfre, 1977), as does electroconvulsive shock (e.g., Dorworth and Overmier, 1977; Lambert, Harrell
and Emmett-Oglesby, 1978). Finally, forced exposure to the response
contingency (e.g., dragging a dog across the shuttlebox barrier,
thereby forcing the response) also eliminates the interference effect
(Seligman, Maier and Geer, 1968; Seligman, Rosellini and Kozak, 1975).

Theories of Behavioral Effects of Uncontrollability

A range of accounts of the proactive interference with behavior
arising from experience with uncontrollable events has been offered.
In general they have focused upon uncontrollable aversive events
and the aversive-aversive interaction class of experiment, and this
has colored the nature of the theories. The theories may for

---

* (continued from page 13) sensitivity can lead to artifactual differ-
    ences between master and yoked groups. Seligman (1978; versus Levis,
    1976; Costello, 1978) notes that the variety of stimuli that have
    been used to induce the interference effect counters such an explan-
    ation of it.

convenience sake be grouped as those which invoke (a) induced
neurochemical imbalances which impair motor response initiation,
(b) changes in motor response repertoire, or (c) cognitive
constructs.   Each merits comment in light of the extensive current
controversy (Alloy and Seligman, in press; Anisman, 1975; Anisman and
Waller, 1973; Levis, 1976; Maier and Jackson, in press; Maier and
Seligman, 1976; Weiss and Glazer, 1975.)

     Neurochemical. The time course of the proactive interference
effect reported by Overmier and Seligman (1967) led Miller and Weiss
(1969) to suggest that a time-bound neurochemical depletion-recovery
process underlay the behavioral observations. Weiss, Stone and Harrel
(1970) soon initiated a continuing series of experiments to give
plausibility to the hypothesis that changes in neurotransmitter levels
were causally involved in the impaired escape/avoidance responding
observed in Maier, Overmier and Seligman's experiments. The basic
strategy was to replicate in rats the full range of behavioral
effects--often with better control--and show that these were exactly
paralleled by appropriate changes in brain chemistry. Additionally,
they sought to show that alternative manipulations of brain chemistry
also led to the expected behavioral effects. This elegant series of
experiments is reviewed by Weiss, Glazer and Pohorecky (1976) and
Glazer and Weiss (1976a). A sampling of experiments and data will
provide insights.

     Weiss, et al. (1970; 1973) used matched triplets of escape/
avoidance trained, shock-yoked, and unshocked naive animals (the
triadic design) in a wheel turning apparatus. Their usual finding
was that brain norepinephrine levels in all brain regions were
depleted in the uncontrollably-shocked, yoked animals relative to
the master and the naive control animals. Similarly, after
noting that exposure to cold water swim (2°C) depletes brain
norepinephrine (Stone, 1970), Weiss and Glazer (1975) showed that
cold water swim impaired escape/avoidance learning in a shuttlebox
30 min later, while warm water swim (a treatment which does not
deplete brain norepinephrine) did not.

     There are, however, criticisms of interpretations of the classic
proactive interference effects in terms of neurotransmitter levels.
The post-stress brain assay or behavioral test interval used by
Weiss was not the 24-hour interval Maier, Overmier and Seligman used
to establish the proactive interference effect. Overmier and
Seligman (1967) were, in fact, concerned with preventing misattribu-
tion of interference effects to a short-term physiological exhaustion. This was the reason for the 24-hour treatment test interval.
Weiss and Glazer's (1975) own data (Exp. 3) suggest rapid dissipa-
tion of the neurochemical effects of stressors. Additional data
from several other sources indicate that stress-induced depletions
of brain amines are fully recovered within six hours (Barchas and
Freedman, 1963; Bliss, Ailion and Zwanziger, 1968; Bodnar, Kelly and

Glusman, 1978; Paulsen and Hess, 1963). Without neurochemical data
from subjects tested at the 24-hour interval, attempts to explain
the classic proactive interference effect in such terms must be
viewed with considerable caution.

A series of experiments on chronic exposures to stress (Weiss,
Glazer, Pohorecky, Bruck and Miller, 1975) also directly contradicts
their thesis. The logic behind the experiments was that if repeated
exposures to stressors block later norepinephrine depletion (Zigmond
and Harvey, 1970), then to the extent that the proactive interference
effect is dependent upon norepinephrine depletion, interference also
should be blocked by repeated exposures to stressors. Of concern
were four pairs of groups; one of each pair was tested for escape/
avoidance and one was assayed for brain norepinephrine. One pair
of groups was simply naive before tests (either behavioral or assay);
one pair received no pretreatments prior to the inescapable shocks;
one pair received repeated daily exposures to shocks prior to the
inescapable shocks; and finally, one pair received repeated daily
cold swims prior to the inescapable shocks which antedated the tests.
The desired effect was obtained in that the group pretreated with
repeated daily shocks showed no depletion of brain norepinephrine
and no behavioral interference, relative to both naive and no-pre-
treatment controls. These data are shown in Figure 3. However,
note that the group pretreated with cold swims showed substantial
norepinephrine depletion but no impairment in escape/avoidance
learning! This is inconsistent with the hypothesis that norepinephrine depletion directly mediates the proactive interference effect.

Recently, Glazer and Weiss (1976a,b) have differentiated
between a short-term response impairment (presumably based upon
neurotransmitter depletion) and a long-term proactive interference
effect. The former is obtained under conditions of exposure to
severe stressors followed promptly (e.g., 30 min) by testing for
escape/avoidance while the latter is obtained under conditions of
exposure to more moderate stressors followed by delayed testing
(e.g., 72 hours).

Glazer and Weiss (1976a,b) continue to argue that the phenomenon
found by Overmier and Seligman (1967) is an instance of the short-
term impairment process. They do so despite (a) their lack of any
evidence whatsoever of any neurotransmitter depletion in dogs, or
even rats, at the 24-hour stress test interval used by Maier,
Overmier and Seligman, (b) the independence of the interference
effect from the time constraints which neurochemical mediation
demands (e.g., Overmier, 1968; Overmier and Seligman, 1967, as
discussed above, Seligman and Groves, 1970), and (c) their own
data (1976a) which show that the "long-term" effect appears within
three hours after inescapable shock and is found at 24, 72, and
168 hours after the exposure to inescapable shocks--a range which
includes that used by Maier, Overmier and Seligman.

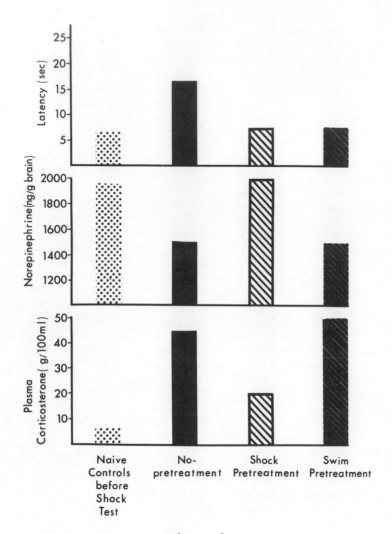

Figure 3

Effects of chronic exposure to stress upon plasma corticosterone, hypothalamic norepinephrine, and test performance (from
Weiss et al., 1975). Rats were pre-exposed to either daily cold-
water swims or electric shocks and then to a series of inescapable
shocks which were followed 30 minutes later by either a behavioral
test or chemical assays. Note that the group pre-exposed to cold-
water swims showed substantial norepinephrine depletion but no
escape/avoidance impairment.

Response Repertoire Changes. To account for impairment of escape
and avoidance behaviors after exposure to a series of uncontrollable
electric shocks, some theoreticians have hypothesized that changes in
the animal's response hierarchy or repertoire occur during the shock
pretreatment sessions (e.g., Anisman and Waller, 1973; Bracewell and
Black, 1970; Glazer and Weiss, 1976a,b; Levis, 1976; Weiss, Kriekhaus
and Conte, 1968). All further suggest that the responses which
become pre-eminent during the inescapable shock pretreatment later
emerge in the escape/avoidance task and successfully interfere with
the occurrence of the criterion response. The theorists differ
regarding the processes thought to mediate the development of these
incompatible responses.

Anisman and Waller (1973), for example, suggest that an
organism exposed to noxious stimuli reflexively engages in its
species specific defense reactions (flight, fighting and struggling,
and freezing) in a search for an effective coping response. They
argue further that when no effective flight or struggling response
is found, freezing becomes the dominant defense reaction. Later, in
the test task, freezing is elicited by the noxious stimulus and
prevents successful escape. Weiss, et al. (1968), based on the
observation that prior classical conditioning of rats impaired later
avoidance learning, also argue that proactive interference is caused
by freezing. However, they see freezing as a response elicited by
fear classically conditioned during the inescapable shock treatment.

Although shocks in the pretreatment phase may be response independent, shock presentations do evoke behaviors and those occurring
at shock termination may be reinforced by virtue of this contiguity.
Thus, a third account of the proactive interference effect argues
that if such behaviors are learned and if they are incompatible with
the test task, interference would be observed. This account has been
offered in several versions (Anisman, et al., 1978; Bracewell and
Black, 1974; Glazer and Weiss, 1976a,b; Levis, 1976). Consistent
with this hypothesis, Bracewell and Black showed that if shock
intensity during the pretreatment phase was positively correlated
with activity so as to punish activity and reward immobility, then
some impairment of subsequent escape learning resulted.

Anisman et al.(1978) measured activity during inescapable shock
treatments and related it to performance in escape tasks (see also
Anisman and Waller, 1972, for a related effort). They showed that
activity did indeed decrease with increasing durations of shocks
(Exp. 1, 8 and 11), and that exposure to inescapable shocks of
6-sec duration, but not 2-sec, resulted in proactive interference
with escape responding when opportunity to make the escape response
was delayed a few seconds (e.g., Exp. 5 and 9). In addition,
activity levels during the 6-sec inescapable shocks, but not during

the 2-sec ones, were significantly correlated with later escape
performance in a shuttlebox (Exp. 11). These results were taken as
confirmation of Glazer and Weiss' (1976a) hypothesis that the proactive interference effect is related to the decline in activity
that occurs with long inescapable shocks.

One implication of Anisman et al.'s (1978) hypothesis (see also
Glazer and Weiss, 1976a,b) and data is that proactive interference
should only arise from inescapable shocks of more than a few
seconds duration. This seems false. Kelsey (1977) reported
proactive interference in rats exposed inescapably to shocks of
mean durations of less than 2.9 to 3.9-sec. And, Overmier and
Seligman (1967) reported that a large number of half-second
uncontrollable shocks resulted in proactive interference in dogs.

A second implication is that a series of long inescapable
shocks leads to the learning of inactivity and thus activity level
during the inescapable shocks should predict later test task escape
performance. As a test, Lawry, Lupo, Overmier, Kochevar, Hollis and
Anderson (1977) exposed dogs to a series of 5-sec inescapable shocks,
measuring activity during the inescapable shocks, later escape
performance, and the correlation between the two. Parameters of
the shock (AC versus DC, constant versus pulsed) were varied in
order to generate a wide range of activity patterns. No significant predictive relationship obtained between activity during the
inescapable shock series (initial shocks, last shocks, the change
from initial to last shocks, and total activity over all shocks;
all $p > .16$) and later performance in the shuttlebox test. The
absence of any meaningful correlation between activity during the
pretreatment shocks and performance on the criterion task stands in
opposition to the theory of Glazer and Weiss (1976a,b) and the
relevant data of Anisman, et al. (1978). One source of the discrepancy may be Anisman et al.'s use of a type of shock source which
directly promotes the learning of immobility.

It is one thing to argue that inescapable shocks may lead to
reductions in activity, learned or otherwise (Anderson, Crowell,
Koehn and Lupo, 1976; Levine, Madden, Conner, Moskal and Anderson,
1973), and quite another to assert that such reductions are
responsible for all instances of the proactive interference effect
(see also Jackson, et al. 1978; Maier and Jackson, 1977). While
presence of the predicted correlations in some experiments lent
plausibility to the freezing and inactivity hypotheses, their
absence--and even inversion--in others disconfirms these hypotheses
as general accounts of proactive interference based upon exposure
to uncontrollable shocks.

Learned Helplessness Theory. While not denying that transfer of previously learned incompatible responses may contribute to observed proactive interference, nor that it must have some physiological substrate (e.g., Ellison, 1977), it seems that an adequate account of the phenomenon does not lie with the two possibilities discussed so far. In their original paper, Overmier and Seligman (1967) offered another hypothesis: they suggested that the source of the interference was a general "learned helplessness" which developed as a result of experiencing absence of control. This initial suggestion was presented without precision but "learned helplessness" was intended to mean some general cognitive state that transcended stimulus conditions and specific response learning. Seligman, Maier and Solomon (1971; Maier, Seligman and Solomon, 1969; Maier and Seligman, 1976; Seligman, 1975) have elaborated a theory based upon the learning of a cognitive state of helplessness arising from the experience with uncontrollable shock. It asserts that exposing naive animals to uncontrollable, inescapable, noxious events has three consequences. First, the emotional state of the organism is altered, with generalized anxiety and then emotional depression becoming predominant (Engle and Schmale, 1972; Seligman, 1975), both typically accompanied by physiological changes (e.g., Weiss, 1968; Engle and Schmale, 1967). Second, the incentive to respond in the face of aversive stimuli is reduced (Maier and Seligman, 1976). Third, there is an expectational or perceptual bias which impairs later learning about response-dependent reinforcers (Alloy and Seligman, in press). All three consequences arise from the cognition that hedonically important events are uncontrollable and independent of behavior.

The "learned helplessness" hypothesis as given is clearly a high abstraction about the mental processes of organisms. It is this emphasis on beliefs, expectations, and cognitions that is the source of criticisms of "learned helplessness" as an account of the proactive interference resulting from exposures to uncontrollable inescapable aversive events (e.g., Levis, 1976; Weiss, Glazer and Pohorecky, 1976). In one sense, the criticisms reflect metatheoretical biases and are simply one more instantiation of the controversy over mechanistic versus cognitivistic theories. Let us consider the evidential basis for the three components of learned helplessness.

A change in emotional state is both the least controversial and least emphasized (cf. Maier and Jackson, in press) postulate of helplessness theory, perhaps because it is not an intrinsic aspect of the proactive interference phenomenon. Much evidence for this effect was marshalled from outside the proactive interference literature (e.g., Anderson and Liddell, 1935; Broadhurst, 1960; Mineka and Kihlstrom, 1978; Mowrer and Viek, 1948; see reviews by Seligman, 1975; Maier and Seligman, 1976).

An incentive-motivational deficit has been inferred from the failures of animals previously exposed to inescapable shocks to initiate responding in escape-avoidance tasks. This failure to initiate responding, a performance deficit, is the primary feature of the proactive interference seen in dogs (Overmier and Seligman, 1967) and cats (Thomas and DeWald, 1977). Maier and Seligman (1976) argued that experiencing conditions under which shocks are independent of responding (i.e., $p[Sh/R] = p[Sh/no R]$) can lead to a belief in the inefficacy of responding--an expectancy that future responses will be futile; this belief/expectancy is the primary feature of learned helplessness and causes the loss of incentive for initiating responses in the presence of noxious events.

An associative deficit was inferred primarily on the basis of retarded learning (Baker, 1976; Jackson et. al., 1978; Overmier, 1968; Seligman and Maier, 1967). For example, Overmier and Seligman (1967) reported that if dogs which had previously been exposed to inescapable shocks did successfully escape in the test task, they were much more likely to revert back to passively accepting the escapable shock on the next trial than naive dogs.

Most of the work which has attempted to demonstrate an associative deficit (Baker, 1976; Jackson, et al., 1978; Maier, 1970; Maier and Testa, 1975; Overmier, 1968; Seligman, et al., 1975; Testa, Juraska and Maier, 1974) has failed to unambiguously implicate such a factor by ruling out other possibilities such as motivation, incentive, and even attention. The detailed criticisms of Anisman, et al. (1978) and Alloy and Seligman (in press) make it clear that most of the above data implicating associative deficit can be accounted for equally well by performance deficits. Other studies failed to establish that the effects were atributable to experience with uncontrollable events.

In an effort to unconfound learning and performance, Maier and Jackson (in press) have begun using a choice test task. Rats are placed in a Y-maze and at the onset of the escapable shock, movement into the correct arm is required to terminate the shock; movement into the wrong arm does not terminate shock. There is no necessary relation in this task between vigor of motor activity and the correctness of choices. Maier and Jackson found that inescapably shocked rats made many more total errors than escapably shocked or naive control rats (Figure 4). Not only was the rate of learning different, but the groups reached different asymptotes of percentage correct choices. Because failures to respond were essentially absent (although latency differences did exist) and because there was no correlation between latency and trials with errors, this experiment provides the best available animal data demonstrating an associative deficit as a result of prior exposure to inescapable shocks.

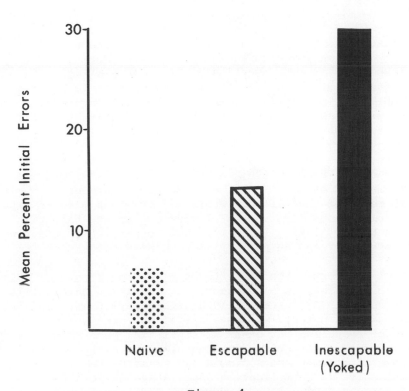

Figure 4
    Data of Maier and Jackson (in press) showing the associative
deficit resulting from prior exposure to uncontrollable (inescapable)
shock. The behavioral test was a choice task in which subjects had
to choose the correct arm of a Y-maze in order to escape shock.

    One weakness of "learned helplessness" arises from its view
of the expectancy about future response-outcome contingencies as a
single causal entity. This implies that the three effects, whenever they can be independently assessed, ought to show substantial
positive correlations. This implication has not been consistently
confirmed. The Maier and Jackson (in press) Y-maze escape experiment discussed above provides one example of dissociation of these
effects. Recall that there was no correlation between response
latencies and likelihood of correct choices--that is, between the
incentive-motivational effect and the associative effect. With

respect to dissociation between response initiation and emotionality, as indexed by gastric ulceration, Weiss (1971a) has reported that those rats which show the lowest degree of response initiation, reflecting the greatest loss of incentive under the learned help-lessness hypothesis, also showed the least alteration in emotionality.

Comment. Although the three theories discussed above represent the major accounts of the proactive interference effect, it seems clear that all have difficulty explaining significant portions of the data. It should be recognized that the three classes of theory--neurochemical, response, and cognitive--currently represent competing accounts. They, however, also repre-sent different levels of analysis which are not in themselves incompatible. We look forward to a unified theory which views the effect from all three perspectives.

ABSENCE OF CONTROL: SOMATIC EFFECTS

In the preceding section we reviewed the behavioral effects of control over events and the theoretical interpretations of them, but indicated that there were significant somatic effects as well. Here we shall summarize these effects.

Basic Phenomena

Weiss has provided elegant demonstrations of the somatic effects of exposures to uncontrollable shocks. Using the triadic design, so as to separate the effects of shocks from their controllability, Weiss (1968) demonstrated that rats yoked to those receiving escape/avoidance training showed more weight loss and greater gastric ulceration than the escape/avoidance trained group which, in turn, differed from naive rats. This makes clear that absence of some degree of control over the aversive shocks produced adverse somatic consequences; control over the shocks ameliorated these. Furthermore, Weiss (1971a) found that rats exposed to unsignaled stress--independent of whether or not they had control--showed more severe ulceration than did the corresponding groups stressed with signaled shocks and that, under both the signaled and the unsignaled conditions, yoked rats showed more gastric ulceration than escape/avoidance trained rats. Figure 5 shows this interactive effect of predictability and control-lability upon physiological strain.

A Theory of Somatic Effects

To account for the complex interactions of behavior and environmental contingencies which result in deleterious somatic effects, Weiss (1971a) proposed a theory of coping and ulceration. The theory identified two interacting factors. The first factor is the number of responses (coping attempts) the animal makes.

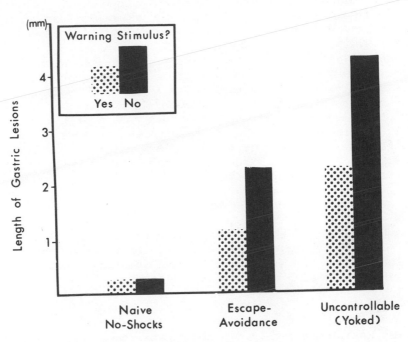

Figure 5

Length of gastric lesions in rats as a function of predictability of electric shock. Note that the absence of a warning
signal adds to the already large effect produced by the uncontrollable shocks (data from Weiss, 1971a).

The second factor is the feedback for the responses: if the
responses produce stimuli associated with termination or absence
of shock, the feedback is said to be "relevant." Responding when
every response produces relevant feedback results in little ulcerative stress (Weiss, 1971c), while responding in the absence of
relevant feedback results in considerable ulcerative stress (Weiss
1971b) and this increases with the number of responses emitted.
Thus, degree of somatic stress is the product of an interaction
between the number of coping attempts made by the animal and the
amount of relevant feedback received for those responses.

This theory accounts well for the data Weiss has obtained (1971a,b,c), especially the differential ulceration found under unsignaled and signaled avoidance conditions, which in his experiments, afforded identical degrees of control. Because the number of coping attempts emitted are greater under unsignaled shock avoidance conditions than under signaled avoidance conditions, the theory readily accounts for the increased ulceration seen in rats trained in unsignaled avoidance (and their yoked partners) relative to those trained in signaled avoidance (and their yoked partners). What is left unexplained by this account is why the animals respond more frequently in the unsignaled conditions than in the signaled conditions and whether the responding per se is causal or merely reflective of some other process.

Weiss' theory is of interest in light of the interaction between behavioral and physiological management of stress presented in TABLE I and the possibility of a trade-off between behavioral strain and physiological strain. His theory of coping (1971a) predicts that if the animal makes few responses under conditions of exposure to unsignaled, uncontrollable electric shocks--that is gives up behavioral coping efforts--the animal will suffer less ulceration than a more responsive animal. Of course, absence of behavioral coping efforts is the essence of the proactive interference effect. Thus, "learned helplessness" may in fact be a partially successful adaptive strategy.

LOSS OF CONTROL

Mandler (1964) argued persuasively that the withdrawal of effective coping responses is emotionally (and behaviorally) significant. Consistent with this view, Mason, Brady and Tolson (1966) showed that while exposure of monkeys to free shocks alone or to temporally paced avoidance resulted in only modest increases in plasma norephinephrine and corticosterone, the presentation of unavoidable shocks to the monkeys after they had learned the avoidance response produced dramatic increases in both of these endocrines (see also Coover, Ursin and Levine, 1973; Mason et al., 1966; Sidman, Mason, Brady and Thach, 1962). That such signs of increased stress cannot be attributed to the increased number of shocks or frustration experienced when animals are deprived of control may be demonstrated by removing the manipulandum with which the organism exerts control without delivering further shocks. Animals which experience this sort of loss of control still show dramatic increases in steroids (Mason, et al., 1966; Coover, et al., 1973).

As suggestive as these experiments are, they all lack critical yoked-control groups to demonstrate that the change in contingency is the causal factor rather than the changes in the frequency or distribution of reinforcer events. Fortunately, a small number

of demonstrations incorporating yoked controls are available and they confirm that it is the change in the response-reinforcer contingency which is responsible for the deleterious effects observed. Both Wald and Desiderato (1973; Wald, 1972) and Weiss (1971b) have shown that rats which lose control through reduction in the effectiveness of the escape/avoidance response show more ulceration than rats which never had control. The latter rats, in turn, show more ulceration than rats which are never shocked.

Perhaps the clearest demonstration was provided by Hanson, Larson, and Snowdon (1976). They exposed monkeys to stressful loud noises (>100 dBa). One group was kept naive with respect to noises. A second group was exposed to a series of noises the duration of which was determined by the third group. This third group, and one of special interest, was exposed to a minimum duration of noise; when this minimum duration of noise had elapsed, a lever was inserted which the monkey could press to terminate the noise for himself and his yoked partner in the second group. Thus, in this last group, the monkeys had some control after the minimum duration had elapsed. Halfway through the last day of the experiment, the lever was inserted but presses on it no longer terminated the loud noises; terminations were independent of responses.

The effects of this loss of control were dramatic. So long as the monkeys had some control their cortisol levels were less than those of monkeys that had no control. When control over the noise was withdrawn, the level of cortisol increased significantly.

Taken together, the experiments in this section suggest that loss of control over noxious stimuli is more stressful than never having had control at all.

INTERACTIONS BETWEEN PREDICTION AND CONTROL

With respect to experiments which study the effects of uncontrollable events upon subsequent behavior, most have actually confounded uncontrollability and unpredictability. That is, events which were uncontrollable were also unpredictable. One exception is the study by Weiss (1971a). He studied the quantity of gastric lesions which occur as a function of the predictability and controllability of electric shock. It was found that absence of predictability and absence of control of electric shock both increased the incidence of gastric lesions (see Figure 5). Also, the effect of the two variables appeared additive. Whether parallel effects can be obtained in the behavioral realm is unknown, but we are currently evaluating this possibility. By assaying cortisol levels in our dogs we are also testing the generality of the physiological effects found by Weiss.

In pilot work we have demonstrated that dogs pre-exposed to signaled, uncontrollable electric shocks perform better on a choice avoidance task than dogs pre-exposed to unsignaled, uncontrollable shocks. During the induction phase, subjects were secured in a Pavlovian sling and exposed to a series of uncontrollable shocks. For one group of subjects (predictable shock group) a tone preceded the delivery of each shock. A second group (unpredictable shock group) experienced the same series of shocks but the tones were presented on a random schedule independent of shock presentations. In the next phase the subjects were presented with the following choice avoidance problem: avoidance/escape trials began with presentation of a flashing white light under the right or left front paw of the subject. The dog could escape or avoid shock by lifting the paw under which the light was flashing. Figure 6 shows the mean time per trial during which the subject was engaged in performing an incorrect response as a function of blocks of 40 trials. Acquisition of the correct response was slower in the group which had experienced uncontrollable and unpredictable shock compared to the group pre-exposed to shocks that were only uncontrollable. Thus, the predictability of a stressor does seem to modulate future behavioral coping.

Future research in our laboratories will seek to specify how predictability and controllability interact to contribute to the proactive interference effect. Several alternatives may be suggested. It is possible that the additivity found by Weiss (1971a) is paralleled in behavioral indices. This model would suggest that intermediate levels of proactive interference might be produced by signaled, but uncontrollable, events or, contrary to learned helplessness theory, by controllable but unsignaled events.

Other relationships between predictability and controllability have been suggested. Averill (1973) suggests that control is important because of the predictability which it provides. Conversely, it has been argued that predictability is important because it allows efficient control (Biederman and Furedy, 1970, 1973, 1976; Furedy and Biederman, 1976; Lykken, 1962; Lykken & Tellegen, 1974). Experimentally distinguishing these three models is problematic. Not only are the two factors difficult to independently manipulate for technical reasons, but all three models appear to make identical predictions regarding the outcome of the critical factorial experiment (e.g., Weiss, 1971a). An additive model might predict that the greatest behavioral (or somatic) dysfunction would be seen in those animals which could neither control nor predict the stimulus event. Animals which could either predict or control the event should show intermediate levels of dysfunction, while those which can both control and predict the event should show the least dysfunction. This is in fact the result shown in Figure 5. However, if predictability and controllability reduce to a single common factor, the same predictions

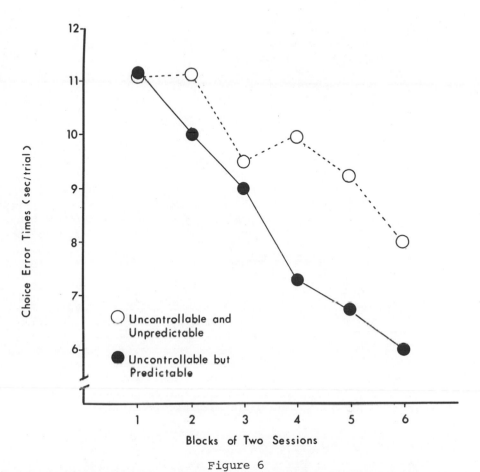

Figure 6

Mean incorrect time per trial for a group of dogs exposed to
uncontrollable and unpredictable shocks and a group exposed to
uncontrollable and predictable (preceded by a tone) shocks.

hold: animals which have neither prediction nor control experience
the least of this common factor; animals which have one or the
other experience intermediate levels of it; and animals which can
both predict and control events will experience the greatest
amount of the single underlying factor. It is thus unlikely that
any technically feasible experiment can differentially support any
of these three models.

We would like to suggest an alternative. It is possible that
prediction and control operate independently on different components of a general proactive interference syndrome. Figure 7
illustrates such a model. Uncontrollability is viewed as predominantly disruptive of motivation. This concurs with the classic
learned helplessness theory (Maier and Seligman, 1976; Maier,
Seligman and Solomon, 1969; Seligman, Maier and Solomon, 1971).

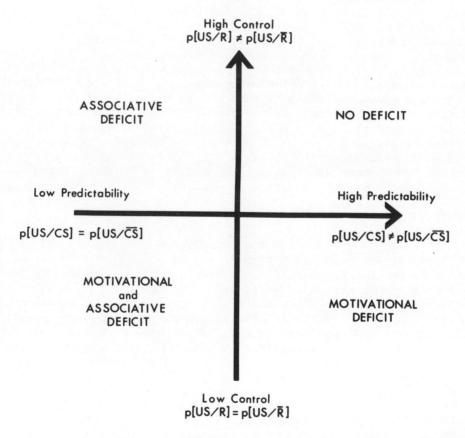

Figure 7

A preliminary model of the interactive effect of predictability
and controllability upon the motivational and associative components
of the proactive interference effect. In this case predictability
and controllability act independently upon the associative and
motivational deficits, respectively.

Unpredictability, on the other hand, yields associative deficits. These may be either response-outcome associations--the associative deficit postulated by helplessness theory and demonstrated by Maier and Jackson (in press)--or stimulus-stimulus associations (Baker, 1976; Popik and Frey, 1978; Tomie, 1976). This model recognizes the importance of unconfounding prediction and control in future experiments. Furthermore, it is congruent with the dissociation of interference indices (Testa et al., 1974; Weiss, 1971; see above) which is problematic for learned helplessness theory.

Unanswered empirical questions remain regarding the proactive interference effect. We should like to know, for instance, what aspects of the experience of uncontrollability affect the extent to which it disrupts future learning and motivation. Considerable evidence indicates that the effects are quite pervasive (see Generality, above; also, Tondat, 1973). On the other hand, Dweck and Reppucci (1973) have evidence that the interference effect may be under rather precise stimulus control. We also wonder whether specific response learning systems can be disrupted by exposure to uncontrollable or unpredictable events. The data presented in Figure 2, page 10, indicate that avoidance and escape responses are differentially sensitive to proactive interference. Moreover, Prindaville and Stein (1978) offer evidence that the avoidance responding of human subjects is more sensitive to the effects of unpredictability than is escape responding.

CONCLUDING COMMENTS

It seems clear that control is psychologically and biologically important to the organism. Animals prefer control over environmental events to its absence when given a choice. Moreover, absence of control is demonstrably stressful. The resulting pathogenesis, however, follows laws which can be integrated with the animal's "normal" psychological structure, as opposed to indicating the collapse of normal systems. Since ethical and practical considerations restrict similar research in man, theoretical advances must be made via animal models such as those discussed above. To the extent that analogous processes are operative in animals and man, a clear danger to the health of individuals is presented by excessive exposure to uncontrollable events or by inordinate loss of control. Finally, the availability of alternative means of coping with stress suggests that valuable work might be directed toward determining the most effective and efficient ways for man to deal with lack of control.

References

Alloy, L. B., and Seligman, M. E. P., in press, On the cognitive
    component of learned helplessness and depression, in: "The
    Psychology of Learning and Motivation," G. Bower ed., Vol. 13.
Altenor, A., Kay, E., and Richter, M., 1977, in press, The generality
    of learned helplessness in the rat, Learn. Motiv., 8:54.
Anderson, D. C., Crowell, C., Koehn, D., and Lupo, J. V., 1976,
    Different intensities of unsignaled inescapable shock treatments
    as determinants of non-shock-motivated open field behavior: A
    resolution of disparate results, Physiol. Behav., 17:391.
Anderson, O. D., and Liddell, H. S., 1935, Observations on experimental
    neurosis in sheep, Arch. Neurol. Psychiat., 34:330.
Anisman, H., 1975, Time-dependent variations in aversively motivated
    behaviors: Non-associative effects of cholinergic and catechol-
    aminergic activity, Psychol. Rev., 82:359.
Anisman, H., and Waller, T. G., 1971, Effects of methamphetamine and
    shock duration during inescapable shock exposure on subsequent
    active and passive avoidance, J. Comp. Physiol. Psychol., 77:143.
Anisman, H., and Waller, T. G., 1973, Effects of inescapable shock
    on subsequent avoidance performance: Role of response repertoire
    changes, Behav. Biol., 9:331.
Anisman, H., Decantanzaro, D., and Remington, G., 1978, Escape
    performance following exposure to inescapable shock: Deficits
    in motor response maintenance, J. Exp. Psychol. [Anim. Behav.],
    4:197.
Averill, J. R., 1973, Personal control over aversive stimuli and its
    relationship to stress, Psychol. Bull., 80:286.
Baker, A. G., 1976, Learned irrelevance and learned helplessness:
    Rats learn that stimuli, reinforcers, and responses are
    uncorrelated, J. Exp. Psychol. [Anim. Behav.], 2:130.
Barchas, J. D., and Freedman, D. X., 1963, Brain Amines: Response
    to physiological stress, Biochem. Pharmacol., 12:1232.
Biederman, G. B., and Furedy, J. J.,1970, The preference-for-signaled-
    shock phenomenon: Signaling shock is reinforcing only if shock
    is modifiable, Quart. J. Exp. Psychol., 22:681.
Biederman, G. B., and Furedy, J. J., 1973, Preference-for-signaled-
    shock phenomenon: Effects of shock modifiability and light
    reinforcement, J. Exp. Psychol., 100:380.
Biederman, G. B., and Furedy, J. J., 1976, Preference for signaled
    shock in rats? Instrumentation and methodological errors in
    the archival literature, Psychol. Rec., 26:501.
Bliss, E. L., Ailion, J., and Zwanziger, J., 1968, Metabolism of
    norepinephrine, serotonin, and dopamine with stress, J.
    Pharmacol. Exp. Ther., 164:122.
Bodnar, R. J., Kelly, D. D., and Glusman, M., 1978, Stress-induced
    analgesia: Time Course of pain reflex alterations following
    cold water swims, Bull. Psychonom. Soc., 11:333.
Bracewell, R. J., and Black, A. H., 1974, The effects of restraint
    and noncontingent preshock on subsequent escape learning in
    the rat, Learn. Motiv., 5:53.

Brady, J. V., Porter, R. W., Conrad, D. G., and Mason, J. W., 1958,
    Avoidance behavior and the development of gastroduodenal ulcers,
    J. Exp. Anal. Behav., 1:69.
Braud, W., Wepmann, B., and Russo, D., 1969, Task and species gener-
    ality of the "helplessness" phenomenon, Psychonom. Sci., 16:154.
Brennan, J. F., and Riccio, D. C., 1975, Stimulus generalization of
    suppression in rats following aversively motivated instrumental
    or Pavlovian training, J. Comp. Physiol. Psychol., 88:570.
Broadhurst, P. L., 1960, Abnormal animal behavior, in: "Handbook
    of Abnormal Psychology," H. J. Eysenck ed., First Edition,
    Basic Books, New York.
Catania, A. C., 1971, Elicitation, reinforcement, and stimulus
    control, in: "The Nature of Reinforcement," R. Glaser ed.,
    Academic Press, New York.
Church, R. M., 1964, Systematic effect of random error in the yoked
    control design, Psychol. Bull., 62:122.
Church, R. M., LoLordo, V. M., Overmier, J. B., Solomon, R. L., and
    Turner, L. H., 1966, Cardiac responses to shock in curarized
    dogs, J. Comp. Physiol. Psychol., 62:1.
Coover, G. D., Ursin, H., and Levine, S., 1973, Plasma-corticosterone
    levels during active-avoidance learning in rats, J. Comp.
    Physiol. Psychol., 82:170.
Corson, S. A., 1971, Pavlovian and operant conditioning techniques
    in the study of psychosocial and biological relationships, in:
    "Society, Stress and Disease," Vol. 1, Oxford University Press,
    London.
Costello, C. G., 1978, A critical review of Seligman's laboratory
    experiments on learned helplessness and depression in humans,
    J. Abnorml. Psychol., 87:21.
Davis, H., 1979, Behavioral anomalies in aversive situations, in:
    "Psychopathology in Animals," J. D. Keehn ed., Academic Press,
    New York.
Desiderato, O., and Newman, A., 1971, Conditioned suppression
    produced in rats by tones paired with escapable or inescapable
    shock, J. Comp. Physiol. Psychol., 77:427.
Dorworth, T. R., and Overmier, J. B., 1977, On "learned helplessness":
    The therapeutic effects of electroconvulsive shocks, Physiol.
    Psychol., 5:355.
Dweck, C. S., and Reppucci, D. N., 1973, Learned helplessness and
    reinforcement responsibility in children, J. Pers. Soc. Psychol.,
    25:109.
Ellison, G. D., 1977, Animal models of psychopathology: The low
    norepinephrine and low serotonin rat, Am. Psychol., 32:1036.
Engle, G. L., and Schmale, A. H., 1967, Psychoanalytic theory of
    somatic disorder. Conversion, specificity, and the disease
    onset situation, J. Am. Psychoanal. Assoc., 15:344.
Engle, G. L., and Schmale, A. H., 1972, Conservation-withdrawal:
    A primary regulatory process for organismic homeostasis, in:
    "Physiology, Emotions, and Psychosomatic Illness," CIBA
    Foundation Symposium, Elsevier, Amsterdam.

Faircloth, K. P., 1974, The importance of subject control in rein-
    forcing brain stimulation, Learn. Motiv., 5:16.
Fox, M. W., 1971, Towards a comparative psychopathology, Z. Tier-
    psychol., 29:416.
Friedman, S. B., Ader, R., and Glasgow, L. A., 1965, Effects of
    psychological stress in adult mice inoculated with Coxsackie B
    viruses, Psychosom. Med., 27:361.
Furedy, J. J., and Biederman, G. B., 1976, Preference-for-signaled-
    shock phenomenon; direct and indirect evidence for modifiability
    factors in the shuttlebox, Anim. Learn. Behav., 4:1.
Gibbon, J., Berryman, R., and Thompson, R. L., 1974, Contingency
    spaces and measures in classical and instrumental conditioning,
    J. Exp. Anal. Behav., 21:585.
Glazer, H. I., and Weiss, J. M., 1976a, Long-term and transitory
    interference effects, J. Exp. Psychol. [Anim. Behav.], 2:191.
Glazer, H. I., and Weiss, J. M., 1976b, Long-term interference
    effect: An alternative to "learned helplessness," J. Exp.
    Psychol. [Anim. Behav.], 2:202.
Goodkin, F., 1976, Rats learn the relationship between responding
    and environmental events: An expansion of the learned helpless-
    ness hypothesis, Learn. Motiv., 7:382.
Gray, J. A., 1964, "Pavlov's Typology," Pergamon Press, Oxford.
Hanin, I., and Usdin, E., 1977, "Animal Models in Psychiatry and
    Neurology," Pergamon Press, Oxford.
Hanson, J. D., Larson, M. E., and Snowdon, C. T., 1976, The effects
    of control over high intensity noise on plasma cortisol levels
    in rhesus monkeys, Behav. Biol., 16:333.
Hiroto, D. S., 1974, Locus of control and learned helplessness, J.
    Exp. Psychol., 102:187.
Hull, C. L., 1943, "Principles of Behavior," Appleton-Century-Crofts,
    New York.
Jackson, R. L., Maier, S. F., and Rapaport, P. M., 1978, Exposure to
    inescapable shock produces both activity and associative
    deficits in the rat, Learn. Motiv., 9:69.
Jenkins, H. M., and Ward, W. C., 1965, "Judgment of Contingency
    Between Responses and Outcomes," Psychological Monographs,
    79:1 (whole no. 594).
Keehn, J. D., 1979a, Psychopathology in animal and man, in:
    "Psychopathology in Animals," J. D. Keehn ed., Academic Press,
    New York.
Keehn, J. D., 1979b, "Psychopathology in Animals: Research and
    Clinical Implications," Academic Press, New York.
Kelsey, J. E., 1977, Escape acquisition following inescapable shock
    in the rat, Anim. Learn. Behav., 5:83.
Kimmel, H. D., 1971, "Experimental Psychopathology: Recent Research
    and Theory," Academic Press, New York.
Knapp, R. K., Kause, R. H., and Perkins, C. C., Jr., 1959, Immediate
    vs. delayed shock in T-maze performance, J. Exp. Psychol., 58:357.

Lambert, P. L., Harrell, E. H., and Emmett-Oglesby, M. W., 1978, Electroconvulsive shock improves responding in an animal model of depression. Paper presented at the 86th Annual Convention of American Psychological Association, Toronto, August.

Lawry, J. A., Lupo, V., Overmier, J. B., Kochevar, J., Hollis, K. L., and Anderson, D. C., 1978, Interference with avoidance behavior as a function of qualitative properties of inescapable shocks, Anim. Learn. Behav., 6:147.

Lehmann, H. E., 1972, The impact of scientific models on clinical psychopharmacology: A psychiatrist's view, Sem. Psychiat., 4:255.

Levine, S., Madden, J., Conner, R. L., Moskal, J. R., and Anderson, D. C., 1973, Physiological and behavioral effects of prior aversive stimulation (preshock) in the rat, Physiol. Behav., 10:467.

Levis, D. J., 1976, Learned helplessness: A reply and an alternative S-R interpretation, J. Exp. Psychol. [Gen.], 105:47.

Lewis, M., 1964, Some nondecremental effects of effort, J. Comp. Physiol. Psychol., 57:367.

Lewis, M., 1965, Psychological effect of effort, Psychol. Bull., 64:183

Liddell, H., 1956, "Emotional Hazards in Animals and Man," Charles C. Thomas, Springfield, IL.

Looney, T. A., and Cohen, P. S., 1972, Retardation of jump-up escape responding in rats pre-treated with different frequencies of noncontingent electric shock, J. Comp. Physiol. Psychol., 78:317.

Lykken, D. T., 1962, Preception in the rat: Autonomic response to shock as a function of length of warning interval, Science, 137:665.

Lykken, D. T., and Tellegen, A., 1974, On the validity of the pre-ception hypothesis, Psychophysiology, 11:125.

Maier, S. F., 1970, Failure to escape traumatic shock: Incompatible skeletal motor responses or learned helplessness? Learn. Motiv., 1:157.

Maier, S. F., and Jackson, R. L., 1977, The nature of the initial coping response and the larned helplessness effect, Anim. Learn. Behav., 5:407.

Maier, S. F., and Jackson, R. L., in press, Learned helplessness: All of us were right (and wrong): Inescapable shock has multiple effects, in: "The Psychology of Learning and Motivation," G. Bower ed.

Maier, S. F., and Seligman, M. E. P., 1976, Learned helplessness: Theory and evidence, J. Exp. Psychol. [Gen.], 105:3.

Maier, S. F., and Testa, T. J., 1975, Failure to learn to escape by rats previously exposed to inescapable shock is partly produced by associative interference, J. Comp. Physiol. Psychol., 88:554.

Maier, S. F., Albin, R. W., and Testa, T. J., 1973, Failure to learn to escape in rats previously exposed to inescapable shock depends on nature of escape response, J. Comp. Physiol. Psychol., 85:581.

Maier, S. F., Anderson, C., and Lieberman, D. A., 1972, Influence of control of shock on subsequent shock elicited aggression, J. Comp. Physiol. Psychol., 81:94.

Maier, S. F., Seligman, M. E. P., and Solomon, R. L., 1969, Pavlovian fear conditioning and learned helplessness, in: "Punishment and Aversive Behavior," B. A. Campbell and R. M. Church eds., Appleton-Century-Crofts, New York.

Mandler, G., 1964, The interruption of behavior, in: "Nebraska Symposium on Motivation," D. Levine ed., 12:163.

Maser, J. D., and Seligman, M. E. P., 1977, "Psychopathology: Experimental Models," W. H. Freeman, San Francisco.

Mason, J. W., Brady, J. V., and Tolson, W. W., 1966, Behavioral adaptations and endocrine activity: Psychoendocrine differentiation of emotional states, in: "Endocrines and the Central Nervous System," R. Levine ed., Williams & Wilkins Company, Baltimore.

Masserman, J. H., 1943, "Behavior and Neurosis," University of Chicago, Chicago.

Miller, N. E., and Weiss, J. M., 1969, Effects of the somatic or visceral responses to punishment, in: "Punishment and Aversive Behavior," B. A. Campbell and R. M. Church eds., Appleton-Century-Crofts, New York.

Mineka, S., and Kihlstrom, J. F., 1978, Unpredictable and uncontrollable events: A new perspective on experimental neurosis, J. Abnorm. Psychol., 87:256.

Mowrer, O. H., and Viek, P., 1948, An experimental analogue of fear from a sense of helplessness, J. Abnorm. Soc. Psychol., 83:193.

Neuringer, A. J., 1969, Animals respond for food in the presence of free food, Science, 166:399.

Osborne, S. R., 1977, The free food (contra-freeloading) phenomenon: A review and analysis, Anim. Learn. Behav., 5:221.

Overmier, J. B., 1968, Interference with avoidance behavior, J. Exp. Psychol., 78:29.

Overmier, J. B., and Seligman, M. E. P., 1967, Effects of inescapable shock upon subsequent escape and avoidance responding, J. Comp. Physiol. Psychol., 63:28.

Padilla, A. M., Padilla, C., Ketterer, T., and Giacolone, D., 1970, Inescapable shocks and subsequent avoidance conditioning in goldfish (Carrasius auratus), Psychonom. Sci., 20:295.

Paulsen, E. C., and Hess, S. M., 1963, The rate of synthesis of catecholamines following depletion in guinea pig brain and heart, J. Neurochem., 10:453.

Payne, R. J., Anderson, D. C., and Mercurio, J., 1970, Preshock-produced alterations in pain-elicited fighting, J. Comp. Physiol. Psychol., 71:258.

Popik, R. S., and Frey, P. W., 1978, Retarding effect of unsignaled shock presentations: Potential mediation by background stimuli, Paper presented at Midwestern Psychological Association, Chicago, May.

Porsolt, R. D., Bertin, A., and Jalfre, M., 1977, Behavioral despair
    in mice: A primary screening test for antidepressants, Arch.
    Int. Pharmacodynam., 229:327.
Porsolt, R. D., LePichon, M., and Jalfre, M., 1977, Depression: A
    new animal model sensitive to antidepressant treatments, Nature,
    266:730.
Prindaville, P., and Stein, N., 1978, Predictability, controllability,
    and inoculation against learned helplessness, Behav. Res. Ther.,
    16:263.
Rapaport, P. M., and Maier, S. F., 1978, Inescapable shock and food-
    competition dominance in rats, Anim. Learn. Behav., 6:160.
Rhue, J. W., and Brown, R. T., 1978, Appetitive learned helplessness:
    The effects of free food parallel those of uncontrollable shock,
    Paper presented at meeting of Psychonomic Society, San Antonio,
    Texas, November.
Rosellini, R. A., 1978, Inescapable shock interferes with the
    acquisition of an appetitive operant, Anim. Learn. Behav., 6:155.
Rosellini, R. A., and Bazerman, M. H., 1976, Exposure to noncontin-
    gent food interferes with the acquisition of a response to
    escape shock. Paper presented at Midwestern Psychological
    Association, Chicago, May.
Rosellini, R. A., and Seligman, M. E. P., 1978, Role of shock
    intensity in the learned helplessness paradigm, Anim. Learn.
    Behav., 6:143.
Sandler, J., 1972, Physiology, emotion and psychosomatic illness,
    CIBA Foundation Symposium: R. Porter and J. Knight eds.,
    Elsevier, Amsterdam, 388.
Seligman, M. E. P., 1975, "Helplessness: On Depression, Development
    and Death," W. H. Freeman, San Francisco.
Seligman, M. E. P., 1978, Comment and integration, J. Abnorm. Psychol.,
    87:165.
Seligman, M. E. P., and Beagley, G., 1975, Learned helplessness in
    the rat, J. Comp. Physiol. Psychol., 88:534.
Seligman, M. E. P., and Groves, D. P., 1970, Nontransient learned
    helplessness, Psychonom. Sci., 19:191.
Seligman, M. E. P., and Maier, S. F., 1967, Failure to escape
    traumatic shock, J. Exp. Psychol., 74:1.
Seligman, M. E. P., Maier, S. F., and Geer, J., 1968, The allevia-
    tion of learned helplessness in the dog, J. Abnorm. Psychol.,
    73:256.
Seligman, M. E. P., Maier, S. F., and Solomon, R. L., 1971,
    Unpredictable and uncontrollable aversive events, in: "Aversive
    Conditioning and Learning," F. R. Brush ed., Academic Press,
    New York.
Seligman, M. E. P., Rosellini, R. A., and Kozak, M. J., 1975,
    Learned helplessness in the rat: Time course, immunization and
    reversibility, J. Comp. Physiol. Psychol., 88:542.
Serban, G., and Kling, A., 1976, "Animal Models in Human Psycho-
    biology," Plenum Press, New York.

Sidman, M., Mason, J. W., Brady, J. V., and Thach, J., 1962, Quantitative relations between avoidance behavior and pituitary-adrenal cortical activity, J. Exp. Anal. Behav., 5:353.

Singh, D., 1970, Preference for bar pressing to obtain reward over freeloading in rats and children, J. Comp. Physiol. Psychol., 73:320.

Solomon, R. L., and Brush, E. S., 1956, Experimentally derived conceptions of anxiety and aversion, in: Nebraska Symposium on Motivation, M. R. Jones ed., 4:212.

Spencer, H., 1855, "The Principles of Psychology," Longman, Brown, Green, & Longmans, London.

Stolk, J. M., Conner, R. L., Levine, S., and Barchas, J. D., 1974, Brain norepinephrine metabolism and shock-induced fighting behavior in rats, J. Pharmacol. Exp. Ther., 190:193.

Stolz, S. B., and Lott, D. F., 1964, Establishment in rats of a persistent response producing a net loss of reinforcement, J. Comp. Physiol. Psychol., 57:147.

Stone, E. A., 1970, Behavioral and neurochemical effects of acute swim stress are due to hypothermia, Life Sci., 9:877.

Testa, T. J., Juraska, J. M., and Maier, S. F., 1974, Prior exposure to inescapable electric shock in rats affects extinction behavior after successful acquisition of an escape response, Learn. Motiv., 5:380.

Thomas, E., and DeWald, L., 1977, Experimental neurosis, in: "Psychopathology: Experimental Models," J. D. Maser and M. E. P. Seligman eds., W. H. Freeman, San Francisco.

Tolman, E. C., 1955, Principles of performance, Psychol. Rev., 62:315.

Tomie, A., 1976, Retardation of autoshaping: Control by contextual stimuli, Science, 192:1244.

Tondat, L. H., 1973, Is the effect of preshock treatment on shock-elicited aggression independent of situational stimuli? Paper presented at Midwestern Psychological Association, Chicago.

Ullman, L. P., and Krasner, L., 1969, "A psychological approach to abnormal behavior," Prentice-Hall, Englewood Cliffs.

Ursin, H., Coover, G. D., Kohler, C., Deryck, M., Sagvolden, T., and Levine, S., 1975, Limbic structures and behavior: Endocrine correlates, in: "Hormones, Homeostasis, and the Brain: Progress in Brain Research," W. H. Gispen, T. B. vanWimersma Greidamus, B. Bohus, and D. deWied eds., 42:263.

Wald, E. R., 1972, Endocrinological correlates of stress-induced ulcers, unpublished master's thesis, Connecticut College.

Weiss, J. M., 1968, Effects of coping responses on stress, J. Comp. Physiol. Psychol., 65:251.

Weiss, J. M., 1971a, Effects of coping behavior in different warning signal conditions on stress pathology in rats, J. Comp. Physiol. Psychol., 77:1.

Weiss, J. M., 1971b, Effects of punishing the coping response (conflict) on stress pathology in rats, J. Comp. Physiol. Psychol., 77:14.

Weiss, J. M., 1971c, Effects of coping behavior with and without a feedback signal on stress pathology in rats, J. Comp. Physiol. Psychol., 77:22.

Weiss, J. M., Glazer, H. I., 1975, Effects of acute exposures to stressors on subsequent avoidance-escape behavior, Psychosom. Med., 37:499.

Weiss, J. M., Glazer, H. I., and Pohorecky, L. A., 1976, Coping behavior and neurochemical changes: An alternative explanation for the original "learned helplessness" experiments, in: "Animal Models in Human Psychobiology," G. Serban and A. Kling eds., Plenum Press, New York.

Weiss, J. M., Krieckhaus, E. E., and Conte, R., 1968, Effects of fear conditioning on subsequent avoidance behavior and movement, J. Comp. Physiol. Psychol., 65:413.

Weiss, J. M., Stone, E. A., and Harrell, N., 1970, Coping behavior and brain norepinephrine level in rats, J. Comp. Physiol. Psychol., 72:153.

Weiss, J. M., Glazer, H. I., Pohorecky, L. A., Brick, J., and Miller, N. E., 1975, Effects of chronic exposure to stressors on avoidance-escape behavior and on brain norepinephrine, Psychosom. Med., 37:522.

Weiss, J. M., Pohorecky, L. A., Salman, S., and Gruenthal, M., 1976, Attenuation of gastric lesions by psychological aspects of aggression in rats, J. Comp. Physiol. Psychol., 90:252.

Weiss, J. M., Pohorecky, L. A., Dorros, K., Williams, S., Emmel, D., Whittlesey, M., and Case, E., 1973, Coping behavior and brain norepinephrine turnover. Paper presented at Eastern Psychological Association, Washington, D. C., May.

Welker, R. L., 1976, Acquisition of a free-operant response in pigeons as a function of prior experience with response-independent food, Learn. Motiv., 7:394.

Wheatley, K. L., Welker, R. L., and Miles, R. C., 1977, Acquisition of barpressing in rats following experience with response-independent food, Anim. Learn. Behav., 5:236.

White, R. W., 1959, Motivation reconsidered: The concept of competence, Psychol. Rev., 66:297.

Wight, M. T., and Katzev, R. D., 1977, Noncontingent positive reinforcers retard later escape/avoidance learning in rats, Bull. Psychonom. Soc., 9:319.

Zigmond, M. J., and Harvey, J. A., 1970, Resistance to central norepinephrine depletion and decreased mortality in rats chronically exposed to electric shock, J. Neuro-Visc. Rel., 31:373.

Zubin, J., and Hunt, H., 1967, "Comparative Psychopathology - Animal and Human," Grune and Stratton, New York.

PSYCHOBIOLOGY OF COPING IN ANIMALS:

THE EFFECTS OF PREDICTABILITY

Joanne Weinberg
Seymour Levine

Department of Psychiatry
and Behavioral Sciences
Stanford University
School of Medicine

The term stress had a common usage in everyday life as well as in biology and medicine long before Hans Selye's initial report in 1936. However, the development of the stress field as a popular and important area of research can generally be traced to Selye's concept of the "general adaptation syndrome" (Selye, 1936). Selye was surprised to find that a variety of very different agents such as cold, heat, x-rays, hormones, bacteria, toxins or muscular exercise produced essentially the same triad of symptoms. This was true despite the fact that a highly specific adaptive response existed for any one of these agents by itself. The triad of symptoms included (1) adrenal cortical hypertrophy (indicative of increased adrenocortical activity); (2) involution or shrinkage of the thymus, spleen, lymph nodes and all other lymphatic structures; (3) gastrointestinal ulceration. These symptoms were named the "alarm reaction" and were thought to represent a nonspecific adaptive response of the body. This nonspecific demand upon the body, according to Selye, was the essence of stress (Selye, 1973).

The concept of nonspecificity obviously raised a critical question--through what mechanism could so many diverse agents transmit the common "message of stress". Selye speculated that there must be some physiological "first mediator" of stress; that is, some nonspecific chemical or by-product of biological reactions which produced the symptoms indicative of stress (Mason, 1975). However the search for physiological "first mediators of stress" was largely unproductive.

Over the past 20 or 30 years there has been an increasing

awareness of the fact that psychological and social factors can have
effects which are similar to and perhaps even more potent than those
of physical stressors; and further, that the pituitary-adrenal system
(one of Selye's original indicators of alarm) is particularly sensitive to these psychological stimuli (Mason, 1968). To cite just a
few examples: In studies on mice, it has been suggested that many of
the physiological effects observed in experiments on fighting behavior are due more to psychological factors than to factors such as
attack or wounding. Thus previously defeated mice placed in the
presence of a trained fighter show as much pituitary-adrenal activation as mice that are actually attacked and defeated (Bronson and
Eleftheriou, 1965). On the other hand, rats exposed to electric
shock in pairs and thus able to fight in response to that shock show
much lower levels of ACTH than animals exposed to the same shock
singly (Conner, Vernikos-Dannellis and Levine, 1971). Still other
studies have shown that simply exposing an animal to a novel chamber
can produce plasma corticoid elevations as great as those produced by
exposure to painful electric shock (Bassett, Cairncross and King, 1973;
Friedman and Ader, 1967).

In view of our current understanding of psychological variables,
Mason (1975) suggests that the unrecognized "first mediators" in
many of Selye's experiments may have been the CNS substrate involved
in emotional arousal. The fact that pituitary-adrenal activation
frequently occurs during novel or aversive stimulation is therefore
not surprising since the pituitary-adrenal system appears to be an
excellent indicator of arousal (Hennessy and Levine, 1979). This
alters the concept of nonspecificity, at least in terms of the
pituitary-adrenal response to stress. Instead of viewing the
hormonal response as being elicited by a great diversity of stimuli,
we can now view the hormonal response as being elicited largely by
a single stimulus or stimulus configuration common to a variety of
situations, i.e., factors in these situations which elicit emotional
arousal.

Recently it has been shown that psychological factors can not
only lead to increased arousal, but can also decrease arousal, as
indexed by decreased pituitary-adrenal activity, by altering the
response to even intense or noxious stimuli. The psychological
variables which have been studied most often are those related to
(1) the predictability of stressors; (2) control or the ability to
make coping responses (e.g., avoidance or escape) during stress;
(3) the amount of feedback or information which the organism
receives following a noxious stimulus or the response to that
stimulus; and (4) the previous history of an organism with regard
to these factors. Overmier (this volume) has discussed the effects
of previous experience with control. This paper will focus on the
variable of predictability, and on how control and feedback information relate to predictability.

PREDICTABILITY

In a variety of studies it has been observed that predictable shock seems less aversive and that animals prefer predictable over unpredictable shock. For example, in a shock situation where animals can bar press to escape from shock, it has been shown that animals which receive a signal prior to shock behave very differently from animals which receive no such signal (Badia and Culbertson, 1970). Subjects in the signaled condition hold the bar much less, and leave the bar area and explore more freely than animals in the unsignaled condition. Furthermore, if given a choice, rats will choose signaled over unsignaled shock situations not only when shock is avoidable or escapable, but also when shock is unavoidable and inescapable (Badia and Culbertson, 1972; Badia, Culbertson and Lewis, 1971). Similarly, related research has shown that animals choose fixed time shock (which is regular and therefore predictable) over variable time shock (which is irregular and unpredictable) when both conditions are unsignaled. However that choice can be reversed if signals are introduced into the variable time shock situation thus making that condition more predictable (Badia, Harsh and Coker, 1975). This behavioral preference for signaled or predictable shock appears to be so strong that animals will choose signaled shock which is 4-9 times longer and 2-3 times more intense than unsignaled shock (Badia, Culbertson and Harsh, 1973). The procedure in all of the studies by Badia and associates which involve choice was to provide a lever by which animals could change over from unsignaled to signaled shock. In other words, while receiving unpredictable shock subjects could press a lever and thereby change the conditions so that predictable shock then occurred. Once they had learned to do this, subjects appeared to continue responding to change over to the signaled condition.

Others have reported similar findings using different methods. In a 2-compartment test chamber where a warning signal (CS) precedes shock on one side and no signal precedes shock on the other side, it was found that rats not only show a strong behavioral preference for the signaled side of the chamber (Lockard, 1963; Gliner, 1972) but also develop fewer gastric ulcers than animals receiving unpre- dictable shock or yoked controls which cannot make a choice for one side of the chamber (Gliner, 1972). Using tail shock Weiss (1970) observed that animals receiving unpredictable shock not only develop more severe gastric ulcers, but also show greater increases in body temperature, higher plasma corticosterone concentrations, increased body weight loss, greater suppression of food and water intake, and more defecation than animals receiving predictable shock. Similarly, Seligman and Meyer (1970) found that unpredict- able shocks presented to rats bar pressing for food produce a pronounced suppression of bar pressing throughout the test session, while rats receiving signaled shock show a transient suppression of bar pressing only during the CS, but not in its absence. In the

bar-pressing situation, as in the 2-compartment chamber and tail
shock conditions, animals experiencing unpredictable shock develop
the most sever stomach and intestinal ulcers.

In contrast, other studies indicate that under some conditions
signaled or predictable shock may be more aversive than unpredictable
shock. For example, both rats (Brady, Thornton and Fisher, 1962)
and mice (Friedman and Ader, 1965) have been shown to lose more weight
in situations where electric shocks are preceded by a warning signal
than when the same number of shocks are not signaled. In addition
to weight loss, both adrenal hypertrophy and increased stomach
ulceration (Pare, 1964) as well as increased mortality (Brady et al.,
1962) have also been shown to occur when warning signals are presented prior to shock. Similar results have been found using an
increase in plasma corticosterone as the index of stress. For
example, Bassett et al. (1973) observed greater elevations of plasma
corticosterone when a CS preceded shock than when shock was unsignaled, regardless of whether shock was presented on a regular or an
irregular schedule. Hennessy and co-workers (Hennessy, King,
McClure and Levine, 1977) also found that signaled shock produced
pituitary-adrenal activation. These investigators altered predictability of shock by altering the regularity of the intershock
interval (ISI). Three groups of animals were tested. One group
experienced no variability in the ISI (i.e., a Fixed Interval
schedule) and thus could use the temporal regularity of the schedule
to predict shock. A second group experienced highly variable ISIs
and thus had no cues with which to predict shock. The third group
experienced moderate amounts of variability in the ISI and thus had
some moderate degree of predictability of shock. The adrenocortical
response following four sessions of training on these schedules
appeared to follow a curvilinear function. Both highly predictable
and highly unpredictable shock were the most aversive and produced
the greatest pituitary-adrenal activation. In contrast, the group
experiencing moderate variability in the ISI showed significantly
less elevation of plasma corticoids. It was suggested that the
pituitary-adrenal system is sensitive to variations in uncertainty,
i.e., the amount of information in the environment which can be
used to predict shock. Highly predictable situations lend themselves to rather intense preparatory responding which was reflected
in pituitary-adrenal activation. Highly unpredictable situations
place the organism in chronic anticipation of shock which also led
to pituitary-adrenal activation. In contrast, moderate levels of
uncertainty allowed some predictability of shock, so that subjects
were not responding as intensely as those in the highly predictable
group, yet allowed fairly long intervals of time-safe, so that
subjects were less aroused than those in the highly unpredictable
group. This last condition appeared to be the least aversive.
Davis et al. (unpublished), using a conditioned emotional response
(CER) paradigm, likewise found that signaled shock was aversive.
Rats were first trained on a variable interval (VI) food reinforce-

ment schedule, and then received daily sessions of either signaled shock (paired CS-US) presentations or unsignaled shock (random CS-US) presentations, while the VI schedule was in effect. Behaviorally, subjects in the unsignaled shock group showed a much greater suppression in responding than subjects in the signaled shock group. When plasma corticosterone levels were measured at the end of the 30-min session, no differences between the signaled and unsignaled groups were observed, similar to the observation of Hennessy et al. (1977) cited above. However, in a follow-up experiment animals were trained under the same VI schedule and exposed to the same shock conditions (i.e., blood samples were obtained on a test day during which animals were exposed to 8 min of the VI schedule alone in the absence of any CS-US presentations. Under these conditions subjects which had received signaled shock showed significantly higher steroid levels than subjects which had received unsignaled shock. Thus, it was suggested that once an animal has been exposed to signal-shock experience, being placed in that situation leads to intense pituitary-adrenal activity and thus essentially to a greater stress response. This is similar to the hypothesis of Hennessy et al. (1977). That is, in a highly predictable (i.e., signaled) situation animals may show intense responding in anticipation of the signal and hence of shock.

In summary, after reviewing these studies we can conclude that the data on the effects of predictability are both complex and confusing. There appears to be a large body of evidence which suggests that predictable shock is less aversive than unpredictable shock, and an equally large body of evidence suggesting that predictable shock is more aversive for an organism. How can we begin to reconcile these results?

One reason results may differ from study to study is because different physiological measures are used to index stress. For example, it is somewhat difficult to compare ulcer formation with other physiological measures of stress since the testing procedures used to induce ulceration are unique. Animals are always tested while food deprived and test sessions are of long duration. (In the studies discussed above sessions ranged in length from 6 hours to 48 hours; and in the Seligman and Meyer (1970) study 50-min sessions were given over 70 consecutive days.) In fact, given these chronic conditions, the bar-pressing task used by Seligman and Meyer (1970) presents some problems. During the 50-min test sessions the groups receiving unpredictable shocks bar pressed very little and showed no recovery of bar pressing over sessions, while the other groups pressed at a high rate over sessions. Chronic fear, measured by suppression of bar pressing, was correlated with ulceration. Thus there is a confounding factor in this study in that animals which suppressed bar pressing also

received few reinforcements compared to animals which pressed at a
high rate.   Lack of food during the test sessions may have contributed to ulcer formation in these animals.   In any case, it is
apparent that the independent variables in studies using ulceration
as an index of stress are quite different form those found in studies
using a more acute measure such as pituitary-adrenal activation.

A second source of conflict in these studies on the effects of
predictability may arise from the use of behavioral as opposed to
physiological measures to assess the stress response.   In the studies
discussed above it was noted that, in a test situation where animals
can make a choice, they will always choose predictable over unpredictable shock (e.g., Badia and Culbertson, 1972; Badia et al., 1971;
Badia et al., 1973; Gliner, 1972; Lockard, 1963).   Thus behaviorally,
animals appear to prefer predictable shock.   Physiologically,
however, the effects of predictability are not so clear-cut.   Some
investigators claim that animals receiving predictable shock show
fewer somatic or physiological stress responses (e.g., Gliner, 1972;
Weiss, 1970) while others claim that subjects receiving predictable
shock are more stressed (e.g., Friedman and Ader, 1965; Pare, 1964).

The "preparatory response" hypothesis has been proposed to
explain the behavioral choice for signaled shock.   This hypothesis
suggests that a signal allows a subject to make preparatory postural
responses and thus actually to reduce the amount of shock it receives
(Lockard, 1963).   In fact, Furedy and Biederman (1976) demonstrated
that no preference for signaled shock occurs in a situation with
completely scrambled shock, i.e., where no postural adjustments
can alter the amount of shock received.   In their study, the preference for signaled shock emerged only during unscrambled shock
when animals developed the capacity for external shock modification
by standing on grids of the same polarity.   Thus animals placed in
a situation where they had little control over the modification of
shock spent less than 20% of their time on the signaled side of the
apparatus.   However, animals which received unscrambled shock and
could make postural adjustments which had a large impact on amount
of shock received, spent 60-70% of their time on the signaled side
of the apparatus.   This finding highlights a potential problem for
studies purporting to measure choice for signaled shock and using
a grid floor for shock delivery.   One must be aware that unless care
is taken to properly scramble the shock and to insure that no
external shock modification is possible, what appears to be a choice
for predictability might in fact be a choice for a signal which
then permits preparatory postural responses.

In studies using primarily physiological rather than behavioral
measures, this notion of preparatory responses has been proposed to
explain why signaled shock appears to be _more_ aversive than unsignaled shock.   It has been suggested that physiological responses
are not just indices of aversiveness but are also all associated

with the organism's preparedness for and response to shock (Bassett et al., 1973; Hennessy et al., 1977). Accordingly, intense responding (for example, elevated levels of plasma corticosterone) makes the animal optimally prepared, physiologically, to respond to the physical stressor. Furthermore, because the signal provides the animal with an identifiable shock period, preparatory responses can be precisely timed, more intense responding can occur during the warning signal (Hennessy et al., 1977) and responses to the environment in general can be extinguished (Perkins, 1968).

Although the factors we have described so far--use of behavioral as opposed to physiological measures, and choice of the physiological response to be measured--are helpful in explaining some of the problems inherent in the data on predictability, there still remains a fair amount of controversy as to whether predictability of shock is more or less aversive for an organism. There are two other factors which are involved in most of the experiments on predictability and which may help to further explain these discrepant results. These factors are control and feedback.

CONTROL

Control can be defined as the ability to make active responses during an aversive stimulus. These responses are frequently effective in allowing the animal to avoid or escape from the stimulus, but might also provide the animal only with the opportunity to change from one set of stimulus conditions to another (i.e., to modulate the environment) rather than to escape from shock entirely. Control in itself appears to be a factor which can reduce an organism's physiological response to a stimulus such as shock. For example, it has been observed that rats able to press a lever to avoid shock show less severe physiological disturbances (weight loss, gastric lesions) than yoked controls which cannot respond, even though both groups receive the same amount of shock (Weiss, 1968). Similarly, animals able to escape from shock show less elevation of plasma corticosterone over the course of testing than animals receiving the same amount of inescapable shock (Davis, Porter, Livingstone, Herrmann, MacFadden and Levine, 1977). Control over high intensity noise can also reduce plasma cortisol levels. Hanson, Larson and Snowdon (1976) observed that rhesus monkeys which had control over noise showed plasma cortisol levels similar to animals which were not exposed to noise, and that both of these groups were significantly less elevated than animals with no control over the aversive stimulus. When animals in the group which had control suddenly lost control (lever pressing no longer terminated noise), cortisol levels rose to those of the no-control group.

Another interesting example which contrasts the effects of having and then losing control can be seen using a conditioned taste aversion situation. In the version of this task which has

been developed in our laboratory (Smotherman, Hennessy and Levine, 1976), animals are given five exposures to a sweetened milk solution, and immediately following the 5th exposure are injected with LiCl (an i.p. injection of 0.40 M LiCl). This treatment makes them ill, and a single injection will cause the animals to avoid the milk solution when reexposed to it several days later. Furthermore, we have observed that the physiological response to the reexposure session depends upon the animals' food and water intake during the interval between conditioning and reexposure. If the animals are maintained on ad lib food and water during this interval, then plasma corticoid levels measured at the end of the 30-min reexposure session are similar to basal levels. If however, animals are deprived during this interval, plasma corticoid levels are markedly elevated. It has been suggested that this corticoid elevation reflects the fact that deprived animals are in a conflict situation (Smotherman, Margolis and Levine, in press; Weinberg, Smotherman and Levine, 1978). That is, they are hungry and thirsty yet presented only with a substance which has been paired with illness. Under these conditions they are, in a sense, "forced" to consume a small amount of the milk solution. The arousal produced by this approach-avoidance conflict is reflected in elevated corticosteroid levels. Nondeprived animals, on the other hand, do not experience such conflict and thus do not exhibit any steroid elevations. We suggest that one can also interpret these data in terms of control and loss of control. Animals in the nondeprived condition have control in this situation. Because they are neither hungry nor thirsty they can effectively avoid the milk solution on the reexposure day. Once animals are deprived however, they lose control. When reexposed to the milk solution they can no longer make an effective avoidance response, and this loss of control produces elevated levels of plasma corticosterone.

We can also view extinction of an established operant response as loss of control. For example, Coover, Ursin and Levine (1973) observed that during extinction of a shuttlebox avoidance response, plasma corticoid elevations occurred whether extinction was accomplished by punishing the on-going crossing response or by blocking the crossing response with a Plexiglas barrier and presenting only the CS. The fact that corticoid elevations occurred in the latter case, where the response was simply prevented from occurring, clearly indicates that it was not the physical stimulus of shock itself which was causing the increased arousal. It is possible that the psychological factor--loss of control--may have been one of the factors which produced the plasma corticoid elevations which were observed. In this situation animals had learned the task and thus had established a high level of control, i.e., they could make an effective avoidance response. When this control was suddenly removed by blocking the on-going response, plasma corticoids became elevated. Furthermore, this phenomenon is not limited to loss of

control over noxious stimuli. Extinction of an appetitive response can also activate the pituitary-adrenal system. For example, if an animal has learned to bar-press for food in an operant chamber, and food is suddenly withdrawn in this situation, there is a marked elevation of plasma corticoids (Coover, Goldman and Levine, 1971; Davis, Memmott, MacFadden and Levine, 1976). Once again, these data can be viewed within the context of loss of control.

Thus, having control is helpful; losing control is aversive; and previous experience with control can significantly alter the ability to cope with subsequent aversive stimuli (Overmier, this volume).

How does control relate to the concept of predictability? Authors of all of the studies on predictability discussed at the start of this paper stated that they were investigating the effects of predictability. Yet in many of the experiments animals not only had predictability but also had control, even though control was not mentioned as a parameter in the experiment. For example, in the studies where animals could choose one side or the other of an experimental chamber (Lockard, 1963; Gliner, 1972) the ability to make that choice actually gave the animals control over the stimulus conditions in that situation. Similarly, in the studies by Badia and co-workers where animals could make a bar press response to change over from unsignaled to signaled conditions, this bar press response provided control over the test conditions. Unfortunately this particular "changeover" procedure presented the animal with an "asymmetrical" choice, in that an active bar-press response produced a signal while a passive (withholding-of-barpress) response produced unsignaled shock (Furedy and Biederman, 1974). Therefore it was not simply predictability of shock which varied in these situations but also the availability of an active vs. a passive response. Yet only the issue of predictability was discussed in explaining the results.

In summary, the evidence suggests that in situations where animals also have control over shock, signaled shock may be less aversive. In situations where animals cannot make a response, either to avoid or escape, or to change the stimulus conditions, signaled shock frequently appears to be more aversive in terms of hormonal or physiological responses (e.g., Bassett et al., 1973; Brady et al., 1962; Pare, 1964). Whether control in itself is the important variable, or whether control and predictability interact to produce their effect, is difficult to determine at this time. What seems clear, however, is that adding control to a signaled shock situation may be one of the factors which is critical in making predictable shock less aversive for an organism. And conversely, predictability alone, without control, may actually be more aversive.

FEEDBACK OR INFORMATION ABOUT SAFETY

Feedback is the second factor which may be involved in studies
on predictability. Feedback can be defined as stimuli occurring
after a response and not associated with the stressor (Weiss, 1971a).
These stimuli provide information to an organism, indicating that it
has "done the right thing" and/or that the aversive stimulus is over,
at least for some interval of time.

In a number of studies it has been shown that relevant information or feedback can have a pronounced effect on the response to
an aversive stimulus. In one study (Weiss, 1971a) animals were
assigned to one of three signal conditions: (1) warning signal--a
20-sec beeping tone preceded shock; (2) progressive signal--30-sec
after shock offset there was a series of tones of increasing frequency and amplitude leading up to the beeping tone; (3) no signal
preceded shock. It should be noted that both of the signal conditions, and particulary the progressive-signal condition, are designed
to provide more information about timing of shocks than the typical
CS employed in most studies. Three groups of animals were tested
in each of these signal conditions. The triplet consisted of:
(1) a subject which could avoid and/or escape shock: (2) a subject
yoked to the avoidance/escape animal; (3) a nonshocked control. It
was found, first that animals which could avoid/escape shock
developed less severe gastric ulcers than yoked subjects which
received the same shocks but could not alter them by their behavior.
Thus, in keeping with the discussion above, having control or being
able to perform an effective coping response was less stressful (in
terms of ulceration) under all signal conditions. However, here we
can also see the effects of feedback; avoidance/escape animals in
the signaled conditions developed fewer ulcers than avoidance/
escape animals in the no-signal condition. The signals, particularly
the progressive signal, provided high levels of feedback information;
responses prior to shock or just following shock onset terminated
the tone (as well as the shock, if shock onset had occurred), and
produced a stimulus condition (i.e., silence) not closely associated
with shock. On the other hand, most of the responses made in the no-
signal condition produced low feedback. At best, shock was terminated; at worst if responses occurred prior to shock onset, no
change in the stimulus conditions of the environment occurred and
animals received no feedback. Thus, in this study, shock did not
produce ulceration under all conditions; the psychological variables
of control and feedback primarily determined the response to shock.
This statement is further supported by the finding that the avoidance rate was not very high for animals in the signaled condition.
In fact, 70% of these animals never learned to avoid shock, only to
escape it. Therefore these animals actually received a high number
of shocks. Yet it appears that because feedback for responding was
also high, these subjects in the signal groups developed fewer
ulcers than animals in the no-signal condition.

The effects of feedback can be seen even more dramatically in two subsequent studies by Weiss. In one experiment (Weiss, 1971b) animals in the signaled shock condition received a brief pulse of shock whenever they performed a well learned avoidance-escape response. These animals developed more severe ulcers and exhibited higher corticosterone levels than yoked animals which received exactly the same shocks but could not perform the avoidance-escape response (Weiss, 1971b). It is unlikely that the additional shocks received increased the ulceration or the plasma corticoid levels in the avoidance group, since both avoidance and yoked subjects received extra shocks, yet only animals which actively made avoidance responses showed increased ulceration. Instead, it appears that altering the feedback information is what increased the ulceration in this situation. For avoidance-escape animals the additional shocks dramatically altered relevant feedback. Whereas in the normal signal condition responding produced stimuli that were not associated with shock (e.g., signal offset, shock offset), when punishment shocks were added, responses now produced stimuli associated with shock--in fact, responding produced the shock itself.

Similarly, increasing feedback for animals in the no-signal condition was shown to significantly reduce ulceration (Weiss, 1971c). While rats which can avoid and/or escape shock normally develop considerable ulceration when in the no signal condition, it was found that if a brief feedback signal (5-sec tone) followed each response, ulceration was reduced almost to the level of nonshock controls.

We have also obtained evidence in our own laboratory indicating that feedback or signals providing information for the animals is more important than amount of shock received in determining an animal's responses. In one study we used a 2-way active-avoidance paradigm designed to assess plasma corticosterone responses over the course of training (Coover et al., 1973). Animals were tested for 10 sessions per day for 16 days. It was observed that levels of plasma corticosterone were significantly elevated over basal levels on Day 1 of testing, were slightly diminished during the acquisition phase (Day 6-7) when approximately an 80% performance rate was obtained, and were further decreased late in learning when performance was stabilized (Day 16-17). This pattern in the plasma corticosterone response was intriguing. A large decrease in number of shocks occurred between Day 1 and Day 6-7, yet only a small decrease in corticosterone levels occurred at this point. Further, animals were receiving about the same number of shocks on both Day 7 and Day 17, yet on Day 17 a large decrease in corticoid levels occurred. It thus appears that the decrease in number of shocks received was not the critical factor in determining the animal's hormonal response. This notion was further supported by the results from a second study using the same avoidance paradigm (Weinberg and Levine, 1977). In that study we observed that,

particularly at higher shock intensities (0.8 mA vs. 0.5mA), there
were a number of nonlearners, i.e., animals which never learned to
avoid shock, but only to escape once shock onset had occurred.   Nonlearners by definition never experienced the reduction in shock
frequency experienced by the avoiders, and received a high number of
shocks per session. However the steroid response over the 16 days
of testing was similar to that of the avoiders--elevated on Day 1,
a slight decrease on Day 6-7, and a more significant decrease by
Day 16 (see Table 1). How could animals which never learned to avoid
shock (and thus received a large number of shocks over the 16 days
of testing), show a drop in corticoids equivalent to that shown by
animals which did learn to avoid shock (and thus received virtually
no shock at all for the last 10 days of testing)? We suggest that
receiving feedback or information about safety enabled these animals
to show reduced arousal indicative of coping, whether or not there
was a reduction in number of shocks received.

     This hypothesis was supported by data from another study in
which both "avoiders" and "nonlearners" were again tested in this
same avoidance paradigm (Weinberg, 1977). In that study, nonlearners
were produced by subjecting the animals to differential pretreatments
prior to testing them in the active avoidance task. For one group,
animals were placed singly into a test chamber and given five
sessions of shock. In a second group animals were placed in the
chamber in pairs and thus were able to fight during the five shock
sessions (i.e., shock-induced fighting). The third group of animals
was exposed to the chamber alone without shock. When tested 2 weeks
later in the shuttlebox task it was observed that animals previously
subjected to shock-induced fighting were significantly impaired in
avoidance performance compared with the other two groups. These
subjects reached a criterion of only 30% correct avoidance responses,
while nonshocked controls achieved 55% correct responses and animals
shocked individually achieved over 80% correct responses (Figure 1 A).

TABLE 1

Plasma Corticosterone

		Day 1	Day 6-7	Day 16
♀	Avoiders	62.6*	59.1	45.7
	Nonlearners	60.2	51.2	44.9
♂	Avoiders	32.1	27.3	18.8
	Nonlearners	33.8	28.5	22.1

*Mean value: μg%

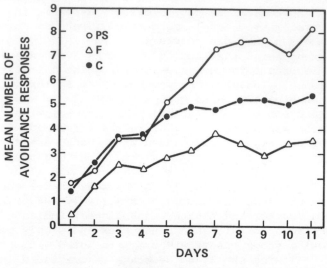

Figure 1 A

Mean number of correct (avoidance) responses for animals shocked singly (PS), animals shocked in pairs (F), and animals exposed to the chamber alone without shock (C).

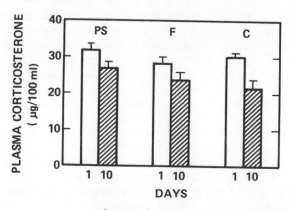

Figure 1 B

Plasma corticosterone levels following the avoidance session on Day 1 and Day 10 of testing.

However, despite these differences in level of performance, all
three groups showed similar physiological responses in this situation.
All had elevated levels of plasma corticosterone on Day 1 of testing
and all showed a significant decrease by Day 10 (Figure 1 B). Thus
once again it appeared that number of shocks avoided (or received)
was not the important factor in determining the animal's physiological response. Instead, the psychological factor of feedback
information enabled all three groups of animals to show reduced
arousal, regardless of their actual performance in the task. In
this task there was a high level of relevant feedback--animals
changed location, signals associated with shock were terminated,
and shock itself was terminated. Although one might speculate
that having control (i.e., ability to escape) was also an important factor for these animals, it is unlikely that escape in itself,
without relevant feedback, could as effectively reduce arousal.
Previous data (Walker and Levine, unpublished) indicate that if
animals are placed in this same shuttlebox and simply permitted to
escape following shock onset but never presented with either a CS
or a signal following shock, no decrease in corticoid levels occurs.
In that experiment each experimental animal (Group E) was yoked to
a partner which was matched to it by weight (Group Y). The test
chambers were wired in series so that the shocks received by the
two subjects in a pair were identical in number, duration and
intensity. Animals were tested for 22 sessions with 10 trials per
session. Following a 90-sec intertrial interval animals received
shock of 0.8 mA. Group E subjects could terminate shock by jumping
the barrier. Group Y subjects could also freely cross the barrier
but they had no control over shock. Blood samples were collected
from each subject immediately following the 10th trial on sessions
1, 5, 9, 14, and 20. Analysis of plasma corticosterone levels
(Figure 2) revealed that there were no differences between groups
and that neither group showed a decrease in corticoid levels over
sessions. Thus, over the 220 trials in this experiment, control
(i.e., ability to escape from shock) had no effect on the plasma
corticoid response to shock; animals in the escape group were not
different from animals in the yoked group, and both groups remained
elevated over basal levels across sessions. Control alone was not
sufficient to alter the hormonal response under these conditions.
In escape paradigms other than those using a shuttlebox (e.g.,
leverpress escape) corticoid decreases have been observed in escape
subjects over the course of testing, but only after as many as
750 trials (e.g., Davis et al., 1977). It thus appears that by
adding feedback signals to an escape situation one can significantly alter the animal's ability to cope with shock. Feedback
information enables an animal to show reduced arousal indicative
of coping in tasks where control alone is not as effective in
doing so.

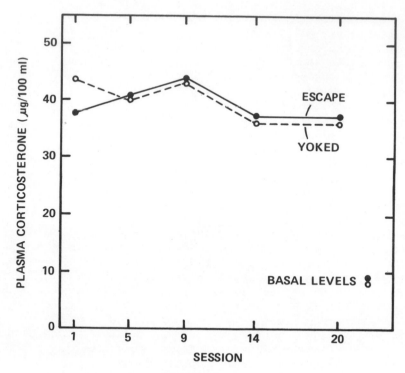

Figure 2
Plasma corticosterone levels measured across sessions in
subjects with control (escape) and subjects with no control (yoked).

In summary, feedback is an extremely important variable in
determining an organism's response in aversive situations. Lack of
feedback can increase stress responses such as ulceration and
pituitary-adrenal activity, and increased feedback can reduce these
same stress responses.

How does feedback relate to the concept of predictability? In
attempting to reconcile the conflicting results found in many of
the studies on predictability some have hypothesized that, if shock
is inescapable, predictability may only be effective in reducing
stress if it provides feedback for an organism. One statement of
this idea is known as the "safety signal" hypothesis. The "safety-
signal" hypothesis states that in situations where a reliable CS
predicts shock, the absence of the CS is a reliable predictor of
safety; and what controls behavior in these shock situations is

really the ability to predict safe or shock-free periods (Seligman, 1968). Further, animals may prefer signaled shock conditions because of the information value of the signal. When shock is unpredictable virtually the entire test session is spent in anticipation of shock, and animals remain in a chronic state of fear. With predictable shock, however, a safety signal exists; animals only show fear during the CS and not in the absence of the signal (Seligman and Meyer, 1970). Fear of the experimental chamber in general is diminished; and in the absence of the signal preparatory responses can be relaxed (Lockard, 1963; Perkins, 1968). In addition, the stimulus conditions which predict safety are fear reducing and therefore acquire reinforcing properties on their own (Badia, et al., 1971; Badia and Culbertson, 1972; Badia et al., 1973; Gliner, 1972; Perkins, 1968). Thus it has been suggested that predicting safety is more important than predicting shock (Weiss, 1970).

In addressing this issue, several studies have been designed specifically to test whether feedback, i.e., signals about safety, is in fact more important than predictability, i.e., warning signals, in altering an animal's response to an aversive stimulus. In a study by Hennessy et al. (1977) the effects of a warning signal vs. a safety signal were contrasted by varying the CS-US contingencies. One group received shock only in the presence of a tone (warning signal), one group received shock only in the absence of a tone (safety signal), and for a third group tones and shock were programmed independently (unpredictable shock). Animals in the safety signal group, for whom tones signaled a time-out from shock, had corticoid levels which were elevated to only 25% above the plasma corticoid response of nonshocked subjects. However, animals receiving warning signals showed as great an elevation as subjects receiving totally unpredictable shock. Thus both highly predictable and highly unpredictable shock conditions were found to be the most stressful. Animals which had a safety signal, i.e., a tone which indicated time out from shock, were the least stressed.

In another study using a choice procedure, Badia, Harsh, Coker and Abbott (1976) questioned whether choice of a signaled condition was in fact based on having identifiable shock periods, identifiable shock-free periods, or on both periods being identifiable. In their first experiment a signal or CS preceded (and thus predicted) shock. They found that subjects chose the signaled condition both when the signal predicting shock was dependable (i.e., shock always occurred in the presence of the signal) and when the signal predicting shock was undependable (i.e., shock only sometimes occurred in the presence of the signal.) Thus the dependability of the signal as a predictor of shock was relatively unimportant as a factor determining choice. However, in their second experiment they found that the dependability of the signal identifying shock-free (safe) periods was an important

determinant of choice. As the dependability of safety was systematically degraded, the amount of time spent in the signaled condition
systematically decreased. These authors suggested that the safety-
signal hypothesis was strongly supported by the data, i.e., dependability of the safe stimulus was more important for the animal than
was dependability of the warning or unsafe stimulus.

In yet another study (Arabian and Desiderato, 1975) animals
were exposed to unavoidable shock, and predictability of shock vs.
safety was tested by manipulating signal-shock contingencies
(Table 2A). In one condition--NS/NP--animals received no information about shock. Lights, tones and shock were randomly related,
i.e., tones and shocks occurred independently, regardless of whether
lights were on or off in the test chamber. Therefore animals in
this condition had neither predictability nor a safety signal. In
a second condition--S/NP--animals received some information; in
this case, a safety signal. The lights in the chamber provided the
signal: shock only occurred during lights on, and lights off
indicated completely shock-free time. The safety signal was thus
absence of the stimulus, or lights off. During lights on, both
tones and shocks occurred but they were randomly related. Therefore these animals had a safety signal but no predictability.
Finally, in the third condition--S/P--animals received a great deal

TABLE 2

A. Light-Tone-Shock Contingencies

S/P = safety signal + predictability
        no shock during lights off
        tone signals shock

S/NP = safety signal, no predictability
        no shock during lights off

NS/NP = no safety signal, no predictability
          light, tone, and shock randomly related

B. Test Conditions

	Side 1	Side 2
A.	S/P	NS/NP
B.	S/NP	NS/NP
C.	S/P	S/NP

of information about shock occurrence. For these animals, shock
only occurred during lights on, and a tone preceded each shock.
Shock was thus completely predictable. In addition, shock never
occurred during lights off and therefore lights off was a safety
signal. Thus this group had both a warning signal (or predictability) and a safety signal. Animals were tested in a two-sided
chamber. Shock was unavoidable, that is shock came on in both sides
of the chamber simultaneously; however animals could move from one
side of the chamber to the other. The test conditions for the
three groups of animals are described in Table 2B.

It was observed that both Groups A and B preferred Side 1 over
Side 2. However, there was a stronger preference for the signaled
side in Group B than in Group A animals. Note that Group A
subjects had both warning and safety signals while Group B subjects
had only safety signals. The finding that Group B spent more on the
safety signal side, despite the fact that the tone was not available
as a predicting stimulus, indicates that a warning signal does not
necessarily increase the attractiveness of situations in which
inescapable shock is encountered. It is the results for Group C,
however, which most clearly separate the effects of safety signals
from those of warning signals. Where the safety signal was present
on both sides of the box, the inclusion of the warning signal
produced a preference for the opposite side of the box. In addition,
only Group C animals gained weight during the study. Group A and B
animals lost weight. These results strongly support the notion that
a safety signal or some signal which predicts absence of shock is
what is reinforcing for an animal. A warning signal per se is not
preferred; rather, animals seek to avoid it. This would suggest
that when a warning signal is preferred or when somatic responses
are reduced in a signaled situation, it may be because that signal
can be used to predict the absence rather than the occurrence of
shock.

From the discussion above it appears that prediction of safety
is more important, in terms of reducing an animal's stress responses,
than prediction of shock. It may be that signaled shock is prefer-
able and causes less stress only when the contingencies between
warning and shock are such that the subject has an identifiable
safe period and can therefore relax during the intershock interval.
If the parameters of the task are such that a signal accurately
predicts shock but provides the organism with little feedback or
information about safety, then predictable shock may well be more
aversive.

CONCLUSION

In discussing the psychological variables which can ameliorate
a stress response, predictability is often cited as an important
factor. However, a careful review of studies which have tested the

effects of predictability reveals that the results are both complex
and confusing. While many find that predictable shock is less
aversive for an organism, many others find that predictable shock
is more aversive. Why is there such a discrepancy in the results?

It appears that although many investigators claim to be studying predictability, in fact they have introduced other variables
into their design, and it is these other variables which may be
primarily responsible for the results obtained. The two most
frequently occurring variables are <u>control</u> and <u>feedback</u>. Control
has been defined as the ability to make active responses which are
effective in allowing an animal either to avoid or escape from an
aversive stimulus, or simply to modify its environmental conditions.
Feedback has been defined as stimuli which provide information to
an organism, indicating that its responses have been effective and/
or that the aversive stimulus is over, at least for some interval
of time. Both control and feedback are, in themselves, potent
variables in ameliorating physiological or somatic responses to
stress. If either or both of these factors are present in a
signaled shock situation then the response to shock will be altered.
It is possible, in fact, that these two factors can account for most
if not all of the effects currently attributed to predictability in
experiments where a noxious stimulus is employed. The positive
aspects of predictability might be attributed primarily to control,
while the negative aspects of predictability might be attributed to
lack of information about safety. Thus predictability of a noxious
stimulus may always be more aversive unless the organism also has
control or unless the contingencies of the situation enable the
organism to gain information about safety. If experiments are
structured or analyzed with these two factors in mind, it may be
possible to actually eliminate the variable of predictability from
the literature on aversively motivated behavior.

REFERENCES

Arabian, J. M., and Desiderato, O., 1975, Preference for signalled
    shock: a test of two hypotheses, <u>Anim. Learn. Behav.</u>, 3:191.
Badia, P., and Culbertson, S., 1970, Behavioral effects of signalled
    vs. unsignalled shock during escape training in the rat, <u>J.
    Comp. Physiol. Psychol.</u>, 72:216.
Badia, P. and Culbertson, S., 1972, The relative aversiveness of
    signalled vs. unsignalled escapable and inescapable shock,
    <u>J. Exp. Anim. Behav.</u>, 17:463.
Badia, P., Culbertson, S., and Harsh, J., 1973, Choice of longer or
    stronger signalled shock over shorter or weaker unsignalled
    shock, <u>J. Exp. Anim. Behav.</u>, 19:25.
Badia, P., Culbertson, S. and Lewis, P., 1971, The relative aversive-
    ness of signalled vs. unsignalled avoidance, <u>J. Exp. Anim.
    Behav.</u>, 16:113.

Badia, P., Harsh, J., and Coker, C. C., 1975, Subjects choose fixed
    time over variable time shock and vice versa: shock distribu-
    tion and shock-free time as factors, Learn. Motiv., 6:264.

Badia, P., Harsh, J., Coker, C. C. and Abbott, B., 1976, Choice and
    the dependability of stimuli that predict shock and safety,
    J. Exp. Anim. Behav., 26:95.

Bassett, J. R., Cairncross, K. D., and King, M. G., 1973, Parameters
    of novelty, shock predictability and response contingency in
    corticosterone release in the rat, Physiol. Behav., 10:901.

Brady, J. P., Thronton, D. R., and Fisher, D. C., 1962, Deleterious
    effects of anxiety elicited by conditioned pre-aversive stimuli
    in the rat, Psychosom. Med., 24:590.

Bronson, F. H., and Eleftherion, B. E., 1965, Adrenal response to
    fighting in mice: separation of physical and psychological
    causes, Science, 147:627.

Conner, R., Vernikos-Danellis, J., and Levine, S., 1971, Stress,
    Fighting and Neuroendocrine Function, Nature, 234:564.

Coover, G. D., Goldman, L., and Levine, S., 1971, Plasma cortico-
    sterone increases produced by extinction of operant behavior
    in rats, Physiol. Behav., 6:261.

Coover, G. D., Ursin, H., and Levine, S., 1973, Plasma-Cortico-
    sterone levels during active-avoidance learning in rats,
    J. Comp. Physiol. Psychol., 82:170.

Davis, H., Memmott, J., MacFadden, L., and Levine, S., 1976,
    Pituitary-adrenal activity under different appetitive extinction
    procedures, Physiol. Behav., 17:687.

Davis, H., Porter, J. W., Livingstone, J., Herrmann, T., MacFadden,
    L., and Levine, S., 1977, Pituitary-adrenal activity and lever-
    press shock escape behavior, Physiol. Psychol., 5:280.

Friedman, S. B., and Ader, R., 1965, Parameters relevant to the
    experimental production of "stress" in the mouse, Psychosom.
    Med., 27:27.

Friedman, S. B., and Ader, R., 1967, Adrenocortical response to
    novelty and noxious stimulation, Neuroendocrinology, 2:209.

Furedy, J. J., and Biederman, G. B., 1976, Preference for signalled
    shock phenomenon: direct and indirect evidence for modifiability
    factors in the shuttlebox, Anim. Learn. Behav., 4:1.

Gliner, J. A., 1972, Predictable vs. unpredictable shock: preference
    behavior and stomach ulceration, Physiol. Behav., 9:693.

Hanson, J. D., Larson, M. E., and Snowdon, C. T., 1976, The effects
    of control over high intensity noise or plasma cortisol levels
    in rhesus monkeys, Behav. Biol., 16:333.

Hennessy, J. W., King, M. G., McClure, T. A., and Levine, S., 1977,
    Uncertainty, as defined by the contingency between environmental
    events, and the adrenocortical response of the rat to electric
    shock, J. Comp. Physiol. Psychol., 91:1447.

Hennessy, J. W., and Levine, S., 1979, Stress, arousal, and the
    pituitary-adrenal system: a psychoendocrine hypothesis, in:
    "Progress in Psychobiology and Physiological Psychology,"
    J. Sprague and A. Epstein, eds., Academic Press, New York.

Lockard, J. S., 1963, Choice of a warning signal or no warning signal
    in an unavoidable shock situation, J. Comp. Physiol. Psychol.,
    56:526.
Mason, J. W., 1968, A review of psychoendocrine research on the
    pituitary-adrenal cortical system, Psychosom. Med., 30:576.
Mason, J. W., 1975, A historical view of the stress field, Part II,
    J. Hum. Stress, 1:22.
Pare, W. P., 1964, The effect of chronic environmental stress on
    stomach ulceration, adrenal function and consummatory behavior
    in the rat, J. Psychol., 57:143.
Perkins, C. C., Jr., 1968, An analysis of the concept of reinforce-
    ment, Psych. Rev., 75:155.
Seligman, M. E. P., 1968, Chronic fear produced by unpredictable
    electric shock, J. Comp. Physiol. Psychol., 66:402.
Seligman, M. E. P., and Meyer, B., 1970, Chronic fear and ulcers in
    rats as a function of the unpredictability of safety, J. Comp.
    Physiol. Psychol., 73:202.
Selye, H., 1936, A syndrome produced by diverse nocuous agents,
    Nature, 138:32.
Selye, H., 1973, The evolution of the stress concept, Amer. Sci.,
    61:692.
Smotherman, W. P., Hennessy, J. W., and Levine, S., 1976, Plasma
    corticosterone levels during recovery from LiCl-produced
    taste aversions, Behav. Biol., 16:401.
Smotherman, W. P., Margolis, A., and Levine, S., in press, Flavor
    pre-exposures in a conditioned taste aversion situation: a
    dissociation of behavioral and endocrine effects, J. Comp.
    Physiol. Psychol.
Weinberg, J., 1977, Modulation of the deleterious effects of pre-
    shock by shock-induced fighting in rats or fighting is its own
    reward, unpublished doctoral dissertation, Stanford University.
Weinberg, J., and Levine, S., 1977, Early handling influences on
    behavioral and physiological responses during active avoidance,
    Devel. Psychobiol., 10:161.
Weinberg, J., Smotherman, W. P., and Levine, S., 1978, Early handling
    effects on neophobia and conditioned taste aversion, Physiol.
    Behav., 20:589.
Weiss, J. M., 1968, Effects of coping responses on stress, J. Comp.
    Physiol. Psychol., 65:251.
Weiss, J. M., 1970, Somatic effects of predictable and unpredictable
    shock, Psychosom. Med., 32:397.
Weiss, J. M., 1971a, Effects of coping behavior in different warning
    signal conditions on stress pathology in rats, J. Comp. Physiol.
    Psychol., 77:1.
Weiss, J. M., 1971b, Effects of punishing the coping response (con-
    flict) on stress pathology in rats, J. Comp. Physiol. Psychol.,
    77:14.
Weiss, J. M., 1971c, Effects of coping behavior with and without a
    feedback signal on stress pathology in rats, J. Comp. Physiol.
    Psychol., 77:22.

ASSOCIATIVE AND NON-ASSOCIATIVE

MECHANISMS IN THE DEVELOPMENT OF

TOLERANCE FOR STRESS

Jeffrey A. Gray, Susan Owen,
Nicola Davis and Joram Feldon

Department of Experimental Psychology
Oxford

It has been known since Pavlov's (1928) early experiments on counter-conditioning that it is possible to rob a painful event of some of its capacity to act as a stressor by associating it with an appetitive event. In these experiments an electric shock to the skin was used as a conditioned stimulus (CS) signalling the unconditioned stimulus (UCS) of food. Not surprisingly, the dog used as a subject in the experiment at first reacted to the shock by howling, barking and struggling to get out of the apparatus. But after the shock had been paired with the food a number of times this reaction disappeared; instead, the animal took the shock calmly and salivated in anticipation of the food.

Counter-conditioning as demonstrated by Pavlov involves a direct association between the painful CS and the desirable UCS. The effects of the counter-conditioning do not spread very far beyond the particular circumstances in which it is carried out. Indeed, in these early experiments, they were very limited indeed. It was sufficient for the experimenter to shift the shock to another part of the dog's body for the initial reaction of pain and fear to return. But since then it has become clear that it is possible using similar techniques to affect an animal's behaviour so widely that one is sometimes tempted to talk about a change in the animal's general personality rather than a change in a particular form of behaviour.

What is not always clear is the extent to which these other techniques depend on an associative mechanism, as did Pavlov's counter-conditioning experiment, as distinct from non-associative

mechanisms. This paper will attempt to unravel these possibilities
and it will also consider what brain events may underlie the development of tolerance for stress by either route.

BEHAVIOURAL TOLERANCE FOR STRESS

Two experimental paradigms have been influential in shaping
theories in this field: one is concerned with the 'partial reinforcement extinction effect' (PREE), the other with the closely analogous
'partial punishment effect' (PPE). Both kinds of experiment have
most often been conducted with rats rewarded with food for running
in an alley. In the PREE two groups of rats are compared. One is
given a reward on every trial during   training (a 'continuous
reinforcement' or CRF schedule), the other a reward on a randomly
chosen proportion (typically 50%) of trials (a 'partial reinforcement' or PRF schedule). Both groups are then tested in extinction.
The PRF group is found to be more resistant to extinction (i.e., it
runs faster to the empty goalbox than the CRF group): this is the
PREE. The PPE also depends on a comparison of two groups, one of
which is given CRF training as in the PREE experiment. The other
group is also given food reward on a CRF schedule, but in addition
it receives shock in the goalbox. The shock may occur on every
trial or only on a randomly chosen proportion of trials; it is
usually of low intensity on early trials and is then gradually
increased to a maximum. By analogy with the PRF schedule we shall
describe these methods of presenting shock during training as 'partial punishment' (PP) schedules. After training is complete, both
groups are tested with CRF food and the maximum intensity of shock
punishment on every trial. It is found that the PP group is more
resistant to punishment (i.e., it runs faster to the electrified
goalbox than the CRF group): this is the PPE.

Theory-building has concentrated in particular on the PREE
(Sutherland and Mackintosh, 1971; Mackintosh, 1974). A variety
of different explanations have been offered for this phenomenon,
but only two have proved to have wide explanatory power. Capaldi
(1967) proposed that rats trained on a PRF schedule learn to associate the after-effect or memory trace of a nonrewarded trial with
reward for running on the next rewarded trial. Thus running is a
more probable response to after-effects of nonreward during
extinction in PRF- than in CRF-trained rats, giving rise to the
PREE. Amsel (1962) also proposes that nonreward produces an after-
effect, which he specifies as a negative emotional state termed
'frustration'. As a result of experiencing unconditioned frustration in the presence of apparatus cues the animal develops a
Pavlovian conditioned reflex of 'conditioned' or 'anticipatory
frustration' to these cues. The immediate effect of anticipatory
frustration is to inhibit the running response (observed as a
period of slowed and erratic running in the PRF group early in
training). However, since the PRF-trained animal is rewarded on

a proportion of trials, the internal cues emanating from the state
of anticipatory frustration themselves become associated with reward
for performing the running response, a process Amsel terms 'counter-
conditioning'. After counter-conditioning is complete, the internal
cues of anticipatory frustration come to control continued running
rather than the inhibition of running, giving rise to the PREE. It
is clear that both theories depend on an associative process of
counter-conditioning. Capaldi supposes this to involve as the
counter-conditioned stimulus the after-effect or memory of nonreward;
Amsel supposes it to involve stimuli arising from anticipatory
frustration.

Capaldi's and Amsel's theories are not mutually exclusive, but
rather complementary. And the evidence suggests that the PREE is
produced by (at least) two routes, which perhaps correspond to
the processes postulated by these two theorists (Mackintosh, 1974).
Capaldi's route appears to be favoured by short inter-trial intervals (ITI), up to 10-20 minutes, and relatively few training trials
(of the order of 50-70); Amsel's route is favoured by a long ITI
(especially one of 24 hours) or (if short ITIs are used) many
training trials (Mackintosh, 1974). Both theories are well
supported, in the sense that each makes predictions which the other
does not and which have been demonstrated experimentally. But the
nature of these predictions and the supporting experimental data
is different in the two cases. In the case of Capaldi's theory
these are of a kind that only an associative process could easily
generate. In the case of Amsel's theory, they are consistent with
an associative process, but in many cases a non-associative
process could give rise to the same or closely similar effects.
This is a problem to which we shall return later.

The possibility that tolerance for aversive events (such as
shock or nonreward) might arise from a non-associative mechanism
has been brought into sharp focus by the experiments of Weiss and
Glazer (1975), working in Neal Miller's laboratory. Following up
earlier research on 'learned helplessness' (Seligman, Maier and
Solomon, 1971), Weiss and Glazer showed that a single session of
inescapable shock impairs the rat's ability subsequently to learn
escape or avoidance responses in a shuttlebox; but the disruptive
effect of inescapable shock disappeared if the rats were pre-
exposed to fifteen, rather than one such session. Thus repeated
exposure to inescapable shock allows the rat to overcome the
deleterious effects of a single session of inescapable shock.
Miller (1976) has termed this effect 'toughening up'. Notice that
the animal does not receive any reward during exposure to
inescapable shock, so counter-conditioning of the Pavlovian kind
(shock becoming a CS for a desirable UCS) could not take place. It
is difficult to rule out entirely the possibility that the animal
learned an instrumental response (presumably minimising the felt
intensity of shock) which transferred to its later behaviour in

the shuttlebox (in the general manner postulated by Amsel and
Capaldi for the PREE).   But there are features of Weiss and Glazer's
experiments that render this type of explanation extremely implaus-
ible.   For example, they showed that it was possible to nullify the
disruptive effects of inescapable shock not only by repeated exposure
to shock itself, but also by repeated exposure to swimming in cold
water ('cold swim') or by repeated injection of a drug which depletes
brain monoamines (Weiss and Glazer, 1975; Glazer, Weiss Pohorecky
and Miller, 1975; Weiss, Glazer, Pohorecky, Brick and Miller, 1975).
It is difficult to see how these varied treatments could have in
common the generation of an instrumental response.   Thus toughening
up seems to require no specific association, whether stimulus-
stimulus or stimulus-response.

There appear, then, to be at least three ways of increasing
behavioural tolerance for stressful events.   The first is by
Pavlovian stimulus-stimulus association: an aversive event is made
a direct signal for an appetitive one (Dickinson and Pearce, 1977).
The second is by stimulus-response association, and is best exemplified by Capaldi's work on the PREE: stimuli produced by nonreward (or the memory of nonreward) become cues for performing the
rewarded instrumental response.   The third is by non-associative
repeated exposure to the stressful event (Miller's toughening up);
it is best exemplified by Weiss and Glazer's experiments.

As pointed out above, Pavlovian counter-conditioning is
apparently quite narrow in its behavioural effects: a small change
in the location of the counter-conditioned shock CS on the skin may
be sufficient to disrupt the acquired tolerance for its aversive
effects (Pavlov, 1927).   Toughening up, in contrast, has extremely
widespread effects.   Weiss et al.   (1975) showed that repeated
exposure to inescapable shock prevents cold swim from impairing
shuttlebox performance (an impairment which is produced by a
single session of cold swim not preceded by repeated inescapable
shock).   Similarly, repeated exposure to cold swim prevented a
single session of inescapable shock from having this effect.
Exposure to repeated inescapable shock has also been shown to
produce increased resistance to extinction (Chen and Amsel, 1977).

To these instances of 'cross-tolerance' between stressors
produced by non-associative techniques we can add two more whose
mode of production is more equivocal: training on a PRF schedule
gives rise to increased resistance to punishment, and training on
a PP schedule produces increased resistance to extinction (Brown
and Wagner, 1964).   These effects have usually been considered in
associative terms.   It has been argued that a PRF schedule gives
rise to Amselian counter-conditioning of the internal stimuli
characteristic of frustration and a PP schedule to counter-
conditioning of the internal stimuli of fear; that these two
classes of hypothetical stimuli resemble each other; and that this

resemblance is sufficient to permit transfer of counter-conditioning from nonreward to punishment and vice versa (Amsel, 1962; Gray, 1967). It is possible to test this assumption by presenting the shock of a PP schedule outside the goalbox where food is received, thus breaking the associative link. This control was used in an investigation of the PPE itself by Miller (1960), who showed that this was produced associatively, since shock during training but outside the goalbox failed to increase resistance to punishment when high-intensity shock was later presented in the goalbox. But, to our knowledge, there is no report of a control for non-associative effects in cross-tolerance between PP training and extinction testing. In view of Chen and Amsel's (1977) demonstration that repeated inescapable shock can increase resistance to extinction, such controls are essential before one can conclude that cross-tolerance can be produced by associative, as well as non-associative, mechanisms.

ANTI-ANXIETY DRUGS AND STRESS TOLERANCE

Part of the evidence that there are two kinds of PREE, one due presumably to Capaldi's process and one to Amsel's comes from the observed effects of anti-anxiety drugs, i.e., barbiturates, benzodiazepines and alcohol (Gray, 1977).

The drug which has so far been most investigated is the barbiturate, sodium amylobarbitone (SA). If the conditions of the experiment are such as to favour Capaldi's mechanism (a short ITI and very few trials), SA has no effect on the PREE (Ziff and Capaldi, 1971): if they are such as to favour Amsel's mechanism (a 24-hour ITI), SA given during training virtually eliminates the PREE (Feldon, Guillamon, Gray, de Wit and McNaughton, 1979); if they do not favour either mechanism very clearly (a short ITI and relatively many trials), mixed effects are obtained (Ison and Pennes, 1969; Gray, 1969). These results are broadly consistent with the hypothesis that SA impairs conditioned frustration, but does not influence the after-effect of nonreward (Gray, 1977; Feldon et al., 1979). If the PREE is largely determined by after-effects, it is not affected by the drug; if it is largely determined by conditioned frustration, it is blocked by the drug; and if it is determined by both types of process, the drug produces only a partial effect. Also consistent with this interpretation is the failure of SA to affect the frustration effect (FE: Amsel and Roussel, 1952) in the double runway (Gray, 1977), assuming this to be an after-effect of nonreward. However, we shall see that there are other findings which are harder to fit into this picture.

Recently, investigation of the anti-anxiety drugs has been extended to the benzodiazepine, chlordiazepoxide (CDP), and to PP schedules. Previous experiments using CDP have produced state dependency (Overton, 1966) of the running response (Iwahara, Nagamura and Iwasaki, 1967; Willner and Crowe, 1977). We overcame

this problem by gradually decreasing (or increasing) the dosage of the drug over the last few days of training in groups which received a switch in drug state between training and testing. Using this method, and an ITI of 24 hours, we have shown that 5 mg/kg CDP given during training abolishes both the PREE and the PPE (Figure 1), and that these effects are in neither case due to state dependency since they appear also in groups treated with the drug during both training and testing (Feldon, Davis and Gray, unpublished). In a similar experiment, also at one-trial-a-day but using SA, Dyck, Lussier and Ossenkopp (1975) found that SA in training abolished the increased resistance to punished extinction produced by a PP schedule. Thus, at a 24-hour ITI, the anti-anxiety drugs block acquired tolerance to both nonreward and punishment.

Notice, however, that the one-trial-a-day PREE and PPE differ in one respect which is crucial for their bearing on Amsel's and Capaldi's theories. When nonreward occurs on a PRF schedule, there is (at least) a 24-hour interval before the next rewarded trial. Presumably, Capaldi's after-effects or memories have less likelihood of living through a 24-hour ITI than one of a few minutes. It is for this reason that after-effects should play a very limited role in determining the one-trial-a-day PREE. But on a PP schedule, whenever shock occurs, it is immediately followed by food reward. Thus the hypothesis that anti-anxiety drugs block conditioned emotional states rather than the after-effects of aversive events (Feldon, et al., 1979) does not predict that these agents should have particularly marked effects on the PPE at one-trial-a-day. Since the effects we have obtained with CDP in the one-trial-a-day PREE and PPE are strikingly similar (Feldon et al., unpublished), some doubt must also be cast on the adequacy of this hypothesis as applied to the PREE.

THE SEPTO-HIPPOCAMPAL SYSTEM AND STRESS TOLERANCE

For some years we have been using the observed effects of anti-anxiety drugs as a base from which to investigate the brain mechanisms which underlie anxiety (Gray, 1978) and the development of behavioural tolerance for stress (Gray, Davis, Feldon, Owen, and Boarder, in press). Our first guess as to the nature of these mechanisms implicated the septal area, the hippocampus and their interconnections, and attributed a particularly important role to the hippocampal theta rhythm (known to be controlled by pacemaker cells in the medial septal area) in a narrow frequency band centered on 7.7 Hz (Gray, 1970).

Part of the evidence for this hypothesis was that the anti-anxiety drugs raise the threshold for production of hippocampal theta by electrical stimulation of the septal pacemaker ('theta-driving') specifically at 7.7 Hz (Gray and Ball, 1970; McNaughton, James, Stewart, Gray, Valero, and Drewnowski, 1977). This suggested that

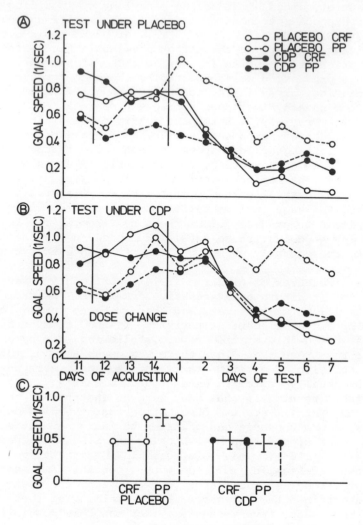

Figure 1

Effects of 5 mg/kg chlordiazepoxide HCl (CDP) or saline (placebo) given during acquisition on the partial punishment effect. (CF: continuous reinforcement. PP: partial punishment.) A: goal speeds during 7 trials (1/day) of testing with food and shock on every trial and saline injections for all groups. B: as in A, but with CDP injections for all groups. C: goal speeds as a function of acquisition training and drug conditions, averaged across test drug conditions and test days. Between Days 11 and 14 of acquisition the dose of CDP was gradually changed in groups switched from drug to placebo or vice versa.

the anti-anxiety drugs might act on behaviour by impairing septal
control of hippocampal theta specifically in this frequency band
(Gray, 1970; Gray and Ball, 1970). This argument implies that
septal driving of theta at this frequency should have effects on
behaviour which are opposite in sign to those of the anti-anxiety
drugs. This prediction was supported by the demonstration that 7.7
Hz theta driving, given in the goalbox of an alley in conjunction
with CRF food reward, increased subsequent resistance to extinction
(Gray, 1972). Gray (1972) interpreted this finding along associative lines. It was supposed that 7.7 Hz theta (the observed
hippocampal electrographic response to nonreward in the alley:
Gray and Ball, 1970; Kimsey, Dyer, and Petri, 1974) is a signal of
nonreward, and that its conjunction with food allows it to be counter-
conditioned as in Amsel's theory of the PREE. Glazer (1974) subsequently used the same interpretation of an experiment in which he
trained animals to produce 7.7 Hz theta by directly rewarding them
with food for so doing; these rats, like those in Gray's (1972)
experiment, subsequently showed greater resistance to extinction.

     Certain features of Glazer's (1974) experiment, however, are
difficult to fit within an associative framework. He trained rats
to generate 7.7 Hz theta first, and then (without further manipulation of hippocampal electrical activity) trained them to barpress on
a fixed ratio schedule of food reward, following this by extinction
of the barpress response. Thus there was never any possibility for
direct association of experimentally induced theta with the barpress
response eventually tested in extinction. Glazer's (1974) own
account of his results is that they were an instance of the
'generalized PREE', i.e., the observation that training on a PRF
schedule with one response can transfer to increased resistance to
extinction of a second response which is not itself learned on a PRF
schedule (Ross, 1964). This is a possible interpretation. But, in
view of Chen and Amsel's (1977) demonstration that non-associative
effects may strengthen resistance to extinction, the possibility
must be entertained that Glazer's (1974) training of theta also
engaged a non-associative mechanism. Nor can this possibility be
ruled out for Gray's (1972) results.

     A further line of evidence implicating the septo-hippocampal
system in the development of tolerance for nonreward is provided
by lesion studies. It was reported by Gray, Quintão and Araujo-
Silva (1972) that damage to the septal area weakens the PREE. Gray
et al. (1972) attributed their results to destruction of the medial
septal area, containing the pacemakers for theta. Later work,
however, has shown clearly that the critical site of damage lies in
the lateral septal area, which receives the major hippocampo-septal
projection (Feldon and Gray, 1979a,b). Gray et al. (1972)
found only a small effect of their lesion on the PREE. Henke's
(1974, 1977) experiments show that this was due to the particular
number of training trials used. Like Gray et al. (1972), Henke

(1974) used a short ITI (4-5 minutes). With 48 training trials, he found a complete abolition of the PREE by total septal ablation, but with 96 trials there was no effect of the lesion on the PREE; Gray et al. (1972) used an intermediate number of trials (72) and obtained an intermediate effect. We have replicated Henke's (1974, 1977) findings using lateral septal lesions, and find the same dependence of their effects on number of training trials (Feldon and Gray, 1979b).

This pattern of results runs counter to the hypothesis that septal lesions affect conditioned frustration as distinct from the after-effect of nonreward. This hypothesis leads to the expectation that the lesion should produce bigger effects (at short ITIs) the larger the number of training trials, since conditioned frustration is thought to play an increasingly important role (relative to after-effects) as acquisition progresses (Mackintosh, 1974; Feldon et al., 1979). This expectation as applied to the anti-anxiety drugs, is broadly confirmed if one compares studies that have used SA with different numbers of training trials (Gray, 1977; Feldon et al., 1979); but it should be noted that none of these experiments has directly compared different training lengths. We have recently made such a comparison, using CDP and the same training parameters as Henke (1974). The drug reduced the PREE with 48 training trials, but had no effect with 96 (Feldon et al., unpublished). This result is consistent with the hypothesis that septal lesions and anti-anxiety drugs affect behaviour in similar manners; but not with the hypothesis that these treatments selectively eliminate conditioned frustration.

The obvious alternative hypothesis to account for Henke's findings is that septal lesions impair Capaldi's after-effects but not conditioned frustration. This leads directly to the prediction of a bigger effect of the lesion on the PREE at short ITIs as training lengthens. But this hypothesis is ruled out for septal lesions by the same facts which rule it out for the anti-anxiety drugs; there is a very large effect of lateral septal lesions on the PREE at one trial a day (Feldon and Gray, 1979a); and there is no effect of septal lesions on the double-runway FE (Mabry and Peeler, 1972; Henke, 1977). Thus, at present, we are unable to accommodate all of the data concerning the effects of either septal lesions or the anti-anxiety drugs on the PREE within one hypothesis. One possibility is that Henke's effect is due to vicarious functioning of systems in the brain other than the damaged septal area. The parallel findings with CDP might arise in the same general way.

BRAIN MONOAMINES AND STRESS TOLERANCE

As indicated above, it is possible to drive the hippocampal theta rhythm at any desired frequency within the naturally occurring theta range (about 6 to 12 Hz) by stimulating the septal area via

chronically implanted electrodes. If one now plots the threshold
current able to drive theta in this way as a function of stimulation
frequency, a characteristic function is found in the free-moving male
rat, with a minimum threshold at 7.7 Hz (Gray and Ball, 1970; James,
McNaughton, Rawlins, Feldon, and Gray, 1977). This minimum is
abolished by anti-anxiety drugs, which raise the threshold selectively
at 7.7 Hz (Gray and Ball, 1970; McNaughton et al., 1977). We
attempted to mimic this effect by altering the function of a number
of putative neurotransmitters. Only by selective blockade of noradrenaline (NA) could we achieve this effect (McNaughton et al.,
1977). Our results indicated that, in the undrugged rat, thresholds
for septal driving of theta are maintained relatively low at 7.7 Hz
by a noradrenergic mechanism, and relatively high at frequencies
above and below 7.7 Hz by a serotonergic mechanism. We have been able
to define the noradrenergic mechanism more precisely. Injection of
the selective neurotoxin, 6-hydroxydopamine (6-OHDA) (Ungerstedt,
19), into the dorsal ascending NA bundle, reducing hippocampal NA
content by more than 90%, also eliminated the 7.7 Hz minimum in the
theta-driving curve (Gray, McNaughton, James, and Kelly, 1975).
Thus it seems likely that the anti-anxiety drugs alter septo-hippocampal electrophysiology by impairing the noradrenergic input which
travels in the dorsal bundle to these structures from the locus
coeruleus (Ungerstedt, 1971).

These findings suggested that the behavioural effects of the
anti-anxiety drugs might be produced in the same way (Gray, et al.,
1978). Findings consistent with this suggestion had already been
published by Fuxe's group in Sweden, who showed that stress
increases the turnover of forebrain NA and that this increase is
reversed by anti-anxiety drugs (Lidbrink, Corrodi, Fuxe, and Olson,
1973). But note that Lidbrink et al. (1973) also showed that stress
increases the turnover of 5-hydroxytryptamine (5-HT) in the brain,
and that this increase too is reversed by anti-anxiety medication.
Other evidence (Stein, Wise and Berger, 1973) also supports the
hypothesis that brain 5-HT plays an important role in mediating
responses to stress, especially punishment, and the action of anti-
anxiety drugs. Our own electrophysiological results (Gray et al.,
1975; McNaughton et al., 1977) were consistent either with the
hypothesis that forebrain NA alone is critical in the mediation of
anti-anxiety action (since destruction of the dorsal NA bundle is
sufficient to eliminate the 7.7 Hz minimum in the theta-driving
curve); or with the hypothesis that both monamines play important
roles (since both are necessary to maintain the normal shape of the
theta-driving curve).

In the last few years we have begun to test these hypotheses
by investigating the behavioural effects of destruction of the
dorsal NA bundle, using injection of 6-OHDA into the bundle; and by
investigating the effects of destruction of forebrain 5-HT pathways
by injection of the neurotoxin, 5, 7-dihydroxytryptamine (5, 7-DHT)

(Bjorklund, Baumgarten, and Rensch, 1975) into the ventromedial
tegmentum. The former treatment produces substantial depletion
(> 90%) of NA in the terminal areas of the dorsal bundle (hippocampus,
neocortex), with only small depletion of NA (about 30-40%) in the
hypothalamus, and no significant reduction of dopamine or 5-HT levels.
The latter treatment is similarly selective for 5-HT, whose levels
in the hippocampus are reduced by about 70%.

   We have looked at animals with destruction of the dorsal NA
bundle in three versions of the PREE: 50 and 100 training trials with
a short ITI (Owen, Boarder, Feldon, Gray, and Fillenz, 1979),
equivalent to Henke's (1974) two training conditions; and the one-
trial-a-day PREE. There was a complete abolition of the PREE with
50 trials (Figure 2), and no effect of the lesion with 100 trials at
the short ITI in agreement with the effects of total septal (Henke,
1974) and lateral septal (Feldon and Gray, 1979b) lesions; but
unlike the two septal lesions, which also impair the one-trial-a-day

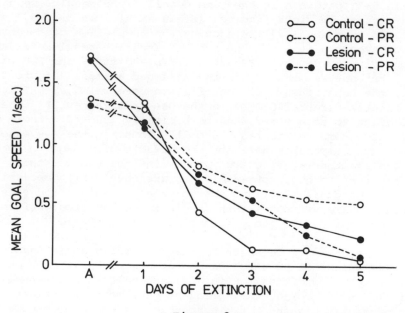

Figure 2

   Effects of 6-hydroxydopamine injection in the dorsal noradrenergic bundle (lesion) on the partial reinforcement extinction
effect. CR: continuous reinforcement. PR: partial reinforcement.
A: final day of acquisition. Control animals underwent a sham
operation.

PREE (Feldon and Gray, 1979a), dorsal bundle lesions failed to affect the PREE in this paradigm. This pattern of results is consistent with an effect of the dorsal bundle lesion, not on conditioned frustration, but on the after-effect of nonreward. To look at this more closely, we investigated the double-runway FE in animals with dorsal bundle lesions. The results of this experiment were not entirely clear; but they afforded very little evidence of disruption of the FE in the lesioned animals. We have also looked at the one-trial-a-day PPE in the dorsal-bundle animals. In contrast to the equivalent PREE experiment, the lesion had a massive effect: as shown in Figure 3, the PPE was abolished in the lesioned animals. This result shows that the failure of the lesion to affect the one-trial-a-day PREE was not due to the ITI per se. But, as noted above, the significance of the ITI is different in the two paradigms. A 24-hour ITI minimises the role of after-effects in the PREE, but does not necessarily affect it in the PPE. Thus, with the exception of the failure to alter the FE, all the effects of the dorsal bundle lesion fit the hypothesis of an impairment in the control of behaviour by the after-effects of nonreward and punishment.

We have not yet investigated the effects of destruction of forebrain 5-HT pathways in the same detail. The results we have to date conform previous findings (Stein et al., 1973; Tye, Everitt and Iversen, 1977) in showing that depletion of forebrain 5-HT increases resistance to punishment (see the results for the CRF group given 5,7-DHT in Figure 3). In addition, the PPE was reduced, but not eliminated, in the lesioned animals (Figure 3). Overall, the behavioural effects of intra-cerebral 5, 7-DHT and those of intra-cerebral 6-OHDA in the one-trial-a-day PPE were quite similar to each other, and both closely resembled those of systemic CDP (compare Figures 1 and 3). Thus, in the one case for which we have comparable data for the effects of damage to forebrain NA and 5-HT neurons, respectively, our findings support the hypothesis that both neurotransmitters are involved in mediating the effects of punishment; and that both also mediate the effects of the anti-anxiety drugs. This conclusion is in broad agreement with the work of Fuxe's group (Lidbrink et al., 1973).

These experiments demonstrate that forebrain NA is involved in the development of both tolerance for nonreward (though only under restricted conditions: Figure 2) and tolerance for punishment (Figure 3). By so doing, they bring us once more up against the problem of distinguishing between associative and non-associative mechanisms in tolerance for stress. For Weiss et al. (1975) and Glazer et al. (1975) have shown that this same neurotransmitter is involved in the clearly non-associative phenomenon of toughening up.

Weiss et al. (1975) and Glazer et al. (1975) advance several lines of evidence, in support of this conclusion. First, in the

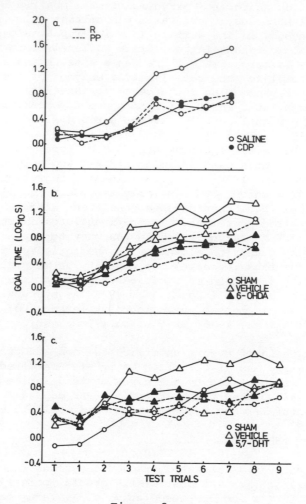

Figure 3

Effects of (a) 5 mg/kg chlordiazepoxide HCl (CDP), (b) 6-hydroxy-
dopamine injection into the dorsal noradrenergic bundle (6-OHDA), or
(c) 5, 7-dihydroxytryptamine injection into the ventromedial
tegmentum (5, 7-DHT on the partial punishment effect. 'Vehicle'
groups were injected with vehicle alone; 'sham' groups were subjected
to surgery, but the injection cannula was not lowered into the brain.
R: continuous reinforcement during training. PP: partial punishment
during training. T: last day of training. During the test trials
(1/day) all animals received food and shock on every trial.

animals in which shuttlebox performance was impaired by acute
exposure to a stressor, there was a concomitant fall in the level of
brain NA.   Second, in the animals in which repeated exposure to a
stressor produced toughening up, brain NA levels returned to normal.
Third, in the latter animals there was a rise in the activity of
tyrosine hydroxylase, the rate-limiting enzyme for the synthesis of
NA.   This may represent an instance of 'trans-neuronal induction' of
tyrosine hydroxylase, which has been shown to occur under conditions
of increased neuronal activity in the peripheral nervous system
(Thoenen, 1975; Fillenz, 1977), and also in the central nervous
system in response to reserpine (Reis, Joh, Ross, and Pickel, 1974),
a drug which depletes catecholamine stores, and cold stress (Zigmond,
Schon, and Iversen, 1974).   Fourth, repeated injection of tetrabenazine, a drug which acts similarly to reserpine, also produced
toughening up.   These findings are consistent with the hypothesis
that: (1) impaired performance in the shuttlebox is due to a fall
in the levels of NA in the brain in response to acute stress; (2)
repeated stress causes an elevation in the activity of tyrosine
hydroxylase and thus increases the capacity of NA systems in the
brain to resist depletion of their neurotransmitter under conditions
of stress; and (3) this induction of tyrosine hydroxylase underlies
the observed development of behavioural tolerance for stress (Weiss
et al., 1975; Miller, 1976; Gray et al., in press).

     If this chain of events underlies the non-associative phenomenon
of toughening up, and if forebrain NA is also involved in the PREE
and the PPE, as suggested by the experiments described above, the
question arises whether the PREE and the PPE depend on a similar
chain of events; if they do, they might similarly be non-associative.

QUESTIONS FOR THE FUTURE

     This paper has deliberately raised questions rather than
proposed answers. For, at most of the crucial points of choice
between associative and non-associative mechanisms, data by which
to guide the choice are scarce. In this concluding section, therefore, we shall summarise the questions that remain open, both at the
psychological and the physiological level, and indicate some of the
ways the answers to these questions might interact with each other.

     We have asked the question 'associative or non-associative?'
in three major connections.   (1) Is the second process (besides
Capaldi's) that contributes to the PREE associative, as supposed by
Amsel, or is it non-associative? (2) Does the experimental induction
of theta increase resistance to extinction, as in Gray's (1972) and
Glazer's (1974) experiments, by an associative or a non-associative
path? (3) Is forebrain NA part of an associative mechanism for the
production of tolerance for nonreward (in the PREE) and punishment
(in the PPE); or is it exclusively part of a non-associative
mechanism, as in the case of toughening up? Two other, closely

related, questions have been implied by much of the discussion.
(4) Is there an associative mechanism which can produce cross-
tolerance between different stressors, or are associative effects
limited to the production of direct tolerance (as in Pavlov's
original counter-conditioning experiments)? (5) Do the anti-anxiety
drugs affect Amsel's associative process or a non-associative one?
None of these questions yet has a definitive answer. But they are
all capable of being given one.

     The problem posed by the first question arises in part out of
the data that have been considered to discriminate between Capaldi's
(1967) and Amsel's (1962) rival theories of the PREE. Much of the
experimentation dealing with the PREE over the last fifteen years
has been concerned to support or refute one or other of these
theories (Mackintosh, 1974). From our present point of view, there
has been an important asymmetry in the data and arguments generated
by this dispute. By and large (Mackintosh, 1974), it has been counted
as evidence in favour of Capaldi's theory when it has been shown
(usually at short ITIs) that resistance to extinction varies as a
function of the precise details of the training schedule (sequence
of rewarded and nonrewarded trials, numbers of transitions between
such trials, lengths of repeated sequences of nonrewarded trials,
etc.). Similarly, it has been counted as evidence for Capaldi's
theory when extinction performance has been shown to deteriorate as
a function of change between the parameters of training and extinction
respectively. Thus, evidence for Capaldi's theory has as the same
time constituted evidence for the essentially associative nature of
the process he postulates. Conversely, it has usually been counted
as evidence for Amsel's theory when it has been shown that the
effects of training with a PRF schedule do not depend very much on
the details of the training schedule, when it has been shown that
resistance to extinction transfers across wide differences between
training and extinction conditions, and when cross-tolerance between
different stressors has been demonstrated. But most of this evidence
(while it supports the view that there is a second process in the
PREE besides Capaldi's) does not, by its very nature, discriminate
between an associative process of wide generality and a process that
is not associative at all.

     To be sure, there are some experiments (e.g., Ross, 1964) which
have been performed within the framework provided by Amselian theory
and which have come up with clear evidence of associative effects.
But these were not concerned to discriminate Amsel's theory from
Capaldi's, and it is possible that the associative effects observed
in these experiments were due to Capaldi's process. Conversely, the
experiments which have been concerned to rule out the operation of
Capaldi's process did not also attempt to provide evidence for
associative effects. Thus, now that evidence from Amsel's own
laboratory (Chen and Amsel, 1977) has demonstrated that a non-associative process can generate increased resistance to extinction, it

is necessary to look for effects that are simultaneously consistent with frustration theory, inconsistent with Capaldi's theory, and incompatible with a non-associative process.

One way to do this (and at the same time to investigate Questions 4 and 5) might be to exploit the capacity of the anti-anxiety drugs to block the one-trial-a-day PREE (Feldon et al., 1979), and PPE (Dyck et al., 1975; Feldon et al., unpublished; and see Figure 1). If we assume that the two drug effects depend on the same mechanism (and the detailed similarities between them make this a reasonable assumption, Feldon et al., unpublished), then we may rule out an action on Capaldi's process (since this plays at best only a small role in the one-trial-a-day PREE). It remains, therefore, to distinguish between an associative process that is not Capaldi's (and would therefore reasonably be identified as the one postulated by Amsel) and a non-associative process. It is not difficult to control for non-associative effects in the PPE; one simply shocks the animal outside the goalbox, thus breaking the association between shock and reward or between shock and the rewarded response (Miller, 1960). This control has not yet been carried out in a one-trial-a-day experiment. Suppose we carry it out. There are then two possibilities: the non-associative treatment will produce a PPE, or it will not. If it does not, it follows that the PPE is associative and that the effect of SA or CDP on the PPE is also mediated by an associative process. If it does, then one could investigate the effects of these drugs on the non-associative PPE. If they block the non-associative PPE, the most parsimonious inference would be that the PPE as usually run is also non-associa-tive; that there is no need to postulate an additional, Amselian process; and that the anti-anxiety drugs block a non-associative process. If the anti-anxiety drugs do not block the non-associative PPE, it would follow that there is both a non-associative process and an Amselian one, and that the anti-anxiety drugs block only the latter.

Controlling for non-associative effects in the PREE is much more difficult, and perhaps impossible. Since nonreward necessarily occurs under conditions in which the animal expects reward, the converse must also be true: reward will occur when nonreward is expected, thus permitting direct counter-conditioning of Amsel's postulated anticipatory frustration by reward. But it might be possible to gain at least some insight into the role of non-associative effects in the PREE by studying cross-tolerance between nonreward and punishment. This has apparently not yet been investigated at one trial a day, though Dyck et al. (1975) showed transfer from a PP schedule to punished extinction. If cross-tolerance could be established at one trial a day, and if the experiments suggested in the previous paragraph were successful, it would be possible to determine whether the same roles of associative and non-associative factors, and the same drug sensitivities, which

hold for the PPE also hold for the increased resistance to extinction produced by a PP schedule. Such experiments might also tell us (in answer to Question 5) whether cross tolerance can be produced associatively or only non-associatively.

Question 2--whether the experimental induction of theta works associatively or non-associatively--is easier to answer. As we have seen, the design of Glazer's (1974) experiment strongly suggests that non-associative factors could have been involved in the genera-tion of his results. In the first pase of his experiment rats were rewarded for the production of 7.7 Hz theta; in a second phase (without further experimental induction of theta) they were trained to press a bar for food reward; and in the final phase the experi-mental animals showed increased resistance to extinction relative to controls. This design is basically the same as Chen and Amsel's (1977) experiment, in which inescapable shock in the first phase gave rise to increased resistance to extinction in the third. There seems little doubt that Chen and Amsel's (1977) finding arises from non-associative processes; so it is possible that Glazer's (1974) result has the same origin. It is not possible to test this using Glazer's procedure for the induction of theta, since rewarding the animal for theta obviously allows direct counter-conditioning to occur. But the experiment can be done using septal stimulation to drive theta. The appropriate comparison is between a group given theta-driving paired with food in phase 1 of the experiment, and a group given theta-driving and food according to a truly random procedure. Lee Holt is currently running this experiment in our laboratory.

It is in relation to Question 3--whether forebrain NA is part of an associative or a non-associative mechanism for the develop-ment of behavioural tolerance for stress--that the existing data are most contradictory. As indicated above, our own experiments have generated a pattern of data which is most consistent with the conclusion that destruction of the dorsal NA bundle eliminates Capaldi's process in the production of the PREE, and this of course is associative. But the experiments of Weiss et al. (1975) and Glazer et al. (1975) clearly implicate brain NA (though not necessarily forebrain NA) in the non-associative phenomenon of toughening up. We are currently approaching this problem by looking at changes in tyrosine hydroxylase activity in different brain regions as a function of different behavioural experiences (Owen et al., 1979; Fillenz, Graham-Jones and Gray, 1979); but these experiments are only in a preliminary stage.

CLINICAL CODA

In this paper we have taken a rather fine-grained look at behavioural tolerance for stress, emphasising problems of psycho-logical or physiological interpretation. But if one stands back

and looks at the experiments more grossly, two findings stand out as being of potentially great importance for clinical practice, whatever the mechanism by which they are produced. First, it is clear that exposure to one kind of stress can give rise, not only to tolerance for that stress, but also to tolerance for stress generally (Brown and Wagner, 1964; Weiss and Glazer, 1975; Chen and Amsel, 1977). Second, it is possible to block the development of behavioural tolerance for stress by administering anti-anxiety drugs (Gray, 1977; Dyck et al., 1975; Feldon et al., 1979; Figure 1). If these agents have similar effects in Man, the cost of using them to purchase immediate tranquility may be rather high.

ACKNOWLEDGEMENTS

     The experimental work described in this paper has been supported by the United Kingdom Medical Research Council. J. Feldon held the Kenneth Lindsay Scholarship awarded by the Anglo-Israel Association.

REFERENCES

Amsel, A., 1962, Frustrative nonreward in partial reinforcement and
     discrimination learning; some recent history and a theoretical
     extension, Psychol. Rev., 69:306.
Amsel, A., and Roussel, J., 1952, Motivational properties of
     frustration: I. Effect on a running response of the addition of
     frustration to the motivational complex, J. Exp. Psychol., 43:363.
Björklund, A., Baumgarten, H. G., and Rensch, A., 1975, 5, 7-Di-
     hydroxytryptamine: improvement of its selectivity for serotonin
     neurons in the CNS by pretreatment with desipramine, J. Neuro-
     chem, 24:833.
Brown, R. T., and Wagner, A. R., 1964, Resistance to punishment and
     extinction following training with shock or non-reinforcement,
     J. Exp. Psychol., 68:503.
Capaldi, E. J., 1967, A sequential hypothesis of instrumental
     learning, 1967, in: "The Psychology of Learning and Motivation,"
     K. W. Spence and J. T. Spence, eds., Vol. 1, Academic Press,
     New York, London.
Chen, J. S., and Amsel, A., 1977, Prolonged, unsignaled, inescapable
     shocks increase persistence in subsequent appetitive instru-
     mental learning, Anim. Learn. Behav., 5:377.
Dickinson, A., and Pearce, J. M., 1977, Inhibitory interactions
     between appetitive and aversive stimuli, Psychol. Bull., 84:690.
Dyck, D. G., Lussier, D., and Ossenkopp, K. -P., 1975, Partial
     punishment effect following minimal acquisition training:
     sodium amobarbital and the stimulus properties of early
     punished trials, Learn. Motiv., 6:412.

Feldon, J., and Gray, J. A., 1979a, Effects of medial and lateral
    septal lesions on the partial reinforcement extinction effect
    at one trial a day, Quart. J. Exp. Psychol., 31, (in press).

Feldon, J., and Gray, J. A., 1979b, Effects of medial and lateral
    septal lesions on the partial reinforcement extinction effect
    at short inter-trial intervals, Quart. J. Exp. Psychol., 31,
    (in press).

Feldon, J., Guillamon, A., Gray, J. A., DeWit, H., and McNaughton, N.,
    1979, Sodium amylobarbitone and responses to nonreward, Quart.
    J. Exp. Psychol., 31:19.

Fillenz, M., 1977, The factors which provide short-term and long-
    term control of transmitter release, Progr. Neurobiol., 8:251.

Fillenz, M., Graham-Jones, J., and Gray, J. A., 1979, The effect of
    footshock on synaptosomal tyrosine hydroxylation in rat brain
    regions, J. Physiol., (in press).

Glazer, H. I., 1974, Instrumental conditioning of hippocampal theta
    and subsequent response persistence, J. Comp. Physiol. Psychol.,
    86:267.

Glazer, H. I., Weiss, J. M., Pohorecky, L. A., and Miller, N. E.,
    1975, Monamines as mediators of avoidance-escape behaviour,
    Psychosom. Med., 37:535.

Gray, J. A., 1967, Disappointment and drugs in the rat, Adv. Sci.,
    23:595.

Gray, J. A., 1969, Sodium amobarbital and effects of frustrative
    nonreward, J. Comp. Physiol. Psychol., 69:55.

Gray, J. A., 1970, Sodium amobarbital, the hippocampal theta rhythm
    and the partial reinforcement extinction effect, Psychol. Rev.,
    77:465.

Gray, J. A., 1972, Effects of septal driving of the hippocampal theta
    rhythm on resistance to extinction, Physiol. Behav., 8:481.

Gray, J. A., 1977, Drug effects on fear and frustration: possible
    limbic site of action of minor tranquilizers, in: "Handbook
    of Psychopharmacology," Vol. 8, L. L. Iversen, S. D. Iversen,
    and S. H. Snyder, eds., Plenum Press, New York.

Gray, J. A., 1978, The neuropsychology of anxiety, Brit. J. Psychol.,
    69:417.

Gray, J. A., and Ball, G. G., 1970, Frequency-specific relation
    between hippocampal theta rhythm, behavior and amobarbital
    action, Science, N.Y., 168:1246.

Gray, J. A., Davis, N., Feldon, J., Owen, S., and Boarder, M., in
    press, Stress tolerance: possible neural mechanisms, in:
    "Psychosomatic Approaches in Medicine, Vol. 1, Behavioural
    Approaches," M. Christie and P. Mellett, eds, Wiley and Sons,
    London.

Gray, J. A., McNaughton, N., James, D. T. D., and Kelly, P. H., 1975,
    Effect of minor tranquillisers on hippocampal theta rhythm
    mimicked by depletion of forebrain noradrenaline, Nature,
    258:424.

Gray, J. A., Quintão, L., and Araujo-Silva, M. T., 1972, The partial
    reinforcement extinction effect in rats with medial septal
    lesions, Physiol. Behav., 8:491.

Henke, P. G., 1974, Persistence of runway performance after septal
    lesions in rats, J. Comp. Physiol. Psychol., 86:760.
Henke, P. G., 1977, Dissociation of the frustration effect and the
    partial reinforcement extinction effect after limbic lesions
    in rats, J. Comp. Physiol. Psychol., 91:1032.
Ison, J. R., and Pennes, E. S., 1969, Interaction of amobarbital
    sodium and reinforcement schedule in determining resistance
    to extinction of an instrumental running response, J. Comp.
    Physiol. Psychol., 68:215.
Iwahara, S., Nagamura, N., and Iwasaki, T., 1967, Effect of chlor-
    diazepoxide upon experimental extinction in the straight
    runway as a function of partial reinforcement in the rat,
    Jpn. Psychol. Res., 9:128.
James, D. T. D., McNaughton, N., Rawlins, J. N. P., Feldon, J., and
    Gray, J. A., 1977, Septal driving of hippocampal theta rhythm
    as a function of frequency in the free-moving male rat,
    Neuroscience, 2:1007.
Kimsey, R. A., Dyer, R. S., and Petri, H. L., 1974, Relationship
    between hippocampal EEG, novelty and frustration in the rat,
    Behav. Biol., 11:561.
Lidbrink, P., Corrodi, H., Fuxe, K., and Olson, L., 1973, The effects
    of benzodiazepines, meprobamate and barbiturates on central
    monoamine neurons, in: "The Benzodiazepines," S. Carattini,
    E. Mussini, and L. O. Randall eds., Raven Press, New York.
Mabry, P. D., and Peeler, D. F., 1972, Effect of septal lesions on
    response to frustrative nonreward, Physiol. Behav., 8:909.
Mackintosh, N. J., 1974, "The Psychology of Animal Learning,"
    Academic Press, London.
McNaughton, N., James, D. T. D., Stewart, J., Gray, J. A., Valero,
    I., and Drewnowski, A., 1977, Septal driving of hippocampal
    theta rhythm as a function of frequency in the male rat: effects
    of drugs, Neuroscience, 2:1019.
Miller, N. E., 1960, Learning resistance to pain and fear; effects
    of overlearning, exposure and rewarded exposure in context,
    J. Exp. Psychol., 60:137.
Miller, N. E., 1976, Learning, stress and psychosomatic symptoms,
    Acta Neurobiol. Exp., 36:141.
Overton, D. A., 1966, State-dependent learning produced by depress-
    ant and atropine-like drugs, Psychopharmacologia, 10:6.
Owen, S., Boarder, M. R., Feldon, J., Gray, J. A., and Fillenz, M.,
    1979,   Role of forebrain noradrenaline in reward and
    nonreward, in: "Catecholamines: Basic and Clinical Frontiers,"
    E. Usdin, J. D. Barchas, and I. J. Kopin eds., Pergamon Press,
    Elmsford, NY.
Pavlov, I. P., 1928, "Conditioned Reflexes," Trans. W. H. Gantt,
    Liverwright, New York.
Reis, D. I., Joh, T. H., Ross, R. A., and Pickel, V. M., 1974,
    Reserpine selectively increases tyrosine hydroxylase and
    dopamine-β-hydroxylase enzyme protein in central noradrenergic
    neurones, Brain Res., 81:380.

Ross, R. R., 1964, Positive and negative partial reinforcement
    extinction effects carried through continuous reinforcement,
    changed motivation, and changed response, J. Exp. Psychol.,
    68:492.

Seligman, M. E. P., Maier, S. F., and Solomon, R. L., 1971,
    Unpredictable and uncontrollable aversive events, in: "Aversive
    Conditioning and Learning," F. R. Brush ed., Academic Press,
    New York.

Stein, L., Wise, C. D., and Berger, B. D., 1973, Anti-anxiety action
    of benzodiazepines: decrease in activity of serotonin neurons
    in the punishment system, in: "The Benzodiazepines,"
    S. Garattini, E. Mussini, and L. O. Randall eds., Raven Press,
    New York.

Sutherland, N. S., and Mackintosh, N. J., 1971, "Mechanisms of
    Animal Discrimination Learning," Academic Press, London, New York.

Thoenen, H., 1975, Transsynaptic regulation of neuronal enzyme
    synthesis, in: "Handbook of Psychopharmacology, Vol. 3, "
    Plenum Press, New York.

Tye, N. C., Everitt, B. J., and Iversen, S. D., 1977, 5-Hydroxy-
    tryptamine and punishment, Nature, 268:741.

Ungerstedt, U., 1968, 6-hydroxydopamine induced degeneration of
    central monoamine neurons. Europ. J. Pharmacol., 5:107.

Ungerstedt, U., 1971, Stereotaxic mapping of the monamine pathways
    in the rat brain, Acta Physiol. Scand., 82:1, Suppl. 367.

Weiss, J. M., and Glazer, H. I., 1975, Effects of acute exposure to
    stressors on subsequent avoidance-escape behaviour, Psychosom.
    Med., 37:499.

Weiss, J. M., Glazer, H. I., Pohorecky, L. A., Brick, J., and
    Miller, N. E., 1975, Effects of chronic exposure to stressors
    on avoidance-escape behavior and on brain norepinephrine,
    Psychosom. Med., 37:522.

Willner, P. J., and Crowe, R., 1977, Effect of chlordiazepoxide on
    the partial reinforcement extinction effect, Pharmacol. Biochem.
    Behav., 7:479.

Ziff, P. R., and Capaldi, E. J., 1971, Amytal and the small trial
    partial reinforcement effect: stimulus properties of early
    trial non-rewards, J. Exp. Psychol., 87:263.

Zigmond, R. E., Schon, F., and Iversen, L. L., 1974, Increased
    tyrosine hydroxylase activity in the locus coeruleus of rat
    brain stem after reserpine treatment and cold stress, Brain Res.,
    70:547.

ASSOCIATIVE AND NON-ASSOCIATIVE MECHANISMS

IN THE DEVELOPMENT OF TOLERANCE FOR STRESS:

THE PROBLEM OF STATE-DEPENDENT LEARNING

J. N. P. Rawlins

Department of Experimental Psychology

University College, Oxford

It is proposed by Gray, Owen, Davis and Feldon (1979) that there are at least three ways of increasing behavioural tolerance for stressful events. The first is by Pavlovian stimulus-stimulus association (e.g., Dickinson and Pearce, 1977); the second is by stimulus-response association (e.g., Capaldi, 1967); and the third is by non-associative repeated exposure to stressful events (e.g., Chen and Amsel, 1977). I wish to consider this third category, and to suggest that effects such as increased resistance to extinction induced by repeated, inescapable shock outside the testing apparatus need not be dependent upon a non-associative mechanism. Instead they could result from an effect on associative memory.

Early demonstrations of state-dependent learning in animals (Overton, 1964) showed that learning which takes place when the animal is drugged (in this case with sodium pentobarbital) may be completely ineffectual in controlling behaviour when retested in an undrugged condition. The animal behaves as though no learning at all had taken place. However, on being re-tested in the drugged condition, the animal can be shown to have learnt. Thus information which is learned in the drugged condition cannot be retrieved in the undrugged condition; the converse is often true as well, in which case the drug would be described as having symmetrical state dependent effects. In cases where learning which took place in one drug state can be retrieved in another, but the converse relationship does not hold, the drug is said to have asymmetrical state dependent effects.

Although early experiments demonstrated state dependency by

using drugs to alter the animal's state, it has more recently been
shown that endogenous changes of a natural kind can also produce
state dependency. Apparent state dependent effects have been shown
to result from deprivation of rapid eye movement sleep (Joy and
Prinz, 1969), from mood changes in cycling manic depressives
(Weingartner and Murphy, unpublished, cited in Eich, Weingartner,
Stillman and Gillin, 1975), and from diurnal rhythms (Wansley and
Holloway, 1976). In all these cases, performance of a learned task
was significantly better when the internal state at retention
testing was identical to that during training. I propose that state
dependent learning of a related kind can provide an explanation for
some aspects of 'non-associative toughening up'. There are two
important propositions which must hold for this to be possible. The
first suggests that punishment (typically by electric shock) and
non-reward (that is, omission of an expected reward) are in many
respects equivalent events. The second, that receiving shock
produces marked, discriminable changes in an animal's internal
state.

The supporting evidence for the first of these suggestions is
reasonably strong; some of it has been covered in the preceding
paper by Gray et al. In general terms it is true to say that
both punishment and non-reward reduce the probability of emitting
a response which produces them; that in both cases this response
inhibition can be blocked by treatment with tranquillising drugs;
and that experience with either punishment or non-reward can
modify the response to the other (Wagner, 1966; Gray, 1967). In
addition, both give rise to conditioned emotional states which can
themselves control behaviour in similar ways. It has been suggested
(Gray, 1977) that the same central nervous structures control the
behavioural response to both classes of event.

The evidence for the second of the propositions is derived
from an experimental paradigm introduced by Kamin (1957). Kamin's
aim was to study memory retention in animals, and in order to do
this he partially trained rats in a two-way active avoidance task.
He then tested their performance using a variety of intervals
between initial training and retesting. He found, somewhat surprisingly, that performance of the avoidance response did not follow
a monotonic function typical of forgetting, but had a U-shaped
curve. Thus performance at very short (1 minute) or long (24 hours)
intervals was good, but performance at intermediate (1 and 6 hours)
intervals was poor; so much so that at the 1 hour testing interval
it was indistinguishable from that of naive animals being trained
for the first time.

A variety of explanations have been put forward to account for
this striking observation. The one with the greatest explanatory
power seems to be a state dependent model (Bryan and Spear, 1976).
The authors propose that stressful events cause changes in pituitary-

adrenal activity, and that animals only perform well when their levels of corticosteroids and of adrenocorticotrophic hormone (ACTH) are the same at the time of testing as they were at the time of learning. In support of this suggestion, they have demonstrated that good perfor- mance can be reinstated at intermediate test intervals in a variety of ways. First, giving extra footshock just before testing improves performance at intermediate test intervals, while leaving performance at short or long intervals intact. Second, water stress 5 minutes before testing also improves performance at intermediate test intervals (Klein, 1972), thus showing that the nature of the stressor itself is unimportant; the critical thing is simply to have been stressed. Finally, administration of ACTH also restores performance at intermediate test intervals, thus clearly implicating the adreno- pituitary system (Klein, 1972), though there is no reason to suppose that other endogenous changes--e.g., in noradrenaline and acetyl- choline levels (Anisman, 1975)--do not also contribute to the post- stress state. The critical point being made here is that animals can be shown to be in a discriminably altered state following stress, which becomes associated with the animal's learned response; learning in the aftermath of stress is somehow stored separately from learning in an unstressed condition, and either will tend to be retrieved dependent on the animal's state at the time of testing.

In considering, therefore, whether an animal will perform a learned response like running down an alley it is clear that running will be more probable if the conditions remain as they were when it was learnt. Changing conditions will result in a drop in performance. This point forms the basis of the 'generalisation decrement' theory of extinction (Capaldi, 1967). I propose, on the basis of the evidence I have briefly reviewed, that exposure to stressful events, which category includes nonreward (Levine, Goldman and Coover, 1972), even if outside the testing apparatus, will produce an internal state in the animal which is associated with the animal's ability to retrieve and perform a learned response. Thus an animal trained to run down an alley when in a post-stress state in acquisition--and this state may be produced by punishment in the goalbox, by non- reward in the goalbox, or by any stressor outside the apparatus--will continue to carry out this learned response when in a stressful extinction- or punishment-induced conflict. Conversely, an animal which has never been trained to respond when in a post-stress state will be unlikely to emit the learned response following stress. This point of view emphasises a novel approach to 'toughening up'. Instead of animals learning to respond in spite of the consequences of the response, it suggests that they may, perhaps additionally, learn to respond in spite of the circumstances under which the response is to be made. To characterise such a process as being non-associative is clearly a mistake; however, further experimental analysis is required before the relative contribution of this fourth way of increasing tolerance to stress can be assessed.

REFERENCES

Anisman, H., 1975, Time-dependent variations in aversively motivated
    behaviors: Nonassociative effects of cholinergic and catechol-
    aminergic activity, Psych. Rev., 82:359.
Bryan, R. G., and Spear, N. E., 1976, Forgetting of a discrimination
    after intervals of intermediate lengths: The Kamin effect with
    choice behaviour, J. Exp. Psychol. (Anim. Behav. Proc.), 2:221.
Capaldi, E. J., 1967, A sequential hypothesis of instrumental
    learning, in: "The Psychology of Learning and Motivation,"
    K. W. Spence and J. T. Spence eds., Vol. 1, Academic Press,
    New York, London.
Chen, J. S., and Amsel, A., 1977, Prolonged, unsignaled, inescapable
    shocks increase persistence in subsequent appetitive instru-
    mental learning, Anim. Learn. Behav., 5:377.
Dickinson, A., and Pearce, J. M., 1977, Inhibitory interactions
    between appetitive and aversive stimuli, Psychol. Bull., 84:690.
Eich, J. E., Weingartner, H., Stillman, R. C., and Gillin, J. C.,
    1975, State-dependent accessibility of retrieval cues in the
    retention of a categorised list., J. Verb. Learn. & Verb. Behav.,
    14:408.
Gray, J. A., 1967, Disappointment and drugs in the rat, Adv. of Sci.,
    23:595.
Gray, J. A., 1977, Drug effects on fear and frustration: possible
    limbic site of action of minor tranquilizers, in: "Handbook
    of Psychopharmacology," L. L. Iversen, S. D. Iversen, and
    S. H. Snyder eds., Vol. 8, Plenum Press, New York.
Gray, Owen, Davis, and Feldon, 1979, preceding paper in this
    symposium.
Joy, R. M., and Prinz, P. N., 1969, The effect of sleep altering
    environments upon the acquisition and retention of a conditioned
    avoidance response in the rat, Physiol. Behav., 4:809.
Kamin, L. J., 1957, Retention of an incompletely learned avoidance
    response, J. Comp. Physiol. Psychol., 50:457.
Klein, S. B., 1972, Adrenal-pituitary influence reactivation
    avoidance-learning memory in the rat after intermediate
    intervals, J. Comp. Physiol. Psychol., 79:341.
Levine, S., Goldman, L., and Coover, G. D., 1972, Expectancy and the
    pituitary adrenal system, in: "Physiology, Emotion and Psycho-
    somatic Illness," CIBA Symposium, 1972.
Overton, D. A., 1964, State-dependent or "dissociated" learning
    produced with pentobarbital, J. Comp. Physiol. Psychol., 57:3.
Wagner, A. R., 1966, Frustration and punishment, in: "Current
    Research in Motivation," R. M. Haber ed.,
Wansley, R. A., and Holloway, F. A., 1976, Oscillations in
    retention performance after passive avoidance training,
    Learn. Motiv., 7:296.

A COPING MODEL OF MOTHER-INFANT RELATIONSHIPS

Seymour Levine

Department of Psychiatry
and Behavioral Sciences
Stanford University
School of Medicine

Although there are striking species-specific differences in mother-infant interactions in nonhuman primates, in general the initial relationship between the primate mother and the neonate is continuous and the infant plays an active role in the maintenance of dyadic interaction. The maintenance of contact between mother and infant monkey, for example, is largely dependent upon the infant's clinging and following behaviors. The squirrel monkey infant, for example, almost immediately after birth assumes a position upon the dorsal surface of the mother and maintains that position actively for a considerable period of time until it ultimately begins to leave the mother, initially for brief periods of time, and finally, for sustained periods of time. However, observations of squirrel monkey mothers and infants indicate very clearly that although the infant may be spending time away from the mother, the presence of stimuli which may signal threat or elicit distress results in the infant almost immediately seeking the mother and once again resuming the clinging position. Although squirrel monkey mothers are also active in maintaining proximity to the infant, they do not retrieve their infants in the usual sense; they will, again under conditions of stress, seek the infant and present themselves so that the infants can more easily assume the clinging position. In other primates such as the rhesus, the expressions of the mother-infant relationship are different in that the infant spends considerably more time in a ventral-ventral position. Once again, however, observations of the mother-infant pairs in a group living situation very clearly indicate that the infant, when distressed, will actively seek the mother and achieve proximity either by clinging or by maintaining a position close to the mother. The mother also responds to the infant's distress signals by actively seeking the infant and retrieving the infant vigorously.

In a group living situation in which mothers and infants are not separated at weaning, this process appears to go on for a considerable length of time. Year-old infants seek proximity to the mother when conditions in the environment appear to be unstable or when the infant is subject to some distressful experience. The response of the mother and infant to achieve proximity or contact under conditions of stress appears to be characteristic of most of the primate species including humans. For most primate species, with a few notable exceptions (Rosenblum & Kaufman, 1967), the only salient animal in the environment to which the infant will respond in such a manner is the mother. Conversely, the mother appears to respond only to those signals emitted by her own infant. This selective preference has been dealt with extensively by attachment theorists and is one of the criterions for the presence of an attachment relationship. A second, major criterion is response to the loss of the attachment figure.

Perhaps the most widely used method for studying attachment has been the separation procedure. Both the behavioral and the physiological responses of mothers and infants have been examined in reaction to the absence of either figure from the normal environment. The earlier studies (Kaufman, 1973; Seay, Hansen and Harlow, 1962; Seay and Harlow, 1965) of separation primarily examined the behavioral responses of the infant to loss of the mother. The initial responses to loss of the mother have been described as protest, involving distress vocalizations and agitated activity. Upon sustained separation however, it has been described that the infant moves from this protest phase to a phase of despair and "depression" which are manifested by extremely low levels of activity, a general lethargy and apparent withdrawal from the environment.

Although the protest reaction of the infant appears to be invariant, the expression of depression is dependent upon the conditions of separation (Mineka and Suomi, 1978). Depression is most likely to occur when the infant remains behind in the social group after the mother has been removed. The responses of the mother have not been examined in as much detail although one of the major theories of attachment, that of Bowlby (1969, 1973), does predict that the response of both mother and infants should be similar under conditions of separation.

More recently, our own laboratory has been investigating the effects of separation on the endocrine responses of both mother and infant squirrel monkeys and rhesus. In general, we have found that both infant and mother squirrel monkeys show a vigorous endocrine response to brief periods of separation (30 min)(Mendoza, Lowe, and Levine, 1978). The squirrel monkey mother shows a striking elevation in plasma cortisol following separation from her infant. This response occurs whether the mother is permitted to remain in

her own cage, permitted to remain with her group, or removed from
the group. The uniformity of this response is striking (Coe,
Mendoza, Smotherman and Levine, 1978). Every mother in at least
four different studies has responded with a marked increment in
cortisol values following the separation procedures. The effects
of separation occur under conditions when the infant is removed to
another room and the infant cues are not available to the mother.
Thus, the primate mother appears to be responding to the absence of
the infant and not to the particular stimulus emitted by that infant
as a consequence of the agitation caused by separation. Furthermore,
the plasma cortisol response of the mother squirrel monkey following
separation from her infant is as high (and often higher) as that
which has been observed using more traditional types of stressful
stimuli in nonpregnant squirrel monkeys.

The behavioral response of the infant to separation has also
been described and infant squirrel monkeys, like other primate
infants, show increased locomotion and vocalizations as well as a
reduction in object manipulation, activity play and social play as
a consequence of involuntary separation (Kaplan, 1970; Jones and
Clark, 1973). In our initial studies which examined the influence
of brief periods of separation on the infant's endocrine response,
we clearly demonstrated that separating the infant from the mother
or separating the infant from an inanimate surrogate mother (Kaplan,
1977) resulted in a striking elevation in plasma cortisol. In these
studies, where the infant was removed from the mother it was
difficult to assess whether the effects of separation were a consequence of the separation per se, or confounded by the additional
variable that the infant is both separated and in a novel
environment.

In a subsequent experiment we attempted to parcel out the effects
of separation from the effects of novelty. Thus a group of squirrel
monkey mother-infant pairs was tested under the standard conditions
utilized in our laboratory for assessing the effects of separation.
These conditions involve obtaining a basal sample from the mother
and infant upon immediate removal from the group; another sample is
obtained following separation-reunion in which the mother and infant are
separated briefly and immediately reunited and blood-sampled 30 min
later. Other blood samples were taken when the mother was removed,
leaving the mother in a group with her social partners. Under some
circumstances, female squirrel monkeys which do not have infants will
show maternal behavior in that they will permit infants to ride dor-
sally and also will frequently attempt to retrieve infants. This
phenomenon is particularly evident in late pregnant females. In our
group living situation, there was one late pregnant female who, when
the mother was removed, aunted the separated infants. The infants,
when aunted by the female, showed few signs of the usual protest
behavior observed immediately following separation.

The phenomenon of reduced behavioral agitation, when an infant is with an "aunt," has been interpreted by Rosenblum (1972) as indicating that aunting reduces the effect of separation. Our data (Coe, et al., 1978) indicated that although aunting does tend to reduce the behavioral agitation which is observed in separated infants, the infant still showed a striking pituitary-adrenal response which was significantly elevated over basal and separation-reunion conditions and was just as elevated as when the infants were removed from their mothers and from their social group. We interpreted these data as indicating that the infant shows specific recognition of his mother and that only the mother has the capacity to serve the function of arousal reduction for the infant. Since normal mothers do not normally aunt other infants, it is difficult to assess whether the infant also has the same specific arousal reduction function for the mother.

Although we have focused largely on the effects of separation and the stressful consequences of separation, perhaps the more important finding in this series of studies is not the influence of separation, but the effects which were observed under our separation-reunion condition. Recall that the separation-reunion condition involved removing the mother and infant, separating them, which clearly appears to be disturbing in view of the excessive vocalizations that are emitted by both infant and mother, and immediately reuniting the pair and returning them to their home cage. Under these conditions we observed no change in plasma cortisol in either the mother or infant even though the procedure appeared to be extremely disturbing. These data were indeed surprising since we have previously demonstrated that removing a nonlactating female from her cage and immediately returning her to the home cage does lead to a significant elevation of plasma cortisol as measured 30 min later. This is not surprising since handling has been used by some investigators (Ader, 1970) as a standardized procedure for activating the pituitary-adrenal system.

Two hypotheses were entertained to account for these data. The first was that the mother and infant have the capacity to buffer each other from stress and therefore the presence of the mother and infant, under some conditions, prevents an increase in arousal, as measured by activity of the pituitary-adrenal system. However, an alternate explanation of these data is that both mother and infant cortisol levels could have been significantly elevated initially, but by 30 min could have returned to basal levels. Thus separation could indeed have constituted a stress, both for the 30 min separated condition and for the separated-reunited condition. However, contact between the mother and infant in the immediate reunion condition could have reduced that stress to permit a return to basal values by 30 min. A subsequent study (Levine, Coe, Smotherman and Kaplan, 1978) demonstrated that indeed the first hypothesis more accurately described the process. Thus, blood

samples were obtained from mothers and infants under the separated-reunited condition, 5 min, 10 min and 30 min after being reunited. Under no circumstances did the observed rises in plasma cortisol approach that seen under 30 min separation. This evidence clearly indicates that the mother and infant serve a mutual function to reduce the response to stress under the experimental circumstances present in this experiment.

We have recently demonstrated a similar phenomenon in rhesus macaques (Gunnar, Cochran and Levine, unpublished). Mothers and infants (5-7 mos of age) were removed from their social group and housed as dyads in standard laboratory primate cages. The capture procedure is most stressful. As a control group, adult multiparous females who did not have an infant during that breeding season were also captured and rehoused in individual cages. Following capture and rehousing, blood samples were taken 3 hours, 3 days, and 5 days while the monkeys were adapting to the new housing conditions. Three hours following capture, all adult females showed highly elevated levels of plasma cortisol. However, by the third day the females with their infants had returned to basal levels whereas the other adult females were still showing elevated levels. Thus the presence of the infant facilitated the adaption to the novel housing condition. Perhaps more striking was that the infants with their mothers show no change in plasma cortisol levels at any time during the capture and rehousing procedure. These findings are similar to those reported by Smotherman, Hunt, McGinnis and Levine, 1979).

The data presented on the effects of separation and mother-infant contact on arousal as measured by changes in pituitary-adrenal activity are pertinent not only to the understanding of mother-infant interactions, but also are relevant to the general topic of this conference, which is coping.

We propose that under conditions of stress, proximity and contact with the mother results in the modulation and reduction of the infant's arousal levels. Since coping requires control as a mechanism for reducing stress, proximity-seeking behavior which results in arousal reduction, can best be viewed within the context of coping. We would like to further propose that for the infant, the primary experiences with coping occur in the context of the mother-infant interaction.

Mother-infant relationships are truly dyadic. The mother certainly imposes control over the infant's behavior and there is more and more evidence which indicates that the infant, by use of certain specific signals, is capable of controlling its mother's behavior. Research on rodents has indicated that the signals emitted by the young influence the behavior of the mother (Bell, 1974; Noirot, 1972; Smotherman, Bell, Starzek, Elias and Zachman,

1974). The neonatal infant rodent emits very specific ultrasonic signals which lead to an increase in certain aspects of maternal behavior, particularly retrieving. The infant rodent, however, is limited in his motoric responses and therefore requires a different set of stimuli which are capable of modifying the mother's behavior. In the primate, the more advanced motor development permits the infant to actively seek proximity and to achieve contact in addition to emitting vocal signals which elicit both retrieval and proximity-seeking behavior on the part of the mother. Thus the infant is functioning in a contingent environment in which it can control outcomes through specific responses it emits.

The previous papers in this conference have emphasized several important aspects of the organism's behavior which are capable of modifying and reducing the response to stressful events. One of the most important dimensions of these behaviors is control. Thus the infant very early in development learns to control its environment by developing contingent relationships between its responses and outcomes which, at this early stage, usually involve a modification of maternal behavior. Both Watson (1967) and Seligman (1975) have also proposed that the infant is involved in a contingency analysis of the relationship between its responses and their outcomes. We further hypothesize that the capacity of the infant to modify its stress response by maintaining contact with the mother not only affects the organism's capacity to cope later in life, but serves as an integral part of the process whereby specific attachments are formed.

This capacity of the infant to use control to modify its stress response by maintaining contact with the mother is consistent with a number of the hypotheses which have attempted to account for attachment. Bowlby (1969) and Ainsworth (1969, 1972) have argued that mothers and infants are biologically predisposed to assure proximity and in the case of the mother, such proximity leads to the protection of the infant. They proposed that both adults and infants behave in a manner designed to increase the amount of interaction the infant has with particular adults.

Bowlby proposes four principles to explain the development of specific and discriminating attachment. (1) A built in bias toward looking at certain patterns in preference to others and toward things that move; (2) exposure learning by which the familiar comes to be distinguished from the strange; (3) a built-in bias to approach familiar and later to withdraw from the strange; (4) feedback of results by which a behavioral sequence is augmented when it is followed by certain results and diminished when it is followed by others.

The coping model of attachment which is being elaborated on in this paper focuses only on the fourth of these principles proposed

by Bowlby, and argues that the feedback results are a reduction in
arousal in the infant as a consequence of the contingent relationship between the infant's responses and the mother's responses.
This position is probably more consistent with the formulation of
Lamb (1978), that argues that the adult emits appropriate and
sensitive responses to the infant's behavior. Any simple contingent
response on the part of an adult will not be sufficient. Thus,
certain individuals do respond appropriately to the infant's signals
more often than others. They retrieve it when it cries, comfort it
with physical contact rather than vocalizations, and sensitively
pace their interactions with the infant. It is to these individuals
that the infant will become attached. In the case of humans, the
evidence that human infants become attached to their fathers as
well as their mothers even when the amount of father-infant interaction is minimal, would support this position. When dealing with
most subhuman primates, however, there is little evidence that the
father responds appropriately to the signals of the infant. This
may be different in some of the species in which the male plays a
more active part in the caretaking of the infant. However, data on
infant attachment in subhuman primates to fathers are not available.

ATTACHMENT IN SURROGATE-REARED MONKEYS?

The original paper by Harlow and Zimmerman in 1959 which has
proved to be a landmark experiment in psychology disproved the
hypothesis that rhesus infantile attachment was based solely on the
pleasures of feeding. This experiment argued that the overriding
factor in such attachment was contact comfort and was based on the
finding that young monkeys formed a clear preference for cloth
surrogates over wire surrogates regardless of which surrogate was
involved with feeding. To quote Mason (1971), "We know from Harlow's
celebrated experiments that contact is a significant factor in the
development of filial attachment and we have reasons to conclude
that the affected mechanism is a reduction in emotional arousal."
Mason's theory of the development of filial attachment in monkeys
is based primarily on the phenomenon of clinging. Among the
numerous postulates he presents on the development of clinging,
critical are the two postulates which say that any object that is
used repeatedly for the performance of clinging can become the focus
of emotional dependence (attachment), and that the average strength
of attachment to a given object is an increasing function of the
motivation to cling, the frequency with which the object has served
to reinforce clinging in the past, and the efficacy of the object
as a reinforcer for clinging. Thus, there is nothing in Mason's
formulations which would preclude the formation of attachment to
an inanimate surrogate. That the relationship between the infant
and its surrogate mother is considered attachment is further
evidenced by a recent review by Rajecki, Lamb and Obmasher (1978)
in which the data on surrogate-reared animals are cited frequently
as critical tests of attachment theory. Clearly, however, any view

which postulates contingency relationships as a central mechanism
for the development of attachment is antithetical with the notion
that infants become attached to inanimate objects. If infants do
indeed become attached to inanimate objects we would expect that all
of the criteria of attachment including preference, recognition,
and response to loss should be evidenced when the appropriate
manipulations are conducted with the surrogate-reared infant.

    A close examination of the available data indicates that this
is not the case. Surrogate-reared animals do show an extensive
amount of clinging to the surrogate object, show signs of behavioral
agitation when the surrogate object is removed and may use the
surrogate object as a way of reducing arousal when placed in
unfamiliar environments (Hill, McCormack and Mason, 1973). Although
these behaviors would appear to be indicative of attachment, a more
recent evaluation of the physiological responses to separation show
clear evidence of marked differences between surrogate-reared and
mother-reared infants. Meyer, Novak, Bowman and Harlow (1975)
examined plasma cortisol in mother-reared and surrogate-reared rhesus
infants prior to and following separation and following placement
into a novel enclosure with fear-producing stimuli. Prior to
separation, the plasma cortisol levels of the surrogate- and mother-
reared animals were identical. However, two weeks following separation the plasma cortisol levels of the mother-reared infants were
still elevated by almost two-fold, whereas the plasma cortisol levels
of the surrogate-reared animals were identical to those previously
observed when the animal was with the surrogate. Although these
data would indicate that there appears to be no response as measured
by pituitary-adrenal activity to separation, since the preimposed
measures were separated by two weeks, one cannot dismiss the
possibility that there is a differential recovery from the response
to separation and that initially both surrogate-reared and mother-
reared infants showed a significant separation response.

    Recent data (Hennessy, Kaplan, Mendoza, Lowe and Levine, in
press) from our laboratory also indicates that, in contrast to
mother-reared infants, the removal of the surrogate from the home
cage resulted in some behavioral agitation as shown by increased
vocalizations and activity levels, but under no circumstances did
the infant exhibit any change in plasma cortisol levels. The
surrogate-reared infant squirrel monkey appears to have the capacity
to show a significant elevation of plasma cortisol under certain
circumstances, i.e., exposure to novelty, but does not appear to
show any change in plasma cortisol levels following removal of the
surrogate when kept in its home environment. These data are in
direct contrast with the physiological response observed when
mother-reared infants are deprived of their mothers and the
physiological response is observed in both separated squirrel
monkeys and rhesus macaques even following repeated separations.

Similar discrepancies between mother and surrogate rearing have been found. Using other physiological measures, Reite, Short and Seiler (1978) found an increase in heart rate and body temperature compatible with the state of hyperarousal in separated group-living pigtail monkeys. Further, disturbances in sleep patterns were also observed; however, when infant pigtail monkeys were reared on surrogate mothers and the surrogate mother was then removed, the changes in the physiological responses observed were quite different. "Our observations following separation from the surrogate, both behavioral and physiological, are generally in marked contrast to previous studies on the effects of maternal separation in mother-reared group-living pigtail infants. Although behavioral and physiological arousal was evident, possibly an attenuated agitation reaction immediately following separation, neither behavioral nor physiological accompaniments of a subsequent depressive reaction were observed." These authors go on to further state, "Thus, one might conclude that infant surrogate attachment bond, although seemingly real and strong to the observer of the dyad, is not of sufficient intensity to produce, when disrupted, a particular marked psychobiological reaction." Although these authors do not conclude that pigtail infants are not attached to their surrogates and appear to offer the hypothesis that attachment is of less intensity, these data could also be interpreted as indicating a failure of attachment to occur as evidenced by the absence of a response to separation.

There is another aspect of these separation studies which indicates a marked difference between surrogate- and mother-reared infants. In the studies reported on the surrogate-reared squirrel monkeys, a number of experimental conditions were imposed following removal of the surrogate (Hennessy et al., in press). These conditions were imposed in order to determine the specificity of the response of the infant reared on surrogate cloth mothers. Thus, following removal of the surrogate, either the infant was left alone or on separate occasions one of a variety of surrogates was placed in the cage, i.e., its own surrogate, a clean cloth surrogate, or a surrogate from another infant. All of these surrogates were capable of reducing the behavioral agitation in response to surrogate removal.

A similar finding was reported by Mason, Hill and Thompson, 1974. Increased vocalization was observed in surrogate-reared macaques following the removal of the surrogate. However, either its own surrogate or a totally novel surrogate was capable of reducing this response to removal. Bowlby defines attachment as a strong affectional tie that occurs between an individual and his or her most intimate associates. Bowlby postulates that organisms who are attached will behave so as to maintain proximity to one another. However, a further requirement is that attachment behaviors have a specific target. The presence of other animals in

a social group in no way ameliorates the effects of separation on
the infant rhesus or pigtail macaque or squirrel monkey, and, in
fact, these circumstances result in even a more severe reaction
(depression) on the part of the animal following separation from
the mother (Mineka and Suomi, 1978). This specificity is lacking
in surrogate-reared infants since a similar.clingable object
appears to be capable of ameliorating the behavioral effects of
separation.

One cannot ignore, however, the fact that infants do indeed
utilize the surrogate to reduce arousal under certain circumstances
(Hill et al., 1973). It would appear that the responses of the
infant to the surrogate represent dependency behaviors rather than
attachment. A clear distinction has been made by a number of
theorists between emotional dependence and attachment. Thus
Ainsworth (1972) states, "The behavioral hallmark of attachment is
the seeking of proximity or contact with an attachment figure.
The traditional concept of dependency also includes these behaviors,
but without the implication they are directed toward a specific
person or persons."

COPING AND CONTINGENCY

Although we have dealt primarily with the role of contingency
relationships in the formation of attachment, the importance of
contingency for the developing infant has been speculated upon by
many individuals. Thus, Lewis and Goldberg (1969) say that,
"Contingency is important not only because it shapes the acquisition
of specific behaviors but because it enables the child to develop a
motive, which is the basis for all future learning. The main
characteristic of this motive is the infant's belief that his actions
affect his environment. The mother is important because it is the
contingency between the infant's behavior and her responses that
enables the infant to learn that his behavior does have consequences."
Mason (1978) in discussing the differences between infant rhesus
monkeys that were raised with stationary surrogates (hobby horses)
and infant rhesus monkeys that were raised with dogs, comments,
"I believe that the critical distinction between attachment figures
in these experiments is the presence or absence of response
contingent stimulation. Stationary surrogates and hobby horses show
they provide few opportunities for the developing individual to
experience the fact that his behavior has affects on the environment
and to learn that the events going on around him are amenable to his
control. Inert mother substitutes make no demand, occasion no
surprises, do not encourage the development of attentional processes
and the acquisition of simple instrumental behaviors that are the
fabric of social interaction."

That mothers are the prime resource of response contingent
stimulation needs little elaboration. In the normal course of

development, the infant requires these early contingent relationships in order to learn certain aspects of his environment which permit it to make adaptive coping responses to its environment. The hypotheses contained in this paper, however, are different from other attachment theories in only one major regard: namely, that attachments are formed only to response contingent figures, and that the function of attachment is to provide the infant with response contingent relationships which ultimately provide the infant with primary coping responses which permit the organism to behave adaptively and respond appropriately to its environment throughout the rest of its life.

ACKNOWLEDGEMENT

This research was supported by NICH & HD-02881 from MH-23645 from NIMH; Dr. Levine is supported by USPHS Research Scientist Award K5-MH-19936 from NIMH.

REFERENCES

Ader, R., 1970, The effects of early experience on the adrenocortical response to different magnitudes of stimulation, Physiol. Behav., 5:837

Ainsworth, M. D. S., 1969, Object relationships, dependency and attachment. A theoretical review of infant-mother relationships, Child Devel., 40:969.

Ainsworth, M. D. S., 1972, Attachment and Dependency: A Comparison, in: "Attachment and Dependency": J. L. Gerwitz, ed., Winston & Son, Washington, D. C.

Bell, R. W., Ultrasounds in small rodents: arousal-produced and arousal producing, Devel. Psychobiol., 7,1:39.

Bowlby, J., 1969, Attachment, in: "Attachment and Loss," Vol. 1, Basic Books, New York.

Bowlby, J., 1973, Separation, in: Attachment and Loss," Vol. 2, Hogarth, London.

Coe, C. L., S. P. Mendoza, W. P. Smotherman and S. Levine, 1978, Mother-infant attachment in the squirrel monkey: adrenal response to separation, Behav. Biol., 22:256.

Harlow, H. F. and R. R. Zimmerman, 1959, Affectional responses in the infant monkey, Science, 130:421.

Hennessy, M. B., J. N. Kaplan, S. P. Mendoza, E. L. Lowe and S. Levine (in press), Separation distress and attachment in surrogate-reared squirrel monkeys, Physiol. Behav., 23(6).

Hill, S. D., S. A. McCormack and W. A. Mason, 1973, Effects of artificial mothers and visual experience on adrenal responsiveness of infant monkeys, Devel. Psychobiol., 6:421.

Jones, B. C. and D. L. Clark, 1973, Mother-infant separation in squirrel monkeys living in a group, Devel. Psychobiol., 6(3):259.

Kaplan, J., 1970, The effects of separation and reunion on the behavior of mother and infant squirrel monkeys, Devel. Psychobiol., 3(1):43.

Kaplan, J., 1977, Perceptual properties of attachment in surrogate reared and mother-reared squirrel monkeys, in: "Primate Bio-Social Development," S. Chevalier-Skolnikoff and F. E. Poirier, eds., Garland Publishing, Inc., New York.

Kaufman, I. I., 1973, Mother-infant separation in monkeys, in: "Separation and Anxiety: Clinical and Research Aspects," J. P. Scott and E. C. Sinay, eds., A.A.A.S., Washington, D.C.

Lamb, M. E., Social interaction in infancy and development of personality, in: "Social and Personality Development," M. E. Lamb, ed., Holt, Rhinehart and Winston, New York.

Levine, S., C. L. Coe, W. P. Smotherman and J. N. Kaplan, 1978, Prolonged cortisol elevation in the infant squirrel monkey after reunion with mother, Physiol. Behav., 20:7.

Lewis, M., and S. Goldberg, 1969, Perceptual-cognitive development in infancy: a generalized expectancy model as a function of the mother-infant interaction, Merrill-Palmer Quart., Behav. Devel., 16:81.

Mason, W. A., 1971, Motivational factors in psychosocial development, in: Nebraska Symposium on Motivation, 1970, W. J. Arnold and M. M. Page, eds., University of Nebraska Press, Lincoln.

Mason, W. A., 1978, Social experience in primate cognitive development, in: "The Development of Behavior: Comparative and Evolutionary Aspects," G. M. Burdhardt and M. Bekoff, ed., Garland STPM Press, New York.

Mason, W. A., S. D. Hill and C. E. Thomsen, 1971, Perceptual factors in the development of filial attachment, Proc. 3rd Congr. Primat. Zurich, Vol. 3, S. Karger, Basel.

Mason, W. A., S. D. Hill and C. E. Thomsen, 1974, Perceptual aspects of filial attachment, in: "Ethology and Psychiatry," M. F. White, ed., Univ. of Toronto Press, Toronto.

Mendoza, S. P., E. L. Lowe and S. Levine, 1978, Social organization and social behavior in two subspecies of squirrel monkeys (Saimiri sciureus), Folia Primatol., 30:126.

Meyer, J. S., M. A. Novak, R. E. Bowman and H. F. Harlow, 1975, Behavioral and hormonal effects of attachment object separation in surrogate-peer-reared and mother-reared infant rhesus monkeys, Devel. Psychobiol., 8(5):425.

Mineka, S. and S. J. Suomi, 1978, Social separation in monkeys, Psychol. Bull., 85:1376.

Noirot, E., 1972, Ultrasounds and maternal behavior in small rodents, Devel. Psychobiol., 4:371.

Rajecki, D. W., M. E. Lamb and P. Obmasher, 1978, Towards a general theory of infantile attachment. A comparative review of aspects of the social bond, Behav. Brain Sci., 1:417.

Reite, M., R. Short and C. Seiler, 1978, Physiological correlates of maternal separation in surrogate-reared infants: A study in altered attachment bonds, Devel. Psychobiol., 11:427.

Rosenblum, L. A., 1972, Sex and age differences in responses to infant squirrel monkeys, Brain Behav. Evol., 5:30.

Rosenblum, L. and C. Kaufman, 1967, Variations in infant development and response to maternal loss in monkeys, Am. J. Orthopsychiat., 38:418.

Seay, B. M., and H. F. Harlow, 1965, Maternal separation in the rhesus monkey, J. Nerv. Ment. Dis., 140:434.

Seay, B., E. Hansen and H. F. Harlow, 1962, Mother-infant separation in monkeys, J. Child Psychol. Psychiat., 3:123.

Seligman, M. E. P., 1975, "Learned Helplessness: On Depression, Development and Death," W. H. Freeman, San Francisco.

Smotherman, W. P., L. E. Hunt, L. M. McGinnis and S. Levine, 1979, Mother-infant separation in group-living rhesus macaques: A hormonal analysis, Devel. Psychobiol., 12(3):211.

Smotherman, W. P., R. W. Bell, J. Starzec, J. Elias and T. Zachman, 1974, Maternal responses to infant vocalizations and olfactory cues in rats and mice, Behav. Biol., 12:55.

Watson, J. B., 1967, Memory and "contingency analysis" in infant learning, Merril-Palmer Quart., 17:139.

CONTINGENT STIMULATION: A REVIEW

OF ITS ROLE IN EARLY DEVELOPMENT

Megan R. Gunnar

Department of Psychiatry
and Behavioral Sciences
Stanford University
School of Medicine

The last decade has seen a change in emphasis regarding the
role of stimulation in sustaining and fostering cognitive,
motivational and emotional development. Whereas, during the '60's
such diverse pathologies as dwarfism, mental retardation,
depression and affectionless psychopathology were attributed to
lack of sufficient stimulation, particularly maternal stimulation,
during infancy (Ainsworth, 1962; David and Appell, 1961; Levine,
1969; Province and Lipton, 1962; Rheingold, 1960), during the
'70's these same pathologies have been attributed to lack of
sufficient response-contingent, or controllable stimulation
(Levine, this volume; Lewis and Goldberg, 1969; Seligman, 1975;
Watson, 1966). This change in emphasis from stimulation, per se,
to contingent stimulation has been brought about by an increasing
recognition of the importance of control for normal functioning
and for coping with stress (see reviews by Averill, 1973;
Lefcourt, 1976; Seligman, 1975; and other articles in this volume).
It has been argued that experiences with control alter one's
motivation to respond, ability to learn contingent relationships,
and behavioral and physiological responses to aversive stimulation
(Bandura, 1977; Levine and Hennessy, this volume; Overmier, this
volume; Seligman, 1975). Therefore, how the child deals with
events later in life may be expected to be affected by early
experiences with controllable versus uncontrollable stimuli (Lewis
and Goldberg, 1969; Seligman, 1975; Watson, 1966). The child who
experiences controllable stimulation during infancy is expected
to approach the world with the conviction that he or she can affect
the occurrence of events, while the child who experiences uncontrollable stimulation during infancy is expected to approach the world
with the conviction that he or she is helpless. These expectancies

of control versus helplessness are expected to affect three domains
of functioning: learning and cognitive development, exploratory
behavior, and emotional state. Noncontingent or uncontrollable
stimulation is expected to (1) impair the infant's capacity to
learn contingent relationships and thus depress learning and cognitive
development (Watson, 1966); (2) reduce motivation to respond and
thus reduce exploration of the environment (W. Bronson, 1971); and
(3) produce negative emotional states, anxiety and depression
(Seligman, 1975). Conversely, contingent or controllable stimulation
is expected to foster cognitive development, stimulate exploration
of the environment, and produce positive emotional states. Given
the current emphasis on control and its role in coping, it is
appropriate at this time to consider the extent to which research on
contingent stimulation in infancy supports these claims.

CONTINGENCY AWARENESS PARAMETERS

     Two factors limit the infant's capacity to experience response-
contingent stimulation during early infancy. First, the infant's
limited repertoire of voluntary responses means that, during the
first few months, there are actually few events which are contingent
on voluntary actions (Watson, 1966). Second, the infant's limited
memory span reduces the likelihood that events will be perceived
(on some level) as response-dependent (Watson, 1966). Thus, Millar
(1972) and Ramey and Ourth (1971) have shown that temporal delays
of as little as 3 seconds between an action and an event will
prevent learning of an instrumental response throughout the first
year. Even delays of as little as 1 and 2 seconds will weaken the
strength or frequency of the instrumental response. Spatial displacement may also influence learning during the first half of the first
year. Millar and Schaffer (1972) found that 9 and 12 month old
infants could learn to activate a stimulus which was displaced 180°
from the response of touching a cylinder, but 6 month old infants
could not learn under these conditions. At 6 months both the action
and the outcome had to be in the same spatial orientation, perhaps
because infants of this age were not able to keep both the stimulus
and the response in working memory if they were not both visible at
the same time.

     The recovery period of a voluntary action also influences
contingency learning early in infancy. Watson (1967) showed that
the 2 to 3 month old infant must reexperience the response-event
contingency within 2 to 7 seconds after the initial occurrence in
order for learning of the response to take place. Responses which
take longer than 7 seconds to recover (to be organized and repeated),
or which recur too rapidly (in less than 2 seconds) are not ones
which the infant can easily learn to associate with outcomes. Thus,
during the early months of life there appear to be rather severe
limits on the response-dependent events which the infant can
respond to as being controllable. They must be dependent on

voluntary actions which are sufficiently developed to be repeated fairly rapidly. They must occur almost immediately following the response, and recur within 7 seconds. Further, in certain cases, at least, they must occur within the same spatial orientation as the response.

Such data have led Watson (1966) to argue that the early months of life constitute a period of natural deprivation in regard to contingency or control experiences. This, if true, would indicate that in the normal course of events, the responsiveness of the environment during the early months would have little effect on later functioning. However, it is important to note that this argument is based on studies using, what could be termed "artificial" contingencies. That is, these studies have involved response-event relationships which would not occur in the infant's natural environment. Thus, for example, a slide show might be made contingent on the infants' visual fixations ("artificial" contingency), rather than making social stimulation contingent on visual fixation ("natural" contingency). There is some evidence that in the young of other species certain response-contingencies are learned more readily than others (Riccio, Rohrbaugh and Hodges, 1968). These appear to be ones which occur predictably in the infant's natural environment, and which involve outcomes which have important survival consequences for the organism at that stage of development. It may well be that contingency-awareness parameters are less severe when such "natural" contingencies are involved, and thus, that the work on contingency awareness underestimates the infant's capacity to experience events as response-contingent during the early months of life.

EXPERIMENTALLY MANIPULATING RESPONSE-CONTINGENT STIMULATION

Clearly, one way of examining the effects of experiences with controllable versus uncontrollable stimulation is to experimentally manipulate the infant's environment. A number of such studies have recently been conducted in order to determine whether contingent stimulation increases the infant's capacity to learn later response-contingent relationship, and, conversely, to determine whether noncontingent stimulation impairs later learning (Finkelstein and Ramey, in press; Ramey and Finkelstein, 1977; Watson and Ramey, 1972). In general, it does appear that training on one task which involves the pairing of a voluntary response with a given outcome does facilitate learning of other response-event relationships. Watson and Ramey (1972) showed that when an outcome is made immediately contingent on a response over which the infant has a good deal of voluntary control, then even infants as young as 2 months of age can learn to "control" the outcome. They gave one group of 2-month-olds control over making a mobile spin. The response was turning the head on an air pressurized pillow.

A second group experienced a noncontingent spinning mobile, while
the third saw a stationary mobile. Ten minute trials on each of
14 consecutive days produced a high rate of responding in the
contingent-mobile group, and no change over base rates in the other
two groups. Furthermore, 6 weeks later positive transfer effects
were observed in a second task which involved learning to activate
a second mobile (Watson and Ramey, 1969). Infants who had experienced the contingent mobile learned to control the second mobile
faster than did infants in the other groups.

Similarly, Ramey and Finkelstein (1977) have shown that 3-month-
olds who had experienced 5 days of training on a task which involved
vocalizing to turn on lights and sounds, on the 6th day could learn
to turn on a slide by focusing their gaze on one of a set of slides.
Infants who had not had the additional stimulation could not learn
this second task. Finkelstein and Ramey (in press) have also
demonstrated similar positive transfer effects for 6- to 10-month-old
black infants classified as being at risk because of the poor quality
care they receive at home. They have also shown that experiences
with response contingent feedback increases the ability of these
infants to distinguish between periods of contingent and noncontingent stimulation.

While prior experiences with controllable stimulation do appear
to enhance later learning, it is not clear that experiences with
uncontrollable stimulation interfere with later learning. When the
learning situations are highly similar, and a number of preexposures
to noncontingent stimulation are given, proactive interference is
observed. Thus, Watson and Ramey (1969) showed that 14 preexposures
to a noncontingent mobile were sufficient to interfere with the
infant's ability to learn to control the same mobile 6 weeks later.
Brief preexposure to noncontingent stimuli may not interfere with
later learning. Millar (1972) showed that one 3-minute preexposure
to a noncontingent audio-visual stimulus led to an increase, rather
than a decrease, in learning rate when that stimulus was made
contingent on the infant's actions.

When learning situations are dissimilar noncontingent stimulation has been shown to both facilitate and interfere with later
learning (Finkelstein and Ramey, 1974; Ramey and Finkelstein, 1977).
However, the evidence more strongly supports a facilitating effect.
Thus, in one study using 6-month-olds Finkelstein and Ramey (1974)
found that two 8-minute exposures to a noncontingent stimulation
only tended (p < .10) to suppress response rates on a second,
different, task. Conversely, in another study with 3-month-olds
they found that five exposures to a noncontingent stimulation in
the home significantly enhanced learning on a second task in the
laboratory (Ramey and Finkelstein, 1977).

Thus, although it has been argued that noncontingent stimulation interferes with later learning during infancy (Finkelstein and Ramey, 1974; Watson, 1977), it is not clear that this is the case. All of the above studies have involved positive or affectively neutral stimuli such as light arrays, auditory and visual stimulation, and spinning mobiles. It is difficult to believe that brief bouts of such noncontingent stimulation could produce significant detrimental effects on later learning, at least for infants reared in home environments where they are also experiencing considerable contingent stimulation.

CONTINGENT STIMULATION AND EXPLORATORY BEHAVIOR

There have been relatively few studies of the characteristics of stimuli which elicit exploratory behavior. One factor which does affect exploration is the novelty of the stimulus, with novel objects eliciting more attention and manipulation than familiar objects (McCall, 1974). The number of movable parts, and the amount of feedback contingent on the infant's actions, however, also seems to be important (W. Bronson, 1971). Thus McCall (1974) showed that during the last quarter of the first year infants spent more time playing with objects which made more noise when they manipulated them than they did with objects which made less noise. Similarly, Rheingold (1963) showed that younger infants also attended more to an object if it "did something" when they manipulated it. Thus, it does appear that contingent stimulation facilitates or motivates exploratory behavior.

AFFECTIVE CONCOMITANTS OF CONTINGENT STIMULATION

From a therapeutic standpoint, some of the most exciting work on contingent stimulation during infancy comes from studies of the effects of control on the infant's affective, or emotional responses to events. Controlling the environment appears to be pleasurable for the infant (White, 1959). Events which are contingent on the infant's actions develop reward properties merely because they are controllable. Watson and Ramey (1972) found that the 2 month old infants in their study who had the controllable mobile began to smile and coo at it, something which did not happen for the infants who had the noncontingent or stationary mobile. More interestingly, some of the infants appeared to develop mild depressive responses when the contingent mobile was removed, suggesting that they may have developed some sort of positive relationship to it.

Along similar lines, several researchers have noted distress responses during extinction periods in operant learning studies. Extinction can be viewed as loss-of-control, as the subject's actions no longer produce the reinforcing stimulus. Rheingold, Gewirtz and Ross (1959) found that during extinction of a vocalization response which had previously been paired with

social reinforcement (experimenter smiled and said "good baby"),
the infants refused to look at the now unresponsive experimenter.
In fact, they even vigorously avoided eye contact when their heads
were propped to prevent them from turning away. In another study
(Ramey and Finkelstein, 1977) the extinction/re-conditioning
phases of a study with 3 month old infants had to be discontinued
because too many of the infants cried and showed distress. Such
reactions do not occur when infants receive noncontingent positive
stimulation. Therefore, it seems that loss-of-control is more
aversive for the infant than lack-of-control, per se.

Contingent stimulation is also now beginning to be used as a
therapy for Failure-to-Thrive infants (Ramey, Hieger and Klisz, 1972;
Ramey, Starr, Pallas, Whitten and Reed, 1975). Failure-to-thrive
is a syndrome characterized by physical, intellectual and social
retardation which persists even though no organic etiology can be
determined. There is usually, in addition, some history of maternal
neglect. Ramey and his colleagues (1972) have shown that experiences with response-contingent feedback produces marked changes in
such infants. In an initial study they conditioned two failure-to-
thrive infants to vocalize in order to turn-on a visual stimulus.
After several conditioning sessions the infants began to show an
increase in vocalization rates. Concomitant with these increases
were changes in affective behavior, which generalized beyond the
conditioning setting. Specifically, both infants ceased to show
the apathetic behavior patterns characteristic of such infants
(gaze aversion, a hands-over-the-face posture, and peculiar,
guttural vocalizations). Instead, both infants began to be more
responsive to hospital staff, to babble, and to show increased
competence in social responding, in general. In later work,
Ramey (1975, above) has shown that similar changes can be insti-
tuted by training the mother to engage in contingency-play with
the infant. Bouts of such play over a 3 month period also
resulted in significant increases in social responsiveness and in
the infants' scores on the Bayley test of mental and motor development.

Thus far we have been concerned with the affective consequences
of the infant's control over positive or affectively neutral events.
However, most studies of control and coping, in animals and in
adult humans, have focused on the effects of the subject's control
over negative or aversive events (see reviews by Averill, 1973;
Seligman, 1975). Under most conditions, controllable aversive
events appear to be less frightening and stressful than uncontrollable aversive events.

At birth, and for many months thereafter, there is little that
the infant can do to directly control aversive stimulation. The
infant can, however, perform a variety of behaviors which elicit
responses from caretakers (Bowlby, 1969). Furthermore, physical

contact with the mother or other attachment figure is a potent
stimulus for reducing distress (Wolff, 1969). In fact, in nonhuman
primates physical contact has been shown to reduce physiological
responses indicative of stress (see Levine, this volume). Thus,
the human infant can reduce distress by performing responses which
elicit physical contact and comforting from caretakers.

By the last half of the first year the infant's ability to
achieve or control contact with the mother has potent fear-reducing
effects (G. Bronson, 1971). For example, Rheingold and Eckerman
(1969) found that 10 month old infants who had access to the mother
entered and explored a novel room without distress, while infants
who were not allowed access to the mother were highly distressed in
the novel room. Similarly, Morgan and Riciutti (1969) noted that
negative emotional responses to the approach of a stranger were
greater when the infant was confined in an infant seat than when
the infant was free to crawl to the mother's side. Thus, by the
last part of the first year it appears that the infant's control
over achieving proximity and contact with the mother has significant
fear and distress reducing effects.

However, at this point there is no evidence that the infant's
direct control over the occurrence of aversive stimulation reduces
distress until the end of the first year. In a recent series of
studies (Gunnar, 1978; Gunnar-v. Gnechten, 1978) infants were
observed responding to an arousing and potentially frightening toy
which they either turned on themselves, or which came on independent
of their actions. In three studies 12-month-olds who controlled the
activations of the toy cried less and approached the toy more than
did 12-month-olds who had no control over when the toy was activated.
This was not the case for infants younger than 12 months. One study
examined developmental changes in the effects of this type of control.
The results showed that at 6 and 9 months controlling the toy did
not reduce distress (crying) and in fact at 9 months infants who
turned the toy on themselves were more distressed than were infants
of the same age who had no control over activating the toy.

These data may not indicate that all types of direct control
over aversive stimuli are ineffective in reducing distress prior to
12 months. Few studies of control and fear have employed control
over producing the aversive stimulus as the type of control examined
(Pervin, 1963). Instead, control has usually meant performing an
action to avoid or escape aversive stimulation (Averill, 1973).
When a subject controls the onset of an aversive stimulus, then he
or she does have control over avoiding that stimulus. By inhibiting
the action the stimulus can be avoided. However, in order for
such control to increase expectations of safety, the subject must
in some sense, anticipate the consequences of not performing the
controlling response. This may be beyond the cognitive capacities

of younger infants. Expectations of safety may, however, be
increased for younger infants by pairing a response with the absence
of the aversive stimulus.

To summarize, in the laboratory prior experiences with response-
contingent stimulation do appear to facilitate later instrumental
learning. Furthermore, objects which provide contingent stimulation
elicit and sustain exploratory behavior. There is also evidence
that events which are contingent on the infant's actions develop
reward properties as a function of their controllability. When
the outcome is pleasant, then controlling the occurrence of that
event appears to produce positive emotional responses. Control
over safety, in the form of achieving contact with the mother,
appears to reduce distress during the second half of the first
year. However at this point, at least, there is no evidence that
direct control over aversive stimulation is distress-reducing until
the end of the first year. Noncontingent stimulation does appear
to elicit distress if it follows a period of contingent stimulation
(loss of control). However, there is no strong evidence that
noncontingent positive stimulation interferes with later learning
unless the event to be controlled is highly similar to the one
which the infant has experienced as being uncontrollable.

MATERNAL RESPONSIVENESS

Especially during the early months of life the human infant
can do little to directly manipulate the inanimate environment.
Contingent stimulation during these early months must be provided
by the infant's caretakers. This has led researchers to focus on
the mother or caretaker's role in providing the initial experiences
upon which the infant's expectancies of control will be based.
Thus, Seligman (1975) argues that maternal deprivation can be viewed
as the primary model of helplessness, and Levine (this volume)
argues that maternal responsiveness can be viewed as providing
the infant with his or her first experiences of coping with stressful
events. Similarly, Lewis and Goldberg (1969) argue that maternal
responsiveness forms the basis of the infant's expectancy of control,
and thereby affects all later learning. Finally Ainsworth, Bell and
Stayton (1971), and Bowlby (1969) argue that the mother's responsiveness influences both the development and the security of the attachment relationship, and thus influences the extent to which the
infant can use the mother as a secure base from which to explore the
environment. Research on the effects of maternal responsiveness
on infant learning and cognitive development, exploration, and fear
or timidity provides only partial support for these hypotheses.

This can be seen in Tables 1 through 3. While maternal
responsiveness to positive infant behaviors (smiling, cooing, etc.)
is related to infant learning and cognitive development, there is
really no indication that the mother's responsiveness to distress

TABLE 1

MATERNAL RESPONSIVENESS AND INFANT LEARNING AND COGNITIVE DEVELOPMENT

Study	Maternal Responsiveness at:	Infant tested at:	Test Given	Responsiveness to:	
				Positive Signals	Distress Signals
Lewis & Goldberg, (1969)	3 mo	3 mo	Habituation Rate	.53	.44
Yarrow et al., (1975)	5-6 mo	5.5 mo	Bayley Test	N.S.	N.S.
Beckwith et al., (1976)	1 and 3 mo	9 mo	Sensori-Motor Develop.	N.S.	N.S.
	8 mo	9 mo	Sensori-Motor Develop.	.60	N.S.
Yarrow, (1963)	1-6 mo	6 mo	D.Q. (not specified)	.59	N.S.
Ainsworth and Bell, (1973)	9-12 mo	9-12 mo	Griffith Scales	(rating of combined responsiveness .46)	
Clarke-Stewart, (1973)	10.5-11.5 mo	11.5 mo	Bayley Test	N.S.	N.S.
	10.5-11.5 mo	17 mo	Bayley Test	.50	N.S.

TABLE 2

MATERNAL RESPONSIVENESS AND INFANT EXPLORATORY BEHAVIOR

Study	Maternal Responsiveness at:	Infant Exploration at:	Measure of Exploration	Maternal Responsiveness to:	
				Positive Signals	Distress Signals
Yarrow, (1963)	1–6 mo	6 mo	Rating of amount of exploration	.51	.33
Yarrow et al., (1975)	5–6 mo	6 mo	Time manipulating novel object	.31	N.S.
Yarrow, (1977)	6 mo	12 mo	Amount of exploration	N.S.	N.S.
Gunnar-v. Gnechten, (1976)	6 mo	12 mo	Time exploring novel object	N.S.	N.S.
Clarke-Stewart, (1973)	10.5–17 mo	12 mo	Number of toys manipulated	-.34	N.S.
			Time per toy	.35	N.S.

TABLE 3

MATERNAL RESPONSIVENESS AND INFANT TIMIDITY

Study	Maternal Respon- siveness at:	Infant Fear at:	Stim- u- lus	Maternal Responsiveness to:	
				Positive Signals	Distress Signals
Gunnar-v. Gnechten (1976)	6 mo	12 mo	Mechanical toys	N.S. combined	N.S. (.32)
	9 mo	9 mo	Mechanical toys	.30	.35
Clarke-Stewart (1973)	10.5-17 mo	12 mo	Stranger	N.S. combined	N.S. (.35)

signals bears any relationship to this aspect of infant functioning
(Table 1). The one study (Lewis and Goldberg, 1969) which found a
significant correlation between learning (habituation rate) and the
mother's responsiveness to distress, while widely quoted, has one
severe methodological problem. Maternal responsiveness was measured
immediately prior to when the infant test was administered. Clearly,
the mothers who were more responsive to the infant's signals may have
kept their infants in a state which was more appropriate for testing.
The reported correlation may, therefore, reflect a transient rather
than a stable relationship between maternal responsiveness and infant
learning.

Similarly, there is no evidence that maternal responsiveness to
cries is related to exploration (Table 2). Furthermore, the relationship of exploration and responsiveness to positive infant
behaviors is weak, with only those studies which measure maternal
responsiveness and infant exploration concurrently showing any
significant, positive correlations. Finally, in regard to fear
or timidity (Table 3), by the end of the first year maternal
responsiveness, if anything, is related to more rather than less,
fearful responses to arousing/aversive stimuli.

The failure of these studies to find strong support for the
hypothesis that maternal responsiveness facilitates learning, stim-
ulates exploration and reduces fear probably reflects problems in
how the hypothesis has been tested, rather than problems with the
hypothesis, per se. These problems can be identified. The first
is methodological, the second involves the predictions derived
from theories regarding the effects of expectancies of control, and
the third involves a failure to consider the effects of other
sources of contingent stimulation.

The first problem is how we should operationally define
maternal responsiveness. As noted earlier, several studies indicate
that temporal delays of as little as 3 seconds between a response
and an outcome can prevent learning of contingent relationships
throughout the first year (Millar, 1972; Ramey and Ourth, 1971).
Furthermore, temporal delays between response-event trials may
also interfere with the infant's capacity to learn that an action
is associated with a given outcome (Watson, 1967). In studies of
maternal responsiveness these factors have not been taken into
account in determining how "responsiveness" is defined. This is
especially the case in regard to the amount of time permitted
between the infant's behavior and the mother's response. Depending on the study a maternal response may mean that the mother's
behavior occurred immediately following the infant's behavior
(Yarrow, 1963: responsiveness to vocalizations) or within 45 seconds
of the infant's behavior (Clarke-Stewart, 1973: responsiveness to
distress). There is also within study variability in the time
permitted depending on the type of infant behavior under consider-

ation. In general, the mother's response to positive behaviors
must be more immediate than her response to distress in order to
be scored as contingent (Clarke-Stewart, 1973; Yarrow, Rubenstein
and Pederson, 1975). This may explain why significant correlations
have been found more often with responsiveness to positive behaviors
as compared to responsiveness to distress. Clearly, what we need to
do is to determine what defines a "contingent" maternal response
from the infant's standpoint, and then define "responsiveness"
accordingly, before we can adequately assess the effects of maternal
responsiveness.

The second problem involves the predictions made regarding
fear and exploration. Do we really expect that early contingent
stimulation should have a general facilitating effect on exploratory
behavior, and an inhibitory effect on fear? As noted earlier, fear
and exploration are behavioral systems which are sensitive to variations in the controllability of the environment. When the infant
has access to the mother (control over proximity) and when there are
objects to manipulate which respond to the infant's actions then more
exploration and less fear are observed. However, when the infant has
little control over the events occurring in the situation then less
exploration and more fear or distress reactions are observed. Rather
than generally reducing fear and increasing exploration, prior
contingent stimulation should increase the infant's responsiveness
to variations in the controllability of the environment. Infants
who have had more experience with control should be more distressed
by lack of control in arousing and potentially frightening situations,
and should be less distressed and exhibit more exploratory behavior
in arousing situations where they are permitted control over the
occurrence of events.

Tangential support for this argument can be found in at least
one study with infant rhesus monkeys (Smotherman, Hunt, McGinnis
and Levine, 1979). It was found that infants of dominant females
were aroused (as indexed by plasma cortisol levels) when forcibly
separated from their mothers (loss-of-control) than were infants
of less dominant mothers. In rhesus, the infants' dominance is
related to the mother's dominance (Sade, 1967), thus offspring of
more dominant females may receive more positive social stimulation,
and have more control over preferred aspects of the environment
than do offspring of less dominant females. If so, their greater
response to separation may reflect a greater discrepancy between
their expectancies of control, and their lack-of-control in the
situation than was experienced by offspring of less dominant
females.

In both studies with human infants which related fear to
maternal responsiveness, the fear-provoking situations were ones in
which the infant was permitted little control. Therefore we would
expect more fearful responses from infants who had experienced more

contingent stimulation from the mother. What needs to be
determined now is whether negative correlations between fear and
maternal responsiveness are observed in situations where the
infant is permitted control.

The third problem is more conceptual in nature. It is the case
that especially during the early months of life contingent stimulation is more likely to involve social rather than nonsocial objects.
However, with age the infant develops the motor skills necessary to
manipulate inanimate objects, and begins to spend time eliciting
contingent stimulation from virtually any object which comes to hand.
Therefore it does not make much sense to examine the effects of early
contingent stimulation by focusing attention solely on the mother's
role in providing such experiences.

Home environments vary in the number and variety of objects
available for the infant to manipulate, the amount of floor freedom
permitted once the infant has learned to crawl and later walk, and
in the feedback potential (e.g., number of movable parts) of the
objects which the infant is permitted to explore. Only a few
researchers have systematically examined the effects of these variables. These data are shown in Tables 4 and 5. As can be seen,
these variables are positively related both to learning and cognitive development and to exploration of the environment. In many
cases these correlations are higher than those found with maternal
responsiveness as measured in the same study (Yarrow, 1963; Yarrow,
Rubenstein and Pederson, 1975).

This cannot be taken to indicate that maternal responsiveness
and contingent nonsocial stimulation are interchangeable. These
correlations with aspects of the inanimate environment were
observed for infants who were living in home environments with
mothers who were at least minimally responsive to their signals.
However, they do suggest that by focusing solely on the mother we
miss a good deal of important information about aspects of the
child's early experiences which should affect the child's expectancies of control. Especially in the human species, where our
capacity to directly manipulate the physical environment plays an
important role in how well we function in life, it is only reasonable to expect that children's early experiences with controlling
objects, as well as their early experiences with controlling social
stimulation, will bear strongly on later expectations of being able
to control their environment.

TABLE 4

ASPECTS OF THE INANIMATE ENVIRONMENT AND INFANT LEARNING AND COGNITIVE DEVELOPMENT

Study	Environment at:	Infant Tested at:	Infant Measure	Environment Measure	Relationship (Pearson r)
Yarrow, (1963)	1–6 mo	6 mo	I.Q.	Age approp. of obj. and exper.	.85
Yarrow et al., (1975)	5–6 mo	5.5 mo	Bayley Test	Responsiveness	N.S.
				Variety	.51
Bell, (1971)	8 mo	8 mo	Griffith Scale	Floor Freedom	.61
				Variety	.43
	11 mo	11 mo		Floor Freedom	.57
				Variety	.41
Ainsworth and Bell, (1973)	9–12 mo	9–12 mo	Griffith Scale	Floor Freedom	.46

TABLE 5

ASPECTS OF INANIMATE ENVIRONMENT AND INFANT EXPLORATORY BEHAVIOR

Study	Environment at:	Infant Ex-ploration at:	Infant Measure	Environment Measure	Relationship (Pearson r)
Yarrow, (1963)	1-6 mo	6 mo	Rating of amount of exploration	Age approp-riateness of objects	.69
Yarrow et al., (1975)	5-6 mo	6 mo	Time manip-ulating novel object	Feedback potential	N.S.
Yarrow, (1977)	6 mo	12 mo	Amount of exploration	Feedback potential	.49
				Variety	N.S.

REFERENCES

Ainsworth, M. D. S., 1962, The effects of maternal deprivation: a review of findings and controversy in the concept of research strategy, in: "Deprivation of Maternal Care: A Reassessment of its Effects," World Health Organization, Geneva.

Ainsworth, M. D. S., and Bell, S. M., 1973, Mother-infant interaction and the development of competence, in: "The Growth of Competence," K. Connolly and J. Brunner, eds., Academic Press, New York.

Ainsworth, M.D.S., Bell, S., and Stayton, D.J., 1972, Individual differences in the development of some attachment behaviors. Merrill-Palmer Q., 18:123-143.

Averill, J., 1973, Personal control over aversive stimuli and its relationship to stress, Psychol. Bull., 80:286

Bandura, A., 1977, Self-efficacy: Toward a unifying theory of behavioral change, Psychol. Rev., 84:191.

Beckwith, L., Cohen, S., Kopp, C., Parmelee, A., and Marcy, T., 1976, Caregiver-infant interaction and early cognitive development in preterm infants, Child Devel., 47:579.

Bell, S., 1971, Early cognitive development and its relationship to infant-mother attachment: A Study of disadvantaged Negro infants, Report prepared for the U.S. Office of Education, Project No. 00542.

Bowlby, J., 1969, "Attachment and Loss, Vol. 1: Attachment," Basic Books, New York.

Bronson, G., 1971, Fear of the unfamiliar in human infants, "Origins of Human Social Relations," H. R. Schaffer, ed., Academic Press, New York.

Bronson, W., 1971, The growth of competence: Issues of conceptualization and measurement, "Origins of Human Social Relations," H. R. Schaffer, ed., Academic Press, New York

Clarke-Stewart, K., 1973, Interactions between mothers and their young children: Characteristics and consequences, Soc. for Research in Child Development Monographs, 38:6 #153.

David, M., and Appell, G., 1961, A study of nursing care and nurse-infant interaction: a report on the first half of an investigation, in: "Determination of Infant Behavior," Vol. 1, B. M. Foss, ed., Methuen, London.

Finkelstein, N., and Ramey, C., in press, Learning to control the environment in infancy, Child Devel.

Gunnar, M., 1978, Control and fear in infancy. Unpublished doctoral dissertation, Stanford University.

Gunnar-v. Gnechten, M., 1976, The relationship between maternal responsiveness and infant timidity. Paper presented at meetings of the Western Psychological Association, April.

Gunnar-v. Gnechten, M., 1978, Changing a frightening toy into a pleasant toy by allowing the infant to control its actions, Devel. Psychol., 14:157.

Lefcourt, H., 1976, "Locus of Control: Current Trends in Theory and Research," Wiley and Sons, New York.

Levine, S., 1969, Infantile stimulation: A perspective, in: "Stimulation in Early Infancy," A. Ambrose, ed., Academic Press, London.

Lewis, M., and Goldberg, S., 1969, Perceptual-cognitive development in infancy: A generalized expectancy model as a function of the mother-infant interaction, Merrill-Palmer Quart., 15:81.

McCall, R., 1974, Exploratory manipulation and play in the human infant. Monograph of the Society for Research in Child Development, 39(2), Serial #155.

Millar, W. S., 1972, A study of operant conditioning under delayed reinforcement in early infancy. Monograph of the Society for Research in Child Development, 37, Serial #147.

Millar, W. S., and Schaffer, H. R., 1972, The influence of spatially displaced feedback on infant operant conditioning, J. Exp. Psychol., 14:442.

Morgan, G., and Riciutti, H., 1969, Infant responses to strangers during the first year, in: "Determinants of Infant Behavior, Vol. 4, Wiley, New York.

Pervin, L., 1963, The need to predict and control under conditions of threat, J. Personal., 31:570.

Provence, S., and Lipton, R., 1963, "Infants in Institutions," International Universities Press, New York.

Ramey, C., and Finkelstein, N., 1977, The effects of responsive stimulations in early infancy. Paper given at meetings of the Society for Research in Child Development, New Orleans.

Ramey, C. and Ourth, L., 1971, Delayed reinforcement and vocalization rates of infants, Child Devel., 42:291.

Ramey, C., Hieger, L. and Klisz, D., 1972, Synchronous reinforcement of vocal responses in failure-to-thrive infants, Child Devel., 43:1449.

Ramey, C., Starr, R., Pallas, J., Whitten, C., and Reed, V., 1975, Nutrition, response-contingent stimulation and the maternal deprivation syndrome: Results of an early intervention program, Merrill-Palmer Quart., 21(1):45.

Rheingold, H., 1960, The measurement of maternal care, Child Devel., 31:656.

Rheingold, H., 1963, Controlling the infant's exploratory behavior, in: "Determinants of Infant Behavior," B. M. Foss, ed., Methuen, London.

Rheingold, H., and Eckerman, C., 1969, The infant's free entry into new environments, J. Exp. Child Psychol., 8:271.

Rheingold, H., Gewirtz, J., and Ross, H., 1959, Social conditioning of vocalizations in the infant, J. Comp Physiol. Psychol., 52:68.

Riccio, D., Rohrbaugh, M., and Hodges, L., 1968, Developmental aspects of passive and active avoidance learning in rats, Devel. Psychobiol., 1:108.

Sade, D., 1967, Determinants of dominance in a group of free-
    ranging rhesus monkeys, in: "Social Communication among
    Primates," S. Altman, ed., University of Chicago Press.
Seligman, M., 1975, "Learned Helplessness: On Depression, Devel-
    opment and Death," Freeman and Company, San Francisco, Calif.
Smotherman, W. P., Hunt, L. E., McGinnis, L. M. and Levine, S.,
    1979, Mother-infant separation in group-living rhesus macques:
    A hormonal analysis, Devel. Psychobiol, 12:211.
Watson, J. S., 1966, The development and generalization of
    "contingency awareness" in early infancy: Some hypotheses,
    Merrill-Palmer Quart., 12:123.
Watson, J. S., 1967, Memory and "contingency analysis" in infant
    development, Merrill-Palmer Quart., 13:55.
Watson, J. S., 1977, Depression and the perception of control in
    early childhood., in: "Depression in Childhood: Diagnosis.
    Treatment and Conceptual Models," J. G. Schulterbrandt and
    A. Raskin, eds., Raven Press, New York.
Watson, J., and Ramey, C., 1969, Reactions to response - contingent
    stimulation in early infancy. Revision of a paper presented
    at meetings of the Society for Research in Child Development,
    March 1969.
Watson, J., and Ramey, C., 1972, Reaction to response-contingent
    stimulation in early infancy, Merrill-Palmer Quart., 18:219.
White, R. W., 1959, Motivation reconsidered: the concept of compe-
    tence, Psychol. Rev., 66:297.
Wolff, P. H., 1969, The natural history of crying and other vocali-
    zations in early infancy, in: "Determinants of Infant Behavior,"
    Vol. 4, Methuen, London.
Yarrow, L., 1963, Research in dimensions of early maternal care,
    Merrill-Palmer Quart., 9:101.
Yarrow, L., 1977, The origins of mastery motivation, working paper
    of National Institute of Mental Health.
Yarrow, L., Rubenstein, J., and Pederson, F., 1975, "Infant and
    environment: early cognitive and motivational development,"
    Wiley and Sons, New York.

EARLY ADOLESCENCE AS A LIFE STRESS

Beatrix A. Hamburg, M.D.

Laboratory of
Developmental Psychology
National Institute
of Mental Health

Relationships between life stress and susceptibility to various physical and psychological disorders has been shown by many studies. These issues deserve careful study in early adolescence in particular. The concept of early adolescence is relatively new. The full range of adolescence in contemporary America is too lengthy and complex to be comprehended as a single undifferentiated entity of "teen-agers" or as "the adolescent." Fortunately, during the past decade, stages of adolescence have been delineated. The earliest recognition of the significance of this specific age cohort was in a collection of stimulating papers in which outstanding investigators reanalyzed their adolescent research and experience with a focus on the twelve to sixteen year old population (Kagan and Coles, 1972). In further studies, early adolescence has emerged as a stressful period of development that has distinctive tasks, challenges and opportunities (Hamburg, 1974a, 1974b).

Prior to this time, late adolescence was the focus of research and interventions. Particularly in the 1960's, it was this older age group whose behaviors presented the most puzzling and alarming concerns. At that time it was widely believed and feared that their patterns of youth alienation and rebellion heralded the emergence of a new secular trend that would continue to characterize adolescent needs and motivations. As we have seen, this did not turn out to be the case. The turbulence of the 1960's largely represented a cohort effect anchored in transient, specific historic events (Hamburg, 1975). In contrast, there have been some enduring social changes and trends in women's roles and behaviors. Female out-of-home employment, personal control of fertility, and sexual "liberation" continue to show rising rates and reflect a true societal change. As we look at early adolescence, it will be useful

121

to try to sort out effects of enduring social change, biologically
based innate stresses, and cohort effects of the vicissitudes of
specific historic context. The transiency of specific historic
context should not be taken to minimize the importance of the
potential impact. For a given cohort, some of those effects are
likely to exert pressures and to shape development in ways that,
in turn, will significantly influence the patterns of adult
functioning.

HEALTH STATUS OF EARLY ADOLESCENTS

     Understanding the developmental tasks and challenges of early
adolescence is of great theoretical importance and intrinsic interest.
It is an understudied period during which major disequilibrium in
physiological and psychosocial systems is modal. In addition, at
the present time, there are many pressing and practical reasons to
try to understand the adaptive challenges involved in negotiation
of the biological, psychological, and social demands that face
early adolescents. They are the group whose behaviors are currently
a major source of profound distress and concern. It is a sad fact
that significant problems, indeed crisis issues, such as high rates
of alcohol abuse, drug use, smoking, promiscuity, unwed pregnancy,
venereal disease, violent behavior, school dropout, runaways,
depression, suicide and preventable accidents are widespread and
are showing their highest rates of increase in early adolescence.
These behaviors are by no means universal; nonetheless, their
prevalence rates are high enough to cause grave concern. In the
aggregate, these behaviors constitute the leading causes of death,
disability, and suffering for this age period. The Final Mortality
Statistics Report (1977) shows that the age-adjusted death rate
declined from 6.3 in 1976 to 6.1 in 1977, the lowest level ever
recorded in the United States. The death rate declined for most
age groups of both sexes. The exceptions were for males aged 10-24
years and females aged 10-24 years and females 45-64 years. The
table on page 3 shows the percent change in death rates for specified age groups. Furthermore, there is increasing awareness that
the bulk of this mortality and morbidity of the early adolescent
period is directly traceable to personal attitudes and behaviors
that are health damaging. Health attitudes and behaviors adopted
in these adolescent years typically define patterns of adult functioning. In this way, events are entrained that will have predictably
devastating health consequences in later life. Early smoking is a
good example. Statistically, smoking is the leading cause of
shortened life span. In addition to lung cancer, smoking contributes to deaths from heart disease, other lung diseases, and
bladder cancer. Smoking is decreasing in most sectors of the
American population but it is rising in teenage girls. Data from
a joint study of the National Cancer Institute and the American
Cancer Society (1977) indicate that cigarette smoking has increased
by 23% since 1969. In 1975, 27% of all teenage girls were smoking

TABLE 1

FINAL MORTALITY STATISTICS REPORT, 1977

Age	Percent Change		
	Total	Male	Female
All ages	-1.3	-1.3	-1.3
Under 1 year	-6.9	-5.9	-8.1
1-4 years	-1.6	-2.2	-0.8
5-9 years	-2.3	-1.0	-4.2
10-14 years	+1.4	+0.9	+2.0
15-24 years	+3.2	+3.0	+3.6
25-44 years	-1.7	-1.0	-3.0
45-64	-2.0	-2.4	+1.5
65-74	-2.3	-2.5	-2.1
75-84	-2.0	-1.3	-2.6
95 years and over	-4.9	-3.8	-5.4

a pack or more of cigarettes per day.

It has long been the conventional wisdom that adolescents enjoy the healthiest period of the lifespan. The necessity for detailed scrutiny of their true medical status is apparent. The recent National Health Examination Survey reveals some significant findings. The data reported are drawn from the two programs of the Health Examination Survey that focused on the impact of illness and disability in probability samples of non-institutionalized children 6-11 years of age and non-institutionalized youth 12-17 years of age. The data collection was carried out over the years 1963-1970 (DHEW, 1974). First is the adolescents' view of their own health status. There is a steep upsurge in bodily concerns about health. At ages 12 to 15 years, roughly 14% of both males and females have from three to five medical symptoms rated by them as definitely requiring a doctor. In fact, almost none of these young people ever are seen by physicians for these symptoms. The National Health Survey Research also indicates that ulcers, skin disorders, and neuromuscular joint disorders are far more common than previously believed. In the same surveys, pediatricians rate more youths (12-17 years) than children (6-11 years) as having some significant abnormality. When examined 21% of youths and 11% of children were found to have abnormalities. In a separate study hypertension was found to be higher than expected (1977). Systolic blood pressure levels showed a mean of 105.9 mm of Hg at 6 years and increased to 134.1 mm of Hg at 17 years. The increase shows a sharp rise between 11 and 12 years of age, average of 9 mm of Hg. This increase accounts for one-third of the increase noted over the 12-year span from 6 to 17 years of age. Similarly, there is a generally consistent increase of diastolic pressure with age but less rapid than the systolic rise.

Also, there is acceleration of rise between 11 and 12 years of age.
There is an interesting finding that the diastolic mean of boys
14-17 years old and girls 12-17 years old, exceed, respectively, the
levels of young men and women 18-24 years of age. The rise in early
pregnancy and childbearing has highlighted health problems for both
the adolescent mother and her vulnerable child.

Health issues in early adolescence have long been neglected.
Nevertheless, there is substantial reason for concern and there is
a significant opportunity for remedial and preventive interventions.
The relation of life stress and effectiveness of coping to health
outcomes continues to be a fruitful area of research. Some of
these stresses and coping strategies will be described for early
adolescents.

STRESSES OF EARLY ADOLESCENCE

A characteristic of stressful transition or crisis is
discontinuity with past situations. Totally novel problems often
defy familiar ways of behaving. Ambiguity is high and individuals
in these circumstances are often unable to obtain relevant information to guide their actions or to receive meaningful feedback from
supportive others. For early adolescents, there is maximal discontinuity. There is almost no sphere in which it is possible to draw
on analagous past experience as a support or guide. During this
time of superimposed environmental and internal demands, the coping
skills of the early adolescent are impoverished and the previously
dependable sources of parental and school support are often weakened
or withdrawn. Anticipatory coping that might serve to attenuate,
regulate or otherwise modify the stressful impacts does not usually
occur because of the general lack of awareness of predictable tasks
and challenges of the period. This, too, is an area that has
received insufficient attention. Some suggestions for anticipatory
coping strategies will be discussed shortly.

There are three sets of new preemptive challenges that inevitably confront the early adolescent. The first set relates to the
multiple impacts of the biological changes of puberty. The second
set of challenges derive from the entry into the totally new school
environment of junior high school. The third set reflects the
problems of sudden entry into the new role status of adolescence
that is conferred by virtue of entering junior high school. The
new role expectations are poorly defined for both the young persons
and the adults who deal with them. This ambiguity concerning role
behaviors becomes a stress in its own right.

Biological Changes of Puberty

The impact of the biological changes of puberty is a dominant
theme of early adolescence. Puberty is a time of drastic and

unpredictable bodily changes. These changes involve all systems of
the body. Tanner has stated "for the majority of young persons, the
years from twelve to sixteen are the most eventful ones of their
lives so far as their growth and development is concerned. Admit-
tedly during fetal life and the first year or two after birth
developments occurred still faster . . . but the subject himself
was not the fascinated, charmed or horrified spectator that watches
the developments or lack of developments, of adolescence" (Tanner,
1971).

    The pattern and sequence of adolescent growth and bodily change
has been shown to be surprisingly consistent across populations.
There are strong suggestions that there have not been appreciable
changes since the time of Early Man. There is a wide variation,
however, both within populations and across populations in the
average age at which each of the events occurs, the rapidity with
which one event follows the other and in the interrelationships
between the different series of events. The bodily changes of
early adolescence have the overall effect of enhancing sexual
dimorphism. This is most obvious in the development of secondary
sex characteristics. It is also manifested in the changes in facial
contours, in shifts in body proportions and in height changes.
However, virtually the entire body participates in anatomical and
physiological changes in the course of the pubertal development.
The net effect is that mature males tend to excel in size, strength
and physical endurance.

    The range of ages for the occurrence of these events is great
for both boys and girls. When there are deviations from the
averages (Clausen, 1975) or significant lack of synchrony between
the different series of events (Eichorn, 1975), these discrepancies
are experienced as stressful.

    Coming to terms with the changing body image is not easy. The
early adolescent perceives, at times erroneously, his emerging, still
developing, size and shape as the physique that will characerize him/
her throughout adult life. In the stage of early adolescence, the
individual must come to terms with his definitive body image through
an integration of his self-perceptions and those reflected to him by
significant others. The negotiation of this task has profound implications for his sense of identity as an adult. The psychological
development of the individual is closely related to the course of
physical development. This concern over body image is pervasive
and there are deep concerns about physical appearance. Differences
between boys and girls in self-perceptions of body weight were striking in reports of the National Health Survey (1975). When asked
about body build or image, less than half reported satisfaction
with their current status. Almost half of the girls would prefer to
be thinner. On the other hand, boys wished to be heavier. Boys were
twice as likely as girls to consider themselves underweight.

Most adolescents have relatively little information about the wide range of normality or the timetables for the appearance of the various physical manifestations that affect his total body image. For many individuals the pubertal changes bring experiences of uncertainty, dissatisfaction, embarrassment, and, above all, a sense of helplessness about bodily events. Recent studies summarized by Janis and Rodin (1979) have shown that in situations of ignorance or high uncertainty individuals are likely to fill in the gaps with speculative inferences which make for erroneous attributions. Developmentally, therefore, early adolescents are exceedingly vulnerable to real or imagined assaults on bodily integrity. This also adds to their problems in coping with medical issues, especially surgery or chronic illness. For example, the control of insulin-dependent diabetes is notoriously more difficult in adolescence than any other time.

During early adolescence there are baffling mood and temperment effects which are probably partially the result of direct effects of the gonadal hormones, but are experienced as interpersonal stress. This is another area that deserves more study. The emerging evidence for endocrine influences on adolescent behavior is stimulating efforts to elucidate factors mediating these influences. Because there are so many widespread physiological and behavioral changes in puberty, psychoendocrine research on early adolescence encounters problems in isolating the events of crucial interest. Some considerations in the design of such studies are briefly noted here.

(1) An endocrine change may be related to intensity of emotional experience. The particular mood exhibited may be a result of the individual's attempt to deal with an increase in drives (e.g., sexuality) which may have no socially acceptable outlet in that age group.

(2) There may be transient hormone-mood relations. During puberty there are drastic shifts within individuals in hormones from minimal pre-pubertal levels to high concentrations that approximate adult values. In longitudinal studies (Faiman and Winter, 1974) ten-fold changes in sex hormone levels have been reported in individuals over the course of a few months. Also, some hormones, notably testosterone, are secreted in pulsatile bursts. Circulating hormone levels cannot be reliably inferred from age of subject or bodily evidence of status of pubertal development. Significant endocrine-behavior interactions can only be studied using techniques of contemporaneous hormone determination and behavioral assessment.

(3) Behavioral effects of a hormone could occur as a result

of an increased behavioral sensitivity to that hormone rather than, or in addition to, increased concentrations of that hormone.

(4) Twenty-four hour rhythms of the hormones should be accounted for in sampling procedures. Also, since the release of several hormones is sleep-related, the patterns of the subject's sleep also must be considered.

(5) Interaction of hormones may be important. The ratios of hormone concentrations may reveal more than measures of only a single hormone per study.

Early versus Late Maturation. Although typical or modal ages have been used for convenience in descriptions of pubertal change, the range of ages for all of these changes is very large. In other words, children mature at different rates. It has been established that the timing of puberty has significant and differential behavioral consequences for boys and girls. Reynolds and Wines (1951) studied onset and end-point of pubertal change in 59 adolsecent boys longitudinally at the Fels Research Institute. The age range for the onset of puberty in boys was 9.5 years to 15 years. The age range for the end-point was 13.5 years to 18.5 years. In a companion study of girls at the Fels Research Institute, Reynolds and Wines (1948) found a range of ages from 8.5 to 13 for the onset of pubertal change as defined by the appearance of the breast bud. It is clear, therefore, that there are instances in which some children have not yet begun any pubertal change at an age at which their peers have entirely completed all of the pubertal events. Therefore, in a mixed group of boys and girls between the ages of 11 and 15 there is enormous variability in the level of maturational development. It should be remembered that this coincides with the junior high school exper-ience.

Mary Cover Jones (1965) and associates did long-term investi-gations of the different impacts and varying outcomes of early versus late maturity in boys and girls. Skeletal age was used as a stable and reliable index of physical maturity. On the average, the physically accelerated and physically retarded adolescents of the same chronological age are separated by two years in skeletal age. In girls, as early as 11 years of age all of the late-matur-ers are shorter than the mean for the early-maturers. At the mean age of 14, the height distributions for early- and late-maturers show an extreme separation with no overlap. At the peak of growth, early-maturing girls are not only taller than their girl classmates, but actually much taller than most of the boys in the class. From that age onward, the differences tend to decrease and by 18 or 19 the mature heights of the early- and late-maturing girls are very similar.

Strength tests in boys show that late-maturers are relatively
weak and are low in tests of athletic ability. Early-maturing boys
are more "masculine" (mesomorphic) in their builds, and late-maturing boys more "childish" (slender and long-legged) in their builds.
Later-maturers are likely to be perceived and treated as immature
by both adults and peers.

These classic studies revealed that systematic comparisons
between the behavior and personality characteristics of early-
and late-maturing adolescents have indicated that acceleration in
growth tends to carry distinct advantages for boys but some dis-
advantages for girls. In early adolescence early-maturing boys
are given more leadership roles, were more popular, excelled in
athletic ability, were perceived as more attractive by adults and
peers and enjoyed considerably enhanced heterosexual status. When
studied (Mussen and Jones, 1957) at 17 years of age, the early-
maturing boys showed more self-confidence, less dependency and
were more capable of playing an adult role in interpersonal
relations. Clausen (1975) in a re-analysis of the data found that
these findings were especially robust for working class youth. The
findings on the late-maturing boys showed more personal and social
maladjustment at all stages of adolescence. When studied on follow-
up at age 17 years, the group showed negative self-concepts,
prolonged dependency needs, rebellious attitudes towards parents,
strong affiliative needs, and profound feelings of rejection by the
group. Interestingly, the groups did not differ in needs for
achievement and recognition.

The early reports of systematic comparisons among girls ages
11 to 17 years (Jones and Mussen, 1958) showed that early-maturing
girls were seen as "submissive, listless, or indifferent in social
situations and lacking in poise. Such girls have little influence
upon the group and seldom attain a high degree of popularity,
prestige or leadership." Late-maturing girls in early adolescent
years were seen as relatively more outgoing and assured. They were
described as being confident and having leadership ability.

In early adolescence early-maturing boys and to a somewhat less
degree late-maturing girls share a fortuitous adaptive advantage.
Early-maturing girls stand in an intermediate position adaptively
despite their extreme position developmentally. A possible explanation for this latter finding may be that while their body configuration and tallness is viewed by the girls themselves and others as
discordant, it occurs while in the elementary school setting. Essentially this means that the task of coping with physical change occurs
as the single major challenge confronting her. She does not have the
superimposed academic and social pressures inherent in junior high
school. Her status with her peer group is buffered by halo effects
which can continue to operate inasmuch as she is remaining in a
stable social setting and does not have to establish herself with

new peers. Also, despite the fact that her appearance is different
both to herself and others, the changes are recognized by all concerned as desirable steps towards maturity. Finally, within the
continuity of the elementary school period, parents are less likely
to alter their expectations of her or drastically change their
accustomed ways of relating to her. She is usually perceived by
them as a "large child" rather than an "adolescent." Again,
needed stability may thus be achieved. In instances where the
parents collaborate in permitting an early shift to "adolescent"
behaviors at ages of 9 to 10, there is much more turmoil as she
strives to find a niche.

The late-maturing boy is at the most severe disadvantage. He
is at least as highly discordant as the early-maturing girl but
under much less favorable circumstances. He continues to look like
an elementary school boy at a time when it is important to him to
be as grown up as possible. He has a developmental lag of about
four years as compared to the average girl of the same age and
perhaps two years in relation to the age-matched boy. This degree
of discordance is experienced as a severe stress. The distress is
heightened by the fact that generally the afflicted individual is
unaware that he will, in fact, catch up to his more fortunate early-
maturing peers. At this critical time in development, however, his
self-esteem is very low and he develops maladaptive patterns of
adaption either in terms of appeasement and over-compliance or
swaggering, pseudo-adult behavior. In both instances, anxiety
level is likely to be high. There is some reason to believe that
for some individuals the ultimate adult adaptive ability is enhanced
if the boy succeeds in mastering this developmental challenge.

Asynchrony in Growth Processes. Just as there is significant
distress associated with deviation from the conventional norms of
timing of pubertal events across individuals, there is comparable
distress when noticeable deviations, spurts or lags, characterize
the course of development within the individual. Ideally, the full
range of changes of puberty involve co-adapted, coordinated sequences
of structural, physiological and psychosocial changes. In vivid
images and vignettes some fiction authors have portrayed the
immediate anguish and the long term effects of physical and psychosocial asynchronies in adolescent development. A striking medical
example of asynchrony occurs in precocious puberty when a 5- or 6-
year old child experiences the sex changes of puberty without the
concomitant cognitive, emotional or socio-cultural developments.
Ausubel (1954) has succinctly described the issues in normal
development:

"As the tempo of development. . . accelerates and as
discontinuities in the growth patterns of particular
functions occur, greater opportunities prevail for wider

disparities to develop between the relative levels of maturity
attained by these different functions . . . at least initially,
glaring discrepancies in rate of growth constitute a characteristic and invariable feature of transitional phases of
development. . . .When growth in one area is a necessary
precondition for or stimulant of growth in another area, a
certain amount of lag is inevitable. Thus, muscle strength
lags behind the increase in muscle mass, but it precedes the
gain in neuromuscular coordination. The growth spurts in
social and emotional development necessarily begin after the
physiological and physical growth spurts. . . . In some cases,
unevenness in the total growth pattern is caused by the lack
of a growth spurt in certain areas."

"Just as maturation in one area may precipitate or facilitate
maturation in another area, the converse holds equally true:
relative retardation in a slowly growing function inevitably
limits the full expression and complete development of a more
rapidly growing function. . . . Thus, whenever growth in a
given function greatly outstrips development in related,
supporting functions, only two possibilities of expression
exist: The relatively precocious function will (1) be utilized
immediately, before the supporting areas are adequately developed, and therefore prematurely; or (2) its utilization will
be deferred until related maturational tasks are completed.
But regardless of the alternative, the results will prove
unsatisfactory. Premature utilization can never be wholly
effective or satisfying and often leads to serious dysfunction.
. . . On the other hand, postponement of functional expression until related maturational readiness would lead to
emotional tension because of the frustration of current needs,
and to developmental retardation resulting from disuse and
insufficient role-playing experience."

In a recent review Eichorn (1975) has refocused attention on
the importance of adolescent asynchrony as a source of psychological
distress. She underscores the fact that the early adolescent is
uniquely attuned to nuances of bodily change and disproportion
because of the stage-related preoccupation with self. At the same
time, developmental pressures for conformity with peers or the
meeting of idealized cultural norms makes these perceived discrepancies in cognitive development for school performance, school
behavior, personality development, and probabilities of school
dropout.

Challenges of Junior High School

Typically, junior high school is the setting in which
the biologically changing adolescents find themselves. In our age-
graded culture, students in junior high school range between 11

and 15 years of age. As generally followed, the educational system
involves elementary school for six years and then junior high school
for two, but usually three years followed by high school for three
or four years. As it works out, the entry into junior high school
is timed with significant pubertal changes in most girls. There
are, however, only a small number of early-maturing boys who have
comparable pubertal changes at this time. The transition to junior
high school involves a radical shift from the experience of a self-
contained classroom and single teacher throughout the day as existed
in the elementary school to a large population, large campus, rotating classes and multiple teacher situation. With this transition,
the student relinquishes the former security of membership in one
stable classroom and is faced with the task of negotiating six or
seven changes of teachers and classes each day with no group support.
There also are greater academic demands and concerns about
achievement. This raises threats of failure in the face of vastly
greater requirements for autonomy. Finally, there is uncertainty
about the ability to make friendships in the new context.

Parents also view the junior high school student as entering
a new world. They expect to treat their child differently and
think of him now as an "adolescent." The stereotype thus evoked
often refers to late adolescents and so parental attitudes and
behaviors tend to derive from this model. The applicability of the
late adolescent model for providing useful prescriptions for dealing with early adolescents is dubious. New freedoms accorded, more
emphasis on independent decision-making, and conscious parental
efforts to foster autonomy may result in a loss of needed support
and guidance at a time of great confusion and ambiguity in all
spheres of functioning.

Entry into junior high school probably represents the most
abrupt and demanding transition of an individual's entire educational career. This is a crisis period that has important
educational as well as personal consequences. A major issue in
early adolescence is the recognition of sharp escalation in
academic demands both in terms of expected output and complexity
of tasks. A great many students have deep seated fears of inad-
equacy and failure. (Some students are buffered by the support of
older siblings who have served as models and sources of information
for them in negotiating the transition. But for many other siblings.
lings are negative and disturbing models or the student himself is
the eldest or perhaps an only child.) Evidence tends to confirm
that their fears may be well-founded. Studies have demonstrated
(Finger and Silverman, 1966) that there is a startling drop in
school performance associated with junior high school. In a study
by Armstrong in New York (1964), 45% of the boys and girls
with good elementary school records performed at a fair or poor
level in junior high school.

The work of Finger and Silverman (1966) replicated this finding
and furthermore has shown that students who experienced a drop in
performance in junior high school were rarely able to improve at a
later point in their careers. It is possible, therefore, to make
rather accurate predictions of eventual academic performance in
junior high school. The authors further note that whereas grades
in elementary school are highly related to intelligence, intelligence was largely unrelated to the change in performance at the
junior high level. In junior high school, motivation seems to be
the important factor.

Despite the fact that <u>intelligence</u> per se is not at issue in
the school performance of early adolescents, it is worthwhile to
re-examine their style of cognitive functioning. By and large, it
has generally been assumed that these early adolescents have moved
on from "formal operational thinking" to logical operations and
abstract thinking (Inhelder and Piaget, 1958). There are several
lines of evidence that would suggest that this is not generally
true. First, teachers who have previously taught high school
students invariably report that they are unable to be successful
with the same approach in junior high school. Martin (1971) states
"when I moved from high school to junior high school teaching I
was an experienced teacher with a reputation for good performance.
I went to my class of eighth graders with confidence. After forty-
five minutes, I knew I had entered a different world and would have
to begin learning about teaching again . . . These were people
who were different from the fifteen to eighteen year olds I had
been teaching." Teachers are frustrated unless they revise their
presentation from the predominantly logical and abstract to a
concrete approach. The typical junior high school student is
deficient in his ability to generalize, use symbols and to process
information with objectivity.

Elkind (1967) has described the egocentrism of adolescence as
showing a peak at the ages which correspond to early adolescence
(12-15). Objectivity is, by definition, inversely proportional to
egocentrism. In this same paper Elkind further states that in his
experience, it is not until ages of fifteen or sixteen that formal
operational thinking becomes firmly established. Clearly in any
transition to a new stage, there are rate differences between
individuals and fluctuations within a given individual until the
newly emerging stage is consolidated. It can be said that abstract
thinking generally appears earlier in areas of science and mathematics because children are given much more experience in learning
these symbols and mediating terms and have more practice in
manipulating these relationships and propositions (Peel, 1960).
Even in these areas, however, early adolescents will tend to
revert to concrete operations if confronted with an unfamiliar or
unusually difficult problem. The egocentrism that Elkind describes,
although pervasive, is most flagrantly to be observed in the early

adolescent's preoccupation with his bodily changes and his concerns with responses of others to his appearance.

Neimark (1975) reviews literature on logical reasoning and concludes that most abstract logical reasoning abilities do not begin to emerge until early adolescence. For young children, the ability to reason logically is situation-specific. They may learn to apply logical processes in an isolated context, but consistent performance using a variety of materials and modalities is not seen. Even in early adolescence, the emergence of abstract logical reasoning is by no means universal. For example, transitive inference and sentential logic do not begin to appear before the age of fourteen or fifteen.

Investigations in other areas of reasoning are also relevant to instruction at the early adolescent level. For example, Tversky and Kahneman (1971) describe experiments showing that many adults tend to regard samples as overly representative of the populations from which they are drawn. The prevalence and significance of logical errors and biases of this kind in early adolescents should be investigated, especially in view of the observed tendency of early adolescents to respond strongly to immediate peer influences and to media messages.

Results so far indicate that some formal operational abilities are emerging during the early adolescent period, but abilities such as "controlling variables" (the strategy of holding other things constant in exploring the effect of one variable on an outcome) may be atypical among early adolescents. The results of Karplus, Karplus, Formisano, and Paulsen (1975) suggest that performance on some of the experimental tasks used in their research may be influenced by instruction, but further research is required to establish the degree of teach-ability of these skills at the early adolescent level. Middle/junior high school teachers need to be made aware of the diversity in cognitive abilities characteristic of early adolescents. A significant amount of information has been collected on these differences. This information is especially critical to science, mathematics, and social science teachers whose subject matter requires logical and reasoning skills. It is also applicable to learning social skills and to decision-making processes for health-relevant behaviors.

Entry to junior high school provides opportunity as well as stress. It is generally acknowledged that cognitive development is susceptible to environmental influence as well as maturation. What passes for an educational approach for teaching early adolescents, in a majority of schools, is either abstracted from philosophies governing elementary or high school education, or some mixture of these separate educational units. The uniqueness of early adolescence is not recognized. The development of an

appropriate conceptual framework should begin with the cognitive,
psycho-social, and biological characteristics of the early
adolescent. The rationale should reflect the secular trends which
characterize the broad social realities of our times such as new
career patterns, changes in life styles, shifts in family organization and parenting, new concepts of health and wellness, factors
of social integration, the changing attributes of the work/leisure
relationship, and others. The school curriculum and associated
educational resources can be valid only to the extent that they
reflect the characteristics of early adolescence and social realities
and recognize what knowledge and which skills representing various
disciplines are most useful.

In addition to the drop in academic performance there are other
indicators of high distress noted in the junior high schools. Many
students, particularly boys, who had been tractable and diligent
in elementary school show rebellious acting-out behaviors which
make them intolerable to teachers. There is a high incidence of
drug abuse and alcohol consumption and other deviant behaviors.
Significant numbers of students are captives of negatively oriented
peer groups. Other students are isolated or alienated. In the
educational field, it is generally acknowledged that junior high
school is the period of highest student turbulence, teacher frustration, and discipline problems. Simmons (1979), in large scale studies
in Baltimore and Milwaukee schools, has found that self-esteem typically drops when students are in junior high school. The young
adolescent white girls (6th grade and 7th grade) showed the lowest
self-esteem of the students tested. Further, it was found that
early-maturing girls with active dating behavior showed the lowest
esteem of all students tested. When a matched group of early-
maturing girls attending 5th and 7th grades in an elementary school
was compared with 6th and 7th grade junior high school girls, the
elementary school girls did not show the comparable fall in self-
esteem. It was postulated that the early maturing girls in the
elementary school situation were shielded from the added social and
sexual pressures that characterized the junior high school experience. In prior studies of youth self-esteem, Rosenberg (1965)
found that low self-esteem is correlated with characteristic attitudes and responses. The individual is more vulnerable in interpersonal relations (deeply hurt by criticism); he is relatively
awkward with others (finds it hard to make talk, does not initiate
contacts); he assumes that others think poorly of him or do not
particularly like him; he tends to put up a 'front' for people; he
feels relatively isolated and lonely. There is low faith in
people. In some "this low faith in people takes the form of
contempt for the great mass of humanity; among others, mistrust,
and among still others, hostility (p. 182)." "Low self-esteem
makes them relatively submissive or unassertive in their dealings
with others. . . It is, thus apparent that the individual's self-
conception is not only associated with attitudes towards other

people, it is also associated with his actions in social life and
the position he comes to occupy in his high school peer groups
(p. 205)." The attributes associated with low self-esteem represent
attitudes and behaviors that would diminish coping potential,
heighten stress and accentuate any pre-existing tendencies to
resort to maladaptive solutions.

In any case, it seems likely that the social environment of
junior high school is inherently stressful. The roots of this
high rate of distress in the junior high school population need to
be further studied. It might be fruitful to study the transition
from elementary school to junior high school in a fashion similar
to the study of the transition from high school to college carried
out by Silber, Hamburg, Coelho, Murphey, Rosenberg, and Pearlin
(1961). Some educators are experimenting with alternatives to the
traditional sequence of elementary, junior high and high school.
These deserve study in terms of the psychosocial and coping outcomes,
in addition to curricular and learning considerations.

Some models of anticipating coping to aid in the transition
from elementary to junior high school have been tried. One example
is the Stanford-Palo Alto Peer Counseling Project (Hamburg, 1972).
Junior high and high school student volunteers were trained in
interpersonal, informational and decision making skills. These
peer counselors were assigned to help students with the stressful
transition from elementary to junior high school. These counselees
are initially seen in the sixth grade towards the end of the school
year when their anxiety about the challenge of junior high school
is starting to mount. It had been previously acknowledged by the
sixth graders that they have strong apprehensions about the transition to junior high school. It was reassuring to them to be able
to obtain specific information about what to expect and to know
that the same Peer Counselor speaking with them would be on hand
at the junior high school when they arrive in the fall. It was
very clear that gaining information and knowledge of a reliable
personal support were of crucial coping importance for them. It
was also useful for them to realize the universality of their fears.
They learned that their classmates felt as they did and also that
the Peer Counselor had been concerned at a comparable stage.

The anxieties expressed were (1) fear of academic failure,
(2) insecurity about their ability to cope with the interpersonal
demand of having to relate to a different teacher and different
group of students on an hourly basis, (3) concern about the ability
to make and hold friends, (4) ignorance about role expectations now
that they would be treated as adolescents, and (5) general sense of
confusion about the bigness and complexity of the new school format.
Many worried about actually getting lost and failing to appear for

classes.

In recruiting for the Peer Counseling Program, the training curriculum was described to the students. In this description it was implicit that individuals taking the training could derive substantial personal benefit. It was clear that the course would give specific training and practice in skills for understanding and getting along with other adolescents. It would also offer a chance to gain peer and adult perspectives on topics of high saliency.

The model of constructive use of peers as a coping adjunct for early adolescents has been extended to other areas of adolescent concern. Some other examples will be discussed later.

The Social Environment of Early Adolescents

In America, our earliest and most consistent rite of puberty is the assignment of the status of adolescence to those individuals who enter junior high school. This entry is linked to chronological age but students differ widely in biological age. In so doing, we thrust the crisis of adolescent role change on an arbitrary assortment of somewhat reluctant initiates. Usually, parents and family members are faintly apprehensive as well. The initiated individual is no longer perceived as a child. He is viewed by himself and others as entering the world of the "teen culture." For almost all early adolescents there are doubts and insecurities with the realization that the mostly comfortable, and in any case, well-understood, phase of childhood is over and a challenging, as yet poorly defined, new phase is about to begin. He feels himself in immediate need of a new set of behaviors, values and reference persons. He is aware that significant adults now have different standards and new ways to relating to him. The unitiated person, when aspiring to a new status, often tends to respond to the most conspicuous and stereotyped features of the new role.

Early adolescents are attentive and responsive to the social environment, especially those aspects that reflect the youth culture. Some of this is learned from peer contacts. Much of the education comes from the media. In a survey of youths 12-17 years, conducted by the National Center for Health Statistics, 70% of those interviewed watched at least two hours of television daily. Twelve per cent of that group watched five or more hours daily. Thirty-four per cent listened to two or more hours of radio each day in addition. Eighty-six per cent reported daily exposure to adolescent-oriented magazines and newspapers. The media are an important source of information customs, language styles, and certain values.

A clearly identifiable "youth culture" is systematically presented to adolescents of all stages. It even has its impacts on the youth-oriented adults in our society. In addition to the media, the advertising, entertainment and clothing industries place heavy emphasis on cultivating and shaping the teen-age consumers. For cognitive and psychological reasons already discussed, the early adolescents are probably the most responsive and loyal audiences for these opinion molders. They are by their marginality, inexperience and immaturity of judgment, particularly susceptible to influence by popular stereotypes. It may take considerable time for some of the early adolescents to realize that these stereotypes do not accurately reflect the actual attitudes, behaviors and values of the average older adolescents. The age segregation in that which typifies our communities prevents many early adolescents from having easy access to their older peers.

Demographic factors play some role in the prominence of youth and competition for the commercial attention of this group. During the past decade adolescents, products of the 1950's baby boom, have been an expanding and significantly large percentage of the total population of the United States. In an affluent society, they have been an important market. In 1950 the 10-19 population was 22 million, 14% of the population. In 1976 the same age group numbered 41 million and was 19% of the population. Starting in 1980 there will be a modest absolute decline. By the year 2000, adolescents will have dropped back to 15% of the population. In the meantime, the cultural prominence given to adolescents can be anticipated to continue for some years to come.

In any case, regardless of demographics, the media will continue to exert an independent and pre-emptive role in gaining the attention, conveying messages and strongly influencing the ways in which adolescents approach their developmental tasks. Until recently, the nature and extent of this influence has not been systematically studied except for the Surgeon General's Report on Violence on Television. This is a fruitful area for continuing research.

There is increasing recognition that the media can also by used by educators, health professionals and youth advocates to convey pro-social, health-promoting and competence-enhancing materials. One example is the "health disc jockey" who intersperses health information and messages in rock music programs using adolescent jargon. Another approach has been the presentation of serious issues such as sexuality, pregnancy, crime, alcoholism or drug abuse in documentary TV in-depth programs. As a part of the format there is often a follow-up discussion of the issues by a live panel of adolescents who air their views in the presence of knowledgeable adults. These are promising health-relevant adjuncts to the socialization processes that are being exerted by the media.

As has been mentioned, early adolescents are experiencing a developmental crisis in which there is pyramiding of a number of challenges, and the sharpness of the discontinuity with the past severely limits the ability to draw on past learning and information in trying to cope with the new tasks. As a result the adolescent is unusually dependent on environmental supports in attempting to anticipate and regulate responses to the challenges he faces. The role of environmental and social support in buffering the effects of stress is a topic of great current interest. The availability of ready support, help and guidance can be minimal or absent in today's social environment.

A number of factors have combined to increase age segregation and decrease interaction among significant others both within the family and in the community. Age segregation is enhanced by a public school system that emphasizes placing of students in groups that are narrow in age range but large in absolute numbers. Exclusion of adolescents from work participation prevents association with a range of potential adult models and mentors. Factors such as urbanization and high mobility for families, rising divorce rates, increase in single parent families, and increase in mother working outside the home have led to declines in neighborhood and extended family ties and increased strain on the nuclear family.

Family. Clausen (1976) has analyzed perceptions of degree closeness, influence on values and control over behavior as reported by parents and their adolescent children. These studies showed that as children began puberty parents felt great concern and helplessness. They saw themselves as having less influence on their children than peers. The children, in turn, saw their parents as having the greatest influence on them. The youngest adolescents more often said that they did not know their parents views on a number of topics. Despite parental exaggeration of peer influence, other studies also indicate that parental influences remain more important than peer influences (Campbell, 1969; Douvan and Adelson, 1966; Kandel and Lesser, 1969; Sewell and Shah, 1968). Existing research confirms that many parents feel poorly equipped to deal with the biological, psychological, and social changes of the early adolescent period. Whatever the underlying reasons for this insecurity and weakening of parental authority, when accustomed parental guidance is withdrawn, the young person is thrust towards uncritical acceptance of the peer group as a model and a major coping resource. While this uncritical allegiance to the peer group may be useful in allaying immediate anxieties, it has serious limitations. The peer group at this stage is usually too shallow and rigid to afford the necessary resources for growth and development. When the peer group is organized around drugs and/or acting-out behaviors,

there is potential for considerable damage. There are significant class and cultural differences in parenting practices and the experiencing of the crisis of adolescent role change within the family.

In summary, available evidence supports the concept that parental interest, guidelines and support, particularly of the same-sex parent, offer the most effective help to the early adolescent in negotiating his tasks. There is a need for public understanding of a differentiated view of adolescence and specific information on early adolescence. Rather than accepting the motion of the "generation gap" as modal and even somehow growth-promoting, parents need education about the underlying needs of early adolescents. They need to be supported in carrying out appropriate parental functions and in learning about effective communication with their children. The roles for adult, non-parental surrogates such as teachers, youth leaders, employers, should be explored.

<u>Peers</u>   There is no doubt that peers play a highly significant role in adolescent development. The extent and nature of peer influence can vary widely when it exists, a reliably constructive peer reference group can be a major coping asset. Some of the adaptive tasks for which positive peer support can be especially valuable are:

    1.   Preserving a satisfactory self-image and sense of
         being valued by significant others.

    2.   Appraisal and reappraisal of the meaning, degree of
         threat and opportunities of new situations; learn-
         ing about new roles.

    3.   Obtaining of new information; development of new
         perspectives, new alternatives for dealing with
         situations; learning from the pooling of information
         from others.

    4.   Seeking appropriate role models whose behavior can
         be adapted or adopted.

    5.   Obtaining reliable feedback about behaviors, plans,
         goals; modifying level of aspiration.

    6.   Acquiring growth-promoting skills, e.g., practice
         in modulation of aggression, learning to be
         assertive, practice in social skills.

7.   Validation of identity and values.

8.   Identifying a supportive group for engaging in
     hobbies, sports or recreational activities that are
     unfamiliar or seem difficult.

9.   Preserving reasonable emotional balance by having
     dependable sources of reassurance and comfort in
     distress; resources for reduction of tension by
     encouragement to express feelings freely.

There are additional opportunities to utilize peer influences
for achieving targeted goals. A model of peer counseling for
easing the transition from elementary school to junior high school
has been described. The potentialities of use of peers for health-
promotion are beginning to be explored. When knowledge of the
developmental issues of early adolescence is coupled with understanding of appropriate use of peers, sound preventive programs in
areas of high health risk can be mounted. An excellent example
is the Stanford-based, McAlister (1979) Adolescent Smoking Program.
The intervention utilizes trained peer leaders who will work with
sixth and seventh grade students who are in the midst of making
decisions about whether or not to initiate smoking behavior. There
is a systematic effort to prevent smoking in this group through the
understanding of the risks and benefits, modeling by older peers,
guided practice and role-playing of resistances and refusals to
smoke when pressured ("psychologic inoculation"). There is also a
goal of elicitation of a public commitment not to smoke. Follow-
up studies have shown the program to be highly effective in
deterring smoking as compared to rates of adoption of smoking by
adolescents in matched control schools.

Adolescence is a time of fluidity of behavior. It is characterized by active exploration of possible directions before
making long term commitments. It is thus one of the most formative
periods of the entire life span. If the social environment of
adolescence is reasonably favorable, there is an exceptional
opportunity to use the stressful transition as an opportunity to
gain in skills and competence. There is now a framework for
conceptualizing the tasks and challenges that are posed by the life
stress of early adolescence. When this is coupled with the knowledge about coping and social support, the opportunity exists to
enhance our ability to prevent many of the troubling disorders of
adolescence. At the same time, a solid foundation can be laid
for encouraging the adoption of health-promoting attitudes and
behaviors which have life-long consequences.

REFERENCES

Armstrong, C., 1964, Patterns of achievement in selected New York
    State schools, paper, New York State Educational Department,
    Albany.
Ausubel, D. P., 1954, "Theory and Problems of Adolescent Develop-
    ment," Grune and Stratton, New York
Campbell, E. W., 1969, Adolescent socialization, in: "Handbook.
    Socialization Theory and Research," D. A. Goslin, ed.,
    Rand McNally, Chicago.
Clausen, J., 1975, The social meaning of differential physical and
    sexual maturation, in: "Adolescence in the Life Cycle,"
    S. Dragastin and G. H. Elder, Jr., ed., Wiley and Sons,
    New York.
Clausen, J., 1976, Adolescent-parent perceptions of influence,
    paper presented at the National Conference on Research Issues
    in Early Adolescence, Bethesda.
Douvan, E., and Adelson, J., 1966, "The Adolescent Experience,"
    Wiley and Sons, New York.
Eichorn, D., 1975, Asynchronizations in adolescent development,
    in: "Adolescence in the Life Cycle," S. Dragastin and G. H.
    Elder, Jr., ed., Wiley and Sons, New York.
Elkind, D., 1967, Egocentrism in adolescence, Child Devel., 4:1025.
Faiman, C., and Winter, J. S. D., 1974, Gonadotrophins and sex
    hormone patterns in puberty, clinical data, in: "Control of
    the Onset of Puberty, M. Grumbach, G. Grane, and F. Meyer, eds.,
    Wiley and Sons, New York.
Finger, J., and Silverman, M., 1966, Changes in academic performance
    in junior high school, Personnel Guid. J., 45:157.
Hamburg, B., and Varenhorst, B., 1972, Peer counseling in the
    secondary schools: A community mental health project for
    youth, Am. J. Orthopsychiat., 42:566.
Hamburg, B. A., 1974a, Coping in early adolescence: The special
    challenges of the junior high school period, in: "American
    Handbook of Psychiatry, Vol. 2," S. Arieti, ed., Basic Books
    New York.
Hamburg, B. A., 1974b, Early adolescence, a specific and stressful
    stage of the life cycle, in: "Coping and Adaptation," G. Coelho,
    D. Hamburg and J. Adams, eds., Basic Books, New York.
Hamburg, B. A., 1975, Social change and the problems of youth, in:
    "American Handbook of Psychiatry, Vol. 4," S. Arieti, ed.,
    Basic Books, New York.
Inhelder, B., and Piaget, J., 1958, "The Growth of Logical Thinking
    from Childhood to Adolescence: An Essay on the Construction
    of Formal Operational Structures," Basic Books, New York.
Janis, I. L., and Rodin, J., 1979, Control, decision-making: Social
    psychology and health care, in: "Health Psychology - A Hand-
    book: Theories, Applications, and Challenges of a Psychological
    Approach to the Health Care System," G. C. Stone, F. Cohen
    and N. E. Adler, eds., Jossey-Bass, San Francisco.

Jones, M. C., and Mussen, P. H., 1958, Self-conceptions, motivations
    and interpersonal attitudes of early and late maturing girls,
    Child Devel., 29:491.
Jones, M. C., 1965, Psychological correlates of somatic development,
    Child Devel., 36:899.
Kagan, J., and Coles, R., 1972, "Twelve to Sixteen: Early
    Adolescence," W. W. Norton, New York.
Kandel, D., and Lesser, G., 1969, Parental and peer influences on
    educational plans of adolescents," Am. Soc. Rev., 34:213.
Karplus, R., Karplus, E., Formisano, M., and Paulson, A., 1975,
    Proportional reasoning and control of variables in seven
    countries: Advancing education through science oriented
    programs, Report 10-25, Lawrence Hall of Science, Berkeley.
Martin, E. C., 1971, Reflections on the early adolescent in school,
    Daedalus, 1087.
McAlister, A. L., Perry, C. and Maccoby, N., 1979, Adolescent
    smoking: Onset and prevention, Pediatrics, 63:650.
Mussen, P. H. and Jones, M. C., 1957, Self-conceptions, motivations
    and inter-personal attitudes of late- and early-maturing boys,
    Child Devel., 28:243.
Niemark, E. D., 1975, Intellectual development in adolescence, in:
    "Review of Child Development Research, Vol. 4," University of
    Chicago Press, Chicago.
Peel, E. A., 1960, "The Pupil's Thinking," Oldbourne, London.
Reynolds, E. L. and Wines, J. V., 1948, Individual differences in
    physical changes associated with adolescent girls, Am J. Dis.
    Child., 75:329.
Reynolds, E. L. and Wines, J. V., 1951, individual differences in
    physical changes associated with adolescence in boys,
    Am. J. Dis. Child., 82:529.
Rosenberg, M., 1965, "Society and the Adolescent Self-Image,"
    Princeton University Press, Princeton.
Sewell, W. H. and Shah, V. P., 1968, Social class, parental
    encouragement and educational aspirations, Am. J. Soc., 73:559.
Silber, E., Hamburg, D., Coelho, G. V., Murphey, E., Rosenberg, M.
    and Pearlin, L., 1961, Adaptive behavior in competent
    adolescents: Coping with anticipation of college, Arch. Gen.
    Psychiat., 5:354.
Simmons, R., Rosenberg, F. and Rosenberg, M., 1973, Disturbance in
    self-image at adolescence, Am. Soc. Rev., 38:553.
Simmons, R., Bulcroft, R., Blyth, D. and Mitch-Bush, 1979, The
    vulnerable adolescent: School context and self-esteem,
    paper presented at the Society for Research in Child Devel-
    opment, San Francisco.
Tanner, J. M., 1971, Sequence, tempo and individual variation in
    the growth of boys and girls aged twelve to sixteen,
    Daedalus, 907.
Tversky, A. and Kahneman, D., 1971, Belief in the law of small
    numbers, Psychol. Bull., 76:105.

VITAL STATISTICS

Blood pressure of youths 12-17 years.   DHEW Publication No. (HRA)
     77-1645, Series 11, No. 163, 1977.
Cigarette smoking among teenagers and young women.   National
     Cancer Institute in cooperation with the American Cancer
     Society.   DHEW Publication No. (NIH) 77-1203, 1977.
Examination and health history findings among children and youths,
     6-17 years.   DHEW Publication No. (HRS) 74-164, Series 11,
     No. 129, 1974.
Monthly Vital Statistics Report: Final Mortality Statistics, 1977.
     DHEW Publication No. (PHS) 79-1129, Vol. 28, No. 1,
     Supplement May 11, 1979.

WHEN IS A LITTLE INFORMATION A DANGEROUS THING?

COPING WITH STRESSFUL EVENTS BY

MONITORING VERSUS BLUNTING*

Suzanne M. Miller

Department of Psychiatry
University of Pennsylvania

Consider two individuals, both of whom must undergo an aversive dental procedure. When the first individual arrives, the dentist describes what is going to take place, including when and under what circumstances the person can expect to feel pain. The second individual receives no such preparation from the dentist. Exactly the same procedure is performed on both individuals. Will the person undergoing the predictable procedure experience more or less stress before, during, and after his dental visit than the person undergoing the identical, but unpredictable procedure?

The experimental evidence on predictability and human stress is conflicting. That is, predictability sometimes decreases, and sometimes increases, stress and anxiety. None of the existing theories can account for these inconsistencies (Miller and Grant, 1979, in press; Miller and Grant, 1978, unpublished manuscript). I therefore propose a hypothesis, "Blunting Hypothesis," which specifies the conditions under which predictability has stress-reducing effects and when it does not. This hypothesis can also be extended to account for individual differences in who prefers predictability under threat ("monitors") and who prefers unpredictability ("blunters").

The paper is organized in the following way: I begin by

* I thank E. Freed, R. Grant, J. Harkavy, M. Hammel, C. Mangan, H. Lief, W. Miller, J. Nelson, and M. Seligman for their help and advice. Partially supported by Grant RR-09069 from the National Institute of Health and Grant MH-19604 from the National Institute of Mental Health.

145

presenting the blunting hypothesis and its predictions, and show
how it integrates the predictability literature. I then go on to
detail how the hypothesis accounts for individual differences in
preference for predictability, with some individuals seeking out
threat-relevant information ("monitors"), while others distract
themselves from threat-relevant information (("blunters"). I also
describe a recently validated scale for identifying "monitors" and
"blunters." Finally, I present the results of a field experiment
where individuals classified as monitors or blunters were exposed
to a predictable or unpredictable aversive gynecologic   procedure.

THE BLUNTING HYPOTHESIS

Statement of the Hypothesis

The blunting hypothesis is concerned with specifying the
conditions under which predictability does and does not reduce the
stress of an aversive event, particularly when the event is
uncontrollable. Controllability means that one can do something
about an aversive event; whereas predictability merely means that
one can know something about the event, whether or not one can do
anything about it. The evidence reviewed here focuses primarily on
the stress-reducing effects of predictability, when the aversive
event is uncontrollable (Miller, 1979a, b, in press, for a review
of the controllability evidence.)

The blunting hypothesis is an extension of Seligman's (1968)
safety signal theory, applied to human beings (see also Miller and
Grant, 1979, in press; Miller and Harkavy, 1979a, unpublished
manuscript. The safety signal theory says that when a signal
reliably predicts danger (predictability), the absence of the signal
reliably predicts safety. For example, in the laboratory, if a tone
predicts shock, then the absence of the tone predicts no shock (or
safety) and the individual can relax during silence. In contrast,
if no signal reliably predicts danger (unpredictability), then no
signal reliably predicts safety (all events equally predict shock).
This means that the individual can never relax, because shock is just
as likely to occur during silence as during tone. Thus, if given a
choice, an individual will prefer predictability, so that he can be
exposed to acute periods of high danger (and long periods of safety
and relaxation) rather than to chronic periods of moderate danger.
Considerable data from the animal literature support this (cf.
Seligman and Binik, 1977).

The problem with safety signal theory, like animal theories
generally, is that it fails to distinguish between the physical and
psychological presence of danger signals. This, in fact, is the
heart of behaviorism: i.e., that it focuses on the physical arrangements of stimuli without considering how an individual psychologically transforms such stimuli. Yet it is obvious that danger signals

must be both physically and psychologically present in order to
produce arousal in the first place. Individuals living on the San
Andreas fault are not generally chronically aroused, even though no
physical signal is a reliable predictor of earthquakes and none of
their absence. This is because most individuals never give much of
a thought to earthquakes in the first place: i.e., the danger signals
are not psychologically present.

Moreover, once an individual has been faced with a physical
(i.e., real or objective) danger signal, and has been made psychologically aware of this danger signal, he can then adopt a variety of
cognitive strategies which remove him from any further psychological
awareness of it. The use of such strategies will, in turn, help to
lower his level of arousal. In other words, an individual who has
been warned about the possibility of an impending earthquake can
still use various cognitive strategies to remove himself psychologically from this state of affairs, and so reduce arousal, even
though the danger signal remains physically (objectively) present.
I shall label those strategies which remove people psychologically
from danger signals as "blunting" strategies, so-called because they
help to blunt the psychological impact of physically present danger
signals. Such strategies include, on the more positive side,
distraction, self-relaxation, and reinterpretation; and on the less
positive side, denial, detachment, and intellectualization (Vaillant,
1977).

Consider Table 1. This specifies the relationships between
the physical presence or absence of a danger signal and its psychological presence or absence. In call A, the danger signal is both
physically and psychologically present and the result is realistic

TABLE I

RELATIONSHIPS BETWEEN THE PHYSICAL AND PSYCHOLOGICAL
PRESENCE AND ABSENCE OF THE DANGER SIGNAL

Physical

		Present		Absent
Psycho-logical	Present	A	Attending to danger cues (realistic fear)	C Brooding, worrying, ruminating, rehears-ing (unrealistic fear)
	Absent	B	Distraction: Also denial, detachment, reinterpretation, intellectualization (unrealistic inhibition of fear)	D Attending to safety cues (realistic inhibition of fear)

fear and heightened arousal. The individual should be aroused in
proportion to the perceived probability, intensity, and duration of
the aversive event. On the other hand, in cell D, the danger signal
is both physically and psychologically absent. This means that the
individual is attending to safety and is realistically inhibiting
fear (i.e., he is relaxed). When the danger signal is physically
present but psychologically absent, as in cell B, the individual is
either unaware of the danger signal or, more interestingly, he is
engaging in a successful cognitive strategy that blunts the impact
of the danger signal. For example, he can be distracting himself
by thinking about other events; relaxing himself by calming self-
talk; or reinterpreting the event as a positive, beneficial experience. The individual should show reduced arousal and should be
processing less external information about the situation. Cell B
will be further discussed below. An individual in cell C is not in
any physical presence of a danger signal, but he continues to be in
the psychological presence of the danger signal. When this is so,
we say that the individual is brooding, ruminating or worrying about
the event, and should manifest heightened arousal. Interestingly
enough, this clinically important cell has largely been uninvesti-
gated (cf. Miller and Grant, 1979, in press, for a discussion of
the clinical implications).

Strategies for Accomplishing Psychological Blunting

    What are the different strategies in cell B for accomplishing
psychological withdrawal from danger signals? First and foremost,
one can distract oneself. Distraction can obviously occur spontaneously inside a subject's head or, better yet, it can be induced by
external means. For example, Averill and Rosenn (1972) and Miller
(1979c, in press) operationalized distraction by giving subjects a
choice between listening for a signal that predicted shock
(predictability) or listening instead to music (distraction).
Preference for distraction was indexed by the amount of time each
subject spent listening to the music. Similarly, in an experiment
by Miller and Harkavy (1979a, unpublished manuscript) subjects
worked on an intelligence test,but could attend as often as they
wished to a clock that signaled how much time had passed and/or a
light that signaled how well they were performing. The less time
spent looking at the clock and/or light, the greater the preference
for distraction. Finally, in a somewhat related vein, subjects who
have undergone or who are about to undergo failure experiences can
choose to attend to negative or positive personality information
about themselves. The less time spent scanning for personality
liabilities, the greater the preference to distract oneself from
ego-threatening information (Mischel, Ebbesen, and Zeiss, 1973;
1976).*

* Mischel (1974) has also investigated the role of distraction and
  other blunting strategies in modulating an individual's response

These experiments constitute a theoretically and practically important variant of studies on choice and arousal. In the more standard choice procedure, subjects can only choose between a predictable and an unpredictable aversive event, with no opportunity to distract themselves. For example, subjects may be offered a choice between listening for a tone that signals shock (predictability), or waiting passively with no signal for shock (unpredictability). In real life, however, individuals who are faced with unpredictable aversive events have limitless opportunities for distraction. Under what conditions, then, do people prefer and make use of such distractions, instead of opting for predictability?

Distraction has at least two other properties besides choice which make it measurable experimentally: It should reduce emotional arousal and it should reduce processing of threat-relevant external information. That is, effectiveness of distraction should be proportional to both reduced arousal and to independently measured reduced processing of external information. Many studies have looked at reduced arousal, most commonly by psychobiological measurement (e.g., Averill and Rosenn, 1972; Miller, 1979c, in press). Yet these indices are ambiguous, confounding attentional and emotional processes (Kilpatrick, 1972). To date, no study has taken advantage of the convenient property of reduced information processing (e.g., Wachtel, 1968; Miller and Harkavy, 1979b, unpublished manuscript).

Other blunting strategies, for the moment less conveniently operationalizable and measurable than distraction, can also accomplish psychological withdrawal from danger signals. For example, individuals who are exposed to aversive films depicting gory and painful scenes can be induced to intellectualize about the film (e.g., "As you can see, the operation is formal and the surgical technique, while crude, is very carefully followed."); or to deny its stressful aspects (e.g., "You will soon see that the words of encouragement offered by the older men have their effect and the boy begins to look forward to the happy conclusion of the ceremony.") The use of such strategies, in turn, reduces the level of psychophysiological and subjective arousal typically associated with vicarious stressors of this sort (Lazarus and Alfert, 1964; Lazarus, Opton, Nomikos, and Rankin, 1965; Speisman, Lazarus, Mordkoff, and Davidson, 1964).

* (continued) to positive, rather than negative, events. He has found, for example, that delay of gratification in young children is most readily facilitated by the use of distraction and other blunting strategies. When children engage in such strategies, they are able to continue goal-directed waiting for a more attractive but delayed reward rather than opting for a less attractive but immediate reward.

Still other studies have investigated the effectiveness of inducing blunting strategies to deal with physical aversive events, such as radiant heat, ice water immersion of the hand, electric shock, and a heavy weight applied to the finger. When subjects are instructed to reinterpret the event (e.g., "Think of the pain as an interesting tingling sensation.") or to intellectualize about it (e.g., "Think of the pain as a protective sensory mechanism."), they again show reduced psychophysiological and subjective arousal and also tolerate more pain (Barber and Hahn, 1962; Blitz and Dinnerstein, 1971; Bloom, Houston, Holmes and Burish, 1977; Holmes and Houston, 1974; Neufeld, 1970). Finally, in dental and surgical populations, the induction of blunting techniques such as reinter- pretation has been shown to reduce psychophysiological and subjective arousal and to facilitate the recovery process (Langer, Janis and Wolfer, 1975; Mead, 1970).

Overall, then, reinterpretation, intellectualization, denial and other blunting strategies seem to share some of the arousal- reducing properties of distraction. Moreover, unlike distraction, these alternative strategies may not have the consequence of turning the individual's attention so far afield from the aversive event, even if they are not as effective at reducing arousal. That is, they may combine some degree of reduced arousal with the continued processing of external threat-relevant information. Certain of these blunting strategies (e.g., reinterpretation, self-relaxation) may be more adequate for this purpose than others (e.g., denial). No evidence presently bears on this, but the issue is an important one. One advantage that an individual gains from engaging in threat-relevant information-processing is that he is able to discriminate changes in the external situation. For example, if a formerly uncontrollable event becomes controllable, he will input that information and be in a position to execute the appropriate controlling response. In contrast, an individual who has completely "tuned out" from external information will not input and thereby benefit from changes in the situation. In situations which may be subject to change--i.e., from uncontrollable to controllable or from more intenst to less intense--then the use of a strategy which accomplishes some degree of arousal reduction but does not completely impede external information-processing may be optimal. However, in chronically uncontrollable or high intensity situations, then the strategy of choice may be one which most effectively reduces level of arousal and concomitant processing of threat-relevant information.

Conditions Which Facilitate Blunting Strategies

The blunting hypothesis predicts that certain real-life and laboratory conditions should be more conducive to distraction than other conditions. Generally speaking, the more psychologically invasive and intrusive the danger signals are, the harder it should be to distract oneself. For example, distraction should be easier when the aversive event is unpredictable than when it is predictable.

Consider the case of predictability, where a tone signals the occurrence of an aversive event, such as shock. Here the individual will be listening for the tone; and the tone itself is invasive and intrusive, even if the individual is trying to block it out. In contrast, in the case of unpredictability, the physical danger signals are more continuous and diluted, and so less psychologically invasive and intrusive. Similarly, it will be difficult or impossible to distract when the aversive event is intense: i.e., when it is high probability, high level, long duration, or imminent. On the other hand, distraction will be relatively easy with low intensity aversive events. In addition, distraction is facilitated when external distractors are available and, in the laboratory, when subjects are explicitly informed how they can distract themselves.

Finally, generally speaking it should be easier to distract when the aversive event is uncontrollable, than when it is controllable. When one can instrumentally control an aversive event by escape or avoidance, one must be attentive for danger signals so that one knows when and how to execute the response. Moreover, the harder and more elaborate the controlling response is to perform, the more one must attend to the ongoing situation. On the other hand, when monitoring for danger signals has no instrumental value for the individual, then he is freer to direct his attention away by using distraction and other blunting techniques. Indeed, laboratory evidence consistently shows that subjects find it easier to distract under unpredictability and under low intensity threat (Averill and Rosenn, 1972; Monat, 1976; Monat, Averill and Lazarus, 1972); under uncontrollable threat (Averill, O'Brien, and DeWitt, 1977; Miller, Grant, and Nelson, 1978, unpublished manuscript; and when external distractors are provided (Bloom, et al., 1977).

Predictions and Evidence

The blunting hypothesis therefore predicts that predictable aversive events should be chosen over unpredictable aversive events, under invasive and intrusive conditions which make distraction difficult. This is because subjects can at least know when they are in safety and thereby relax. In contrast, unpredictable aversive events should be chosen over predictable aversive events, under non-invasive conditions which support distraction. This is because a subject can more effectively reduce arousal by using a blunting strategy, such as distraction, than by scanning for external signals. The experimental evidence confirms these predictions (Miller and Grant, 1979, in press; Miller and Grant, 1978, unpublished manuscript, for details). Subjects who are offered a choice between predictability and unpredictability, with no opportunity for distraction in the unpredictability condition, clearly prefer predictability (Badia, McBane, Suter, and Lewis, 1966; Badia, Suter, and Lewis, 1967; Elliott, 1966; Jones, Bentler, and Petry, 1966; Maltzman and Wolff, 1970; Monat et al., 1972). Conversely, when

the choice is between predictability and unpredictability plus
distraction, then the preference reverses and the majority of
subjects choose unpredictability (Averill and Rosenn, 1972; Miller,
1979c, in press; Rothbart and Mellinger, 1972).

For example, in an experiment by Miller (1979c, in press),
subjects were threatened with a low probability electric shock and
were allowed to choose whether or not they wanted information about
when the shock might occur. This meant, in practice, that subjects
could either listen to a monotone, which would be interrupted by a
high warning tone that signalled possible shock onset. Alternatively,
they could listen to music on another channel, with no warning
stimulus. Thus listening to the monotone showed preference for
information, while listening to music showed preference for distraction. Half of the subjects were told they could avoid shock
altogether by pressing a button, on those trials where they detected
the warning signal (controllability). For the other half, avoidance
of the shock was not possible (uncontrollability). Subjects were
divided into monitors, those who listened to the signal on the majority
of the six trials; and distractors, those who listened to the music
on the majority of the six trials.

Individuals clearly preferred information when they could use
that information to avoid. This makes sense, since only by monitoring for the tone could subjects reduce the probability of shock.
The theoretically relevant finding, however, is that the majority
of subjects did not choose to listen for information when avoidance
of shock was not possible. Table 2 shows these results. Of those
who could avoid, 71% monitored the signal on the majority of six
trials. Among those who could not avoid, only 32% monitored the
high tone for the majority of the trials.

The blunting hypothesis also predicts greater anticipatory
arousal to the danger signal under predictability, than during
comparable periods for unpredictability, since the perceived probability of the aversive event at any moment is higher during the
danger signal. This effect should be particularly evident under
noninvasive conditions which support distraction with unpredictability. Again, the unconfounded experimental evidence bears out
this prediction, with predictable aversive events causing greater
physiological and subjective arousal than unpredictable aversive
events (Geer and Maisel, 1972; Miller, 1979c, in press; Monat, 1976;
Monat et al., 1972). These results obtain both when subjects choose
for themselves whether to undergo predictability or unpredictability;
and when predictability or unpredictability is experimentally
imposed upon them. Those studies that fail to find this effect
confront subjects with invasive and intrusive conditions which do
not support distraction, such as intense, frequently occurring
shocks and extremely short anticipatory intervals (Averill and
Rosenn, 1972; Klemp and Rodin, 1976).

The differential arousal associated with predictable vs. unpredictable aversive events is demonstrated in the experiment cited above by Miller (1979c, in press). For example, there was a clear, consistent effect of monitoring for information on antici-patory non-specific electrodermal responses: Monitoring was accompanied by more arousal than distracting. This was because distractors habituated, but monitors did not. That is, over trials arousal waned for distractors but remained high for monitors. As can be seen in Figure 1, monitors and distractors began on trial 1

TABLE 2

NUMBER OF SUBJECTS WHO ARE MONITORS (LISTEN FOR THE WARNING SIGNAL) AND DISTRACTORS (LISTEN TO THE MUSIC)

	Monitors	Distractors
Avoidance Subjects	24	10
Nonavoidance Subjects	11	23

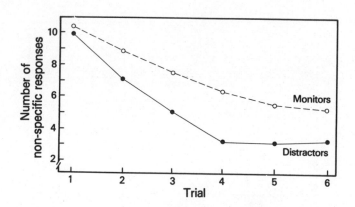

Figure 1
Mean frequency of non-specific electrodermal responses for six trials.

with similar levels of arousal, but then subjects who distracted
themselves showed a rapid decline in number of non-specific
responses, whereas those subjects who were monitoring stayed highly
aroused.

In addition, there was a clear effect of monitoring on ratings
of both anticipatory fear and tension, which wholly paralleled the
physiological effects. Monitors had higher fear and tension scores
than those who distracted. Distractors also had significantly fewer
shock-related thoughts than monitors. As Figure 2 shows, the two
groups thought equally about shock on trial 1, but after the first
trial distractors habituated very rapidly.

The blunting hypothesis makes no prediction about whether or
not a predictable aversive event should actually "hurt" less than an
unpredictable aversive event. To date, the experimental data are
too conflicting to draw any conclusions about the effects of
predictability on impact (see Miller and Grant, 1979, in press).
Finally, the blunting hypothesis predicts that post-impact arousal
may be reduced under noninvasive conditions with unpredictability
because subjects are perseverating less about the aversive event.
Some relevant evidence will be presented below.

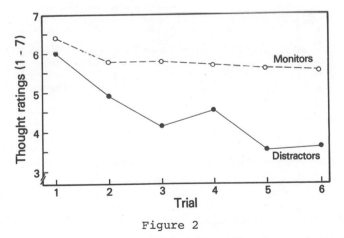

Figure 2

Mean ratings of shock-related thoughts (on a 1 to 7 scale,
where 0 = my thoughts were not at all on the shock, and 7 =
my thoughts were completely on the shock) for six trials.

INDIVIDUAL DIFFERENCES IN PREFERENCE FOR MONITORING VS. BLUNTING

The blunting hypothesis predicts that the ability to successfully distract oneself from danger signals should be subject to wide
individual differences. Some people should find it easy to distract
even under laboratory conditions providing minimal support; while
others should find it difficult to distract even under conditions
providing maximal support. People who believe themselves to be
ineffective distractors should tend consistently to choose predictability over distraction, especially under conditions which do not
support distraction. People who believe themselves to be effective
distractors should tend consistently to choose unpredictability,
even under conditions which do not support distraction. This means
that there should be a consistent minority of subjects choosing
unpredictability under conditions apparently not favoring distraction, who will show lower arousal; and a consistent minority
choosing predictability (and showing higher anticipatory arousal)
under conditions supporting distraction. If these minorities are
forced to their nonpreferred condition, they will show higher
arousal than they did in their preferred condition.

It would seem important, then, to be able to identify
independently and in advance those disposed to distract themselves
or to monitor for danger signals. However, all of the questionnaires that are currently available for identifying information-
seekers and information-avoiders have two main problems. The
first is that they are structurally complex and derived from
psychodynamically-based views of personality (e.g., Byrne, 1961;
Goldstein, 1959); and the second is that they have proven to be of
limited validity in predicting who actually seeks out or avoids
information in objectively aversive situations and in predicting
how aroused individuals become when predictability or unpredictability is imposed upon them (e.g., Averill and Rosenn, 1972; Cohen
and Lazarus, 1973).

The following experiment was conducted to validate a new scale
for identifying monitors and blunters (Miller, 1979, unpublished
manuscript). The Miller Behavioral Style Scale (MBSS) consists of
four hypothetical stress-evoking scenes, of an uncontrollable
nature. Subjects are asked to imagine the following scenes:
1) "Vividly imagine that you are afraid of the dentist and have to
get some dental work done;" 2) "Vividly imagine that you are being
held hostage by a group of armed terrorists in a public building;"
3) "Vividly imagine that, due to a large drop in sales, it is
rumored that several people in your department at work will be laid
off. Your supervisor has turned in an evaluation of your work for
the past year. The decision about lay-offs has been made and will
be announced in several days;" and 4) "Vividly imagine that you are
on an airplane, thirty minutes from your destination, when the
plane unexpectedly goes into a deep dive and then suddenly levels

off. After a short time, the pilot announces that nothing is
wrong, althouth the rest of the ride may be rough. You, however,
are not convinced that all is well."

Each scene is followed by eight statements, which represent
different ways of coping with the situation. Half of the statements
accompanying each scene are of a monitoring variety (e.g., in the
hostage situation: "If there was a radio present, I would stay near
it and listen to the bulletins about what the police were doing;"
or, in the airplane situation: "I would listen carefully to the
engines for unusual noises and would watch the crew to see if their
behavior was out of the ordinary.") The other half of the statements are of a blunting variety (e.g., in the dental situation:
"I would do mental puzzles in my head;" or, in the airplane situation: "I would watch the end of the movie even if I had seen it
before.") The subject simply marks all the statements following
each scene that might apply to him.

To validate the scale, subjects were threatened with a low
probability shock and allowed to choose whether they wanted to
monitor for information or distract themselves with music. In
order to accurately parallel natural stress situations, two kinds
of information were provided. Again, subjects heard a warning
signal that indicated possible shock onset. In addition, they also
heard a series of statements that described the shocks, the
machinery used to deliver shock, and the sensations that shock
produces.

The results showed that the amount of time spent on the
information channel could be predicted by an individual's MBSS score.
In particular, the more blunting items endorsed by a subject on the
scale, the less time spent listening to the tone channel.*

Thus inidividuals differ in the extent to which they choose to
monitor or distract themselves when faced with aversive events; and
these differences in coping style can be predicted on the basis of
questionnaire scores. However, there is an alternative interpretation of these results: It is possible that subjects who chose

---

* The monitoring/blunting dimension bears some relation to the
repression/sensitization dimension of Byrne (1961). Repression/
sensitization scores correlate moderately with the number of
monitoring items endorsed (r = .39, p < .05), but not with the
number of blunting items endorsed. However, the number of
monitoring items that an individual endorses does not predict his
laboratory-information-seeking behavior under threat of electric
shock; whereas the number of blunting items that an individual
endorses does predict such information-seeking.

information were simply more aroused by the prospect of electric shock than subjects who chose distraction. To test for this possibility, self-ratings of anxiety were obtained after subjects were threatened with electric shock but before they knew about the opportunity to monitor or distract. There was no relation between these self-ratings of anxiety and how much time an individual subsequently spent on the information channel. These anxiety ratings were also unrelated to an individual's blunting score. Thus, those who monitor under threat are not simply made more anxious by the event than those who distract. Rather, monitoring and blunting represent different strategies for coping with aversive events of equivalent stress value. Further, the blunting hypothesis assumes that if these two groups are forced into their nonpreferred condition (i.e., unpredictability for monitors and predictability for blunters), they will show increased stress. This issue was addressed in the experiment reported below.

PREPARATORY INFORMATION CONSISTENT OR INCONSISTENT WITH COPING STYLE

One applied setting where it might be crucial to determine whether information helps or hurts an individual is the hospital situation. To date, conflicting results have emerged about the effects of information on a patient's response to diagnostic and surgical procedures. Although individuals sometimes seek out information prior to surgery, such information does not always reduce anticipatory arousal, reduce impact, or promote recuperation from surgery (Egbert, Battit, Welch, and Bartlett, 1964; Johnson and Leventhal, 1974; Sime, 1976; Williams, Jones, Workhoven, and Williams, 1975; vs. Cohen and Lazarus, 1973; Langer, Janis, and Wolfer, 1975; Vernon and Bigelow, 1974).

The blunting hypothesis predicts that individual differences in coping style may integrate this otherwise puzzling range of evidence, with monitors benefiting more from information and blunters benefiting more from distraction. Thus there were four main questions which the present study sought to answer (Miller, Mangan, Freed, and Burtnett, 1979, unpublished manuscript): 1) Does voluminous information hurt or help a patient? 2) Do monitors do better than blunters? 3) Do monitors who crave information and are given it do better than when information is withheld? and conversely, 4) Do blunters do better when not given information than when unwanted information is imposed on them?

To these ends, we studied gynecologic patients about to undergo colposcopy. The colposcopy is a standardized diagnostic procedure to check for the presence of abnormal (cancerous) cells in the uterus. In addition, it is considered a benign procedure from the medical point of view, and so most of the distress associated with it is subjectively generated. Patients were first divided into monitors or blunters, based on our scale. Half of each group was then given (the usual) minimal information. We measured responding

before, during, and after colposcopy, using psychophysiological
reactions, subjective report, and observer ratings.

Prior to the examination patients in the high information
group heard a 20-minute preparatory communication, detailing both
the forthcoming examination procedure and the sensations that
would be experienced. This information was designed to reduce
any uncertainty or misconceptions on the patient's part, and to
discriminate the few parts of the examination which involved some
discomfort from the bulk of the exam, which involved little pain
or discomfort. Patients heard (and viewed) such things as what the
examination room looked like; how they would be placed on the table;
how the doctor would perform the pelvic exam (e.g., "For this
particular exam, the speculum may have to be opened wider than
usual. Remember that the vagina is made similar to a balloon and
is designed to be stretched."); what the Pap smear, biopsy, rectal
exam, and colposcopy each entailed (e.g., "The doctor will then
pull over the colposcope, turn it on, and look through it at your
cervix. He may move the speculum slightly, which may cause you to
feel some minor pressure."); and finally, how the patient could
expect to feel during the days following the procedure (e.g., "You
may observe a brownish discharge. This is from the stiptic
solution.").

In contrast, patients in the low information condition were
given the usual minimal preparation. They were simply told what
class Pap smear they had, and the colposcopy involved looking at
their cervix through a low-powered microscope. To ensure equal
time with the interviewer, these patients were administered a
20-minute questionnaire on nutrition.

Overall 1) Patients' level of psychophysiological arousal
was reduced when the level of preparatory information was consistent
with their coping style; 2) Information increased subjective
arousal; and 3) Monitors showed more self- and observer-rated
arousal than blunters.

Let us begin with the effect of having information which is
consistent vs. inconsistent with an individual's coping style. The
results showed that the degree of consistency between a patient's
coping style and the level of preparatory information she receives
strongly determines her level of psychophysiological arousal, as
indexed by measures of pulse rate. This effect can be seen in
Figure 3. There were initially no pulse rate differences between
gruops on arrival at the hospital. The only group to show a
decrease in pulse rate immediately prior to the exam were blunters
who had been given low information, and they maintained this low
pulse rate throughout. By the end of the exam, monitors who had
been given high information also showed reduced pulse rate, but
low information monitors and high information blunters showed

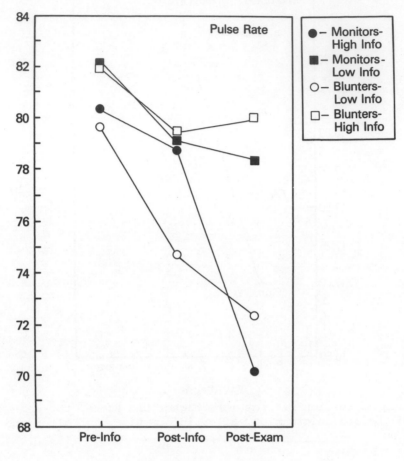

Figure 3

Mean pulse rate readings before information, after information, and after examination.

sustained higher pulse rates (p < .01).

Let us now turn to the results for information. Immediately prior to the examination, but after information was given, patients in the high information condition reported more anxiety than low information patients (p < .01); expected to feel more pain during the procedure (p < .1); and showed more of an increase in depression over when they first arrived at the hospital (p < .05). Figure 4 shows this effect for the self-report of depression. Patients in the two groups did not differ on arrival, but those who recieved

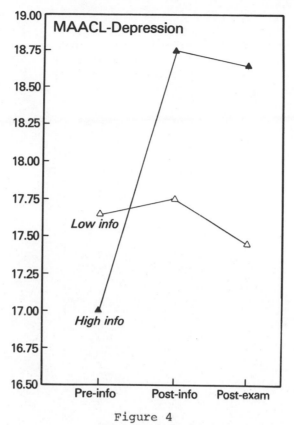

Figure 4

    Mean depression ratings (the higher the score, the more de-
pressed) before information, after information, and after the examination.

high information then increased in anticipatory depression whereas
low information patients did not. Moreover, this elevated
depression did not subside even after the exam for the high
information group. Information not only increased self-reported
distress on the day of the examination but produced greater self-
report of discomfort and pain (p < .05) in the five days afterwards.

    Despite the subjectively arousing cost of high information
before and after the procedure, it is possible that information may
marginally reduce the impact of the procedure itself. As Figure 5
shows, high information patients engaged in less hand clenching than
low information patients (p < .08). High information was also

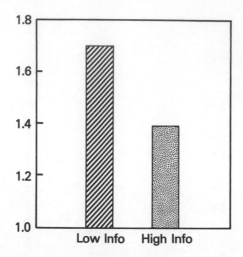

Figure 5
    Mean observer ratings of hand clenching (on a 3.0 point scale,
where 0.0 = no hand clenching, and 3.0 = constant hand clenching)
during the examination.

associated with less crying out (p < .08).

    Finally, what about the effects of being a monitor or a
blunter? On arrival at the hospital, monitors were already more
depressed (p < .05) and anxious (p < .05) than blunters. They were
also more familiar with gynecological procedures than blunters
(p < .05); and more often used medication for physical pain (p < .01).

    During the exam itself, the doctor rated the monitors to be
more anxious than blunters, as indexed by muscular tension in the
vaginal area (p < .0001). This is shown in Figure 6.

    Monitoring was also associated with more exam-related thoughts
(p < .05) and more hostility (p < .08) immediately prior to the
gynecologic procedure than blunting. By the end of the procedure,
monitors decreased in hostility relative to their initial level,
approaching the low level of the blunters which was maintained
throughout (p < .01). The decrease in hostility among monitors
occurred primarily in the high information group (p < .02). Finally, in the five days following the procedure, monitors expressed
more anxiety (p < .05) and discomfort (p < .05) than blunters did.

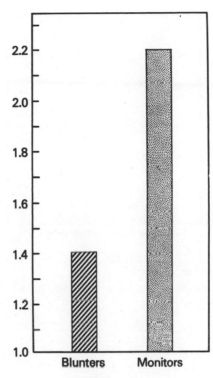

Figure 6

    Mean doctor ratings of tension (on a 3.0 point scale, were
0.0 = no tension, and 3.0 = extreme tension) during the examination.

Figure 7 shows this for discomfort.

    Thus there are four conclusions of the present study. The
first is that voluminous preparatory information may exacerbate
patient distress. Patients given high information showed more
subjective arousal before, immediately after, and in the days
following colposcopy than patients given low information. Yet high
information may have one beneficial aspect: During the brief period
of the examination itself, patients given high information felt less
pain (see also Johnson and Leventhal, 1974; Langer, et al., 1975;
Vernon and Bigelow, 1974). Since high information had no instrumental value, it is unlikely that patients were decreasing impact

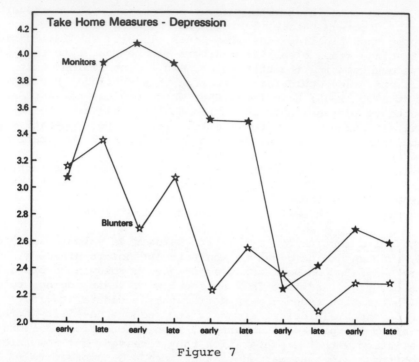

Figure 7

Mean discomfort ratings (on a 1 to 7 scale, where 0 = I do not feel any discomfort, and 7 = I feel extreme discomfort) for the five days after the procedure.

by executing preparatory or controlling responses (Lykken, 1962; Perkins, 1955). Rather, information seemed to make the procedure less surprising for patients (Berlyne, 1960). However, the data suggests that great care should still be exercised when designing preparatory communications to patients, particularly in the case of benign procedures such as colposcopy. The total distress produced by high information (which decreases pain during, but increases distress before and after) seems to outweigh the distress produced by low information.

The second major conclusion is that being a monitor in this setting is a more costly emotional style than being a blunter. Monitors typically seek out threat-relevant information about aversive events; whereas blunters typically cope with aversive events by distracting themselves from threat-relevant information.

Monitoring is associated with greater self-ratings and observer
ratings of distress before, during, and in the days following
colposcopy than blunting (see also Janis, 1958). The implication of
these findings seems clear: If monitors can be taught to cope with
aversive events using the strategies, e.g., distraction, that
blunters use, they would fare better in this setting. For example,
Langer et al., (1975) have found that when surgical patients are
instructed to address their attention to favorable aspects of the
hospital situation,they respond better pre- and post-operatively
than patients who are not so instructed or who have information
imposed upon them. Individuals who are identified as monitors
would seem to be an appropriate target population for preparatory
training in the use of blunting strategies. Future studies should
determine which of these strategies are most optimal for patients,
and how patients can best be instructed in their use.

The third conclusion is that if you do give voluminous inform-
mation, it ought to be given to monitors but not to blunters.
Monitors benefited on some measures by having voluminous preparatory information, and this is consistent with their coping style.
Having information reduced pain during the procedure itself,
reduced psychophysiological arousal, and reduced hostility immediately after the procedure. Further, high information monitors
were satisfied with the preparation they received, but low information monitors said they wanted to know more. On subjective
measures of arousal, however, high information did not help
monitors, but instead increased self-reported distress before and
after the examination.

Finally, the results indicate that blunters show the greatest
benefits when they do not get voluminous information, and this is
consistent with their coping style. Having minimal information
reduced anxiety, depression, discomfort, and psychophysiological
arousal before and after the procedure for the blunters. Further,
low information blunters were satisfied with the level of
information they received. Blunters given voluminous information
showed only one marginal benefit: it slightly reduced level of pain
during the examination itself (see also Andrew, 1970; Cohen and
Lazarus, 1973).

These results must be viewed as preliminary and with caution
for the following reasons. First, colposcopy is a relatively
benign procedure, and these results may not be obtained when more
severe procedures are studied. Under such circumstances, the
greater invasiveness and intrusiveness of danger signals may
interfere with the ability to use distraction. Second, the present
study focused primarily on short-term subjective and psychophysiological distress. It is possible, however, that the physical
recovery process (e.g., amount of days in hospital, use of pain-
killing medication, etc.) is facilitated by voluminous information,
particularly in the case of monitors. Third, and most importantly,

colposcopy patients could not use the information they received
to exert any control or choice over what happened to them. In
other health care situations, individuals can exert control and
choice if information is made available to them, and here
voluminous information must certainly have a more beneficial effect,
at least in the long run. We are currently investigating the above
factors to determine the generality of our findings.

In summary, the results show that voluminous preparatory
information does not necessarily benefit patients; that monitoring
is a more costly emotional style for coping with stressful
procedures than blunting; and that patients generally do better
when the amount of preparatory information they receive is
consistent with their coping style: blunters should get low
information and, perhaps, monitors should get high information.

These results can largely be integrated by the blunting
hypothesis, which emphasizes the stress-reducing effects of
psychologically absenting oneself from danger signals. First,
differences in ease of distraction can account for the fact that
high information increased arousal relative to low information.
When patients are given maximum predictability (as in high
information), it directs their attention toward danger-related cues.
This makes it difficult and even impossible to distract, and so
individuals maintain high arousal. In contrast, when patients are
given minimal predictability (as in low information), it attenuates
the psychological invasiveness of danger-related cues, thereby
facilitating the use of distraction and other blunting techniques,
which minimize arousal. Similarly, the hypothesis can account for
the different arousal of monitors and blunters. Arousal reflects
the psychological presence of danger signals, and is therefore
higher in monitors (who choose to scan for threat-relevant cues);
than in blunters (who ignore threat-relevant cues).

Finally, the blunting hypothesis can also explain the
beneficial effects of coping style consistent preparatory information. Monitors do not believe they can successfully blunt and so
they prefer external signals about danger, because such cues imply
signals about safety. High information, which provides such
signals, marginally reduces their level of arousal; whereas low
information, which does not provide such signals, does not. In
contrast, blunters believe they can successfully remove themselves
from danger signals. They prefer and are less aroused with low
information, because it facilitates the use of blunting techniques;
whereas they disprefer and are more aroused with high information,
because it interferes with the use of blunting techniques.

In summary, I have presented a hypothesis of predictability
and human stress, "Blunting Hypothesis," which emphasizes the
ability of individuals to engage in various cognitive strategies
to blunt the psychological impact of physically present danger

cues, and so reduce arousal. The hypothesis predicts, and the
evidence shows, that predictability is preferred and less arousing
under invasive and intrusive conditions which do not support
blunting strategies; whereas unpredictability is preferred and less
arousing under noninvasive and nonintrusive conditions which do
support blunting strategies. The hypothesis also predicts, and the
evidence shows, that good blunters typically prefer to distract
themselves from danger signals; whereas poor blunters, or monitors,
prefer predictability. Finally, the hypothesis predicts, and the
evidence shows, that blunters show reduced stress when faced with
unpredictable aversive events than when such events are predictable. Conversely, monitors show slightly reduced stress when
faced with predictable aversive events than when such events are
unpredictable.

REFERENCES

Andrew, J. M., 1970, Recovery from surgery, with and without
     preparatory instruction, for three coping styles, J. Personal.
     Soc. Psychol., 15:223.
Averill, J. R., O'Brien, L., and DeWitt, G. W., 1977, The influence
     of response effectiveness on the preference for warning and
     on psychophysiological stress reactions, J. Personal., 45:395.
Averill, J. R., and Rosenn, M., 1972, Vigilant and nonvigilant
     coping strategies and psychophysiological stress reactions
     during the anticipation of an electric shock, J. Personal. Soc.
     Psychol., 23:128.
Badia, P., McBane, B., Suter, S., and Lewis, P., 1966, Preference
     behavior in an immediate versus variably delayed shock
     situation with and without a warning signal, J. Exp. Psychol.,
     72:847.
Badia, P., Suter, S., and Lewis, P., 1967, Preference for warned
     shock: Information and/or preparation, Psychol. Rep., 20:271.
Barber, T. X., and Hahn, K. W., 1962, Physiological and subjective
     responses to pain producing stimulation under hypnotically-
     suggested and waking-imagined "analgesia." J. Abnorm. Soc.
     Psychol., 65:411.
Berlyne, D. E., 1960, "Conflict Arousal and Curiosity," Mc Graw
     Hill, New York.
Blitz, B., and Dinnerstein, A. J., 1971, Role of attentional focus
     in pain perception: Manipulation of response to noxious
     stimulation by instructions, J. Abnorm. Psychol., 77:42.
Bloom, L. J., Houston, B. K., Holmes, D. S., and Burish, T. G.,
     1977, The effectiveness of attentional diversion and situation
     redefinition for reducing stress to a nonambiguous threat,
     J. Res. Personal., 11:83.
Byrne, D., 1961, The repression-sensitization scale: Rationale,
     reliability, and validity, J. Personal., 29:334.

Cohen, F., and Lazarus, R. S., 1973, Active coping processes, coping dispositions, and recovery from surgery, Psychosom. Med., 35:375.

Egbert, L. D., Battit, G. E., Welch, C. E., and Bartlett, M. K., 1974, Reduction of the operative pain by encouragement and instruction of patient: Study of doctor-patient rapport, N.E. J. Med., 270-825.

Elliott, R., 1966, Effects of uncertainty about the nature and advent of a noxious stimulus (shock) upon heart rate, J. Personal. Soc. Psychol., 3:353.

Geer, J. H., and Maisel, E., 1972, Evaluating the effects of the prediction-control confound, J. Personal. Soc. Psychol., 23:314.

Goldstein, M. J., 1959, The relationship between coping and avoiding behavior and response to fear-arousing propaganda, J. Abnorm. Soc. Psychol., 58:247.

Holmes, D. S., and Houston, B. K., 1974, Effectiveness of situation redefinition and affective isolation in coping with stress, J. Personal. Soc. Psychol., 29:212.

Janis, I. O., 1958, "Psychological Stress," John Wiley, New York.

Johnson, J. E., and Leventhal, H., 1974, Effects of accurate expectations and behavioral instructions on reactions during a noxious medical examination, J. Personal. Soc. Psychol., 29:710.

Jones, A., Bentler, P. M., and Petry, G., 1966, The reduction of uncertainty concerning future pain, J. Abnorm. Psychol, 71:87.

Kilpatrick, D. G., 1972, Differential responsiveness of two electro-dermal indices to psychological stress and performance of a complex cognitive task, Psychophysiology, 9:218.

Klemp, G. O., and Rodin, J., 1976, Effects of uncertainty, delay, and focus of attention on reactions to an aversive situation, J. Exp. Soc. Psychol., 12:416.

Langer, E. S., Janis, I. L., and Wolfer, J. A., 1975, Reduction of psychological stress in surgical patients, J. Exp. Soc. Psychol., 11:155.

Lazarus, R. S., and Alfert, E., 1964, Short-circuiting of threat by experimentally altering cognitive appraisal, J. Abnorm. Soc. Psychol., 69:195.

Lazarus, R. S., Opton, E. M., Nomikos, M. S., and Rankin, N. O., 1965, The principle of short-circuiting of threat: Further evidence, J. Personal., 33:622.

Lykken, D. T., 1962, Perception in the rat: Autonomic response to shock as a function of length of warning interval, Science, 137:665.

Maltzman, P. O., and Wolff, C., 1970, Preference for immediate vs. delayed noxious stimulation and the concomitant G.S.R., J. Exp. Psychol., 83:76.

Mead, P. G., 1970, The effect of orientation passages on patient stress prior to dentistry, Psychol. Rec., 20:479.

Miller, S. M., 1979a, Controllability and human stress: Method evidence, and theory, Behav. Res. Ther., 17:287.

Miller, S. M., 1979b, in press, Why having control reduces stress:
    If I can stop the roller coaster I don't want to get off, in:
    "Human Helplessness: Theory and Research," M. Seligman and
    J. Garber eds., Academic Press, New York.
Miller, S. M., 1979c, in press, Coping with impending stress:
    Psychophysiological and cognitive correlates of choice,
    Psychophysiology.
Miller, S. M., 1979, unpublished manuscript, Monitors vs. blunters:
    Validation of a questionnaire to assess two styles for coping
    with threat, University of Pennsylvania.
Miller, S. M., and Grant, R. P., 1979, in press, The blunting
    hypothesis: A theory of predictability and human stress, in:
    "Trends in Behavior Therapy," P. O. Sjoden and S. Bates eds.,
    Academic Press, New York.
Miller, S. M., and Grant, R. P., 1978, unpublished manuscript,
    Predictability and human stress: Evidence theory, and
    conceptual clarification, University of Pennsylvania.
Miller, S. M., and Harkavy, J., 1979a, unpublished manuscript,
    Coping with psychological threat by monitoring vs. blunting,
    University of Pennsylvania.
Miller, S. M., and Harkavy, J., 1979b, unpublished manuscript,
    Monitoring vs. blunting and amount of stress-relevant infor-
    mation processing, University of Pennsylvania.
Miller, S. M., Grant, R. P., and Nelson, J., 1978, unpublished
    manuscript, Choice of potential control under threat of
    electric shock, University of Pennsylvania.
Miller, S. M., Mangan, C. E., Freed, E., and Burtnett, M., 1979,
    unpublished manuscript, Which patients benefit from information
    before a gynecological procedure?: When the doctor should tell
    all, University of Pennsylvania.
Mischel, W., 1974, Processes in delay of gratification, in:
    "Advances in Experimental Social Psychology," Vol. 7,
    Academic Press, New York.
Mischel, W., Ebbesen, E. B., and Zeiss, A. R., 1973, Selective
    attention to the self: Situational and dispositional determi-
    nants, J. Personal Soc. Psychol., 27:129.
Mischel, W., Ebbesen, E. B., and Zeiss, A. R., 1976, Determinants
    of selective memory about the self, J. Consul. Clin. Psychol.,
    46:92.
Monat, A., 1976, Temporal uncertainty, anticipation time, and
    cognitive coping under threat, J. Hum. Stress, 2:32.
Monat, A., Averill, J. R., and Lazarus, R. S., 1972, Anticipatory
    stress and coping reactions under various conditions of
    uncertainty, J. Personal. Soc. Psychol., 24:237.
Neufeld, R. J., 1970, The effect of experimentally altered cognitive
    appraisal on pain tolerance, Psychonom. Sci., 20:106.
Perkins, C. C., Jr., 1955, The stimulus conditions which follow
    learned responses, Psychol. Rev., 62:341.
Rothbart, M., and Mellinger, M., 1972, Attention and responsivity
    to remote dangers: A laboratory simulation for assessing
    reactions to threatening events, J. Personal. Soc. Psychol.,
    24:132.

Seligman, M. E. P., 1968, Chronic fear produced by unpredictable
    electric shock, J. Comp. Physiol. Psychol., 66:402.
Seligman, M. E. P., and Binik, Y. M., 1977, The safety signal
    hypothesis, in: "Pavolvian-Operant Interactions," H. Davis and
    H. Hurwitz eds., Lawrence Erlbaum Associates, Hillsdale.
Sime, A. M., 1976, Relationship of preoperative fear, type of
    coping, and information received about surgery to recovery from
    surgery, J. Personal. Soc. Psychol., 34:716.
Speisman, J., Lazarus, R., Mordkoff, A., and Davison, L., 1964,
    Experimental reduction of stress based on ego-defense theory,
    J. Abnorm. Soc. Psychol., 68:367.
Vaillant, G. E., 1977, "Adaptation to Life," Little, Brown & Co.,
    Boston.
Vernon, D. T. A., 1971, Information seeking in a natural stress
    situation, J. App. Psychol., 55:359.
Vernon, D. T. A., and Bigelow, D. A., 1974, Effect of information
    about a potentially stressful situation on responses to stress
    impact, J. Personal. Soc. Psychol., 29:50.
Wachtel, P. L., 1969, Anxiety, attention, and coping with threat,
    J. Abnorm. Psychol., 73:137.
Williams, J. G. L., Jones J. R., Workhoven, M. N., and Williams, B.,
    1975, The psychological control of preoperative anxiety,
    Psychophysiology, 12:50.

MANAGING THE STRESS OF AGING:

THE ROLE OF CONTROL AND COPING

Judith Rodin

Department of Psychology

Yale University

From many different quarters today, there is the demand for
more personal control: Students complain that they have no control
over the political process, persons in poverty complain that they
have no control over economic resources, and old people complain
that they have little control over anything (Averill, 1973). Of
all these groups, the plight of the aged is probably the most
serious. According to a recent Harris poll conducted in the United
States (1975) the majority of the American public views older
people as passive, sedentary types who have lost the open-mindedness,
mental alertness, and efficiency of the young, and who spend a good
deal of their time off by themselves and dwelling on the past.
Quite clearly, the transition from adulthood to old age often does
represent a loss of control, both physiologically and psychologically
(Birren, 1958; Gould, 1972). However, it is as yet unclear just
how much of this change is biologically determined and how much is
a function of the environment. The ability to sustain a sense of
personal control in old age may be greatly influenced by societal
factors, and this in turn may affect one's physical well-being.

Typically the life situation does change in old age. There is
some loss of roles, norms, and reference groups, events that can
negatively influence one's perceived competence and feeling of
responsibility (Bengston, 1973). Perception of these changes in
addition to actual physical decrements, may enhance a sense of aging
and lower self-esteem (Lehr and Puschner)*. In response to internal

---

*Lehr, K., and Puschner, I., 1963, Studies in the awareness of
aging, paper presented at the 6th International Congress on Geron-
tology, Copenhagen.

developmental changes, the aging individual may come to see himself
in a position of lessened mastery relative to the rest of the world,
as a passive object manipulated by the environment (Neugarten and
Gutman, 1958). Questioning whether these factors can be counteracted,
some studies have suggested that more successful aging--measured by
decreased mortality, morbidity, and psychological disability--occurs
when an individual feels a sense of usefulness and purpose (Bengston,
1973; Butler, 1967; Leaf, 1973; Lieberman, 1965).

CONTROL AND HUMAN BEHAVIOR

The notion of competence is indeed central to much of human
behavior. As early as 1930, Adler described the need to control
one's personal environment as "an intrinsic necessity of life
itself" (p. 398). Or, consider the more recent theorizing of
deCharms (1968), who stated that "man's primary motivation propen-
sity is to be effective in producing changes in his environment.
Man strives to be a causal agent, to be the primary locus of,
causation for, or the origin of, his behavior; he strives for
personal causation" (p. 269).

As operationally defined (Baron & Rodin, 1978), control is the
ability to regulate or influence intended outcomes through selective
responding. Perceived control refers to expectations of having the
power to participate in making decisions in order to obtain desirable
consequences. One aspect of perceived control involves a sense of
freedom of choice, being aware of opportunities to select preferred
goals and means. Another aspect--perceived control over outcomes--
refers to the person's belief in a causal link between his or her
own actions or action capabilities and the consequences that will
ensue. The crucial component is the assumption, held with varying
degrees of conviction by different people and in different situations, that they are responsible for the outcomes that accrue to
them through their own efforts.

Issues regarding control are especially important to health
because there is extensive evidence suggesting that restrictions
in control are often stress-inducing. Seligman and his co-workers
have systematically described the way that decreased control
increases feelings and behaviors associated with helplessness (see
Seligman, 1975). Both the etiology of disease (Glass, 1977) and
death (McMahon and Rhudick, 1964) have been linked to increased
feelings of helplessness and lack of control. Thus it appears that
control-relevant processes are clearly related to health and
survival. Lefcourt (1973) best summed up the essence of this
research in his article on the perception of control when he
concluded that "the sense of control, the illusion that one can
exercise personal choice, has a definite and positive role in
sustaining life."

With so many demonstrations of the negative consequences of reduced control, it is not surprising that other studies have shown that there are positive outcomes associated with increased control. There is now a sizable literature indicating that both actual and perceived control over present or impending harm plays an important role in coping with stress (Bowers, 1968; Houston, 1972; Pervin, 1963; Pranulis, Dabbs, and Johnson, 1975; Staub, Tursky, and Schwartz, 1971). At present there are two dominant views about how control results in stress reduction. One is that self-regulated administration, which allows for actual control, is positively reinforcing and may sometimes decrease the effects of the painful stimulus (Averill, 1973; Kanfer and Seider, 1973; Seligman, 1975). The second holds that an increased feeling of control in the face of threat leads to an increased ability to predict and discriminate periods of safety, which is stress reducing (Ball and Vogler, 1971; Klemp and Rodin, 1976; Pervin, 1963; Weiss, 1970). Both could be true, depending on the type of control that is provided.

Effects of control on health-relevant outcomes

When used in the health domain, some control interventions give patients a great deal of preparatory information, including precise descriptions of expected reactions, medical procedures, and the like, as in Johnson's (1975) work on gastroendoscopy. When these interventions enable patients to make plans for coping with the predicted stress, they enhance feelings of control. Johnson argues that preparatory information not only increases expectancies about likely sensations but also decreases expectancies about unlikely ones. The consequences of such preparation are to reduce significantly the degree of pain experienced, the need for medication following surgery, and the time needed for post-operative recovery (Johnson, 1975).

Other studies have had similar beneficial outcomes by actually providing patients the opportunity to have some degree of control. Work with breast cancer patients, for example, has shown that patients do better, as measured by rate of recovery from surgery, when they have had a two-stage surgical procedure (Taylor and Levin, in press), as compared with those who have undergone a one-stage procedure. The two-stage procedure allows time for orderly planning and evaluation prior to surgery or therapy and often includes active participation of the patient in the decision to resort to surgery. The patient's knowledge that she has a malignancy and her psychological preparation in advance for the removal of the breast, as well as her participation in the relevant planning and decision making are likely to enhance her feelings of personal control.

Control and aging

The implication of all of these studies for research in the

area of aging seemed quite clear to us. Objective helplessness as
well as feelings of helplessness and hopelessness--both enhanced by
the environment and by intrinsic changes that occur with increasing
old age--may contribute to psychological withdrawal, physical disease,
and death. In contrast, objective control and the feelings of
mastery may very well contribute to physical health and personal
efficacy.

While often not working under the theoretical rubric of the
control construct, many researchers have been interested in the
possibility that significant environmental events do have some
relation to health and to subsequent death (c.f., Holmes and Rahe,
1967). Three such environmental events that have been specified
for the elderly, in particular, are loss of a significant other,
relocation, and retirement. With very few exceptions, the studies
that examined these variables have used naturalistic designs.
Usually, the subjects for whom the event occurs form the experimental
group. Other subjects, who have not yet experienced this event, form
the control group. An obvious shortcoming of this type of research
stems from the fact that subjects are not randomly assigned into the
two groups, and so there is always the possibility that the groups
can differ on other characteristics, aside from the one in question.
For example, in many of these studies there is no control for
initial health or age. In many instances then, the experimental
subjects may actually begin the study older or less healthy than
subjects who form the non-critical group.

Relocation studies are an important example of the type of
investigation that focuses on a signficant life event for the elderly.
The data suggest that stress over relocation is related to death in
the elderly, particularly those who are already in poor health. But
most elderly persons in these studies have been relocated, usually
to nursing homes, precisely because they were in ill health. Thus
potential artifacts in these studies abound.

Because of the major sources of experimental error in the few
studies that had been conducted in this area, my colleagues and I
attempted to design experiments that enabled us to look at randomly
assigned environmental gain. In this way, we were able to control
for the role of other factors that I described earlier, such as age
or initial health, which may co-vary with environmental loss and
thus greatly influence death. Because of our theoretical interest
in control as an important mediating process between stress and
health, we first attempted to assess directly the effects of
enhanced personal responsibility and decision-making on a group of
nursing home patients (Langer and Rodin, 1976). In addition to
testing the generalizability of our previous work on control
(Rodin, 1976), we tried in this study to extend the control
conception in two ways.

First, we wanted to consider a broad range of response variables. If control was important, we felt that its effects should generalize to activity, to happiness, to sociability as well as to general well being. Second, we wanted to look at a different way to manipulate the independent variable, by offering a general increase in responsibility and decision-making, that would allow subjects real choices that were not only directed to a single behavior, or to a single stimulus condition. The study was intended to determine whether the decline in health, alertness, and activity that generally occurs when aged persons are put in nursing homes could be slowed or reversed by choice and control manipulations that we and others have shown to have beneficial effects in other contexts.

Subjects in the experimental group had all been randomly assigned to one floor of the nursing home when they entered. In order to administer the intervention, they were called together by the hospital administrator and given a talk that said, in part-- "We want to tell you the kinds of things that you should be doing, and can be doing, here. There are lots of choices that you can be making, you can decide what you want your rooms to look like, what nights you want to go to the movies, and who you want to interact with." Thus this communication emphasized their responsibility for themselves, enumerated things that were possible for them to do in this setting, and explicated where decision-making was possible.

A second, comparison group was comprised of individuals randomly assigned to another floor of the home. Subjects on the two floors did not differ as a function of severity of illness, prognosis, age, sex or length of time in the nursing home. These subjects were called together in the same way, and were given a talk by the administrator that made explicit what was essentially the implicit message in this nursing home, that it was the staff's responsibility to care for them as patients. They were told, for example, "We want to take care of you, we want you to know that we will do for you whatever you need, so just tell us whenever you need something." While this was a benign, caring communication, it was one that greatly implied diminished personal control.

In reality, the choices and avenues for decision-making that we enumerated in the responsibility condition were options that were already potentially available; the administrator simply stated them clearly as possibilities. Thus the institutional readiness was already there, and the experimental induction was intended to bolster individual predispositions for increased choice and self-control.

The data presented in Table 1 give means and change scores in measures taken one month before and three to four weeks after the intervention. They indicate that residents in the responsibility-induced group became more active and reported feeling happier than

TABLE 1

MEAN SCORES FOR SELF-REPORT, INTERVIEWER RATINGS,
AND NURSES' RATINGS FOR EXPERIMENTAL AND COMPARISON GROUPS

Questionnaire Responses	Responsibility Induced (n = 24)			Comparison (n = 28)			Comparison of change scores (p <)
	Pre	Post	Change: Post-Pre	Pre	Post	Change: Post-Pre	
Self-report							
Happy	5.16	5.44	.28	4.90	4.78	-.12	.05
Active	4.07	4.27	.20	3.90	2.62	-1.28	.01
Perceived Control							
Have	3.26	3.42	.16	3.62	4.03	.41	--
Want	3.85	3.80	-.05	4.40	4.57	.17	--
Interviewer Rating							
Alertness	5.02	5.31	.29	5.75	5.38	-.37	.025
Nurses' Ratings							
General improvement	41.67	45.64	3.97	42.69	40.32	-2.39	.005
Time spent							
visiting patients	13.03	19.81	6.78	7.94	4.65	-3.30	.005
visiting others	11.50	13.75	2.14	12.38	8.21	-4.16	.05
talking to staff	8.21	16.43	8.21	9.11	10.71	1.61	.01
watching staff	6.78	4.64	-2.14	6.96	11.60	4.64	.05

the comparison group of residents, who were encouraged to feel that
the staff would care for them and try to make them happy. Patients
in the responsibility-induced group also showed a significant
improvement in alertness and increased behavioral involvement in
many different kinds of activities, such as movie attendance, active
socializing with staff and friends, and contest participation. In
addition to collecting these multiple questionaire and behavioral
measures at the time, we were subsequently able to collect long-
term follow-up data on several variables, including mortality (Rodin
and Langer, 1977). As in the first study, our intent was to gather
as many measures as were accessible for this population with the
goal of increasing accuracy with increased heterogeneity of methodology (Campbell and Fiske, 1959).

In addition to the two treatment groups described earlier, we
also evaluated a small control group of patients who had not
participated in the first study due to a variety of scheduling
problems. Five had previously lived on the same floor as subjects
in the responsibility-induced condition, and 4 lived on the same
floor as the comparison group. All subjects were now living in a
new addition, built after the intervention. The average length of
time in the nursing home was 3.9 years, which was not reliably
different for the three groups.

The mean nurses' ratings are presented in Table 2. On the
average, the patients in the responsibility-induced group were
judged to be significantly more actively interested in their
environment, more sociable and self-initiating, and more vigorous
than residents in the comparison group. The mean ratings also show
the similarity between the comparison group given the "happiness"
induction and the no-treatment group.

Composite scores for all the evaluative items were also available from the questionnaire, which the nurses completed prior to the
original intervention and at the 3-week posttest. The means presented in Table 3 include all residents for whom these two scores
and follow-up data were available (n = 14 for the responsibility-
induced group, and n = 12 for the comparison group). Change scores
between the preintervention means and the 18-month follow-up data
indicate that the decline was significantly smaller for the responsibility-induced group (M = 58.21) than for the comparison condition
(M = 175.42), $t(24)$ = 2.68, p < .02. Change scores calculated between the 3-week postintervention ratings and the 18-month follow-
up showed marginally reliable differences in the same direction,
t (24) - 1.82, p <.10.

Change scores were also calculated between the preintervention
(1974) and follow-up (1976) health evaluation ratings. Health ratings were retrospective, based on the medical records, so change
scores could be calculated for all 43 follow-up subjects. There was
no significant difference among the three groups in the preinterven-

TABLE 2

MEAN RATINGS FOR RESIDENTS 18 MONTHS
FOLLOWING EXPERIMENTAL INTERVENTIONS

Nurses' rating	Responsibility induced (20)*	Comparison (14)*	No treatment control (9)**
Happy	4.35	3.68	3.28
Actively Interested	5.15	3.96	3.95
Sociable	5.00	3.78	3.40
Self-initiating	5.15	3.90	4.18
Vigorous	4.75	3.39	3.33

Note: The difference between the responsibility-
induced and comparison groups was reliable at
p < .05 for all ratings but Happy. Numbers in
parentheses are ns.
* Received experimental treatment in Langer and
  Rodin (1976).
**Not previously tested.

TABLE 3

MEAN COMPOSITE NURSES' EVALUATION
SCORES TAKEN AT THREE DIFFERENT TIME
PERIODS RELATIVE TO THE INTERVENTION

Time Period	Responsibility induced	Comparison
Preintervention	402.38	442.93
Postintervention (3 weeks)	436.50	413.03
Follow-up (18 months)	352.33	262.00

Note: There were seven 10-point items on
the scales used by Langer and Rodin (1976),
making a total of 70 points possible.
There were five items in the follow-up
questionnaire, and the ratings were made on
9-point scales making a total of 45 possible
points. The Langer and Rodin totals were
multiplied by 9 and the follow-up totals
by 14 to make the scores comparable.

tion health evaluations, $F(2.40) = 1.77$. On the follow-up measures, the responsibility-induced group showed a mean increase in general health of .55 on a 5-point scale, which was reliably greater than means for the comparison group ($M = -.29$) and the no-treatment group ($M = -.33$), $F(2.40) = 3.73$, $p < .05$.

The most striking data, however, were obtained in death rate differences between the two treatment groups. Taking the 18 months prior to the original intervention as an arbitrary comparison period, we found that the average death rate during that period was 25% for the entire nursing home. In the subsequent 18-month period following the intervention, only 7 of the 47 subjects (15%) in the responsibility-induced group died, whereas 13 of 44 subjects (30%) in the comparison group had died. The stated causes of death that appeared on the medical record varied greatly among individuals and did not appear to be systematic within conditions, but additional analyses are currently underway to consider possible stress-related contributing factors.

Because these results were so startling, we assessed other factors that might have accounted for the differences. Unfortunately, we simply cannot know everything about the equivalency of these subjects prior to the intervention. We do know that those who died did not differ reliably in the length of time that they had been institutionalized or in their overall health status when the study began. These means are presented in Table 4, which also presents the nurses' evaluations prior to the intervention. From these ratings it is clear that the nurses had given lower evaluations prior to the intervention to those patients who subsequently died than to those who were still living, $F(1.48) = 7.73$, $p < .01$. The inter-action between treatment group and the life-death variable was not significant, however.

It is striking to note that the nurses' evaluations of the patients, and not the overall health ratings, were more closely related to subsequent life and death. Either the psychological variables that the nurses were rating are better predictors of later mortality than medical symptom evaluations or the nurses' views of the residents are significant factors in their potential longevity. One clear area for further study is the patient-nurse interaction to assess if and how this factor is related to patient health. This is a relationship laden with stress and it has been further considered in studies described later in the paper.

We do not conclude from these data that it was control alone, particularly our type of control-relevant intervention, that pro-duced effects as dramatic as these. We believe that the interven-tion set in motion a process that maintained itself throughout this period. This was a setting that was primed and very responsive to the behavior of the patients, and one that was open to change. Control is obviously not adaptive nor is it advantageous in a setting where people try to exercise control, when no control is

TABLE 4

MEAN RATINGS PRIOR TO INTERVENTION GROUPED BY
SUBSEQUENT MORTALITY OUTCOME

	Responsibility Induced		Comparison	
Variable	Dead	Living	Dead	Living
Time				
Institution-alized	2.40 (7)	2.70 (40)	2.80 (13)	2.20 (31)
Health ratings	3.57 (7)	3.85 (40)	3.69 (13)	3.64 (31)
Nurses' evalu-ations	36.20 (5)	44.79 (19)	31.69 (8)	47.39 (20)

Note. The numbers in parentheses represent
       the number of residents on whom each mean is based.

possible. In this instance, control may be stress-inducing.
Another element in the process of change that we observed could
also have been the nurses' behavior. Although they were blind to
the specific hypotheses, they rated the patients and so were aware
of the changes that were occurring. Moreover, if the patients did
show some initial improvement, their interactions with the nurses
and the other relevant people in the setting had to change, trig-
gering a reciprocal set of changes that may have contributed to
better outcomes. The point is that the entire system was obviously
affected very much by the intervention, not only the individual
patients. In other words, increased perception and exercise of
control set a process in motion, which benefited health-relevant
outcomes.

       We then tried a very small study, necessarily small because
we could only find one nursing home to cooperate with what they
perceived as a very strange idea. The more we worked in these
settings, the more we saw an extremely strong tension between the
residents and the nurses. The nurses made the patients feel passive
and helpless, and then they punished them for their dependence.
The nurses' perception was that the patients were always bothering
them and took too much time, and that if only they would stop
complaining, the nurses could get their work done. It was an
extraordinary interaction and fostered a set of stresses and
problems of which we became increasingly aware.

       We assigned each resident in the experimental group a
particular time when he or she could have the nurse's attention--
"Mrs. Jones, the nurse is yours from 9:00-9:15," and "Mr. Smith,
the nurse is yours from 9:15-9:30." We put clocks in all the rooms
and we scheduled times so that if Mrs. Jones wanted the nurse to
come between 9:00 and 9:15, all she had to do was press the
control button, thus making an instrumental response, and the nurse
was required to come in because that was Mrs. Jones' time that day.
We simply had the buttons wired to an event recorder. The nurses
liked the arrangement too because, after all the times had been
assigned, they actually had more apparent free time than they felt
they had before the intervention was introduced.

       In the beginning the patients exercised their control and
called the nurses for very trivial things as well as for some
important problems. But over time it began to taper off and the
patients used the button less and less. While it sometimes
recycled up again, use of the button returned back to an even lower
level, i.e., there were longer and longer periods when they did
not use their control or they used it far less frequently. It
appeared that they sometimes started again, just to show themselves in some way that they still had control if they wanted it.
But over a long period of time, for practically every individual,
there was a clear oscillation of using and then discontinuing use

of the control button.

Relative to untreated controls, general health and sociability improved in the experimental patients. These data suggest that control does not have to continue to be exercised to produce beneficial effects; simply the knowledge that one has control seems to be valuable in this particular instance. This form of control appears to have provided a coping device that made a major problem in the environment appear far less stressful. Indeed we found that a reduction in perceived stress was strongly correlated with increased feelings of control (r = .62, p < .01).

EFFECTS OF ATTRIBUTIONS ON THE INITIATION OF CONTROL RESPONSES

The problem is that without the kinds of explicit interventions described above, many aged people typically do not know or believe that they can exercise control, and their coping repertoire is greatly limited. Why should this be true? One possible cause for reduced coping attempts is the operation of very strong negative labeling processes. But we have observed that chronological age per se is not sufficient to provide a person with the self-definition of "old," although obviously there is some relationship between chronological age and self-perception. Rather a series of events or experiences forces acceptance, although reluctantly, of the fact that one is old, and often these events have the loss of control at their core. Once this occurs, it may be that older people then evaluate themselves on the basis of feelings and behaviors that they attribute to aging rather than to the environment and circumstance.

Negative attributional processes deriving from reduced feelings of control can create at least two different types of problems for older people that may reduce their number of coping attempts and thus detrimentally affect their health (see Rodin, 1978, for a longer discussion of the role of attributions on health in general). First, there is a tendency to over-attribute most of their negative physical symptoms to aging per se, especially to the presumed physical decline with which aging is associated. Biological attributions may incorrectly focus the person away from situational and social factors such as the loss of a loved one or feeling unsafe, which are stress-inducing, in part because they are associated with a loss of control. Recent work has shown that even among healthy college students, loss of control is related to increased experience of symptoms (Pennebaker and Skelton, 1978). Second, when events are attributed to the aging process, they are seen as inevitable; and remedial steps, which could be extremely beneficial, may not be undertaken.

In the next study we interviewed people in the week that followed their entering the nursing home, and selected the 80% who made explicit negative attributions to physical decline associated

with aging as either causing or contributing greatly to some of their problems (Rodin and Langer, in press). We took a variety of premeasures including interviews, health measures, and observations of level of participation. There were three, randomly assigned groups: One group was untreated; one group was simply given information trying to argue against physical decline in aging as being the real source of their problems (using material taken from doctors' reports and journal articles); the third group was given environmental explanations (or at least age-environment interaction attributions) as being the source of their problems. As an example, subjects in the latter group were told that the floors in the nursing home are very slippery because they are tiled in order to keep them clean. Even young people slip on them. Thus we tried to reduce the attribution that slipping was due to weak knees or poor movement that resulted from their age. Or they were reminded that they were awakened at 5:30 in the morning, which would make many people tired by evening. Again we tried to minimize the liklihood that they would attribute their weariness to aging per se. Thus we simply attempted to refocus their explanations for their own feeling and behavior to realistic and possible factors in the environment that could have been producing some of the physical symptoms that they were experiencing.

As a result of the reattribution intervention, patients showed greatly improved behavior, including an increase in active participation and sociability relative to groups given specific information or to untreated controls. These data are presented in Table 5. Thus debilitating and often excessive attribution to physical state can be refocused with beneficial effects to more easily changed sources in the environment. There were also substantial decreases in 24-hour levels of urinary free cortisol and general health. It is to these measures and their relationship to stress and coping, in general, that we turned to next.

STRESS AND COPING

Our data suggest that institutional environments are themselves associated with major sources of stress for the elderly. But if we view stress and its effects as a process involving antecedents or inputs, mediators and outcomes (cf., Lazarus and Cohen)*, the institutional setting is seen as only one of many input variables. Table 6 outlines this process model. Both historical and environmental factors differentiate these institutions and the persons placed there and will influence the degree of stress these people experience. Inputs for the individual are the number and magnitude of recent significant life events, such as the death of a spouse or

---

*Lazarus, R. S., and Cohen, J. B., 1976, Theory and method in the study of stress and coping in aging individuals, paper presented at the 5th W.H.O. Conference on Society, Stress and Disease: Aging and Old Age, Stockholm, Sweden.

TABLE 5

CHANGE SCORES FROM PRE- TO POST-EXPERIMENTAL TREATMENT

Treatment:	Per-ceived Control	Per-ceived Health	Active Activ-ities	Passive Activ-ities	Mem-ory Tasks	Health	UFC
No treatment	-1.6	-1.8	0.4	0.8	-0.8	-2.0	+20.
No attribution (information only)	-1.8	-1.0	-0.6	-0.2	0.4	-1.6	-18.
Environmental attribution (separated from loved ones)	2.4	3.4	2.0	0.6	0.6	2.6	-50.

TABLE 6

PROCESS OF STRESS FROM INSTITUTIONALIZATION OF THE AGED

INPUTS

Institutional	Individual
Institutional policies and procedures Physical environment Social environment Staff attitudes and behavior	Significant recent life events Number and magnitude of chronic daily problems

MEDIATORS

Person-environment fit	Personality characteristics Personal resources Social supports Coping strategies Health

OUTCOMES

Adjustment	Health

the move to a nursing home and the number and magnitude of chronic daily hassles with which a person must deal on a regular basis (Dohrenwend and Dohrenwend, 1974). In other words, stress can come from chronic repeated small nuisances as well as from acute threats, and the former kind are quite likely to occur for the elderly to a substantial degree. The relevant inputs on the institutional level include the physical environment of the institution, the institutional policies and procedures, and the attitude of staff toward the residents and toward elderly people in general.

Once people are placed in a setting where there is a potential for stress, there are institutional and individual attributes and resources that differentiate them with regard to the degree of stress they experience and the coping responses they employ. Institutional mediators are those factors related to person-environment fit. Individual mediators are the personality characteristics of the individual and the social supports and coping resources available to him. Resources are not to be confused with the coping responses made by a person confronting problems but, rather, are better conceived as those dispositional and social network variables that are available to people in developing their coping repertoire and in mediating their response to potentially stressful events (Pearlin and Schooler, 1978). Until we began our work, descriptive studies about life in institutions for the elderly (e.g., Spasoff, Kraus, Beattie, Holden, Lawson, Rodenburg and Woodcock, 1978) failed to delineate systematically which resident reactions and behaviors could be interpreted as methods of coping with stress, which were negative effects of stress, and which were behaviors directly induced by institutionalization per se.

As I am using the term here, coping refers to behavior that protects people from being harmed by problematical experiences, thus mediating, for example, the impact that a particular setting can have on an individual. The protective function of coping behavior can be exercised in three ways: by eliminating or modifying conditions giving rise to problems; by perceptually controlling the meaning of experience in a manner that neutralizes its problematic character; and by keeping the emotional consequences of problems within manageable bounds (Pearlin and Schooler, 1978).

Without yet teaching explicit coping skills, our decision-making interventions had changed individuals in the groups with increased control in ways that enabled them to keep the emotional consequences of their problems within manageable bounds. They appeared to do this by increasing their activity, sociability, and involvement in the setting. With the attribution interventions we enabled them to control perceptually the meaning of their experiences in a way that would neutralize the problematic character of these events.

In the next study (Rodin and White)*, we wished to teach subjects the third type of coping behavior, that is to eliminate or
modify the conditions giving rise to their problems. This is the
response that we believe to be the most desirable form of coping
whenever possible. Its benefits presumably derive first, from
eliminating or reducing the problem; second, from actively engaging in coping attempts and receiving feedback regarding the efficacy
of these responses; and third, from an increased sense of control
and personal efficacy.

Coping skills training

We elected to teach self-regulation skills using a cognitive
strategy. We felt that training regarding cognitions would provide
a particularly important coping skill for the elderly because their
negative self-attitudes and self-statements often interfered with
effective problem solving. One often notices elderly individuals
in nursing homes talking to themselves or repeating instructions
aloud; the self-instructional training procedures developed by
Meichenbaum and his co-workers (Meichenbaum, 1977) could capitalize
on this natural process and serve as a cognitive prosthesis to
overcome age-related deficits (Meichenbaum, 1974).

The following represents a general overview of the self-
regulation, cognitive skills training procedure.

A.   Education phase (Week 1)

1.   We introduced examples to communicate the idea that it
     is not events per se but a persons' thoughts and
     feelings in response to events that determine the degree
     of stress experienced. Events are depressing and
     anxiety-provoking to some extent because of the views
     people take of them and what people choose to attend to
     and think about.

2.   We provided specific examples of negative self-statements,
     which contribute to and exemplify lack of control. For
     example, "nothing ever goes right for me here." Some
     suggestions as to how these self-statements affect
     behavior were introduced. More realistic and "adaptive"
     versions of these negative self-statements were also
     introduced. Residents were encouraged through a role-
     playing exercise to come up with a list of their own
     negative self-statements.

---

*Rodin, J., and White, L., 1979, Coping skills training for elderly
persons, unpublished ms., Yale University.

Summary. As a result of this education phase, subjects were
expected to gain knowledge that they are active contributors to
their own experiences and not helpless victims of their thoughts
and feelings. At the cognitive level, helplessness and lack of
control are reflected in, and maintained by, the specific
appraisals, attributions, expectations, and self-statements that
occur in the context of their daily lives. They were explicitly
made aware of their own forms of negative self-statements.

B.   Introduction of positive self-statements and an opportunity to
     practice these new self-statements in a controlled setting
     (Week 2)

     1.   A memory task where problem solving skills and positive
          self-statements are modeled was the target task. The self-
          instructional training program had the experimenter first
          perform the task, talking aloud to himself while the
          resident observed, then the subject performed the task,
          first talking aloud to himself, and then while not moving
          his lips (covertly). The content of the self-instruction
          was quite broad and included questions about the nature of
          the task, answers to these questions in the form of
          cognitive rehearsal and planning, self-guidance, ways of
          coping with failure, and self-reinforcement. According to
          Meichenbaum (1974), such verbalization rehearsal may
          facilitate behavior in various wasy. Overt verbalization
          may serve to organize information in the stimulus array
          and assist the subject in generating alternatives regard-
          ing the solution. It also provides verbal mediators that
          help to distinguish relevant from irrelevant dimensions
          in both external stimuli and the subject's own thoughts.
          It also may enhance a positive task orientation and provide
          stress inoculation that facilitates coping with possible
          failures.

          A set of self-statements incompatible with negative self-
          statements that interfere with rehearsal were also
          introduced. Negative self-statements now became cues to
          emit new self-statements which could encourage the subjects
          to assess the reality of the situation, cope with negative
          emotions, make choices, control negative self-statements,
          and exert control. Examples of positive self-statements
          are given in Table 7.

     Summary. As a result of this phase residents were to gain a
task orientation to approaching problems and everyday life in the
home which included attending to desired outcomes and implementing
an appropriate behavior strategy. Self-statements were then used
to guide coping behavior.

TABLE 7

EXAMPLES OF POSITIVE SELF-STATEMENTS

1. <u>Identifying source of the problem or negative self-statement</u>

What is it that is bothering you?
How much of a problem is it?
Be honest, think it through, be rational.

2. <u>Preparation for action</u>

What is it that I have to do? What is it that I would like
  to do?
I know that I can work out a plan of action to deal with this.
Don't sit here and feel sorry for yourself; that won't help
  anything. I knew that I would be feeling like this sometime,
  it is no reason to let this get me down further.
No negative statements. I can manage the situation.
You have lots of strategies to call upon. Lots of choices that
  you can make.
I will find something to interest me. I will not sit here and
  do nothing.
What are my choices? What kinds of choices should I be making?
Can I change the situation? Maybe I could just try doing
  something else, or talking to someone else.
I will not be negative. I will feel better. I am alive, I am
  going to do interesting things.

3. <u>Confronting and Handling the Problem</u>

One step at a time while I carry out my plan.
I can meet the challenge.
No negative self-statements, just concentrate on what you
  planned to do.
It is my choice to work this out if I want to. I am in
  control. I know what my options are, and what I can choose
  to do.
I know what I want to do it is just a matter of carrying it out.
You are not going to let today get the better of you.
Don't assume the worst now or jump to conclusions. Look for
  the positives.
It is up to me to work this out as I planned. So you had
  better get on with it. I'll show them.

4. Coping with feelings of being overwhelmed

    Don't quit now after you have gone so far.
    Keep focused on the present, what is it you planned to do.
    Show people and yourself that you won't sit down and watch the
       world go by. Keep it up.

5. Self-reinforcement

    It worked. I feel better already.
    You really handled yourself pretty well.
    If you can control your thoughts, you can work it through.
    It is kind of fun to try to think of different ways of dealing
       with things, and to try out some of the choices which you
       think of.

_____

C. Extended application training (Week 3)

    1. Residents were given an opportunity to apply these new
        coping techniques in attempting to resolve a number of
        potential "helplessness provoking" situations which may
        be encountered in their daily lives (e.g., an expected
        visitor from your family suddenly cannot make it).

    The coping skills study was conducted at an intermediate care
facility in suburban Connecticut. Forty residents were matched on
age, sex, and length of stay in the nursing home, and then randomly
assigned to one of four treatment conditions. All were able to
walk without assistance and some were employed in a special state-
funded program for the elderly and left the facility to work each
day. They were far less ill than the skilled nursing facility
patients we had tested previously and thus were more representative
of a community-based elderly sample. Economic dependency rather
than medical need was often the reason for their continued stay in
the setting.

    Subjects (n = 10) assigned to one of the four conditions
received a slightly modified version of the communication used by
Langer and Rodin (1976) to enhance feelings of personal responsibility and choice in a group of nursing home residents. A second
group (n = 9) received three sessions of self-instructional training. The remaining two groups served as controls. Residents
(n = 10) in one control group spent the same amount of time with
the experimenter as did subjects who received instruction in
cognitive self-guidance but the time was spent chatting and testing.
This attention control afforded an index of change that resulted
from exposure to the materials used in the self-instructional
training (e.g., practicing the recall task) and/or receiving
attention from a professional psychologist without specific coping

skills instruction. Subjects (n = 10) in a fourth condition served
as no treatment controls.

Multiple dependent measures were used to assess the effects of
the experimental interventions including resident self-reports,
nurses' ratings, two types of memory tasks, behavioral measures of
activity and involvement, interviewer ratings, and measures of
physical and psychological stress and general health. In most cases
the measures were administered both prior to and following the experimental interventions in order to provide an index of the amount of
change that resulted from exposure to the various treatments.

The entire experiment was conducted over a nine-month period.
During the first three months we were involved with the collection
of the pretest measures, including a one-hour interview with each
resident. Two months after the pretest assessment was completed,
the experimental interventions began, and continued over the next
two months. Finally, three weeks after the intervention phase was
completed, and during the ensuing two months, the multiple dependent
measures used to assess the impact of the experimental intervention
were administered.

Let us first consider the results reflecting increased
behavioral coping responses. Skills for a memory test constituted
one of the training trials for the self-instruction group. The
first measure of the success of the intervention was taken during
a later training session using a probe recall task. Probe recall
is a test that measures short-term memory of paired items. This
particular measure used five photographs of elderly people, each
paired with a person's name. The photographs were then presented
at various intervals and the subject had to remember the name
associated with each face. As indicated in Table 8, the coping
skills instruction group did reliably better than the attention
control group, which is essentially a check on the manipulation.
During the follow-up period, all subjects were asked questions
requiring them to seek out and remember information about the
setting, e.g., where is the suggestion box located; what is the
name of the movie of the month for October and when will it be
shown? Thus subjects had to remember what information to seek out,
to actively seek it, and then to remember it until the experimenter's
next visit. The data in Table 8 show that the self-instruction and
responsibility-induced groups report reliably more items from
before to after the intervention than subjects in the two control
groups.

Considering the resident interviews next, there were no
significant differences between groups prior to the intervention on
any responses. The first variable listed on Table 8, described as
"control have," is a composite score of items reflecting how much
control subjects felt they had in the setting. For example, "In

TABLE 8

CHANGE SCORES FROM PRE- TO POST-INTERVENTION MEASURES

	Self-Instruction	Attention control	No treatment control	Responsibility-induced	F	p
CONTROL						
Control have	51.55*	42.33***	44.87**	37.77***	3.56	<.03
Value of control (post only)	3.78*	1.44***	1.50**	1.89**	3.52	<.03
Ideas for change (post only)	3.77*	1.77***	1.12**	1.56**	5.09	<.01
ACTIVITY						
(Percentage time observed in various activities)						
Passive	20.00*	50.60**	43.90**	32.00*	2.45	<.09
Active	27.30*	10.60***	10.00***	13.50**	2.81	<.06
Number of new activities (post only)	1.33*	0.33**	0.67***	0.56***	2.96	<.05
MEMORY						
Probe recall	19.00	11.66	--	--	6.48	<.03
Questions about setting	9.23*	4.88**	4.87**	7.93*	3.03	<.05
STAFF RATINGS						
Composite adjustment	24.11**+	34.77**	33.00**	35.33**	2.81	<.06

+ Low numbers are more active, alert, sociable, etc.
Note: Numbers with different asterisks (*, **, ***) are significantly different from one another.

the past month, how much say do you feel that you have had in
determining the kinds of things that go on around here, like the
rules that are established or the types of activities that are
scheduled?" or "At the present time, how much freedom do you have
in deciding how your room should be arranged?" The self-instruction
group increased significantly more than the others on this measure,
with the responsibility-induced group surprisingly expressing the
least feelings of control.

Next we assessed the perceived value of control, a measure
taken in the posttest only. The question was: "how much value do
you think there is in trying to change the way things are around
here?" We also asked their ideas for change: Do you think there
are many things that you can do to change the way things are around
here or do you feel that there is really little or nothing that you
can do to effect change? Table 8 shows that in both measures the
self-instructional group appeared significantly improved relative
to the other groups. On a measure of perceptions of social relationships (family, friends, other residents), there were no significant differences on the change scores for any group. On a measure
of perceived changes in health (hearing, vision, appetite), there
were also no significant changes for any group from pre- to post-
intervention.

Next we measured their activity in several ways. First we
assessed the percentage of time they spent in various activities
grouped as active or passive. These were determined from time
sampling by observers blind to experimental hypotheses. A composite
score for passive represented the percentage of time that the
resident was observed watching people sitting and doing nothing or
sleeping and/or lying down. A composite score for active represented
the percentage of time that the resident was observed actively
participating in activities, or exercising. The data in Table 8
show a smaller percentage of passive activities and a greater
percentage of active participation for the self-instruction subjects.
When we examined staff ratings of activity, however, there were no
significant differences between groups in change scores. It is
interesting that the staff was not aware that changes were actually
occurring. Finally we measured participation in three planned
activities (jelly bean guessing contest, a fall foliage ride, Mystic
Aquarium trip). Again, these direct observations showed the most
active participation in the cognitive coping skills, self-instruction group.

The staff was also asked to evaluate the patients' adjustment
along several bipolar adjective dimensions. A composite of items
including active-passive, happy-sad, sociable-unsociable, vigorous-
listless, and self-initiating-dependent, showed a reliable improvement for the self-instructional group, as is indicated in Table 8.

It is interesting that for these subjects, who were much less
ill than participants in our earlier studies, the simple admonition
to take more responsibility for day-to-day decision making was
insufficient to increase coping responses. It appears that only the
specific training procedures for self-regulation skills were effective in this population.

The data presented thus far suggest that the self-instructional
group felt more in control and was clearly engaged in more active
behavior. But these data alone do not demonstrate that they were
eliminating or reducing their problems better or that they were
experiencing less stress. A second set of measures permitted us to
make these assessments.

A list of 50 problems experienced by persons in nursing home
settings was generated from our prior research. Each subject in the
study was given two packs of cards to sort, each pack containing
all 50 problems. The first pack was sorted into five piles to
indicate the frequency with which they experienced the problem (from
"never" to "constantly"). The second pack, presented in a different
random order, was sorted on the basis of how bothersome or distres-
sing each problem was, when it occurred (from "extremely bad" to
"no bother").

A more global assessment of perceived stress was also obtained.
Following Pearlin and Schooler (1978), we asked subjects the same
question five times with one of five different adjectives each time.
The question was, "When you think of your day-to-day life here,
how_____do you feel?" and the adjectives read in place of
the blank were tense, upset, worried, unhappy, or frustrated. The
first measure, the problem-stress index was computed by multiplying
the frequency by the intensity score for a problem and summing across
problems for each individual. The second measure, the perceived
stress index, was computed by summing across the scores of the five
general stress questions.

It is clear from the data in Table 9 that the coping skills
instruction had a strong effect in reducing the problem-stress index.
This group showed increased ability to eliminate or modify conditions
giving rise to their problems because the frequency component of the
index, as well as the intensity component, was greatly reduced.
Interestingly, the perceived stress index shows that subjects in
all groups except the no-treatment controls felt less stress after
the intervention than they did before. It appears that increased
attention alone may have a short-term stress reducing effect for
these individuals. However, again the change was greatest for the
coping skills group.

Next we asked whether feelings of reduced stress per se were
related to better health-relevant outcomes or whether the coping

TABLE 9

CHANGE SCORES IN PRE- TO POST-INTERVENTION MEASURES ON STRESS INDICES

	Self-instruction	Atten-tion control	No treat-ment control	Responsi-bility induced	F	p
Problem stress index						
Pre	1264.6	1343.3	1402.3	1298.2		
Post	812.4	1238.3	1463.7	1202.8		
(Change)	(452.2)*	(105.0)**	(-61.4)***	(95.4)**	5.62	<.01
Perceived stress index						
Pre	19.4	18.7	19.1	17.8		
Post	14.0	15.3	18.7	14.6		
(Change)	(5.0)*	(3.4)*	(0.4)**	(3.2)*	3.55	<.03

Note: Numbers with different asterisks (*, **, ***) are significantly different from one another.

skills group would have advantages greater than those resulting from
perceived stress reduction alone. We believed that the most critical
test of the efficacy of these coping skills would be found in
measures of pituitary adrenal activity for several reasons.

First, the activation of the pituitary-adrenal system in
response to stress, leading to elevated levels of corticosteroids,
has been well documented, although specification of its exact consequences and antecedent conditions has been greatly debated (Hennessy,
King, McClure and Levine, 1977; Levi, 1972; Mason, 1968; Selye, 1973;
Tennes, Downey and Vernadakis, 1977; Wolff, Friedman, Hofer, and Mason
1964). Further, there is considerable work that relates reduced
adrenocortical activity to the success of a variety of coping mechanisms (i.e., the extent to which they are effective for a particular
individual (e.g., Hamburg and Adams, 1967; Levine, Goldman, and
Coover, 1972; Lipowski, 1970; and Wolff et al. 1964). And finally,
there may be factors related to aging per se that influence
pituitary adrenal responses to stress and coping (Timiras, 1972).
For example, numerous studies have shown that the rates of secretion
and metabolism of adrenocortical hormones decline with age, possibly
in relation to decreases in weight and alterations in tissue components of the cortex (Grad, Kral, Payne and Berenson, 1967; Romanoff,
Morris, Welch, Grace and Pincus, 1963; Serio, Piolanti, Capelli,
Magistris, Ricci, Anzalone and Giusti, 1969). It has also been
reported that cortisol may disappear from circulation of older
subjects at a slower rate (West, Brown, Simons, Carter, Kumagai
and Englert, 1961).

Many deaths in elderly persons can be attributed to a general
weakening of the immune system. Recent data have suggested that
elevated levels of cortisol can hurt the immune system since
corticosteroids display immunosuppressive properties (Gabrielson
and Good, 1967). Indeed, in mice there appears to be an inverse
relationship between plasma corticosterone level and the capacity
of the spleen to synthesize antibodies (Gisler, 1974). In healthy
organisms there are usually homeostatic regulatory mechanisms
effectively counteracting the suppressive properties of corticosteroids (Northley, 1965; Rose and Sabiston, 1971; and Solomon,
1969). But in chronically ill or aged individuals, homeostatic
regulatory mechanisms may be less effective (Timiras, 1972). Thus
stress without effective coping may have an even more debilitating
effect on health in elderly persons, especially if they are also
ill, through its effects on the pituitary adrenal system. This
would occur because the magnitude of the pituitary adrenocortical response to stress becomes greater with aging and environmental uncontrollability might exacerbate this condition. To test
this question, and how effective coping might influence the process,
we measured hypothalamo-pituitary adrenal activity by means of
24-hour urine samples. Three months prior to and four to six
weeks after the intervention phase, urine was collected for free

cortisol (UFC) measurement for 24 hours from 10:00 a.m. to 10:00 a.m.
Cortisol was measured in urine by radioimmunoassay.

Two things are very significant about the cortisol data presented
in Table 10. First is the initial high level of UFC of the whole
sample. Testing healthy active adults, Sokoloff and Hilderbrand
(1977) report a mean value of 20.6 µg/24° for females and 28.9 µg/24°
for males. The upper normal daily limit of UFC excretion is approximately 100 µg (Carroll, Curtis, Davies, Mendels and Sugerman, 1976).
The only other group where there appears to be such high mean levels
on a chronic basis is depressed patients who average 90.1 µg/24°
(Carroll et al., 1976).

Second is the fact that all groups, except the no-treatment
group, showed a significant reduction following the interventions.
It should be recalled from the previous table that perceived stress
was also reduced in all three groups. Thus it may appear that
anything we do can initially decrease perceived stress and cortisol
levels in these subjects. However, before reaching this conclusion,
let us reconsider the earlier data, which suggested that only the
self-instructional group showed greater coping responses, increased
problem-solving activity, and reduced stress from actual problems.
Moreover, individual, within-group correlations indicate that it
was only for this group that increased perceived control and
increased problem-solving activity were strongly and significantly
related to decreases in urinary free cortisol levels (r = .62 and
.54, respectively). Finally, we have just completed collecting data
from a one-year follow-up of these subjects and the cortisol and
perceived stress levels are back up to baseline for everyone except
the self-instructional group. Thus it appears that long-term
benefits are mediated by learning effective coping skills even though
there is some initial benefit for everyone. Currently we are following subjects beginning in the period immediately prior to their
entering the nursing home and taking many more endocrine and
behavioral measures. The goal is to link specific endocrine changes
or patterns of change (cf., Mason, 1971) with specific health-
relevant outcomes.

SIGNIFICANCE OF PITUITARY ADRENAL RESPONSIVENESS IN AGING

Let us conclude by putting our findings in perspective with
other data reported in this volume. Levine and his colleagues
(Hennessy et al., 1977; Levine et al., 1972) have demonstrated that
the pituitary adrenal system responds not only to aversive stimuli
but to changes in environmental contingencies and feedback.
Effective coping requires contingent feedback which should affect
(and lower) corticosteroid level, and it does so in our coping
skills group, over the long-term. According to Ursin, Badia
and Levine (1978), the pituitary adrenal system does not habituate
with experience (as the autonomic system does). It gets actively

TABLE 10

CHANGE SCORES IN PRE- POST- MEASURES ON HEALTH INDICES

	Self-instruction	Atten-tion control	No treat-ment control	Responsi-bility induced	F	p
Physicians' composite ratings						
Pre	26.11	23.88	25.00	23.89		
Post	38.33	25.34	24.44	30.44		
(Change)	(12.22)	(1.47)	(-0.56)	(6.55)	4.62	<.02
Urinary free cortisol (μg/24°)						
Pre	112.0	100.8	107.0	108.7		
Post	62.0	62.5	121.5	62.7		
(Change)	(50.0)	(38.3)	(-14.5)	(46.0)	3.38	<.05

suppressed by informational feedback and control. This is a
significant point, because we are not simply dealing with a
reduction to baseline, but an active suppression of this system as
a result of manipulations involving control and active coping. Such
suppression could be life sustaining for elderly persons with
cortisol levels as high as those in our sample.

To confirm the relationship between explicit contingency training and suppression of corticosteroids in elderly persons, we
conducted another nursing home study (Rodin).* We reasoned that the
requirements for a strong test of the hypothesis were first, that the
person has repeated exposures to the same stressor; and second, that
the characteristics of the stressor remain constant such that if
physiological changes do occur, they would be a function of the
subject's reaction to the stressor and not to a change in the stressor
itself. We decided to focus once again on the nurse-patient interaction as the stress provoking stimulus, since it was one of the
most high frequency-high intensity problems that patients reported.

There were five experimental conditions to which residents were
assigned at random when they entered the nursing home. For one full
week, the following procedures were then followed. In the first
condition--control with information feedback--they were again given
the opportunity to control the time when the nurse came to their
room. After they called but before the nurse entered, an aide came
and gave them feedback about why this was a good or bad time to call
the nurse, what kinds of things the nurse usually has to do during
that time period, and what other demands there were, for example.
The information thus gave them feedback about the utility of the
control response and the best time to make it. The aide then called
the nurse to the subject's room in order to keep nurses blind to
experimental condition, thus keeping their behavior constant.

In another condition--control with no informational feedback--
patients were allowed to exercise control and were then visited
by the aide and then the nurse, but they were not given the explicit
feedback just described. In the third condition--no control with
information feedback--they had visits by the nurse and the nurse's
aide yoked in number to those received by subjects with control and
feedback, and the nurse's aide gave them actual feedback, e.g.,
when it would be a good time to see the nurse, why the nurse was
busy, and so forth. The fourth condition was a no control-no information feedback group, yoked to subjects in the control-no feedback
group for number of visits. Finally there was a no treatment group.
To summarize, everyone was visited by the nurse and the aide about
the same number of times since amount of calling was relatively
equal. The only difference was whether the visit was controllable

---

*Rodin, J., 1979, Control and informational feedbacks: Effects on
  health and adjustment, unpublished ms., Yale University.

or not and whether there was informational feedback provided that
was contiguous with that event. Preliminary analyses suggest that
the group showing the greatest suppression was the control with
informational feedback; and the next best group, but showing
reliably less suppression, was the group given no control but given
feedback. Thus we may conclude that feedback regarding the efficacy
of one's responses seems to be an important variable in suppressing
pituitary adrenal activity for elderly nursing home residents. The
significance of this finding for their health and longevity is
currently being investigated.

To conclude, I would only like to note that I have no doubt
that there are real and very profound biological changes that do
occur with aging; I am only asking that we critically evaluate how
many and which ones. This is especially crucial now because it is
becoming dramatically apparent that presumably objective physical
conditions, such as illness and health, are greatly influenced by
subjective perceptual dimensions and by the feedback that one
receives from attempts at coping. Attributional processes, feelings of control, the efficacy of one's coping responses--all of
these seem to affect the likelihood of developing and of sustaining
a variety of medical disorders. Not only have these facts radically
altered our concepts of health and disease, but they are beginning
to have a profound effect on the nature of medical practice itself.
Aside from their practical significance, I think these studies
elaborating the role of control and feedback show that theory can
also evolve in naturalistic settings that were not specially
contrived for the purpose of testing theory.

REFERENCES

Adler, A, 1929, "The Science of Living," Greenburg, New York.
Averill, J. R., 1973, Personal control over aversive stimuli and
     its relationship to stress, Psychol. Bull., 80:286.
Ball, T. S., and Vogler, R. E., 1971, Uncertain pain and the pain
     of uncertainty, Percept. Motor Skills, 33:1195.
Baron, R., and Rodin, J., 1978, Perceived control and crowding
     stress, in: "Advances in Environmental Psychology," A. Baum,
     J. E. Singer, and S. Valins, eds., Erlbaum, Hillsdale, NJ.
Birren, J., 1958, Aging and psychological adjustment, Rev. Ed. Res.,
     28:475.
Bengston, V. L., 1973, Self-determination: A social and psycholog-
     ical perspective on helping the aged, Geriatrics, 28:118.
Bowers, K. S., 1968, Pain, anxiety, and perceived control, J. Cons.
     Clin. Psychol., 32:596.
Butler, R., 1967, Aspects of survival and adaptation in human
     aging, Am. J. Psychiat., 123:1233.
Campbell, D. T., and Fiske, D. W., 1959, Convergent and discrim-
     inant validation by the multitrait-multimethod matrix, Psychol.
     Bull., 56:81.

Carroll, B. J., Curtis, G. C., Davies, B. M., Mendels, J., and Sugerman, A. A., 1976, Urinary free cortisol excretion in depression, Psychol. Med., 6:43.

deCharms, R., 1968, "Personal Causation: The Internal Affective Determinants of Control," Academic Press, New York.

Dohrenwend, B. S., and Dohrenwend, B. P., 1974, "Stressful Life Events: Their Nature and Effects," Wiley and Sons, New York.

Gabrielson, A. E., and Good, R. A., 1967, Chemical suppression of adaptive immunity, Adv. Immun., 6:91.

Gisler, R. H., 1974, Stress and the hormonal regulation of the immune response in mice, Psychother. Psychosom., 23:197.

Glass, D. C., 1977, Stress, behavior patterns, and coronary disease, Am. Sci., 65:177.

Gould, R., 1972, The phases of adult life: A study in developmental psychology, Am. J. Psychiat., 129:521.

Grad, B., Kral, V. A., Payne, R. C., and Berenson, J., 1967, Plasma and urinary corticoids in young and old persons, J. Geron., 22:66.

Hamburg, D. A., and Adams, J. E., 1967, A perspective on coping behavior: Seeking and utilizing information in major trans- itions, Arch. Gen. Psychiat., 12:277.

Harris, L., 1975, "The Myth and Reality of Aging in America," National Council on Aging, Washington.

Hennessy, J. W., King, M. G., McClure, T. A., and Levine, S., 1977, Uncertainty, as defined by the contingency between environ- mental events, and the adrenocortical response of the rat to electric shock, J. Comp. Physiol. Psychol., 91:1447.

Holmes, T. H., and Rahe, R. H., 1967, The social readjustment rating scale, J. Psychosom. Res., 11:213.

Houston, B. K., 1972, Control over stress, locus of control, and response to stress, J. Personal. Soc. Psychol., 21:249.

Johnson, J. E., 1975, Stress reduction through sensation information, in: "Stress and Anxiety," I. G. Sarason and C. D. Spielberger, eds., Wiley and Sons, New York.

Kanfer, F., and Seider, M. L., 1973, Self control: Factors enhanc- ing tolerance of noxious stimulation, J. Personal. Soc. Psychol., 25:381.

Klemp, G. O., and Rodin, J., 1976, Effects of uncertainty, delay and focus of attention on reactions to an aversive stimulation, J. Exp. Soc. Psychol., 12:416.

Langer, E., and Rodin, J., 1976, The effects of choice and enhanced personal responsibility for the aged: A field experiment in an institutional setting, J. Personal Soc. Psychol., 34:191.

Leaf, A., 1973, Threescore and forty, Hosp. Pract., 34:70.

Lefcourt, H. M., 1973, The function of the illusions of control and freedom, Am. Psychol., 28:417.

Levi, L., 1972, Stress and distress in response to psychosocial stimuli, A. Med. Scandin., Sup. 528:1.

Levine, S., Goldman, L., and Coover, G. D., 1972, Expectancy and the pituitary-adrenal system, in: "Physiology, Emotion, and Psychosomatic Illness," ASP, Amsterdam.

Lieberman, M., 1965, Psychological correlates of impending death: Some preliminary observations, J. Geron., 20:181.

Lipowski, Z. J., 1970, Physical illness, the individual and the coping process, Psychiat. Med., 1:91.

Mason, J. W., 1968, A review of psychoendoendocrine research on the pituitary-adrenal cortical system, Psychosom. Med., 30:576.

Mason, J. W., 1971, A re-evaluation of the concept of 'non-specificity' in stress theory, J. Psychiat. Res., 8:323.

McMahon, A. W., and Rhudick, P. J., 1964, Reminiscing: Adaptational significance in the aged, Arch. Gen. Psychiat., 10:292.

Meichenbaum, D., 1974, Self-instructional strategy training: A cognitive prosthesis for the aged, Hum. Dev., 17:273.

Meichenbaum, D., 1977, "Cognitive-behavior Modification," Plenum Press, New York.

Neugarten, B., and Gutman, D., 1958, Age-sex roles and personality in middle age: A thematic apperception study, Psychol Mon., 72:17.

Northey, W. T., 1965, Studies on the interrelationship of cold environment, immunity and resistance to infection. I. Qualitative and quantitative studies on the immune response, J. Immun., 94:649.

Pearlin, L. I., and Schooler, C., 1978, The structure of coping, J. Heal. Soc. Behav., 19:2.

Pennebaker, J. W., and Skelton, J. A., 1978, Psychological parameters of physical symptoms, Personal. Soc. Psychol. Bull., 4:524.

Pervin, L. A., 1963, The need to predict and control under conditions of threat, J. Personal., 31:570.

Pranulis, M., Dabbs, J., and Johnson, J., 1975, General anesthesia and the patient's attempts at control, Soc. Behav. Personal., 3:49.

Rodin, J., 1978, Somatopsychics and attribution, Personal. Soc. Psychol. Bull., 4:531.

Rodin, J., and Langer, E., 1977, Long-term effect of a control-relevant intervention, J. Personal. Soc. Psychol., 35:897.

Rodin, J., 1976, Crowding, perceived choice and response to controllable and uncontrollable outcomes, J. Exp. Soc. Psychol., 12:564.

Rodin, J., and Langer, E., in press, The effects of labeling and control on self-concept in the aged, J. Soc. Issues.

Romanoff, L. P., Morris, C. W., Welch, P., Grace, M. P., and Pincus, G., 1963, Metabolism of progesterone-4-C^{14} in young and elderly men, J. Clin. End. Metab., 23:286.

Rose, J. E. M. St., and Sabiston, B. H., 1971, Effect of cold exposure on the immunologic response of rabbits to human serum albumin, J. Immun., 107:339.

Seligman, M. E. P., 1975, "Helplessness," W. H. Freeman, San Francisco.

Selye, H., 1973, The evolution of the stress concept, Am. Sci., 61:692.

Serio, M., Piolanti, P., Capelli, G., Magistris, L., Ricci, F., Anzalone, M., and Giusti, G., 1969, The miscible pool and turnover rate of cortisol in the aged, and variations in relation to time of day, Exp. Geron., 4:95.

Sokoloff, R. L., and Hilderbrand, R. L., 1977, Radioimmunoassay of urinary free cortisol, Heal. Lab. Sci., 14:133.

Solomon, G. F., 1969, Stress and antibody response in rats, Int. Arch. All., 35:97.

Spasoff, R. A., Kraus, A. S., Beattie, E. J., Holden, D. E. W., Lawson, J. S., Rodenburg, M., and Woodcock, G. M., 1978, A longitudinal study of elderly residents of long-stay institutions: I. Early response to institutional care, Gerontologist, 18:281.

Staub, E., Tursky, B., and Schwartz, G. E., 1971, Self-control and predictability: Their effects on reactions to aversive stimulation, J. Personal. Soc. Psychol., 18:157.

Taylor, S., and Levin, S., in press, The psychological impact of breast cancer: Theory and practice, in: "Psychological Aspects Of Breast Cancer," A. Enelow, ed., Oxford University Press, London.

Tennes, K., Downey, K., and Vernadakis, A., 1977, Urinary cortisol excretion rates and anxiety in normal 1-year-old infants, Psychosom. Med., 39:178.

Timiras, P. S., 1972, "Developmental Physiology and Aging," Macmillan, New York.

Ursin, H., Baade, E., and Levine, S., 1978, "Psychobiology of Stress," Academic Press, New York.

Weiss, J. M., 1970, Somatic effects of predictable and unpredictable shock, Psychosom. Med., 32:397.

West, C. D., Brown, H., Simons, E. L., Carter, D. B., Kumagai, L. F., and Englert, E., 1961, Adrenocortical function and cortisol metabolism in old age, J. Clin. End. Metab., 21:1197.

Wolff, C. T., Friedman, S. B., Hofer, M. A., and Mason, J. W., 1964, Relationship between psychological defenses and mean urinary 17-OH-CS excretion rates: I. A predictive study of parents of fatally ill children, Psychosom. Med., 26:576.

PSYCHOBIOLOGICAL ASPECTS OF LIFE STRESS*

Marianne Frankenhaeuser

University of Stockholm

and Karolinska Institute, Sweden

The main theme of this paper is the study of psychological mediators of neuroendocrine response patterns in relation to psychosocial conditions. Our recent approaches to these problems will be reviewed against the background of earlier studies from our laboratory (cf. reviews by Frankenhaeuser, 1971, 1976, 1979a, b) and relevant work from other laboratories.

The notion guiding our approach to the study of stress and coping processes is that the effectiveness of psychosocial factors in arousing the sympathetic-adrenal medullary and pituitary-adrenal cortical systems is determined by the person's cognitive appraisal of the balance between the severity of the situational demands on the one hand, and his or her personal coping resources on the other (Frankenhaeuser, 1979b). Another key notion is that the neuroendocrine responses to the psychosocial environment reflect the emotional impact of this environment on the individual and that diverse environmental conditions may evoke the same neuroendocrine responses because they have a common psychological denominator (Frankenhaeuser, 1975a, b). These formulations are linked conceptually to Lazarus' theory (e.g., Lazarus, 1977) of stress and coping as dynamic, transactional processes, as well as with Mason's (1971) "specificity" concept, emphasizing the susceptibility of several neuroendocrine systems to the emotional component in different environmental conditions.

* This paper, prepared for the NATO Symposium on COPING AND HEALTH, held in Bellagio, Italy, March 26-30, 1979, is based on research funded by grants from the Swedish Medical Research Council (Project No. 997), the Swedish Work Environment Fund (Project No. 76/49) and the Swedish Council for Research in the Humanities and Social Sciences.

A characteristic feature of many of our studies is the combination of concepts and methods from psychobiology, social psychology,
and psychosomatic medicine in the study of stress and coping patterns
of persons under both laboratory and natural conditions. It is
hoped that such an integrative approach will facilitate the application of our results, particularly to problems of work environment
and work organization.

NEUROENDOCRINE CORRELATES OF ACHIEVEMENT, EFFORT, AND DISTRESS

The notion of controllability as a major "key to coping" will
be considered in relation to different parameters of achievement,
activation and involvement. The animal models of Seligman and his
coworkers (e.g., Overmier and Seligman, 1967; Seligman, Maier, and
Salomon, 1971), and Weiss (1968, 1970), and the Levine group
(e.g., Levine and Coover, 1976) form the basis of much of the
current research on human beings. In our human studies, to be
outlined below, emphasis has been placed on the dissociation
between sympathetic-adrenal and pituitary-adrenal responses to
controllable and noncontrollable situations.

Assessing Achievement Costs

In our studies of achievement stress, interest has been
focussed on how a person copes when confronted with a sudden
increase in task demand. In principle, he or she may adopt one of
two strategies, either maintaining performance at a constant level
by increasing effort, or keeping effort constant and letting
performance deteriorate. The former strategy exacts a higher
subjective cost as reflected in self-reports of effort and other
aspects of psychological involvement. The physiological cost will
be higher, too, as reflected in indices of, for example, endocrine
and autonomic arousal.

In general, the participants in our experiments, under
laboratory as well as natural conditions, choose to meet situational
demands by investing the effort needed to maintain a high performance
level, often showing a remarkable ability to "raise the body's
thermostat for defense" (Selye, 1974). An example is provided by
experiments in which a color-word conflict test (a modified form
of the Stroop test) was performed at two levels of difficulty, one
denoted "single conflict," the other "double conflict" (Frankenhaeuser and Johansson, 1976). In the latter case, where interfering
auditory color-words were added to those presented visually, the
mental load was markedly higher. This was reflected in higher self-
reports of perceived arousal as well as in higher adrenaline
excretion and heart rate. In other words, the subjects met the rise
in task demand by mobilizing bodily resources; under these circumstances, performance was unimpaired.

The picture was similar in experiments with noise stress
(Lundberg and Frankenhaeuser, 1978) where subjects performed mental
arithmetic during exposure to white noise of either 76 or 86 db(A).
As expected, more effort was invested in doing arithmetic at the
higher noise load, physiological arousal increased and performance
remained intact. The trend was the same for all arousal indices,
i.e., adrenaline, noradrenaline and cortisol excretion as well as
heart rate. However, in another noise experiment (Frankenhaeuser
and Lundberg, 1977), where the subjects' aspiration level was
intentionally lowered, they responded to a rise in noise intensity
by letting performance deteriorate; under these circumstances, the
increase in noise intensity was not accompanied by increased
physiological arousal. Thus, in all these instances, cognitive-
appraisal processes determined the intensity of the physiological
activation.

Data from different laboratories (e.g., Levi, 1972; Frankenhaeuser and Andersson, 1974; Fröberg, Karlsson, Levi, and Lidberg,
1975; O'Hanlon and Beatty, 1976; Ellertsen, Backer Johnsen, and
Ursin, 1978) indicate that, in healthy male persons, catecholamine
secretion tends to correlate positively with achievement. This
positive relationship holds for low to moderate stimulation but not
under conditions requiring rapid information processing (Frankenhaeuser, Nordheden, Myrsten, and Post, 1971). The fact that high
catecholamine secretion may be detrimental to performance in complex
tasks requiring selective attention may be interpreted in terms of
drive theory (Spence and Spence, 1966), according to which high drive
level interferes with the choice between competing response tendencies.
The results are also consistent with Easterbrook's (1959)
interpretation of the Yerkes-Dodson law in terms of a narrowing of
the range of cues utilized when arousal is high.

In male subjects the positive relationship between adrenaline
secretion and psychological efficiency at low to moderate stimulus
levels is not confined to performance in acute situations but applies
to intellectual ability in general (e.g., Johansson, Frankenhaeuser,
and Magnusson, 1973). There is, however, a distinct sex difference
(Collins and Frankenhaeuser, 1978b), correlations between
intellectual ability and catecholamine secretion tending to be low,
or even negative, in females. (Sex differences in catecholamine
secretion will be considered in the last section.)

The relationship between perceived effort and sympathetic-
adrenal medullary activation is well established, but little is
known about the possible modifying influence of affects that
accompany the effort. Will the endocrine profile be the same when
the feelings associated with the effort are predominantly pleasant
(engagement and interest) as when they are indicative if distress?
In other words, do our neuroendocrine techniques differentiate
between "effort without distress" and "effort with distress"?

This question was approached by pooling data from five laboratory experiments (all performed on the same 48 male and female university students) that differed with regard to both effort requirements and affective tone. Under one experimental condition subjects
were passive, watching a "non-engaging" movie, whereas under four
conditions they were active, performing either simple or complex
perceptual or sensorimotor tasks. (For full accounts, see
Frankenhaeuser, Lundberg and Forsman, 1978; Lundberg and Forsman,
1978.) In each experiment, sympathetic-adrenal activity was
assessed by fluorimetric analysis of urinary adrenaline and
noradrenaline (Euler and Lishajko, 1961; Andersson, Hovmöller,
Karlsson, and Svensson, 1974) and pituitary-adrenal activity by
radioimmunoassay of urinary cortisol (Ruder, Guy, and Lipsett, 1972;
Ficher, Curtis, Ganjam, Joshlin, and Perry, 1973). Responses on
the subjective level were assessed by magnitude estimates of effort,
interest, concentration, tenseness, tiredness, impatience, and
boredom. The five experiments took place at different times of the
day, and to eliminate the influence of diurnal variations in endocrine activity and psychological responsiveness, measurements under
each experimental condition were expressed as percentages of measurements obtained in "baseline" sessions at the same hour of a separate
day.

Product-moment correlations between mean scores in each variable
in each of the five conditions were submitted to separate factor
analyses for the male and female groups (Lundberg, in preparation).
Two orthogonal factors were extracted and subjected to varimax
rotation. The pattern of the loadings was almost identical in the
two sex groups. Factor I, which explained 53% of the variance for
the females and 50% for the males, was interpreted as a "distress"
factor with high loadings in variables indicative of negative affect
(boredom, impatience, irritation) and a moderately high loading in
cortisol excretion. Factor II, which explained 35% of the variance
for the females and 34% for the males, was interpreted as an "effort"
factor with high loadings in variables indicative of task involvement and preparedness (effort, concentration, tenseness) as well as
in adrenaline excretion. It is interesting to note the general
resemblance between these two factors and the "cortisol factor" and
"catecholamine factor" reported by Ursin, Baade, and Levine (1978)
in their study of parachutist trainees. The model proposed by Henry
and Stephens (1977) is also relevant in this context since it
emphasizes the association between, on the one hand, sympathetic-
adrenal activation and dominant, aggressive behavior patterns and,
on the other, pituitary-adrenal activation and subordinate, passive
behaviors.

Personal Control as a Determinant of Neuroendocrine Profile

One of the five experiments referred to above is of particular
interest in the present context, because it induced a concomitant
increase of adrenaline release and decrease of cortisol release

(Frankenhaeuser, Lundberg, and Forsman, 1978). Therefore a detailed account will be given of the psychological properties of this situation.

The experiment had been designed for examining neuroendocrine aspects of the role of personal control in stress and coping. Lack of personal control, when accompanied by feelings of fear and help-lessness, will generally activate both the pituitary-adrenal system (e.g., Sachar, 1975) and the sympathetic-adrenal system (e.g., Frank-enhaeuser, 1975a, b). A finding of particular interest is that the pituitary-adrenal system may be actively suppressed under conditions characterized by high levels of controllability and/or predictability (Coover, Ursin, and Levine, 1973; Vernikos-Danellis, Goldenrath, and Dolkas, 1975; Levine, 1978; Levine, Weinberg, and Ursin, 1978; Rodin this volume) or by strong psychological defenses (Friedman, Mason, and Hamburg, 1963).

In our study, great care was taken to create an achievement situation characterized by a high degree of personal control and feelings of competence and mastery. This was attained by starting each session with a preparatory period, in which the subject was encouraged to try out different stimulus rates in order to arrive at his or her "preferred-work pace," i.e., the pace perceived as optimal in terms of wellbeing as well as efficiency. The task did not begin until the subjects felt confident about their choice of pace for the subsequent period of sustained work. Every 5 min the subject was then given the opportunity to modify the stimulus rate so as to maintain an optimal pace throughout the 1-hour session. Hence, the situation was both predictable and controllable to a very high degree.

The results in Figure 1 show that, according to the subjects' self-reports, the experimental arrangements had been successful in creating a work situation where each person felt confident of his or her ability to predict and control the pace of work, and, at the same time, felt pleasantly challenged and motivated to perform well. In short, the situation was characterized by "confident task involve-ment." Under these conditions, sympathetic-adrenal activity increased from baseline ($p < .001$ for adrenaline and noradrenaline excretion), whereas pituitary-adrenal activity decreased ($p < .05$). When interpreted in terms of the psychological properties of the situation, the heightened catecholamine level reflects the challenge to perform well, while the lowered cortisol level reflects the experience of being in control of the situation.

According to our reasoning, the high controllability of the task was the chief reason why the effort that the subjects invested in their performance was associated with positive feelings only. In other words, challenging but controllable tasks are likely to induce effort without distress. On the physiological level this

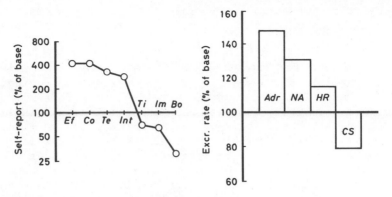

Figure 1

Mean values from an experimental condition where each subject
performed a choice-reaction task at his/her preferred pace,
expressed as percentages of baseline values obtained during an
inactivity period. Left diagram: Magnitude estimates (log scale) of
effort (Ef), concentration (Co), tenseness (Te), interest (Int),
tiredness (Ti), impatience (Im), and boredom (Bo). Right diagram:
Adrenaline (Adr) and noradrenaline (NA) excretion, heart rate (HR),
and cortisol (CS) excretion. Based on Frankenhaeuser, Lundberg,
and Forsman, 1978.

means that catecholamine secretion will rise, whereas cortisol
secretion may be actively suppressed.

Further support for this view was obtained in an experiment
concerned with coping under conditions of control versus no-control
over noise intensity (Lundberg and Frankenhaeuser, 1978). In a
situation where the subjects performed mental arithmetic under noise
exposure, every other subject was offered a choice between noise
intensities, while the next subject, serving as his yoked partner,
had to submit to the same noise. As predicted, the group as a whole
experienced more discomfort and secreted more cortisol when lacking
control. An interesting feature of the results was that the
participants tended to respond to the control versus no-control
situation in accordance with their general expectations about control
as assessed by the Internal-External Locus of Control Scale (Rotter,
1966). Thus, lacking control appeared to be more aversive to
"internals" than to "externals." This suggests that stress responses
to non-controllable situations may be related to the extent to which

persons generally tend to perceive life events as lying beyond or
within their sphere of influence.

Coping and Noncoping in Type-A Persons

Epidemiological investigations have provided convincing support
for the view that the rushed, competitive and achievement-oriented
behavior pattern, labelled Type A, constitutes a major independent
risk factor for coronary heart disease (e.g., Rosenman, Brand, Sholtz,
and Friedman, 1976). The Type A pattern is still an essentially
descriptive notion, and the factors linking this behavior pattern
to coronary heart disease have not yet been identified, although high
catecholamine levels associated with achievement striving are
generally assumed to play a significant part. On the psychological
level, Glass (1977) points to the fear of losing control as a major
threat in the lives of Type A persons. So far, few studies have
compared Type A and Type B subjects with regard to their neuroendocrine
and cardiovascular responses to acute environmental demands, and the
results are equivocal. For example, levels of plasma noradrenaline
were higher in Type As than in Type Bs during competitive, physical
activities (Friedman, Byers, Diamant, and Rosenman, 1975), whereas
studies in our laboratory (Lundberg and Forsman, 1979) showed no
consistent differences in urinary catecholamines during task
activities requiring either prolonged vigilance or rapid information
processing. Interactions between sex and coronary-prone behavior
have also been reported (Manuck, Craft, and Gold, 1978), suggesting
that Type A males, but not females, increase their systolic pressure
in response to a demanding cognitive task.

Insofar as controllability is a significant psychological
concept in coronary-prone behavior, the comparison of stress and
coping responses between Type A and Type B persons in our high-
controllability situation (described above) should yield interesting
information. We wanted to know whether the rush and time urgency
characteristic of Type As would manifest itself in their choosing
a faster work pace than Type Bs and, if so, whether the faster
tempo of the Type A persons would be reflected on the physiological
level.

Figure 2 shows choice of work pace, reaction time, and number
of correct responses over a one-hour session for a total group of
48 male and female subjects, classified as Type A or Type B persons
on the basis of their answers to a Swedish version of Jenkins'
Activity Survey (Lundberg, 1979). Since the sex differences were
negligible, males and females were treated together. As expected,
there were distinct differences in achievement behavior between
the Type A and Type B groups. Not only did the Type-A persons
select a faster work pace (p < .05) thus subjecting themselves to
a greater total work load. They also coped more effectively with
their load than did the Type-B persons with their lesser load.

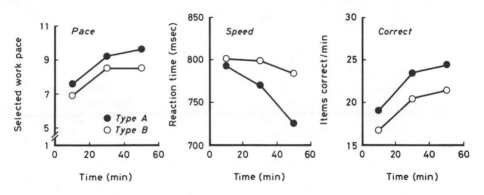

Figure 2

Successive mean scores for Type-A and Type-B subjects for different aspects of performance on a 1-hour choice-reaction task, i.e., self-selected work pace (max. pace=11), reaction time, and number of correct responses. Based on Frankenhaeuser, Lundberg and Forsman, 1978.

Thus, Type As responded faster to individual stimuli (p < .05), yet maintained a higher level of accuracy and hence, achieved a larger number of correct responses in the time allowed (p < .05).

According to self-reports, the superior performance of the Type A persons was not associated with greater costs on the subjective level. For example, the increase in effort from baseline to experimental condition was of the same magnitude in As as in Bs. Nor was there any appreciable difference between Type A and Type B persons with regard to sympathetic-adrenal or pituitary-adrenal activation (Figure 3). It is worth noting, however, that the data do not cover possible aftereffects and, hence, do not tell us whether the Type As took longer to "unwind" and return to base-line. Data from other investigations (Rissler, 1977) suggest that this may have been the case.

We interpret our results as showing that the Type A person, when in control of the situation, sets his or her standards high, copes effectively with the self-selected heavy load, and does so without mobilizing excessive physiological resources. There is an interesting parellel between this experimental illustration of how Type As cope with an acute work load and epidemiological data (Jenkins, Zyzanski, and Rosenman, 1971; Kenigsberg, Zyzanski,

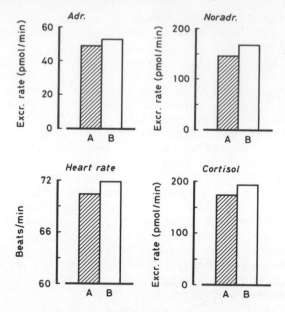

Figure 3

Mean values for adrenaline and noradrenaline excretion, heart rate, and cortisol excretion for Type-A and Type-B subjects. Based on Frankenhaeuser, Lundberg and Forsman, 1978.

Jenkins, Wardwell, and Licciardello, 1974) showing that persons high in "job involvement," i.e., one of the major components of Type-A behavior, had a relatively low incidence of coronary heart disease (cf. Lundberg, 1979). This suggests that conditions calling for effort may be potentially harmful primarily when they evoke feelings of distress, whereas conditions characterized by effort without distress may be less threatening to health. Our data point to controllability as a major key to coping without distress. Support for this view comes both from the laboratory studies reviewed above and from studies of people exposed to job stress in real-life, to be considered in the next section.

The "model of job strain" developed by Karasek (1979) is directly relevant in this context. According to this model,

supported by recent national survey data from Sweden and the United
States, it is the combination of low decision latitude and heavy
job demands, rather than either condition by itself, that leads to
mental strain.

Our suggestion that Type As are generally not worn out by their
heavy work load as such, calls for a search for other behavioral or
life-style characteristics that might contribute to their vulnerability to coronary heart disease. Recent data (Frankenhaeuser,
Lundberg, and Forsman, 1979) point to the lack of strategies for
coping with non-work conditions as a major weakness of the Type A
person. We found that Type B subjects were consistently less aroused
(according to self-reports and physiological indices) when asked to
remain unoccupied in the laboratory than when asked to do arithmetic
under noise exposure. In contrast, Type A persons tended to be equally
or more aroused when deprived of work than when given work to do.
In line with this general tendency to rebel against passivity,
Type As secreted significantly more cortisol than Type Bs during
a prolonged vigilance task, but not during rapid information
processing (Lundberg and Forsman, 1979).

JOB DEMAND, JOB SATISFACTION, AND HEALTH

Our approach to stress in working life (Frankenhaeuser and
Gardell, 1976) has been guided by the notion that the causes
underlying maladjustment and work-related illness can be better
understood if one integrates concepts and methods from psychobiology
and social psychology. Another basic notion is that psychologically
arousing stimuli and events may lead to long-term functional changes
in the sympathetic-adrenal system which, in turn, lead to irrevers-
ible pathophysiological changes (Folkow, 1975).

The social psychological approach emphasizes the chance of
exerting control over one's work pace as a prime determinant of
job satisfaction. In our psychobiological framework, control
over work pace implies that an ability to regulate stimulus input
and rate of responding helps the performer to maintain arousal at
an optimal level, thus minimizing the detrimental effects of underload and overload.

Neuroendocrine Aspects of the Work-Leisure Relationship

Research concerning the work-leisure relationship is of
immediate socio-political interest. Data obtained by social-
psychological methods indicate that ill-effects of psychologically
unrewarding work conditions tend to spread to life outside work
and, hence, may color the individuals total life situation (e.g.,
Gardell, 1976; Wilensky, 1979). The view that the worker would be
able to compensate for a dull and boring job by means of stimulating,
enriching activities during leisure hours, is being replaced by

new insights into the strong links between a job that is circum-
scribed and repetitious and a leisure that is passive and psychologically unrewarding. In other words, those individuals whose
work is restricted and monotonous are less likely to engage in
leisure activities requiring planning, cooperation, and effort.

Viewing our psychobiological research in this context, it
seemed that new knowledge could be gained by using neuroendocrine
techniques for monitoring the aftereffects and cumulative effects
of acute job demands. It seems reasonable to assume that the speed
with which a person "unwinds" after stressful transactions with the
environment will influence the total wear on his or her biological
system. Hence, the speed of unwinding is also likely to influence
the extent to which stress at work is carried over into leisure
time.

There are large interindividual differences in the temporal
pattern of adrenal-medullary stress responses. Experimental results
indicate (e.g., Johansson and Frankenhaeuser, 1973) that "rapid
adrenaline decreasers" tend to be psychologically better balanced
and more efficient in achievement situations than "slow adrenaline
decreasers." An equally important finding is that the time for
unwinding varies predictably with the individual's state of general
wellbeing. Thus, in a group of industrial workers, the proportion
of "rapid adrenaline decreasers" was significantly higher after than
before a vacation period, which had improved the workers' physical
and psychological wellbeing (Johansson, 1976).

An interesting example of slow unwinding was provided in a
recent study of female clerks in an insurance company (Rissler and
Elgerot, 1978). We were particularly interested in stress and
coping patterns during an extended period of overtime at work. The
extra time (an average of 73 hours per employee) was spread over
three months, but most of it occurred within a six-week period. No
new duties were involved, just an increase in the quantity of
regular work. The employees were free to choose the schedule for
their extra hours and most of them opted for work on Saturdays and
Sundays rather than doing more than eight hours on weekdays. Since
these women ordinarily devoted several weekend hours to household
duties, they faced a conflict between responsibilities at home and
at work. It was argued that the additional overtime load would call
for intense adaptive efforts, the effects of which would not
be restricted to the extra work hours, but would also manifest themselves during and after the ordinary workdays. The results supported
this hypothesis in that adrenaline excretion was significantly
increased throughout the overtime period, both during the day and
in the evening.

Figure 4 shows daytime and evening measures of adrenaline
excretion on nine Tuesdays, one before, six during, and two after
the overtime period. (Note that the extra hours were put in on

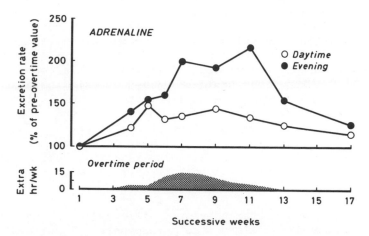

Figure 4

Mean adrenaline excretion in female clerks during the day and evening on nine occasions before, during, and after a period of overtime at work. Values obtained during and after the overtime period are expressed as percentages of those obtained before this period. Most of the extra hours were worked at weekends, and urine samples were obtained on Tuesdays. Based on Rissler and Elgerot, 1978.

Saturdays and Sundays.) The daytime values were determined in urine samples taken at work and the evening values in samples taken at home. Each value during and after the overtime period was expressed as a percentage of the corresponding daytime or evening value before the overtime period. As shown in the diagram, the adrenaline level was consistently elevated throughout the overtime period, and after this it declined towards the typical level for ordinary work conditions. The most remarkable finding was the pronounced elevation of adrenaline output in the evenings, which were spent under non-work conditions at home. This was accompanied by a markedly elevated heart rate as well as feelings of irritability and fatigue. Interview data confirmed that the women had not engaged in any demanding activities but had followed the instructions to relax, e.g., watching the television or listening to the radio. The Tuesday evening television programs were checked in retrospect for any particularly arousal-inducing qualities, but nothing was found that could account for the subjects' high arousal level. It is also worth noting the time lag between the work-load peak, in the

middle of the overtime period, and the peak for adrenaline excretion, which came at the very end of the period. In sum, these results indicate that the effects of overload may spread to leisure hours, and that they may accumulate gradually, which delays their full impact. We will return to this question when discussing sex roles and neuroendocrine activation.

Risk Factors in Machine-Controlled Work

Work on the assembly line, organized according to the principle of the "moving belt," is characterized by the machine system's rigorous control over the worker. The job is understimulating in the the sense that there are no options for variety in either pace or content, and the opportunities for social interaction are minimal. At the same time the work contains elements of overload, such as rapid pacing, coercion, and demands for sustained attention. The worker has no control over the pace, and his body posture and motility are narrowly restricted.

In a study of sawmill workers we focussed on a group classified as high-risk workers on the basis of the extremely constricted nature of their job. This group was compared with a control group of workers from the same mill, whose job was not as constricted physically and mentally.

Figure 5 shows successive measurements of catecholamine excretion, taken during an 8-hour workshift and expressed as percentages of baseline values obtained under work-free conditions at home. The average adrenaline excretion was significantly higher in the high-risk group than in the controls (p <.01). Furthermore, the time course was strikingly different for both amines, catechol-amine release decreasing towards the end of the workday in the control group, but increasing in the high-risk group. The differ-ence between the groups in the last measurements of the day was significant for both amines (p < .01 for adrenaline, < .05 for noradrenaline). In accordance with this rise in arousal in the course of an ordinary workday, interview data showed that inability to relax after work was a serious complaint in the high-risk group. It is noteworthy that absenteeism and frequency of psychosomatic symptoms were exceptionally high in this group, whereas cardiovas-cular symptoms were not. Since the mean age of both groups was 38 years, a comprehensive evaluation of the health data must await supplementary findings for older workers.

We assumed that the high stress level in the acute work situa-tion and the symptoms of failing health had a common origin in the repetitious, coercive nature of the job. In agreement with this, correlational analyses showed consistent, statistically significant relations between psychoneuroendocrine response patterns and job characteristics in terms of monotony, constraint, and lack of

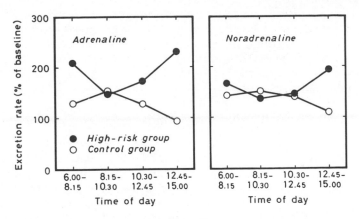

Figure 5

Successive mean values for adrenaline and noradrenaline excretion during an 8-hour workshift in two groups of sawmill workers. Values are expressed as percentages of baselines obtained under non-work conditions. Based on Frankenhaeuser and Gardell, 1976.

personal control (Johansson, Aronsson, and Lindström, 1978). These relationships were examined further by comparing sub-groups of workers who differed with regard to specific job characteristics, as rated by experts. The results, illustrated in Figure 6, indicate that stress, as reflected in adrenaline and noradrenaline excretion, was most severe when the job was highly repetitious, when the worker had to maintain the same posture throughout working hours, and when the work pace was controlled by the machine system. The subgroups were rather small and differences between them not statistically significant, but the trends were consistent and form a meaningful pattern. Self-reports of different aspects of job involvement and negative affect were consistent with the neuroendocrine pattern (Frankenhaeuser, 1979a).

When evaluating these results, two points deserve special notice. The first is that the members of the high-risk group had been selected for their demanding jobs because of their personal qualifications. In short, their jobs are highly skilled and of economic importance for the company which employs them. Hence, there are good reasons for assuming that these workers represent a positive selection at the time of their appointment to the job, not only with regard to skill, but also with regard to health, absenteeism, etc. The fact that the plant that we chose for our study was located in a rural district with extremely stable

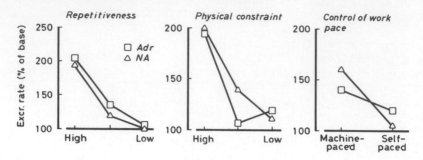

Figure 6

Mean values for adrenaline and noradrenaline excretion in a group of sawmill workers under conditions that differed in repetitiveness, physical constraint and control over work pace. Values obtained during work are expressed as percentages of baselines obtained under non-work conditions. Based on Johansson, Aronsson, and Lindström, 1978.

manpower, of course, increases the probability that symptoms of stress and ill health have been acquired in the present job rather than being due to stressors encountered in previous jobs, or to urban stressors or other factors not associated with work.

The other important point is that conditions in the sawmill are representative of a wide range of mass-production industries. Hence, our data point to potential uses of psychoneuroendocrine techniques in assessing the stressfulness of different aspects of technologically advanced work systems. In this context, one should note the successful outcome, in terms of increased job satisfaction without loss of effectiveness, of technological innovations in some large-scale plants (e.g., Volvo and Saab-Scania in Sweden) that now operate without conventional assembly lines. An important question, being considered in an ongoing study (Johansson and Gardell, in preparation), concerns the risks and benefits involved in the transition to completely automated production systems, where the repetitive, manual elements are taken over by machines and the workers are left with mainly supervisory controlling functions. Such a set-up increases the chances for an active, participatory work role. At the same time, however, it introduces new stress components associated with long, monotonous monitoring periods and with the abstract nature of the work. Possibly, psychoneuroendocrinological techniques may prove useful in identifying potential risk factors and in suggesting ways in which they can be avoided.

Sex Roles and Neuroendocrine Stress Patterns

The high adrenaline secretion associated with overtime work in the group of female clerks (see Figure 4) is particularly noteworthy since, in general, women are less prone than men to respond to achievement demands by increased catecholamine secretion (e.g., Frankenhaeuser, Dunne, and Lundberg, 1976; Frankenhaeuser, Rauste von Wright, Collins, von Wright, Sedvall, and Swahn, 1978). During rest and relaxation, sex differences in catecholamine excretion are generally slight (provided one allows for body weight) and it is only stressful and challenging situations that elicit consistent differences between the sexes. An important point is that the relatively lower sympathetic-adrenal activity of the females does not seem to be accompanied by inferior performance. Thus, on the average, females have consistently performed at least as well as males in all achievement situations to which our subjects have been exposed. Another interesting point is that, in a sample of university students, the correlation between adrenaline release and intellectual achievement was positive in males but negative in females (Collins and Frankenhaeuser, 1978a). Similarly, "overachievement" in school children was positively correlated with adrenaline output in boys, but not in girls (Bergman and Magnusson, 1979).

These psychoneuroendocrine sex differences suggest that the cost of adapting to achievement demands may be lower for females than for males. But why did the female clerks working overtime show the persistent elevation of adrenaline release in the evenings after work? It seems plausible that the heightened adrenaline secretion was not related to the job demands as such, but rather to the intrapsychic conflict associated with letting occupational duties "invade" the time ordinarily reserved for home and family. It is suggestive that not all the women increased their adrenaline output during the overtime period, and that those who did, reported being more "career oriented" than those who did not.

Data from related studies tell us that females who have adopted a "male work role" tend to respond to achievement demands by an increase in adrenaline secretion which we have found to be typical of males. This is true of female engineering students exposed to the same cognitive task as their male fellow students (Collins and Frankenhaeuser, 1978a) as well as female bus drivers exposed to the same traffic and passenger loads as their male colleagues (Frankenhaeuser, Rissler, and Aronsson, in preparation).

One cannot tell for certain to what extent a constitutional tendency to respond to stress and challenge in a "male-fashion" had influenced the vocational choice of the nontraditional females, and to what extent they had acquired a masculine way of responding as a consequence of being exposed to the same challenges as their male colleagues. However, it is suggestive that, as children, the female engineering students (according to retrospective reports)

showed a distinct preference for conventional girls' play activities (Collins and Frankenhaeuser, 1978b). Ongoing studies of neuro-endocrine stress responses in young children of both sexes and their parents may throw some new light on the causal relationships (Lundberg, Frankenhaeuser, deChateau, and Winberg, in preparation). Other studies under way that may illuminate this particular point are concerned with possible interactions between the secretion of sex hormones and catecholamines. Preliminary results indicate that catecholamine secretion during stress in postmenopausal women is not affected by estrogen substitution therapy (Frankenhaeuser, Hagenfeld, Collins, Hansson, and Eneroth, in preparation). This is in agreement with earlier studies showing that catecholamine excretion does not vary much during the menstrual cycle (Pátkai, Johansson and Post, 1974).

In sum, the picture to date suggests that psychological factors related to sex role are more important than biological factors as determinants of different neuroendocrine stress responses in males and females.

Insofar as elevated catecholamine levels are pathogenic, our findings have a bearing on relationships between sex-role patterns and health. It is noteworthy, however that some of the data reviewed above suggest that role conflict may add more to the stress than the job itself. If this is the case, the future sex differential in disease and mortality will be influenced by a number of factors related to sex-role patterns and equality between the sexes.

REFERENCES

Andersson, B., Hovmöller, S., Karlsson, C. -G., and Svensson, S., 1974, Analysis of urinary catecholamines: an improved auto-analyzer fluorescence method, Clinica Chimica Acta, 51:13.

Bergman, L. R. and Magnusson, D., 1979, Overachievement and catechol-amine output in an achievement situation, Psychosom. Med., 41:181.

Collins, A. and Frankenhaeuser, M., 1978a, Stress responses in male and female engineering students, J. Hum. Stress, 4:43.

Collins, A., and Frankenhaeuser, M., 1978b, Interaction of sex-related psychological qualities and psychophysiological stress responses, Report, Dept. Psychology, University of Stockholm, No. 542.

Coover, G., Ursin, H., and Levine, S., 1973, Corticosterone and avoidance in rats with basolateral amygdala lesions, J. Comp. Physiol. Psychol., 85:111.

Easterbrook, J. A., 1959, The effect of emotion on cue utilization and the organization of behaviour, Psychol. Rev., 66:183.

Ellertsen, B., Backer Jo..asen, T., and Ursin, H., 1978, Relationship between the hormonal responses to activation and coping, in: "Psychobiology of Stress: A Study of Coping Men," H. Ursin, E. Baade, and S. Levine, eds., Academic Press, New York, San Francisco, London.

Euler, U. S. v., and Lishajko, F., 1961, Improved technique for the fluorimetric estimation of catecholamines, Acta Physiol. Scand., 51:348.

Ficher, M., Curtis, G. C., Ganjam, V. K., Joshlin, L., and Perry, S., 1973, Improved measurement of corticosteroids in plasma and urine by competitive protein-binding radioassay. Clin. Chemistry 19:511.

Folkow, B., 1975, Vascular changes in hypertension: Review and recent animal studies, in: "Pathophysiology and Management of Arterial Hypertension," C. Berglund, L. Hansson and L. Werkö, eds., Lindgre & Söner, Stockholm.

Frankenhaeuser, M., 1971, Behavior and circulating catecholamines, Brain Res., 31:241.

Frankenhaeuser, M., 1975a, Experimental approaches to the study of catecholamines and emotion, in: "Emotions--Their Parameters and Measurement," L. Levi, ed., Raven Press, New York.

Frankenhaeuser, M., 1975b, Sympathetic-adrenomedullary activity, behaviour and the psychosocial environment, in: "Research in Psychophysiology," Ch. 4, P. H. Venables and M. J. Christie, eds., Wiley and Sons, New York, London, and Sydney.

Frankenhaeuser, M., 1976, The role of peripheral catecholamines in adaptation to understimulation and overstimulation, in: "Psychopathology of Human Adaptation," G. Serban, ed., Plenum Press, New York and London.

Frankenhaeuser, M., 1979a, Psychoneuroendocrine approaches to the study of emotion as related to stress and coping, in: "Nebraska Symposium on Motivation 1978," H. E. Howe and R. A. Dienstbier, eds., University of Nebraska Press, Lincoln.

Frankenhaeuser, M., 1979b, in press, Psychoneuroendocrine approaches to the study of stressful person-environment transactions, in: "Selye's Guide to Stress Research," H. Selye, ed., Van Nostrand Reinhold, New York.

Frankenhaeuser, M., and Andersson, K., 1974, Note on interaction between cognitive and endocrine functions, Percept. Mot. Skills, 38:557.

Frankenhaeuser, M., and Gardell, B., 1976, Underload and overload in working life: Outline of a multidisciplinary approach, J. Hum. Stress, 2:35.

Frankenhaeuser, M., and Johansson, G., 1976, Task demand as reflected in catecholamine excretion and heart rate, J. Hum. Stress, 2:15.

Frankenhaeuser, M., and Lundberg, U., 1977, The influence of cognitive set on performance and arousal under different noise loads, Motiv. Emo., 1:139.

Frankenhaeuser, M., Dunne, E., and Lundberg, U. 1976, Sex differences in sympathetic-adrenal medullary reactions induced by different stressors, Psychopharmacology, 47:1.

Frankenhaeuser, M., Lundberg, U., and Forsman, L., 1978, Dissociation between sympathetic-adrenal and pituitary-adrenal responses to an achievement situation characterized by high controllability: Comparison between Type A and Type B males and females, Report, Dept. Psychol., Univ. Stockholm, No. 540.

Frankenhaeuser, M., Lundberg, U. and Forsman, L., 1979, in press. Note on arousing Type A persons by depriving them of work, J. Psychosom. Res.

Frankenhaeuser, M., Nordheden, B., Myrsten, A. L., and Post, B., 1971, Psychophysiological reactions to understimulation and overstimulation, A. Psychol., 35:298.

Frankenhaeuser, M., Rauste von Wright, M., Collins, A., von Wright, J., Sedvall, G., and Swahn, C. G., 1978, Sex differences in psychoendocrine reactions to examination stress, Psychosom. Med., 40:334.

Friedman, M., Byers, S. O., Diamant, J., and Rosenman, R. H., 1975, Plasma catecholamine response of coronary-prone subjects (Type A) to a specific challenge, Metabolism, 24:205.

Friedman, S. B., Mason, J. W., and Hamburg, D. A., 1963, Urinary 17-hydroxy-corticosteroid levels in parents of children with neoplastic disease, Psychosom. Med., 25:364.

Fröberg, J. E., Karlsson, C. G., Levi, L., and Lidberg, L., 1975, Circadian rhythms of catecholamine excretion, shooting range performance and self-ratings of fatigue during sleep deprivation, Biol. Psychol., 2:175.

Gardell, B., 1976, Technology, alienation and mental health. Summary of a social psychological research programme on technology and the worker, A. Sociol., 19:83.

Glass, D. C., 1977, "Behavior Patterns, Stress, and Coronary Disease," Lawrence Erlbaum Assoc., Hillsdale, NJ.

Henry, J. P., and Stephens, P. M., 1977, "Stress, Health, and the Social Environment. A sociobiological approach to medicine," Springer, New York, Heidelberg and Berlin.

Jenkins, C. D., Zyzanski, S. J., and Rosenman, R. H., 1971, Progress toward validation of a computer-scored test for the Type-A coronary-prone behavior pattern, Psychosom. Med., 33:193.

Johansson, G., 1976, Subjective wellbeing and temporal patterns of sympathetic-adrenal medullary activity, Biol. Psychol., 4:157.

Johansson, G., Aronsson, G., and Lindström, B. O., 1978, Social psychological and neuroendocrine stress reactions in highly mechanized work, Ergonomics, 21:583.

Johansson, G., and Frankenhaeuser, M., 1973, Temporal factors in sympatho-adrenomedullary activity following acute behavioral activation, Biol. Psychol., 1:63.

Johansson, G., Frankenhaeuser, M., and Magnusson, D., 1973, Catecholamine output in school children as related to performance and adjustment, Scand. J. Psychol., 14:20.

Karasek, R. A., 1979, in press, Job characteristics and mental
        strain. Implications for job design, Admin. Sci. Quart.
Kenigsberg, D., Zyzanski, S. J., Jenkins, C. D., Wardwell, W. I.,
        and Licciardello, A. T., 1974, The coronary-prone behavior
        pattern in hospitalized patients with and without coronary
        heart disease, Psychosom. Med., 36:344.
Lazarus, R. S., 1977, Psychological stress and coping in adaptation
        and illness, in: "Psychosomatic Medicine: Current Trends and
        Clinical Applications," Z. J. Lipowski, D. R. Lipsitt, and
        P. C. Whybrow, eds., Oxford University Press, New York.
Levi, L., 1972, Stress and distress in response to psychosocial
        stimuli. Laboratory and real life studies on sympathoadreno-
        medullary and related reactions, A. Med. Scand., Suppl. 528.
Levine, S., 1978, Cortisol changes following repeated experiences
        with parachute training, in: "Psychobiology of Stress: A
        Study of Coping Men," H. Ursin, E. Baade, and S. Levine, eds.,
        Academic Press, New York, San Francisco and London.
Levine, S., and Coover, G. D., 1976, Environmental control and
        suppression of the pituitary-adrenal system, Psychol. Behav.,
        17:35.
Levine, S., Weinberg, J., and Ursin, H., 1978, Definition of the
        coping process and statement of the problem, in: "Psychobiology
        of Stress: A Study of Coping Men," H. Ursin, E. Baade, and
        S. Levine, eds., Academic Press, New York, San Francisco, and
        London.
Lundberg, U., 1979, in press, Type A behavior and its relation to
        personality variables in Swedish male and female university
        students, Scand. J. Psychol.
Lundberg, U., and Forsman, L., 1979, in press, Adrenal-medullary and
        adrenal-cortical responses to understimulation and overstimula-
        tion: Comparison between Type-A and Type-B persons, Biol. Psychol.
Lundberg, U., and Forsman, L., 1978, Adrenal-medullary and adrenal-
        cortical responses to understimulation and overstimulation:
        Comparison between Type-A and Type-B persons, Report, Dept.
        Psychol., Univ. Stockholm, No. 541.
Lundberg, U., and Frankenhaeuser, M., 1978, Psychophysiological
        reactions to noise as modified by personal control over
        stimulus intensity, Biol. Psychol., 6:51.
Manuck, S. B., Craft, S., and Gold., K. J., 1978, Coronary-prone
        behavior pattern and cardiovascular response, Psychophysiology,
        15:403.
Mason, J. W., 1971, A re-evaluation of the concept of "non-specifi-
        city" in stress theory, J. Psychiat. Res., 8:323.
O'Hanlon, J. F., and Beatty, J., 1976, Catecholamine correlates of
        radar monitoring performance, Biol. Psychol., 4:293.
Overmier, J. B., and Seligman, M. E. P., 1967, Effects of inescap-
        able shock upon subsequent escape and avoidance responding,
        J. Comp. Physiol. Psychol., 63:28.
Pátkai, P., Johansson, G., and Post, B., 1974, Mood, alertness and
        sympathetic-adrenal medullary activity during the menstrual
        cycle, Psychosom. Med., 36:503.

Rissler, A., 1977, Stress reactions at work and after work during a period of quantitative overload, Ergonomics, 20:13.

Rissler, A., and Elgerot, A., 1978, Stressreaktioner vid övertids-arbete (Stress reactions related to overtime at work), Rapporter, Report, Dept. Psychol., Univ. Stockholm, No. 23

Rosenman, R. H., Brand, R. J., Sholtz, R. I., and Friedman, M., 1976, Multivariate prediction of coronary heart disease during 8.5 year follow-up in the western collaborative group study, Am. J. Cardiol., 37:903.

Rotter, J. B., 1966, Generalized expectancies for internal versus external control of reinforcement, Psychol. Mono., 80 (Whole No. 609).

Ruder, H. J., Guy, R. L., and Lipsett, M. B., 1972, A radioimmuno-assay for cortisol in plasma and urine. J. Clin. Endocrinol. & Metabol., 35:219.

Sachar, E. J., 1975, Neuroendocrine abnormalities in depressive illness, in: "Topics in Psychoendocrinology," E. J. Sachar ed., Grune and Stratton, New York.

Seligman, M. E. P., Maier, S. F., and Solomon, R. L., 1971, Unpre-dictable and uncontrollable aversive events, in: "Aversive Conditioning and Learning," F. R. Brush ed., Academic Press, New York.

Selye, H., 1974, "Stress without Distress," Lippincott, Philadelphia and New York.

Spence, J. T., and Spence, K. W., 1966, The motivational components of manifest anxiety: Drive and drive stimuli, in: "Anxiety and Behavior," C. D. Spielberger ed., Academic Press, New York.

Ursin, H., Baade, E., and Levine, S., 1978, "Psychobiology of Stress: A Study of Coping Men," Academic Press, New York, San Francisco, and London.

Vernikos-Danellis, J., Goldenrath, W. L., and Dolkas, C. B., 1975, The physiological cost of flight stress and flight fatigue, U.S. Navy Med. J., 66:12.

Weiss, J. M., 1968, Effects of coping responses on stress, J. Comp. Physiol. Psychol., 65:251.

Weiss, J. M., 1970, Somatic effects of predictable and unpredictable shock, Psychosom. Med., 32:397.

Wilensky, H. L., 1979, in press, Family life cycle, work and the quality of life: Reflections on the roots of happiness, despair, and indifference in modern society, in: "Man and Working Life," B. Gardell and G. Johansson eds., Wiley and Sons, New York.

ADRENOCORTICAL RESPONSES OF HUMANS TO

GROUP HIERARCHY, CONFINEMENT AND SOCIAL INTERACTION

Joan Vernikos-Danellis

Biomedical Research Division
Ames Research Center, NASA
Moffet Field, CA

The response of the adrenal gland is the most widely used index of the presence of a stress response. Plasma corticosteroids show a well defined diurnal rhythm, with the peak occurring in the early morning hours in man and other diurnal animals whereas nocturnal rodents show their peak in the evening, at lights-off. In addition, the responsiveness of the adreno-cortical system to stimuli also varies diurnally. Sampling time therefore, becomes of fundamental importance in studies using plasma corticosteroids as an index of stress or other psychophysiological relationships. It should also be noted that the majority of the existing literature on the subject is derived from data obtained by testing and sampling in the morning hours, which coincides with the peak of the rhythm in man and diurnal primates, and the trough of the rhythm in rats, mice and nocturnal primates. Experimental conditions that may disturb this rhythm only compound the problem of reliable data interpretation.

Although previous work indicated that the light-dark cycle and possibly the sleep-wake cycle were the primary or only environmental cues entraining the plasma corticosteroid rhythm in both rats and humans (Critchlow, Liebelt, Bar-Sela and Mountcastle, 1963; Chiefetz, Gaffud and Dingman, 1968; Krieger and Ascoff, in press), more recent evidence suggests that a variety of other factors are similarly effective. For instance, it was found that in rats, the time of food or water presentation could override the entraining influence of the photoperiod (Johnson and Levine, 1973; Krieger, 1974; Krieger and Hauser, 1978). The relative importance of various cues as synchronizers of adrenocortical rhythmicity is still unresolved and particularly so in man.

The present studies were conducted to investigate the effect of
group interaction on the plasma cortisol levels and rhythms or normal
human subjects under conditions of constant light or in a regulated
photoperiod.

METHODS

Nine young, healthy, adult male volunteers, aged 20-25, were
used as the test subjects and were selected following extensive
physical and psychological examinations. They were divided into
three groups of three subjects. Two groups were confined in
acoustically attenuated rooms (North and South Rooms; 11 x 17 feet)
where the environment could be regulated. They were exposed for
periods of several days to either 16L:8D (lights-on at 0800; light
intensity 100±10 ft.c. (1,0764±107.6 lx) or continuous light
(24L:OD; light intensity 15 ft.c. (161.5 lx)). The third group
served as non-confined controls, and were exposed to 16L:8D throughout the study, with freedom to leave the immediate experimental area
during the day. The subjects in the two confinement rooms were
exposed to identical environmental conditions and were deprived of
all time cues. Meal times and composition (with caloric limitations
only) were ad libitum during the continuous light exposures.
Communications were limited to meal and sample collection information.
Meals and samples were passed back and forth through a two-way hatch.
Non-confined controls and confined subjects during the 16L:8D
exposures had the same meals and meal times (0900, 1300 and 1730 hr).
Food consisted of a balanced diet of 2,500 kcal/day.

Blood was drawn by the subjects themselves at 4-hr intervals,
by repeated venipuncture for 24-hr periods, at several time points
throughout the study. Plasma cortisol was determined by Murphy's
competitive protein binding radio-assay (1967) and expressed as
µg/100ml plasma. The time at which the peak plasma cortisol
concentration occurred was calculated from harmonic curves fitted
to each set of 24-hr data from each subject.

RESULTS AND DISCUSSION

Table 1 shows dominance ratings for each group of three
subjects from most (1) to least (3) dominant, and compares them with
their early morning plasma cortisol levels on the third day of the
study. Dominance hierarchies were assessed at the beginning of the
study using a variety of techniques including psychological test
measures on the FIRO-B, interaction counts, clinical data, self-
reports from the subjects and staff impressions. Subjects rated
most dominant in all cases had the lowest plasma cortisol levels on
the third day and vice versa. Although the differences among
subjects in the South room were very small, the Control group and
the North room showed as much as 4-5µg/100 ml plasma difference
between the highest and the lowest concentration of cortisol in the

TABLE I

		Subjects	Leadership Rating	Plasma Cortisol μg/100ml plasma
Day 3	Controls	WCC	1	11.7
		AMM	2	12.8
		GEB	3	15.6
	South Room	JSS	1	11.7
		RBP	2	12.0
		EMS	3	12.4
	North Room	DBW	1	9.4
		KAM	2	11.6
		RVG	3	14.6

Comparison of Plasma Cortisol Levels at 0800 of Day 3 to Leadership/Dominance Ratings in each Group of Three Subjects where 1 is most Dominant.

group. After 20 days none of the subjects in the confinement rooms differed from each other (Figure 1) indicating that once a stable social group is formed there are no differences in plasma cortisol among individuals. This occurred later in the controls (30 days) possibly because these subjects were free to interact with others during the day, thereby delaying the formation of a stable group. Numerous experiments in animals have attempted to correlate dominance with high or low plasma corticosteroid levels (Davis and Christian, 1957; Brain, 1972; Candland and Leshner, 1975) and conflicting reports exist in the literature. Since plasma corticosteroids increase in response to any novelty, it would be expected that the formation of a new group would also result in such a response. Thus corticosteroid levels would be expected to be increased for all the subjects in a group, regardless of dominance status. Figure 1 shows a gradual decline in the plasma cortisol levels over the course of the study in all three groups, although the subordinate subject may have been the slowest to stabilize within each group. The data agree with the recent evidence of Mendoza et al. (1979) who found that successive group formation in squirrel monkeys resulted in increased cortisol levels in all animals regardless of their status.

The occurrence of the daily peak in plasma cortisol in the subjects exposed to 16L:8D also bore no relationship to the hierarchy (Figure 2). In fact, it was remarkably consistent for the three

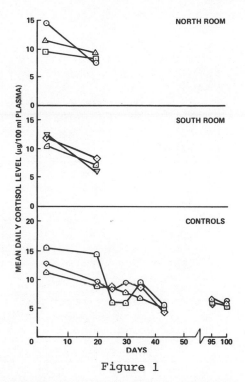

Figure 1

Changes in individual plasma cortisol levels (0800 sample) dur-
ing the course of the study. North Room: RVG = ○ , KAM = △ ,
DBW = □ ; South Room: EMS = ▽ , RBT = ◇ , JSS = ⬡ ; Controls:
GEB = ▽ , AMM = ◯ , WCC = △ .

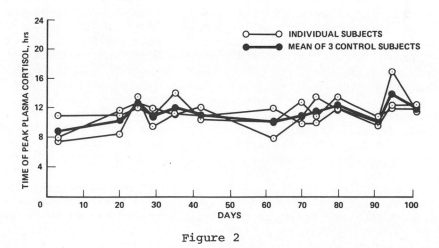

Figure 2

Time of occurrence of peak plasma cortisol level in the three
control subjects maintained in 16L:8D for 102 days.

control subjects over the 102 days of the study, occurring between 0800 and 1200 on 13 different days.

Exposing the two confined groups to constant light, resulted in a steady shift of the plasma cortisol peak (Figure 3). However, in spite of identical environmental conditions in the two rooms, the rate of phase shifting was significantly different for the two groups, although all three subjects within a group phase-shifted at a very similar rate. The subjects in the North room lost 0.691 hr/day and the subjects in the South room lost 0.37 hr/day. Thus although in all the subjects exposed to constant light the plasma cortisol rhythm appeared to be 'free-running' with respect to the environment (period longer than 24 hr), the presence of others in a group seemed to determine the extent to which this rhythm phase-shifted. This phenomenon of the effect of the group on biological rhythms is not singularly limited to the plasma cortisol rhythm, since the rhythms of body temperature and heart rate in these same subjects were similarly influenced by this group interaction (Winget et al., 1975). The importance of social cues in entraining biological rhythms has also been implied by Poppel (1968) and by Aschoff et al. (1971) who attempted to measure the endogenous period of the rhythms of two subjects housed together in continuous darkness for 4 days.

A free-running rhythm describes the endogenous rhythm with a period characteristic of the individual. This endogenous rhythm is believed to be measurable when all environmental factors which serve to synchronize rhythms to the 24 hr day are removed. By definition it should therefore be constant and reproducible whenever the individual is exposed to synchronizer-free environments. This hypothesis was tested in this study. After allowing the plasma cortisol rhythm to recover completely in 16L:8D in all subjects, the two confined groups were again exposed to constant light under conditions that were identical to their first exposure. Figure 3 shows the rate of phase-shifting in both groups was consistent with their previous exposure in that the North room subjects phase-shifted at a rate that was faster than that of the South room. However, the extent and the rate of their phase-shift was considerably less for all subjects during their second exposure to constant light. Since the major known synchronizers were absent in this study it must be concluded that social interaction can entrain the plasma cortisol rhythm in humans, and that man can adapt to repeated photo-periodic change since the degree of phase shifting was less the second time around. Body temperature and heart rate rhythms in these subjects also showed similar changes (Winget, Vernikos-Danellis and Beljan, unpublished observations).

The importance of social interaction within a group in regulating the plasma cortisol rhythm was further tested. A subject (C) who was in the South room during the two successive constant light exposures, had a plasma cortisol rhythm with a peak that shifted at

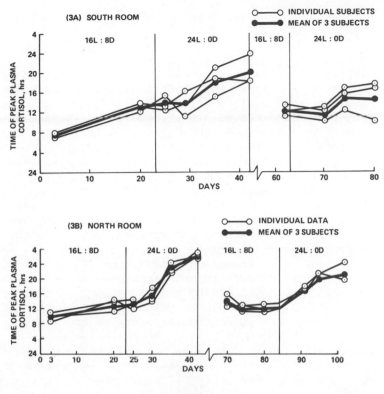

Figure 3

Effect of exposure to constant light (24L:0D) on two successive occasions of two groups of three subjects in South Room (3A) and
North Room (3B). Heavy line represents the mean of the data from the
3 subjects.

a slow rate and parallelled that of the other two members of his
group. In fact during his second constant light exposure he showed
almost no phase shift at all. The other two members of his group
were then replaced by two subjects from the North room and the
environment continued to be constant light. Figure 4 shows that
subject (C) now phase shifted at a rate that was faster than ever
before and paralleling the faster rate of the phase shift of the
other two members of his new group. What factor or which individual
determined the rate of phase-shift of the plasma cortisol rhythm in
constant light cannot be determined from these data. It is evident,
however, that the formation of a new group as well as its composition
affects both the level of plasma cortisol and its rate of desynchronization in a time-free environment. It could further be implied that
resynchronization to a new time environment could be accelerated by

appropriate interaction with a new social group. The importance of such information to occupations that involve shift work or time zone changes and even possibly to disease states characterized by rhythm desynchronization is self-evident.

It is interesting to note that following the formation of a group plasma cortisol levels continue to decrease, and after 30-40 days remain low. There is no evidence of stress at any time, in spite of continued exposure to a situation that is potentially difficult, with changing environmental conditions and changing of group composition. It would appear that following the formation of stable and predictable relationships within the group, the group is used as a coping system to protect and prevent further responses to environmental change.

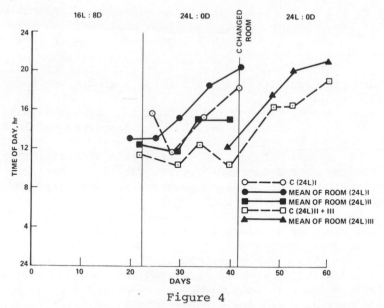

Figure 4

Effect of social interaction on the rate of phase shifting of the plasma cortisol rhythm in 24L:0D. Data show the changes in the time of occurrence of the peak plasma cortisol level in a subject (C) under three constant light exposures (I, II, III) as compared to the mean of the group of subjects with which he was housed.

ACKNOWLEDGEMENTS

I wish to thank Dr. Donald F. Rockwell for his rating the
subjects for dominance, and Dr. L. Rosenblatt for harmonic analyses
of the data used to derive the occurrence of peak plasma cortisols.

REFERENCES

Aschoff, J., M. Fatranska, H. Giedke, P. Doerr, D. Stamm and
    H. Wisser, 1971, Human circadian rhythms in continuous darkness:
    entrainment by social cues, Science, 17:213.
Brain, P. F., 1972, Endocrine and behavioral differences between
    dominant and subordinate male house mice housed in pairs,
    Psychonom. Sci., 28:260.
Candland, D. K. and A. I. Leshner, 1975, Socialization and Adrenal
    Functioning in the Squirrel Monkey (Saimiri Sciureus), Folia
    Primatol., 29:19.
Cheifetz, P., Gaffud, N. and Dingman, J. F., 1968, Effects of Bi-
    lateral adrenalectomy and continuous light on the circadian
    rhythm of corticotropin in female rats, Endocrinology, 82:1117.
Critchlow, V., Liebelt, R. A., Bar-Sela, M. and W. Mountcastle, 1963,
    Sex difference in resting pituitary-adrenal function in the rat,
    Am. J. Physiol., 205:807.
Davis, D. E. and J. J. Christian, 1957, Relation of adrenal weight to
    social rank of mice, Proc. Soc. Exp. Biol. Med., 94:728.
Johnson, J. T. and S. Levine, 1973, Influence of water deprivation on
    adrenocortical rhythms, Neuroendocrinology, 11:268.
Krieger, D. T., 1974, Food and water restriction shifts corticosterone,
    temperature, activity and brain amine periodicity, Endocrinology,
    95:1195.
Krieger, D. T. and H. Hauser, 1978, Comparison of synchronization of
    circadian corticosteroid rhythms by photoperiod and food, Proc.
    Natl. Acad. Sci. USA., 75:1577
Krieger, D. T. and Ascoff, J., 1979, Endocrine circadian rhythms,
    in: "Textbook of Endocrinology," G. Cahill, L. Martini, L. DeGroot,
    D. Nelson, W. Odell, E. Steinberger and A. Winegard, eds.,
    Grune and Stratton, New York.
Mendoza, S. P., C. L. Coe, E. L. Lowe and S. Levine, 1979, The physio-
    logical response to group formation in adult male squirrel
    monkeys, Psychoneuroendocrinology, 3:221.
Murphy, G. E., 1967, Studies of protein-binding of steroids and their
    application to the routine micro and ultramicro measurement of
    various steroids in body fludis by competitive protein binding
    radioassay, J. Clin. Endocrinol. Metab., 29:479.
Poppel, E., 1968, Desynchroniztionen circadiener rhythmen Innerhelb
    einer isolierten gruppe, Pflugers Archiv., 299:364.
Winget, C. M., J. Vernikos-Danellis and J. R. Beljan, 1975, Synchrony
    of physiological rhythms is regulated by social zeitgebers,
    The Physiologist, 18:1025.

COPING WITH MENTAL WORK LOAD

G. Mulder

and L. J. M. Mulder

Department of Experimental Psychology

University of Groningen

INTRODUCTION

In the last thirty years work load has become more a load on the mental capacities of the human operator rather than on his physical capabilities. There is a growing number of activities in which the operator is assigned jobs that involve monitoring and/or supervisory control of complex systems or problem solving of different kinds. Thus instead of acting as a producer of energy, the human operator acts more as a flexible and inventive processor, transforming information into appropriate actions aimed at reaching a special goal.

A (mental) task may be defined as a goal-directed activity pattern which is subjected to certain environmental and structural constraints. The structural constraints involve task variables, believed to affect different mental processes such as perception, memory, attention, decision-making and so forth.

This development has given rise to a number of important questions:

a. Is it possible to develop a concept of mental work load analogous to that of physical work load?

b. Are there physiological indices indicating the amount of effort or costs involved in these activities?

c. Are there conditions of under-or overload?

d. What type of information should be displayed to the operator?

233

e.   What type of decisions can he make effectively and what
     has to be delegated to other information processing systems?

f.   Of special importance to the present conference are issues
     concerning the effects of this type of work on the operator's
     mental and physical health. Is it possible for him to
     cope with the mental load involved in these new jobs?

This contribution will be restricted to the first two and the
latter question. The concept of mental load is somewhat ambiguous.
In a recent article Sanders (1979) distinguished two different
conceptions of mental work load. In the first conception, mental
load is conceived to be only related to the demands required in
mental tasks. We will call this type of load information load. In
the second conception, mental load is conceived to be much wider in
that the task environment, with its physical and in particular its
social and emotional component (e.g., problems around leadership,
management relations, personal relationships, the perception of
threat) is also included. We will call this second type of load
emotional load. It is however questionable if such a distinction
is a real one. In many recent theories cognitive processes are
considered as important determinants of the experienced emotional
state (Mandler, 1975, for example). Hamilton (1977) has argued
that anxiety is at its basic level information which may require
attentional processes and thus compete for space and time with
other external task-relevant information. Also elsewhere (Mulder,
1979) arguments are put forward suggesting that a distinction between
information load and emotional load is not relevant to cardiovascular
responses. These responses have been studied mostly as possible
indices of the costs of mental work and they are the main topic of
this contribution.

In paragraph two we shall discuss the concept of mental work
load and argue that mental work may be considered from modern
theories of attention and information processing. In laboratory
studies on selective attention it has become increasingly clear that
divided attention deficits mainly occur if the operator has to rely
on higher levels of cognitive control and during these moments there
is a characteristic change in cardiovascular state (paragraph 3).
We shall argue that coping with mental work load is determined by
the possibility of relying also on lower levels of control.

In paragraph four we shall explore possible consequences for
physical health and in paragraph five some methods designed for
field applications will be discussed.

MENTAL WORK LOAD, INFORMATION PROCESSING AND COPING

Mental task load, conceived in terms of mental task demands,
supposes a load on mental mechanisms within the information

processing system (Mulder and Mulder-Hajonides van der Meulen, 1973).
Task variables associated with those mental mechanisms that are
concerned with the conscious control of behavior are in particular

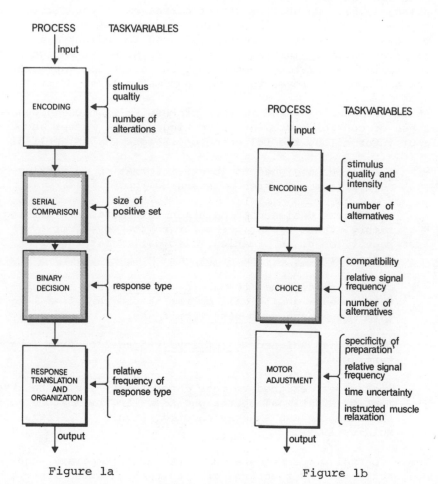

Figure 1a   Figure 1b

Task variables may affect different mental processes. In this
example stimulus quality affects a data limited process, encoding;
memory load affects a resource limited process, the control processes
involved in locating information is a short term store; motor
preparation affects a data limited processes involved in the adjustment of the motor system. Mental load or effort is associated with
controlled processing. Practice may change the level of control
and consequently may reduce mental effort. In that case coping
is said to occur.

loading (Mulder, 1979a). Such a load is potentially threatening to
the organism. Coping with mental work load may either be the result
of problem solving efforts made by the organism and/or arises from a
change in the subjective evaluation of the task situation. In the
first case both performance and physiological activation will change
as a function of practice, while in the second case, performance
will not indicate effective coping but in some way the subject
evaluates his own coping strategy as being effective (Ursin, Baade,
and Levine, 1978). We shall restrict ourselves to the first case.

The changes in performance are believed to reflect a change
in cognitive control: initially the task required attention demanding, controlled information processing, but after considerable
practice the operator moves to a more automatic level of processing.

Attention demanding information processing is closely connected
to the use of control processes in working memory. After encoding
the input information, the following operations may be applied:

-    operations designed to <u>locate</u> information in working
     memory (memory search or scanning);

-    operations designed to <u>maintain</u> information in working
     memory (these operations refer to the covert or overt
     repetition of information, also called <u>maintenance</u>
     rehearsal).

     operations designed to make <u>decisions</u> based on task
     requirements and to call operating programs from long
     term memory and to <u>monitor</u> their use;

-    operations designed to <u>retrieve</u> information from long
     term store;

-    operations designed to <u>code</u> information, i.e., the attach-
     ment of additional operations from long term store to
     the incoming and sensory encoded stimulus (Shiffrin, 1975;
     Mulder, 1979).

These control processes are conceived as a temporary sequence
of nodes, activated under control of, and through attention by,
the subject. Because working memory has a limited processing
capacity, these control processes are extremely resource-limited.
If the task requires it, the subject will have to use these
operations and under these circumstances his performance is highly
dependent on those task variables that affect these resource-limited
processes (see Figure 1a and 1b, shaded area). The more time the
subject has to invest in controlled processing, the more <u>effort</u> the
task requires (Shiffrin and Schneider, 1977; Mulder, 1979).
However, performance is not always dependent on load. Numerous

experiments have shown that the effect of task variables on performance measures such as accuracy or response latency does change after practice. Recently Schneider and Shiffrin (1977) and Shiffrin and Schneider (1977) attempted to mould the research findings on both the effects of practice in memory search and detection tasks into a general theory of information processing and selective attention. If the subject relies on controlled information processing divided attention deficits will occur; if, on the other hand, the information processing occurs automatically, there are no divided attention deficits.

Automatic processes are defined by Shiffrin and Schneider as a sequence of nodes which nearly becomes active in response to a particular input configuration, where input may be externally or internally generated and include the general situational context. Such a sequence is activated automatically without the necessity of active control or attention by the subject. It is an activation of a learned sequence of long term memory elements and occurs only in familiar situations, while controlled processing is a temporary activation of elements and occurs in new situations. The authors have demonstrated convincingly that automatic processing is not a faster form of controlled processing, but is a qualitatively different mode of processing. Though the distinction seems to be quite dichotomously, in practice most tasks will be hybrid, i.e., some components of the task are automatized, while others remain controlled.

An important determinant of the transition to more automatic processing is the consistency of the task. For example, the task may require positive responses to some stimuli, and negative responses to other stimuli. If the task is varied, with positive stimuli on one trial becoming negative on other trials and vice versa, information processing will remain in the controlled mode. Thus a necessary requisite for a change in performance, reflecting a gradual change in the level of control, is therefore that the characteristics of the task must remain constant, as was also demanded by the Ursin et al. (1978) animal model of coping (see also Ursin, this volume).

The above mentioned differences in information processing are not only characteristic of laboratory tasks, they are also found in real life tasks. Rasmussen (1976) for example argued for a hybrid model of the information processing of a plant operator. In his model there is a high capacity parallel processing system related to perception, sensory-motor responses etc. This part of the information processing system is in many respects comparable to a goal-directed, self-organizing associative network, operating by dynamic matching of input information to stored patterns. These patterns constitute an analogue representation of the behaviour of the environment in a time-space structure. This internal world model

directs and controls attention. There is also a conscious processor
which is alerted in the case of a deviation from predictions of the
internal model. The conscious processor is conceived to be versatile,
to constitute the adaptive resources of the operator, but limited in
capacity and speed and it processes the information sequentially.

To summarize this section: Mental work load seems to be
intimately connected to (consciously) controlled, attention demanding
information processing. Under consistent and predictable circumstances, practice will change the level of control. The task will
require less effort, either due to more efficient controlled processing and to the development of automatic processing, performance will
become less dependent on load and the subject is said to cope with
the demands of the task.

In Table I we briefly summarize this conception of coping.

TABLE I

MODES OF INFORMATION PROCESSING

(for details see Mulder, 1979)

Characteristics

AUTOMATIC	CONTROLLED
habitual	non-habitual
pre-attentive	attentive
passive attention	active attention
data limited	resource limited
capacity unlimited	capacity limited
parallel-processing	sequential-processing
analogue representations of the environment	symbolic representations of the environment
long term memory performance is relatively independent of load	working memory performance is highly dependent on load
facilitated by consistent mapping and predictable sequences	occurs if mapping is varied and sequences are unpre- dictable
increased possibility of time sharing	decreased possibility of time sharing

<——— ←——— ←—— ←—— ←

Coping with Mental Work Load

CARDIOVASCULAR STATES

Introduction

Changes in cardiovascular responses may occur within a period of seconds (phasic changes, see Information Processing, Coping and Amplitude of Spontaneous Blood Pressure Oscillations) within a period of minutes to hours (tonic changes, see Information Processing, Coping and Amplitude of Spontaneous Blood Pressure Oscillations, page 243), or over a very extended period of time (chronic changes, see THE DEFENSE REACTION AND CARDIOVASCULAR DISEASE).

These changes are often interpreted within a general activation or arousal model. It must however be realized that indices which in the past have been said to measure "activation" have particular biological functions of their own which need to be fully understood before they can be related to more behavioural concepts. It is very conceivable that some changes in cardiovascular parameters are required in order to enable the organism to process information in a certain way. By studying systematically the effects of task variables, learning etc., on cardiovascular and other parameters, such process-specific states may be discovered. Thus physiological states may be considered as finite and discrete vectors representing distinct and qualitatively different conditions, each of them reflecting different modes of nervous activity.

Recently Pribram and McGuiness (1975) argued for the existence of at least three such states: arousal, related to the encoding of information; activation related to motor adjustment and effort related to controlled processing (see also Figure 1a and 1b). In this section we shall discuss effort-related changes in cardiovascular parameters.

Cardiovascular States and the Concept of Coping

Heart rate (HR), stroke volume (SV), total peripheral resistance (TPR) and venous tone (VT) are important determinants of arterial pressure (P). These parameters are under parasympathetic and sympathetic control. With regard to the heart an increased parasympathetic (or vagal) tone decreases HR, while an increased sympathetic tone increases HR and SV, this latter parameter by increasing myocardial contraction force. However, it has become increasingly clear that numerous combinations of para- and sympathetic cardiovascular control may exist, depending on the nature of demands imposed upon the organism (for details see Manning, 1977; Mulder, 1979c). For example, sympathetic activity is, within a general activation or arousal theory, often characterized as being diffuse, massive and synchronous, whilst sympathetic activity to different organs is now recognized to be different and related to the demands of the activity.

Brod (1970) found that cerebral bloodflow increased during mental activity, cerebral oxygen consumption was also found to increase, while cerebral vascular resistance remained almost unchanged. Recently Lassen (1978) demonstrated even differential patterns of cerebral bloodflow depending on the cortical areas involved in the required mental activity.

During both muscular work and mental work muscle bloodflow increased, though the increase due to mental arithmetic was only minimally accompanied by an increase in O_2 or glucose consumption. The increased muscle bloodflow during mental arithmetic is according to Berdina, Kolenko, Kotz, Savtchencko, and Thorevski (1972) accompanied by an isometric contraction, which is largely anaerobic. Thus on first sight, it appears that the increased blood supply to the muscles is not mediated by a change in metabolic needs, but is partly due to the enhanced release of norepinephrine and partly to a reflex involving cholinergic sympathetic fibres. Brod also indicated that this haemodynamic pattern occurred in animals if stimulated electrically in the defense area of the hypothalamus.

Activation of the defense area in the posterior hypothalamus imposes a cardiovascular state that suggests a resetting of the baroreflex at a different reference level. The baroreflex is mediated by baroreceptors in the aorta and arteria carotis. If arterial pressure (P) increases beyond a certain reference value, the baroreflex causes an increased arterial dilation (decreased TPR); increased venous dilation; a reduction in force of cardiac contraction (decreased SV); a reduction in HR. All these four effects reduce P. If P becomes below a certain reference value or setpoint the reverse occurs. During the defense reaction the heartrate response upon baroreceptor stimulation is in particular diminished. Neurophysiological evidence (for a review see Manning, 1977) shows that facilitation and inhibition of the baroreflex is controlled by different brain sites. Afferents from the carotic sinus reach the medullary reticular formation. A rise in P inhibits pressor activity in this area. The pressor responses are <u>tonically</u> facilitated by diencephalic and cortical regions, because the full range of baroreceptor responses following decerebration is absent. Baroreceptor afferents also reach hypothalamic neurons by ascending projections. The defense area in the hypothalamus makes pre- and postsynaptic connections at the level of the medulla, inhibiting components of the carotis sinus medullary input. In this way a new cardiovascular state has emerged in spite of the increased baroreceptor drive. The above mentioned inhibitory mechanisms helps to account for the functional state of a threatened organism, which simultaneously elevates heartrate and blood pressure, shifts priorities of bloodflow and all the while retains the characteristics of cardio-reflex regulation, only now reset to new levels (Manning, 1977).

During this state oscillations in blood pressure will be less reflected in changes in HR (see fourth paragraph, this page). However the latter state, occurs according to a suggestion of Obrist, Langer, Grignolo, Sutterer, Light, and McCubbin (1977) only under certain circumstances. In some experiments the subject has little control over the environment as, for example, when a person in a classical aversive conditioning paradigm receives periodic electric shocks regardless of his actions. The cardiovascular state which emerges in this situation is characterized by an extreme vagal control and heart rate is directly related to the amount of striate muscle activity. Usually one finds heartrate to decelerate in the CS-UCS interval and a concomitant decrease in "irrelevant" muscle activity.

In other experiments, the subject's actions do influence the environment, for example, when a subject can avoid electric shocks by pressing a button. The cardiovascular state which emerges in this situation is characterized by β-adrenergic influences on myocardial events and these effects are somewhat independent of concomitant striate muscular activity. In these situations one finds heart rate to be increased and also increased Pulse Transmission Time (an indirect measure of systolic pressure) and dp/dt (an indirect measure of contractile force). The subject should also be engaged by this type of task.

In our experiments we used paced cognitive tasks. Engagement in the task was varied by changing the nature of the task demands (Information Processing, Coping and Amplitude of Spontaneous Blood Pressure Oscillations). Sinus arrhythmia, and in particular the amplitude of spontaneous blood pressure oscillations was used as a non-invasive index of vagal control (following paragraph).

Spontaneous Oscillations of Blood Pressure

Invasive measurement of arterial bloodpressure has indicated the existence of spontaneous oscillations (e.g., Hyndman, Kitney, and Sayers, 1971; Sayers, 1973; 1975). These changes are believed to originate from thermoregulator vasomotor activity (main oscillation frequency at 0.03 Hz), from blood pressure regulatory vasomotor activity (main oscillation frequency at 0.10 Hz) and from respiratory activity (usually between 0.25 and 0.40 Hz). The respiratory and non-respiratory linked changes in mean blood pressure are registrated by the baroreceptors and consequently cause via changes in vagal tone similar changes in heartrate.

Katona and Gih (1975) suggested that sinus arrhythmia may be used as a non-invasive indicator of parasympathetic (i.e., vagal) control of the heart. Kalsbeek and Ettema (1963) concluded that sinus arrhythmia tends to be reduced or suppressed during performance on continuous mental tasks. They suggested that sinus arrhythmia

could serve as a physiological index of mental workload. Recent
research has indicated that the suppression of sinus arrhythmia is
mainly due to a reduction or even a loss of the 0.10 Hz component
in the cardiac interval signal (Sayers, 1975; Mulder, 1979b). This
reduction is accompanied by an increase in blood pressure.

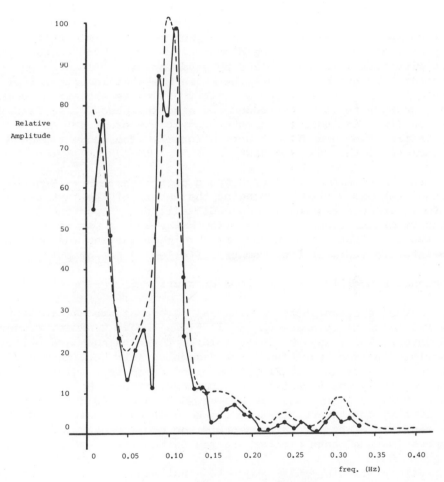

Figure 2

Oscillations in the bloodflow signal (-) or blood pressure
signal are also present in the cardiac interval signal (---). In
this Figure the spectral representation of both the bloodflow and
cardiac interval signal is shown.

(Mulder, 1979c). Also the reverse is true: a decrease in blood
pressure decreased the dominant frequency (from 0.10 Hz to lower
value) and increased its mean power density (Monos and Szus, 1978).
It has been argued that the decrease in amplitude of these vasomotor
oscillations in the heartrate signal is due to the defense reaction
(Mulder, 1979). By means of spectral analysis and digital filtering
we were able to monitor these oscillations during the performance
on mental tasks (Kamphuis, Mulder, and Mulder, 1978; Mulder and
Mulder, 1979; Mulder, 1979c). In the next section we shall
briefly review the most important findings.

Information Processing, Coping and Amplitude of Spontaneous Blood
Pressure Oscillations

On page 234, MENTAL WORK LOAD....we have argued that mental
work load is intimately associated with the amount of time the
subject is engaged in controlled information processing. This
amount of time can be experimentally manipulated. Our tasks were
always paced: the subject was confronted by a sequence of signals
to which he had to react differentially. By manipulating the task
variables the processing time was changed. In some tasks the
processing time almost completely filled the available time interval
(e.g., the interval between successive signals). In other conditions
the available time exceeded the required processing time. The task
we used required almost no physical activity.

In Figure 3 we have depicted the average spectrum (20 subjects)
of the cardiac interval signal. The four different spectra represent
tonic activity during a period of 5 minutes. The thick line represents the average spectrum during rest. There is a sharp spectral
component at 0.10 Hz and less sharp one at 0.24 Hz. The first
component represents oscillations in blood pressure and subjects
do not differ much in the dominant frequency; the second component
represents respiratory activity and it is clear that individuals
differ in mean respiratory rate. The three remaining spectra were
obtained during the performance of a task in which the subject had
to compare the meaning of a sentence (which was exposed 3800 msec)
with the meaning of a picture (which was also exposed for 3800 msec).
The task was designed in such a way that the number of mental comparisons required to perform the match differed over trials. The
spectrum with the highest amplitude of all the components was
obtained in a condition which required an average processing time of
897 msec; the next spectrum was obtained in a condition which
required an average processing time of 1196 msec, whilst the
spectrum with the lowest energy in all components was obtained during
a task which required 2095 msec on the average. This decrease in
energy was interpreted as reflecting a decrease in baroreceptor
sensitivity: fluctuations in blood pressure are less reflected in
the cardiac interval signal. It is also evident that the amplitude
of the vasomotor oscillations (around 0.10 Hz) reflect the

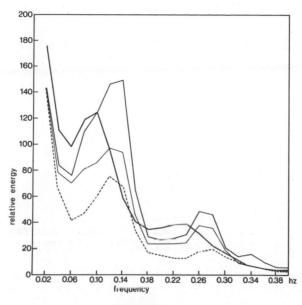

Figure 3

The averaged spectrum of the cardiac interval signal during
rest and three different mental tasks (for explanation see text).

differences between the tasks most clearly. However, during the
tasks the dominant frequency is shifted from 0.10 Hz to 0.14 Hz.
This shift in frequency is due to selective entrainment: the
subject had to perform a decision every 7600 msec. Around each
decision there is a characteristic <u>phasic</u> pattern of cardiac
activity (see Figure 5). This pattern occurs at a frequency of
0.14 Hz and thus entrains the spontaneous component. Frequency
selective entrainment only occurs if the decision rate is near to
the frequency of the spontaneous oscillations.

In Figure 5 we have depicted the amplitude of the spontaneous
component during a task in which the subject was required to keep
an ongoing mental account of his environment, which consisted of
either one or three important events. Whilst tracking one event
was comparatively easy, tracking three events was found to demand
the subject's full attention. Such differences in attentional
demands were clearly differentiated by the spontaneous component.

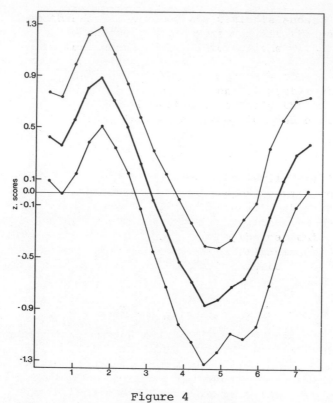

Figure 4

Phasic cardiac responses accompanying decision processes involving a mental task. Heartrate decelerates after the presentation of the sentence, reaching its nadir at about 500 msec after the signal. The maximum acceleration is attained at about 1500 msec after the presentation of the sentence. A sharp deceleration follows until about 800 msec after the presentation of the picture. During the rest of the epoch heart rate accelerates.

(The decision rate in this task was far beyond the critical area, thus no selective entrainment occurred). Finally, we show the results of a memory search task in Figure 6. In the condition DD the search was partly automatized, i.e., performance was relatively independent of the load of the task (see Figure 7); in the condition SD the search was completely controlled. The decision rate was

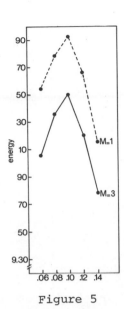

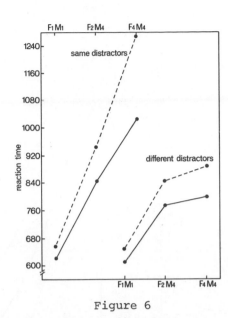

Figure 5

Figure 6

Figure 5. The 0.10 component of the cardiac interval signal during two conditions differing in the memory load.

Figure 6. Performance indicates automatic information processing in condition   Different distractors (DD), while in the condition Same distractors (SD), performance is highly dependent on load, indicating controlled processing. The load of the task is indicated by the amount of elements in a visual display (F_2 or F_4) and the memory load (M_7 or M_4).

around 0.12 Hz and selective entrainment of the spontaneous component occurred. From Figure 7 it is clear that the amplitude of the entrained component is smaller in the condition requiring controlled search.

If a subject is repeatedly exposed to the same task we should expect a decreased cardiovascular activation and improved performance due to coping. In Figure 8 we have depicted the results of a selective attention experiment. In these experiments there are two conditions: a focused and a divided one. These conditions differ in the complexity of the required decision. In both conditions the subject's task is to determine the membership of a visual

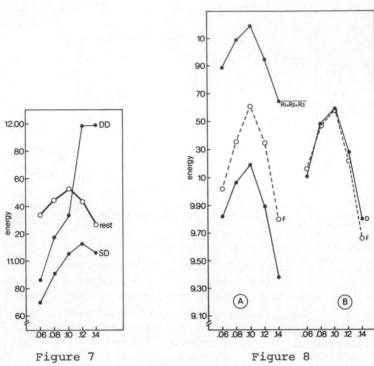

Figure 7

Figure 8

Figure 7. The 0.10 component of the cardiac interval signal during automatic (DD) or controlled (SD) information processing.

Figure 8. The 0.10 component during the first (A) and second (B) exposure to a task. The solid line indicates "divided attention" and the broken line "focused attention." $R_1 + R_2 + R_3$ indicates the mean rest value.

stimulus in a positive or negative set. In the "divided" condition all the attributes of the stimulus are relevant; in the "focused" condition the physical parameters of the stimulus are the same, but the subject is informed before presentation that only a specified subset will be relevant. Divided attention deficits (e.g., errors, long processing times) occur in the "divided" condition. A similar experiment was carried out over 7 training days. The results of day 1, and day 6 and day 7 are shown in Figure 9. Over 7 days the

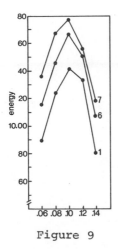

Figure 9

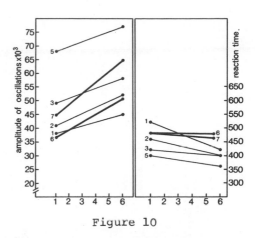

Figure 10

Figure 9.   The increase of the 0.10 Hz component across 7
training days.   The increase accompanies a concomitant decrease in
RT in selective attention tasks.   The phasic component remained.

Figure 10.   The increase of the 0.10 Hz component within and
between seven training sessions.   The increase accompanies a concomitant decrease in RT in a perceptual motor task.   At day 6 the
task changed slightly.   RT increased and the spontaneous component
decreased.   Note that coping with the new task demand occurred very
quickly.

reaction time gradually diminishes and the 0.10 Hz component
increases in amplitude.   It is most important to note that the
phasic changes around each overt decision were still present after
these practice days.   Thus it appears that only the tonic component
is affected by coping, while the phasic component is: "coping-
resistant" (see Ursin this volume).

Finally in Figure 10 we show the results of a tracking task.
The subject had to track a point in this task which followed a
consistent and predictable course through a maze.   There were seven
training days with 6 trials per day.   On the sixth day the point
started to move in a slightly different direction.

In Figure 10 the amplitude of the blood pressure area (ranging
from 0.06 to 0.14 Hz) is plotted as a function of day and trial
number.   The results indicate that both within and across sessions,
the 0.10 Hz component gradually increases.   Similar changes occur
in performance (reaction time).   At day 6, the reaction time is

again considerably increased and the amplitude of the component
strongly reduced. The data indicate that the subjects quickly
cope with these new demands, but the changes in cardiovascular
activation are faster than those in performance.

The amplitude of the spontaneous component is not only an
index of mental task load but also of emotional load. In a recent
experiment we investigated subjects who were subjected to dental
treatment. The treatment period was compared to a "recovery period"
in another environment. The amplitude of the spontaneous component
was very reduced during the dental treatment. Such a result suggests
that with regard to vascular responses, it does not matter whether a
subject is threatened by a dentist or a mental task: both constitute
a threat to the organism and reduce vagal heart rate control.
Thus the decrease of the spontaneous component is unspecific.
Additional behavioral data must indicate whether the subject is
confronted with information or emotional load.

THE DEFENSE REACTION AND CARDIOVASCULAR DISEASE

In this section, we will leave the area of facts and enter
that of speculation. However, even in this area some facts are
available and the search should be directed towards missing links
between them. What are the consequences of a chronic cardiovascular
activation?

It is a well known fact that blood pressure increases with age
and that sinus arrhythmia decreases with age. The spontaneous
components are particularly sensitive to the effects of age and we
found that the older the subject, the higher his blood pressure
and the lower the amplitude of the spontaneous component. (Mulder,
1979c). Eckholdt, Bodmann, Cammann, Pfeifer, and Schubert, (1976)
arrived at a similar conclusion. They found a high correlation
between the duration of hypertension and the amount of sinus arryth-
mia: every 6.3 years of hypertension reduces sinus arrhythmia by
half.

Hypertension may be caused by either an increased cardiac output
or an increased peripheral resistance or by both. Many authors
(see for example Obrist et al., 1977) draw attention to the fact that
younger hypertensives show a more elevated cardiac output due to a
heightened bèta-adrenergic circulatory state, while older hypertensives tend to have a normal cardiac output, but a raised peripheral
resistance. Brod (1972) has hypothesized that the increased
peripheral resistance is predicated upon transient periods of
increased sympathetic activity. He hypothesizes that hypothalamic
systems force a new equilibrium among circulatory parameters by
changing baroreceptor set point. The well-known vascular changes
with morphological abnormalities are late consequences and not the

cause.   This suggests that the observed decrease in amplitude of
the spontaneous component may be partly due to a structural change
in baroreceptor set point and sensitivity and this change is
exaggerated the longer the increased cardiac output existed.

Direct evidence is provided by Folkow, Hallbäck, Lundgren,
Sivertsson, and Weiss (1973).   They found that frequent pressure
rises induced by periodic stimulation of the defense area of the
hypothalamus in spontaneous hypertensive rats caused resistance
vessels to adapt structurally within a few weeks.   This structural
adaptation implied a raised resistance and could account for the
"resting" resistance found in primary hypertension.

Recent research by Weiss (1974) suggests that if the vascular
bed can be protected from such a pressure load from a young age,
these changes are largely pre ented.

The higher sinus arrhythmia, the higher the vagal control of
the heart.   Such control may be very important as a protective
mechanism in acute myocardial infarction.   It has been shown that an
increased sympathetic drive of the heart causes a change in pacemaker
location.   This is believed to be one of the causes of disturbance
in atrial and ventricular rhythm.   Increased sympathetic activity
may also cause a shortened ventricular refractoriness, which may
contribute to the reduction in ventricular fibrillation threshold.
Also beta-blocking drugs, operating against the effects of
circulating catecholamines or neurogenic sympathetic activity are
known to suppress the arrhythmias of ischemic heart disease and
again suggest an important role of sympathetic activity in the
genesis of arrhythmias.

At the cellular level it has been shown that catecholamines
increase diastolic depolarization in Purkinje fibres and pacemaker
cells, leading to repetitive firing.   This all suggests that we
should look for non-invasive measurement techniques to monitor the
subject's tonic and chronic cardiovascular reactions to environmental stressors.   The last section of this chapter is devoted to
these techniques.

POSSIBLE APPLICATIONS IN THE FIELD

The previous sections suggested that the amplitude of the
spectral component related to spontaneous blood pressure oscillations, is very sensitive to the demands required in mental
tasks.   In real life tasks the task demands may suddenly change
and hence it will be important to devise a technique that enables
the researcher to monitor this component from second-to-second.
Digital filtering is such a technique (Mulder and Mulder, 1979).

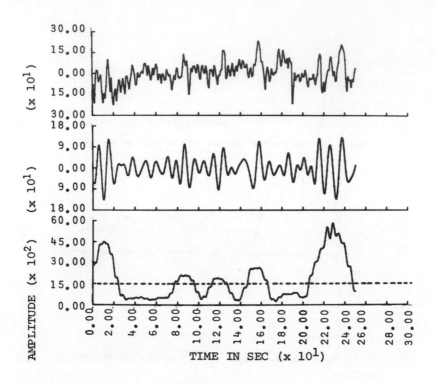

Figure 11

Energy of the spontaneous component in the cardiac interval signal as a function of time.

(a) Momentaneous heart rate; signal variations around the mean in this period.

(b) Band-filtered heart rate signal (passband: 0.06-0.14 Hz).

(c) Energy in the band-filtered heart rate signal, calculated with a moving average window (width = 21 seconds).

Figure 11 illustrates our approach. The cardiac interval signal (A) is filtered in such a way that only a spectral band between 0.06 and 0.14 remains (B). The energy of this filtered signal is obtained by squaring and integrating this signal with the aid of a moving average window (width = 21 seconds). This technique enables us to find momentary periods in which the amplitude

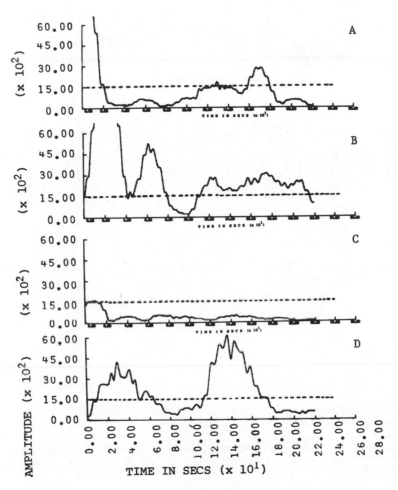

Figure 12

Energy of the spontaneous component in the cardiac interval signal as a function of time, during a laboratory tracking task and during (following) rest periods.

(a) Tracking task, predictable signals, fifth day.

(b) Rest period after task, performance, fifth day.

(c) Tracking task, unpredictable signals, sixth day.

(d) Rest period after previous task, sixth day.

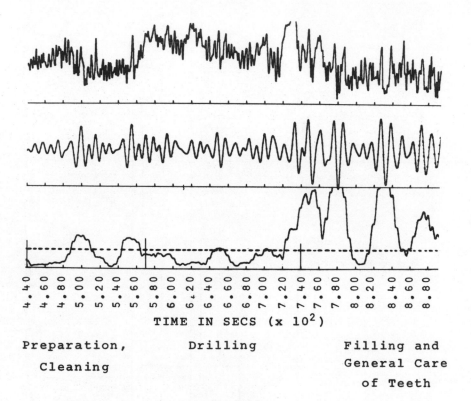

TIME IN SECS (x 10^2)

Preparation,   Drilling   Filling and
  Cleaning   General Care
                                              of Teeth

Figure 13

Energy of the spontaneous component in the cardiac interval
signal as a function of time; the subject is submitted to a treatment of a dentist; different periods in this treatment are indicated.

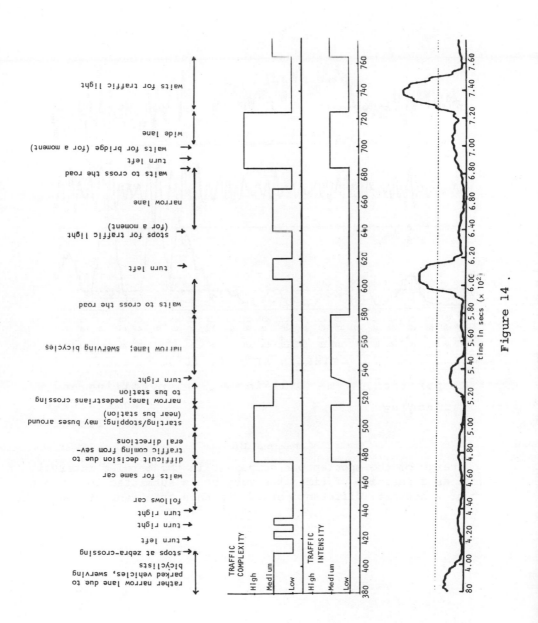

Figure 14 .

of the spontaneous oscillations is severely suppressed (indicating a diminished vagal control) or very large (indicating increased vagal control). These periods are quite evident in Figure 11.

In addition to digital filtering we use also other non-invasive measures; two of these are "carotic dp/dt" and "pulse wave velocity" (PW). Carotic dp/dt is defined as the ascending slope of the pressure wave in the arteria carotis, detected with the aid of a non-invasive pressure transducer; pulse wave velocity is derived from the time distance between the R-wave in the ECG and the moment the pressure wave arrives in the carotis or an other peripheral artery (for example the radialis). Both measures are believed to reflect the effects of β-adrenergic influences on the myocard. A computer program computes continuously dp/dt and PWV for each heart beat.

Artifacts caused by movements are also detected. In order to obtain a template of subject's cardiovascular reactions to severe, mild or light informational stress, they are subjected to series of standard laboratory tasks before performing real tasks.

In Figure 12a the results are depicted of a task trial in which the point in the maze followed a highly predictable route; Figure 12b shows the amplitude of the spontaneous component after completion of the task; in Figure 12c the results are shown in case of an unpredictable route, and Figure 12d depicts the curve for a rest period after this task. Comparing these curves we see that the criterion is exceeded during a shorter period in tasks with unpredictable signals.
signals.
In the first case there is diminished vagal control, while during rest periods the criterion is often exceeded, indicating increased vagal control.

During performance in real tasks, the computer searches for moments in which the subject is mentally taxed in some way, according to criteria obtained in the laboratory. Examples are given in Figure 13 and 14. Figure 13 depicts the energy of the spontaneous component in a situation in which the subject is submitted to a dental treatment, including periods of preparation and cleaning of the teeth, drilling (for most people a threatening event) and finally filling and general care of the teeth. During drilling vagal control is diminished, but during the final period there is a large rebound effect. Figure 14 depicts the energy of the spontaneous component during car driving through a city with a high traffic density. Periods of high and low traffic intensity and complexity are indicated with the aid of two curves. Looking at this picture we see that during periods of waiting for a traffic light, the criterion

criterion is almost never reached. This means a higher vagal control during periods of relatively relaxed driving and lower vagal control during periods of high traffic density and complex driving situations (Wildervanck, Mulder, and Michon, 1978).

FINAL REMARKS AND CONCLUSIONS

In this chapter we have argued that coping is related to the level of cognitive control, either automatic or controlled processing. Automatic processes utilize a relatively permanent set of associative connections in long term store and such a set requires an appreciable amount of practice. While automatic processing reduces the demands made on attentional capacity, it also increased the difficulty of suppressing or altering these processes. In most tasks however a mixture of automatic and controlled processing can be found, i.e., some components of the task may be automatized while others remain controlled. For example, for a child learning to read, the surface structure of a sentence will initially demand controlled processing but with continued practice this will change to the automatic mode and it will be the deep structure that now demands controlled processing. Another example is the pianist who initially pays attention to the playing act per se, but who can later in practice shift his attentional capacity to the emotional interpretation of the piece.

Attention demanding controlled information processing requires a cardiovascular state characterized by low vagal control and increased sympathetic control. Methods described in this chapter may aid the identification of task components which require controlled processing. There may be large individual differences in this respect. Identifying such conditions and individuals is probably the first step in identifying pathogenetic factors, at least for those individuals who are for genetic reasons individuals at risk.

ACKNOWLEDGEMENT

The authors are very grateful to Dr. J. Jackson for the critical way in which she has read the manuscript and improved the English.

REFERENCES

Berdina, N. A., Kolenko, O. L., Kotz, I. M., Savtchencko, A. P.,
    and Thorevski, V. I., 1972, Increase in skeletal muscle
    performance during emotional stress in man, Circ. Res., 6:642.
Brod, J., 1970, Haemodynamics and Emotional Stress, in: "Psycho-
    somatics in Hypertension." M. Koster, H. Musaph, and P. Visser
    eds., Karger, Basel.
Brod, J., 1972, Neural factors in essential hypertension, in:
    "Neural and Psychological Mechanism in Cardiovascular Disease,"
    A. Zanchetti Casa ed., Editrice Il Ponte, Milan.
Eckholdt, K., Bodmann, K. H., Cammann, H., Pfeifer, B., and
    Schubert, E., 1976, Sinus Arrhythmia and Heart Rate in
    Hypertonic Disease, Adv. Card., 16:366.
Folkow, B. M., Hallbäck, M., Lundgren, Y., Sivertsson, R., and
    Weiss, L., 1973, Importance of adaptive changes in vascular
    design for establishment of primary hypertension, studied in
    man and spontaneously hypertensive rats, Circ. Res., Suppl. I.
Hamilton, V., 1977, Cognitive Development in the Neuroses and
    Schizophrenias, in: "The Development of Cognitive Processes,"
    V. Hamilton and M. D. Vernon, eds., Academic Press, London.
Hyndman, B. W., Kitney, R. I., and Sayers, B. McA., 1971, Spontane-
    ous oscillations in physiological control systems, Nature, 233:
    339.
Kalsbeek, J. W. H., and Ettema, J. H., 1963, Scored regularity of
    the heart rate pattern and the measurement of perceptual and
    mental load, Ergonomics, 6:306.
Kamphuis, A., Mulder, L. J. M., and Mulder, G., 1978, Spectral
    analysis of the cardiac interval signal: A comparison of
    different methods, Heymans Bull. Psychol. Instit. Rijksuniver-
    siteit Groningen, Nr. 78-HB-395 EX.
Katona, P. G., and Jih, F., 1975, Respiratory sinus arrhythmia: non-
    invasive measure of parasympathetic cardiac control. J. Appl.
    Physiol., 39:801.
Lassen, N. A., Ingvar, D. H., and Skinhøj, E., 1978, Brain function
    and bloodflow, Sci. Am., 50:59.
Mandler, G., 1975, "Mind and Emotion," Wiley and Sons, New York.
Manning, J. W., 1977, Intracranial mechanisms of regulation, in:
    "Neural Regulation of the Heart," W. C. Randall ed., Oxford
    University Press, New York.
Monos, E., and Szüs, B., 1978, Effect of changes in mean arterial
    pressure on the structure of short-term blood pressure waves,
    Automedica, 2:149.
Mulder, G., and Mulder-Hajonides van der Meulen, W.R.E.H., 1973,
    Mental load and the measurement of heart rate variability,
    Ergonomics, 16:69.
Mulder, G., 1979a, Mental load, mental effort and attention, in:
    "Mental Workload: Its Theory and Measurement," N. Moray ed.,
    Plenum Press, New York.

Mulder, G., 1979b, Sinusarrhythmia and Mental Workload, in: "Mental
     Workload: Its Theory and Measurement," N. Moray ed., Plenum
     Press, New York.
Mulder, G., 1979c, in preparation, "The Heart of Mental Effort:
     Studies in the Cardiovascular Psychophysiology of Mental Work."
Mulder, L. J. M., and Mulder, G., 1979, Digital filtering of the
     cardiac interval signal: Method and applications, Heymans Bull.
     Psychol. Instituten Rijksuniversiteit Groningen.
Obrist, P. A., Langer, A. W., Grignolo, A., Sutterer, J. R., Light,
     K. C., McCubbin, J. A., 1977, Blood pressure control mechanisms
     and stress: Implications for the etiology of hypertension, in:
     "Hypertension: Determinants, Complications and Intervention,"
     G. Onesti and C. R. Klimt eds., Grune and Stratton, New York.
Pribam, K. H., McGuinness, D., 1975, Arousal, activation and effort
     in the control of attention, Psychol. Rev., 82:116.
Rasmussen, J., 1976, Outlines of a hybrid model of the process plant
     operator, in: "Monitoring Behavior and Supervisory Control,"
     Thomas B. Sheridan and Gunnar Johannsen eds., Plenum Press, New
     York.
Sanders, A. F., 1979, Some remarks on mental load, in: "Mental Work-
     load: Its Theory and Measurement," N. Moray ed., Plenum Press,
     New York.
Sayers, B. McA., 1973, Analysis of heart rate variability, Ergonomics,
     16:17.
Sayers, B. McA., 1975, Physiological consequences of information
     load and overload, in: "Research in Psychophysiology,"
     P. H. Venables and M. J. Christie eds., John Wiley, London.
Schneider, W., and Shiffrin, R. M., 1977, Controlled and Automatic
     Information Processing: I. Detection, search, and attention,
     Psychol. Rev., 84:1.
Shiffrin, R. M., 1975, Short-term store: The basis for a memory
     search, in: "Cognitive Theory" Vol. 1, F. Restle et al., eds.
     Erlbaum Associates, Hillsdale, NJ.
Shiffrin, R. M., and Schneider, W., 1977, Controlled and automatic
     information processing: II. Perceptual learning, automatic
     attending, and a general theory, Psychol. Rev., 84:127.
Ursin, H., Baade, E., and Levine, S., 1978, "Psychobiology of Stress:
     A Study of Coping Men," Academic Press, New York.
Weiss, L., 1974, Aspects of the relation between functional and
     structural cardiovascular factors in primary hypertension.
     Experimental studies in spontaneously hypertensive rats,
     A. Physiol. Scand. 409.
Wildervanck, C., Mulder, G., and Michon, J. A., 1978, Mapping
     mental load in car driving, Ergonomics, 21:225.

PERSONALITY, ACTIVATION AND SOMATIC HEALTH

A NEW PSYCHOSOMATIC THEORY

Holger Ursin*

Department of Psychology

University of Bergen

ACTIVATION AND PSYCHOSOMATICS

Over the last decades, brain sciences including psychoneuro-endocrinology have established that the main source of variance in autonomic and endocrine activity is the central nervous system (CNS - Mason, 1971). The somatic response to external and internal CNS Stimulation is a widespread, general response, affecting most or all bodily processes. Some specificity or bias may exist, as individual response profiles, either specific to the stimulation, or to the individual. This general response will be referred to as activation. Activation may lead to somatic pathology under certain circumstances which it now seems possible to describe. This offers a new psychosomatic theory built on several disciplines within experimental and clinical psychology as well as traditional medical disciplines like physiology, endocrinology and epidemiology. Recent multifactorial evidence points to several psychoendocrine response types. Activation is still a general response, but individual variance is present in humans. This individual variance seems related to specific personality traits. Such evidence, together with knowledge of coping and defense mechanisms, suggests hypotheses which make the new psychosomatic theory more specific and perhaps more useful than previous theories.

The neural mechanisms for activation and for the CNS regulation of autonomic and endocrine processes are well mapped, and will not

* Part of this paper was prepared while the author was a visiting scientist to the U.S. Naval Health Research Center, Stress Medicine Division, San Diego, California.

be reviewed here. Activation may be looked upon as a final common
path for all phenomena that lead to higher activity in the CNS. The
psychological conditions for activation have been summarized in the
classical works by Lindsley (1951), Hebb (1955) and Duffy (1972).
Recent data have given additional insight into these processes.
Activation occurs to all novel stimuli, and is an important element
of the orienting response (Sokolov, 1963). Activation also occurs
during exploration of unfamiliar surroundings, need registrations or
registered discrepancies from set values (inborn or acquired), and
emotions. Activation is reduced when set values or expectancies are
being met, and when uncertainties are reduced (Levine, Goldman and
Coover, 1972; Bassett, Cairncross and King, 1973; Ursin, 1978).
Problem solving directs itself at eliminating differences between
set values and actual values (Miller, Galanter and Pribram, 1960;
Vickers, 1973). Activation persists until the problem is solved.

Despite its potential, Activation Theory has met criticisms,
particularly from traditional psychophysiology. In particular, it
has been pointed out that there is a lack of correlation between
indicators, and considerable individual variability (Lacey, 1950).
Some of this is due to the nature of the processes studied by
traditional psychophysiologists. Poor correlations between the
various indicators are to be expected since autonomic processes are
innervated by two opposing systems, the sympathetic and parasympathetic.

Both are active during activation, as pointed out even by Cannon
(1932). The end result, therefore, is affected in two opposing ways
by the brain during activation. This is a serious handicap for
making inferences about the underlying central nervous mechanisms,
or the nature of the psychological response. In addition, response
feed-back systems may be complex, and there are also interactions
with metabolic regulatory processes. Finally, individual variation
is added to these processes from the fact that they are subject to
classical as well as instrumental conditioning (N. Miller, this
volume).

These difficulties are less important for most endocrine systems.
Hormone levels, therefore, may represent a new deal in activation
theory. These processes may also be more directly related to the
possible pathogenic consequences of activation. Quantification of
the responses is reliable, accurate and fairly easy to do with the
modern methods of measuring plasma levels of hormones. Most data
in this report rely on such analyses. The presence of an important,
common "driving" force ("activation") is confirmed, but individual
variance is still meaningful.

ACTIVATION: TRAINING OR STRAINING?

The key issue is when is activation a part of a healthy interaction with the environment, and when does it produce somatic disease.
Activation may be a healthy response which strengthens the system,
in particular skeletal and heart muscles. If so, it represents
training. However, it could also have a deteriorating effect; it
could be using resources which would not be replenished, and there
might be wear and tear. In the latter case, the organism is
subjected to a strain.

Since a certain stimulus giving rise to activation may have
either a training or a straining effect, it is necessary to be
precise in the terminology. To regard any stimulus giving rise to
physiological activation as a "strain" (or "stress") is grossly
inadequate. In living organisms resistance to strain is a dynamic
factor. The breaking point which marks the difference between
training and straining differs between individuals, and differs with
time. It depends on how much load the system has been subjected to
previously. With training, the resistance will be increased. We
have no hard data on any ill effect of moderate degrees of loads.
A certain minimum level of loads has to be present in order to keep
the resistance intact. Absence or deprivation of loads has
pronounced ill effects both in physiology and psychology.

There is no doubt that laymen and many professionals take it
for granted that "stress" produces disease. This implication is
not necessarily true; for many types and degrees of stress it is
simply wrong. It may even mislead people to avoid strains and
challenges that would have given them a training effect. Selye
himself holds that only distress produces disease (Selye, 1974), and
that stress itself is unavoidable, and a necessary life process.
According to him, the only absence of stress is death.

The term "stress" is used partly for the response, partly for
the stimulus, and is not a very useful concept for theoretical
purposes. In this paper, the term will be avoided as a theoretical
construct. All immediate somatic changes that "stress" is said to
produce may be accounted for by activation theory. The key psychosomatic question remains: When is activation a healthy response, and
when does it produce disease?

ACTIVATION DAMPENING MECHANISMS

One very important defect with popular notions on the relationship between "stress" and disease is that it lumps all stimuli.
However, when an organism is subjected to stimuli that produce
activation, it is not the stimulus situation itself that predicts
the response. The most striking feature is the variance in what
the individuals are responding to (Lazarus and Averill, 1972).

There are differences in what drives the activation mechanisms;
there are also personality differences in what dampens activation.
Two such response dampening mechanisms should be identified as
particularly important for the activation that eventually may lead
to somatic pathology. These two mechanisms should be identified as
distinctly different mechanisms. They will be referred to as defense
and coping, respectively.

Perceptual Defense

Perceptual defense is a stimulus dampening mechanism, possibly
only found in humans. A certain stimulus which would otherwise give
a certain response, gives less response due to perceptual mechanisms
which dampen the impact of the stimulus. In the following, defense
primarily includes processes which are measured by The Kragh Defense
Mechanism Test (Kragh, 1960). This test measures defense mechanisms
in the build-up of a percept, and is related to classical defense
mechanisms in the Freudian sense.

The Kragh test, therefore, seems to relate to defense
mechanisms as evaluated by projective techniques and interviews.
Defensive styles may also be evaluated by questionnaires, for
instance the Minnesota Multiphasic Personality Inventory (MMPI),
but these methods give different results. Repressive and denying
defenses on the MMPI scale are related to a low level of self-
reported anxiety, but high physiological reactivity (Dykman, Reese,
Galbrecht and Thomasson, 1959; Lazarus and Alfert, 1964). When
defense mechanisms are evaluated by projective techniques or
interviews, a low level of self-reported anxiety is associated with
a low physiological reactivity (Friedman, Mason, and Hamburg, 1963;
Price, Thaler, and Mason, 1957). Defensive styles that allow for
alteration of the evaluation of a threat, may provide an effective
strategy of reducing the physiological response. How effective it
is in the long run depends on to what extent the individual is able
to solve his real problems (Weinstein, Averill, Opton, and Lazarus,
1968). In certain tasks involving real dangers perceptual defense
may be a serious handicap. Kragh's tachistoscopic method predicts
poor performance in several dangerous occupations where split-second
decisions are necessary for high level performance. This has been
shown for Swedish air pilots (Kragh, 1960), Danish attack divers
(Kragh, 1962), Norwegian parachutist trainees (Baade, Halse, Stenhammer, Ellertsen, Johnsen, Vollmer, and Ursin, 1978) and Norwegian
divers (Vaernes, 1978). Repression and isolation mechanisms may be
used by man performing well, but only when the stress is moderate
or coping develops quickly. When the threat is considerable,
repression and isolation seems to be a serious handicap for
performance, particularly in individuals with high levels of fear
(Baade et al., 1978).

"Defense" should be used for response- or stimulus-dampening processes which direct themselves at reducing the impact of the stimulus situation. The process referred to as "blunting" by S. Miller (this volume) seems to belong to the class of phenomena. If the activation reduction derives from active manipulation of the environment, different processes are involved, the subject is then making successful coping attempts.

Coping

When the response represents a solution, an effective way of dealing with the environment, activation is reduced. This action-induced response decrement will be referred to as coping. Coping, therefore, is not the performance of the response itself, but depends on the appraisal of the situation after the individual has done something to his situation, and then re-evaluates his situation. This second evaluating process is referred to as "secondary appraisal" (Lazarus and Averill, 1972). The animal model for coping has been reviewed by Weinberg and Levine in this volume. In a recent study on parachutist trainees, activation was found to be gradually reduced to basal levels when the trainees learned to master the training situation (Ursin, Baade and Levine, 1978). All physiological variables except heart rate showed a fall as coping developed. However, epinephrine still showed a rise before and after trials even if the total level reached decreased with progressive trials. There was also some suggestion that a short-lasting testosterone fall showed the coping effect. The activation unaffected by coping may be referred to as phasic activation, while the coping sensitive mechanism may be referred to as tonic (Ursin, 1978).

TABLE 1

COMPARISON OF PHASIC AND TONIC ACTIVATION

Characteristics	Phasic	Tonic
Onset	Rapid (seconds)	Slow (minutes)
Duration	Short	Long
Circulation	Heart Rate	Blood Pressure
Catecholamines	Epinephrine	Norepinephrine
Other Hormones	Testosterone rise?	Cortisol, testosterone fall, growth hormone
Blood changes		Blood Glucose, Free Fatty Acids
Effect of coping	Moderate or none	Pronounced

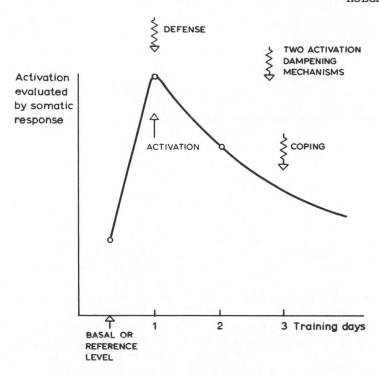

Figure 1

The relationship between defense and coping in situations with repeated exposures to a threatening situation.

Coping is not identical to defense within the definitions offered here. Since coping also includes intrapsychic processes contributing to successful mastery of a psychological challenge, this distinction should be made clear. The gradual development of a response decrement observed in the animal experiments as well as in the human experiments (Ursin et al., 1978) is coping. A reduced initial response is due to defense. The basic thinking is illustrated in Figure 1.

This distinction between defense and coping seems similar to previous references to "conscious" and "unconscious" processes by French, Rodgers and Cobb (1974), Haan (1969), and Kroeber (1963). Defense corresponds to "unconscious" alteration of perception, while coping responds to direct "conscious" action.

Coping is the key term to the understanding of why dramatic and threatening events, even if objectively persistent, do not produce continuous activation and hence pathology in but a minority of cases. In this volume, Weinberg and Levine discuss the term further, and D. Hamburg reviews the historical developments of the

concept. The term has been found useful and even necessary in
clinical psychology and psychiatry, developmental psychology, and
geriatric psychology as is evident from the papers in this volume
by D. Hamburg, Gunnar, and Rodin.

The easiest way to define it is that it is the psychological
operations (except the defense) which reduces activation as
measured in the accompanying physiological state (Levine, Weinberg,
and Ursin, 1978). Coping has not been worked out as a theoretical
construct in any detail within learning theory terms, but is related
to the second factor in two-factor-theory of avoidance learning,
where the essential feature is that the second, instrumental phase
reduces the drive state induced by the first factor (Rescorla and
Solomon, 1967; Coover, Ursin, and Levine, 1973). The relevance of
this formulation of two-factor-theory of avoidance learning for the
animal model has been supported by neuropsychological evidence for
independent neural mechanisms for these two factors (Ursin, Coover,
KØhler, DeRyck, Sagvolden, and Levine, 1975).

Other Response Dampening Mechanisms

Several other clear cases of response decrements have been
identified in neurophysiology and physiological psychology, and
should not be confused with coping or defense. The terms used for
these processes cover well-described physiological events, and
therefore, the conventional terms used for these processes should
be reserved for this use. These mechanisms are less related to
psychosomatic pathogenesis than defense and coping.

Sensory adaptation is an obvious source of response decrement
due to changes in sensory organs following repeated stimulus
presentations or prolonged, continuous stimulus presentations. It
would be fortunate if adaptation was used only for events strictly
concerned with sensory organs. Adaptation is used in many other
meanings, but then covers many physiological and psychological
mechanisms. There is an inherent danger in this term because of
the implication of adaptive mechanisms and purpose in a Darwinian
sense, which invites unwarranted speculations.

Fatigue is most often used for processes involving effector
organs, in particular for response decrements due to muscle fatigue.
It is important to identify this source of response decrement. It
remains an open question whether endocrine organs may show this
phenomenon. However, the traditional Selye concept of stress
diseases being due to an exhaustion of the endocrine system has
never been demonstrated. It cannot be accepted as a cause for
psychosomatic disease or for experimental models of such disease.

Response decrement due to synaptic changes following repeated
nerve or synaptic stimulations is referred to as habituation, in

current usage of that term (Kandel, 1970; Thompson and Spencer, 1966). If the response decrement is not due to repeated firing of a certain neural circuit and the Thompson and Spencer criteria are not met, the term habituation should be avoided. If so, this term may be accepted as a hypothetical construct and retains its high value in our theoretical development.

Extinction refers to response decrements due to absence of reinforcement, and also of response decrements due to other response contingencies that decrease the probability of a conditioned response to a conditioned stimulus. Again, it is important that this term is reserved for its proper use. With the increasing importance of learning theory for understanding autonomic and endocrine responses, we should use the terms from learning theory in the way these terms have been developed within that strong theoretical framework.

The response dampening mechanisms which are most important for the prevention of psychosomatic consequences of activation are defense and coping. A proper understanding of these two dimensions is necessary to account for why most people survive and some even thrive under highly threatening and challenging situations. This understanding depends on the identification of these processes as distinct form all the other response dampening mechanisms described above.

MULTIFACTORIAL ANALYSIS OF ACTIVATION

Since the endocrine indicators of activation are not influenced by the main sources of variance affecting the traditional psychophysiological indicators, it was hoped that analysis of plasma levels of hormones would reveal a clear activation factor. However, factor analyses of plasma levels of hormones do not confirm the existence of one simple and straight-forward activation mechanism, but produce independent factors. There is a fairly consistent principle in this organization, which should be taken into account in future work in psychosomatic relationships. On the other hand, there is no reason to discard activation theory, which still predicts the group data, and predicts when any individual will show activation in all his somatic processes. The individuality affects the relative intensity in the activation response, much in the same way as in traditional psychophysiology (Lacey, 1950).

Rose, Poe, and Mason (1967) analysed circulating hormone levels in 46 men undergoing basic military training. They found five factors, two factors related to androgens and estrogens, one catecholamine factor, one cortisol factor, and one factor related to thyroid function. The suprarenal cortical activity was most consistently correlated with effectiveness of the defensive or coping operations. Low epinephrine levels were associated with the ability to express anger openly. Persky, Zuckerman, and Curtis (1968) analysed 54

male subjects, 29 mental patients and 25 hospital employees, with a
battery of psychological tests and measurements of pituitary hormones
and adrenocortical activity. In a multiple regression analysis they
found that adrenocortical activity predicted anxiety and depression.
Follicle-stimulating hormone, luteinizing hormone, and thyreotropic
activity related to an affect expression factor which derived from
hostility and anxiety scores in an ink-blot test.

In a recent study of hormones in 71 parachutist trainees, and
in 44 trainees in a longitudinal study, Ellertsen, Johnsen, and Ursin
(1978) identified three consistent endocrine factors. Their analysis
included plasma levels of growth hormone, testosterone, blood glucose,
cortisol and free fatty acid (n = 71) and the urine levels of epinephrine and norepinephrine in parachutist trainees (N = 31). Factor
analysis revealed three consistent factors: A catecholamine factor,
a cortisol factor, and a testosterone-free fatty acid factor (see
Figure 2). Inspection of the unrotated factors also revealed no
general activation factor. Oblique rotations gave the same result as
orthogonal rotations. The factors are almost orthogonal or independent of each other (Johnsen, 1979, unpublished). In spite of this,
the group data from the longitudinal study showed a clear relationship between the way all hormone systems reacted to a fear situation
and mastery of the task. All hormones showed a significant and
dramatic rise at the first jump in the mock tower training apparatus,
and all hormones showed a clear and consistent decrease with repeated
exposure and learning to master this particular task. However, factor
analysis on any given level revealed the same consistent factor
picture. Correlations were higher when activation was high, but the
three factors remained independent and consistent regardless of the

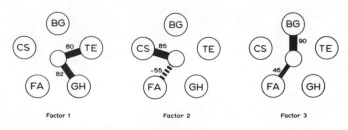

Factor 1   Factor 2   Factor 3

Figure 2

Factor analysis, plasma variables, basal sample, parachutist
trainees (n = 71). Factor 1 is the testosterone (TE) factor, for
this sample also with loadings from growth hormone (GH). Factor 2
is the cortisol (CS) factor, in this case also with a negative
loading from free fatty acids (FA). Factor 3 is interpreted as the
catecholamine factor, with loadings from blood glucose (BG) and free
fatty acids.

level of activation. Ryman and Ursin (1979) have factor analysed
blood values of physiological variables in a study of American Navy
company commanders (n = 31) under considerable physical and psychological work loads (Ward, Rahe, Vickers, Hervig, Conway, and Ryman,
1979). Again no general activation factor was apparent. This was
true also for the unrotated factor matrix. Again, a cortisol factor
and a testosterone factor were evident. Two factors appeared to be
related to catecholamines: One factor involving uric acid, protein
and occasionally systolic pressure. Systolic blood pressure, however,
also related to cortisol. These data, therefore, collected for a
different purpose, seem to confirm the existence of at least three
independent endocrine activation factors.

ENDOCRINE ACTIVATION FACTORS: RELATION TO PSYCHOLOGY

     The three endocrine activation factors relate differently to
important psychological dimensions, and this makes it possible to
arrive at a quite specific psychosomatic hypothesis, specifically
directed at the great variance in psychosomatic data.

     In the two early factor analyses (Rose et al., 1967; Persky
et al., 1968) particular relationships were reported between endocrine
factors and psychological variables. These studies were done on
"joint matrices" where endocrine and psychological data were analysed
at the same time. In the Ellertsen et al. (1978) study, and in the

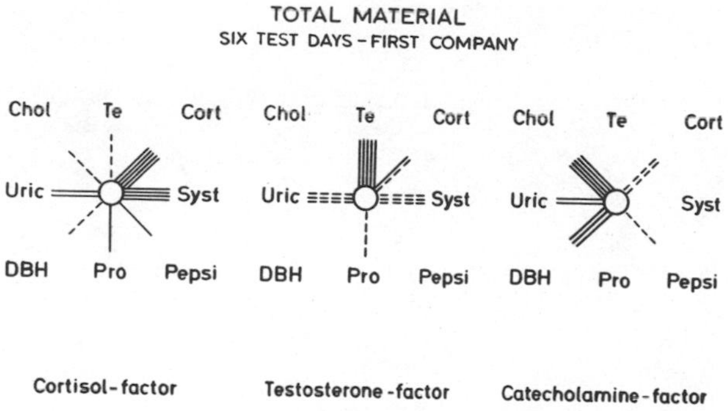

TOTAL MATERIAL
SIX TEST DAYS – FIRST COMPANY

Figure 3

     Consistent factors across six different test days for plasma
variables from 31 commanders under varying degrees of workload and
stress. Each line from one variable to the central circle
represents one day with a significant factor loading from that
variable (Ryman and Ursin, 1979).

Ryman and Ursin (1979) study, the evidence for independent endocrine
activation systems appeared in analyses involving only physiological
variables. When this had been established, analyses were also run
attempting to reveal any psychological specificity of these factors.
In the Ryman and Ursin study of the company commanders, few if any,
such relationships were found. The psychological variables tested
may not have been the important variables for the individual variance
in that sample In the parachutist trainee study, however, consistent
relationships were found. The following discussion is based mainly
on these findings (Baade et al. 1978). Specific relations between
psychological and endocrine variables have also been suggested from
studies of one or a few hormones. These will also be discussed, even
if multivariate studies are required for demonstrating the specificity of such relationships.

The Cortisol Factor

    The cortisol factor related to high defense as measured by the
Kragh Test (1960), and low performance in parachutist jumps, and
with low performance in other performance tests. The correlations
between the cortisol level and performance were consistently negative.
The largest negative correlations were found for any tests with time
pressure. The increase in cortisol was also associated with fear.

    Other studies have also suggested specific relationships between
cortisol and defense (Rose et al., 1967) and depressions (Sachar,
Hellman, Roffwarg, Halpern, Fukushima, and Gallagher, 1973). The
regulation process of the adrenal cortex is disturbed in depressed
patients (Carrol, Curtis, and Mendels, 1976). Plasma hydrocortisone
levels relate to ratings of anxiety (Persky et al., 1968). However,
Sachar et al. (1973) found that the adreno-cortical activity in
depressed patients was related to emotional arousal and psychotic
disorganization, not to depressive illness per se. For many of the
papers suggesting particular relationships between cortisol and
"helplessness" or "conservation-withdrawal" it should be noted that
the increased activation has not been demonstrated to be specific
for the pituitary-adrenal axis. Even so, a specific relationship
between cortisol and specific psychological and psychopathological
processes seems acceptable, and requires further research.

The Catecholamine Factor

    The catecholamine factor found in the parachutist trainees
(Ellertsen et al., 1978) was based on urine samples. This factor
related to performance in intellectual tests and also to performance
in airborne parachutist jumps. This was also true for plasma levels
of free fatty acids, which is another indicator of catecholamine
activity (Norum and Ursin, 1978). Positive correlations between
performance and catecholamines have been demonstrated repeatedly in
single variable studies by Frankenhaeuser and her group (see

Frankenhaeuser this volume). In the parachutist trainees, catecholamines related to activity need and impatience, in particular with
boring routines. The data agree with Roessler (1973), who found
higher psychophysiological reactivity in coping individuals, or in
people with high ego strength. It should also be noted that there
is a suggestive similarity in the description of these catecholamine responders and what has been referred to as Type A behavior
(Jenkins, 1976). Type A behavior is characterized by intense
striving of achievement, competitiveness, easily provoked impatience,
sense of time urgency, abruptiveness of gesture and speech, over-
committment to vocation or profession together with excesses of
drive and hostility. This Type A behavior is claimed to be related
to heart infarctions. Glass (1977) has shown higher autonomic
reactivity in such individuals, but offered a different explanation.

The psychological differences between cortisol responders and
catecholamine responders open several interesting possibilities for
differential psychosomatic involvement, which has also been suggested
by Mason and his group (Mason, Maher, Hartler, Mougey, Perlow, and
Jones, 1976).

The Testosterone Factor

In the parachutist trainees, testosterone was associated
particularly with feminine identifications in the Kragh test and a
particular "masculine" role factor evident from several psychological
tests. Testosterone was also related to preference for thrill and
adventure. It seems as if testosterone picked up particular types
of threats to the individuals, mainly related to the masculine role
in general, and the particular role of becoming a parachutist. Rose
et al., (1967) found that androgens and estrogens correlated with
particular assessments of the psychological state, but this was not
characterised further. This is the least defined factor from a
psychological point of view. The role for somatic pathology is also
uncertain, and this factor will not be dealt with further.

SUSTAINED ACTIVATION PRODUCES SOMATIC PATHOLOGY

The thesis of the present paper is that sustained activation
produces somatic pathology. Shortlasting activation has not been
demonstrated to have any ill effects except when there already is a
somatic change, or a genetic predisposition. The phasic activation
observed in coping subjects is also postulated to be a healthy
response. It is only when the tonic activation variables fail to
decrease that there is a risk for somatic pathology. Persistent
high levels of the tonic activation system may be related to pathology in a variety of ways, high norepinephrine levels might produce
high blood pressure, cortisol may be related to immune mechanisms,
and free fatty acid elevation to cardiovascular disease. The
theory has not been developed in detail for any particular disease

or any particular organ system, but is at least compatible with
available data.

The strongest case for this theoretical position is the
reciprocal set of data on the ulcerations in the non-coping rat (see
N. Miller, this volume), and the reduction of activation observed
in the coping rat (Coover, Ursin, and Levine, 1973). This model is
also the best model for psychosomatic disease from a psychological
point of view. The psychological conditions for ulceration to occur
are reasonably well established, and are accounted for by the concepts
lack of control, and lack of coping (Weiss, 1972; see Murison, this
volume). According to the theory presented here, these psychological
conditions lead to somatic changes through sustained or persistent
activation. Lack of coping, according to the definitions offered
here, means that activation persists. Murison (this volume)
discusses further the application of this theory for the ulceration
model.

Another well developed model is the spontaneous hypertensive rat,
where the vascular changes have been described in detail (Folkow,
1975), but where less details are known about the psychological
factors, except that sustained activation again seems to be a crucial
mediator. Ulcerations and heart infarctions may occur even in
individuals that objectively are performing well, when demands are
very high, requiring constant, sustained activation, as in conflict
situations, or under Sidman schedules (Murison, this volume; Corley,
Shiel, Mauck, Clark, and Barber, 1977).

Sustained activation may be the possible mediator also for
human psychosomatic disease. Life changes do produce disease (Rahe
and Arthur, 1978)., but only in a minority of individuals (Rabkin
and Struening, 1976). The theoretical position of the present paper
is that this is due to the efficiency of the coping mechanisms.
When these mechanisms are insufficient for mastery of the situation,
then health risks occur. Rahe and Arthur (1978) hold that all life
events, including positive ones, constitute health risks, but only
if the life event requires adjustment. Theorell found that distress
was a crucial factor for disease occuring due to life events (Theorell,
1976). Lundberg and Theorell (1976) found that subjective scaling
of life events improved the predictive value of life change indicators.
All positions are compatible with the position of this paper, health
risk arises when activation is sustained for prolonged periods of
time.

This seems also to be true for somatic problems related to
work load. Work load related myocardial infarctions only occur
when there are problems related to the work situation (Theorell and
Floderus-Myrhed, 1977). The importance of job dissatisfaction as a
risk factor has also been pointed out by Sales and House (1971).
Gardell (1977) has reviewed recent Scandinavian data from working

life research which clearly indicate that somatic and psychological
health as well as general well being depend on subjective control
over the work situation. The highest disease risk group is those
that have the highest work load with least control over the work
situation and the time pacing of the work operations. All these data
agree well with the animal model of coping as the important dimension
for somatic health, and the position of this paper that the link
between the psychosocial factors and the somatic health is sustained
activation.

The time course of activation may be a crucial factor in the
pathogenesis of psychosomatic disease. In the coping experiments,
trials or sessions are separated by 24 hours ("spaced learning").
In the ulceration and heart infarction studies, sessions are
continuous, often for 24 hours ("massed trials"). The circadian
rhythm is disturbed, the rats are sleep deprived, and in the ulceration studies also food deprived. Deprivation of food and sleep
produce activation changes by themselves. These models, therefore,
involve sustained activation, and differ from the coping experiments
which involve acute and fairly short lasting activation sessions.
The relevance of the time course of activation is discussed further
by Murison in this volume. The sustained activation seems a
particularly good model for distressful events and chronic unsolvable
conflicts in humans. Weiner (1977) has pointed to the possible role
of disturbed circadian rhythms for producing psychosomatic disease.
This is particularly important for his view that bereavement and
distress are important for the development of psychosomatic disease.

SPECIFICITY OF PSYCHOSOMATIC DISEASE

Alexander (1950) and Dunbar (1954) held that particular
emotional states were channelled into particular physiological
responses. When a particular emotional phenomena had occurred
over a length of time, psychosomatic symptoms occurred in the body
system specific to that emotion. Type of disease and organ selection
was specific and meaningful. Considerable attention has been focused
on demonstrating such relationships between particular emotional
states and particular physiological responses, so-called specific
activation. This has never been demonstrated, and the empirical
basis for this celebrated psychosomatic model does not exist (see
Ursin, 1978 for further discussion). From the data reviewed it
seems likely that personality traits relate to specific endocrine
systems. These personality traits also determine the coping
potential and strategies used when an individual handles threatening
and difficult situations. When sustained activation produces psychosomatic pathology, the pathology may be specific and predictable
from the personality traits and their related dominating endocrine
activation system. It should be stressed that activation is a
general phenomenon acting on all endocrine activities in all subjects.
We treat factors in multidimensional space, where no pure "types"

exist. All individuals load on all factors, but to a varying degree.

Cortisol Responders

In parachutist trainees there was a consistent relationship between cortisol, defense mechanisms and poor performance (Baade et al., 1978). The defense mechanisms interfered with an adequate and accurate evaluation of the threatening environment, which resulted in poor performance in dangerous occupations. The poor performance also affected standard performance tests. The coping level should be relatively low, and correspondingly the risk for psychosomatic disease should be high. However, the high defense mechanisms might defend the individual also against a realistic assessment of his objective performance. Such individuals might reach their incompetence level faster than others, but their psychological traits may also defend them against realisation of their ill fate.

Psychosomatic pathology in this group should be related to cortisol. No specific models for such pathology exist, except for a suggestion by Henry and Stephens (1977) that cortisol pathology may be related to defective immune response mechanisms. Cortisol has also been related to gastric or duodenal ulcers, but this has been questioned recently by Weiner (1977). If cortisol is related to depression and distress, specific pathology may be expected from such states in cortisol responders. As mentioned previously, Theorell found distress to be an important psychosomatic factor. Finally, high defense mechanisms are not always any handicap. It may be of particular importance in surgical emergency situations where body systems are due to collapse, and when even a moderate activation may be more than can be tolerated.

Catecholamine Responders

Catecholamine responders reacted strongly to the situation, they coped well, and showed the corresponding rapid fall in activation (Baade et al., 1978). The same characteristics are true for Roessler's high ego strength person (Roessler, 1973). They should, therefore, be well defended against psychosomatic pathology when coping is possible. However, their mode of physiological and psychological reactivity becomes a handicap if they experience a situation beyond their control. When they reach their "incompetence level" they may be worse off then their well defended cortisol counterpart. In all situations with sustained activation high reactivity may be a risk. Since catecholamine pathology obviously relates to cardiovascular pathology, this may be the underlying mechanism for the claims of relationships between Type A behavior and heart infarctions.

As indiscriminate treatment of all Type A behavior or other

high reactions as undesired seems inadequate. It makes little sense
to reduce general coping potential and ego strength as a therapeutic
endeavour. An effective and gifted performer is more likely to gain
control over his environment, which is the most important aspect of
coping (see Weinberg and Levine, this volume; Frankenhaeuser and
Rissler, 1970; Weiss, 1972). The catecholamine responders should be
recommended to accept challenges and their work situation, but only
as long as their subjective estimate tells them that they master
their situation. The pathological mechanisms involved have been
illustrated in particular for cardiovascular pathology. It has been
demonstrated that in genetically predisposed rats hypertension with
pathological changes of the vascular bed is produced when rats are
subjected to repeated and strong activation (Folkow, 1975). Similar
changes have been produced in rats by sustained conflicts of territory
(Henry and Stephens, 1977). Progressive increase in blood pressure
and heart rate occurred together with atherosclerosis in mice, and
renal damage also occurred.

Catecholamines are also involved in regulation of the plasma
levels of free fatty acids (Norum and Ursin, 1978), and free fatty
acids showed the same relationship to psychological traits as the
catecholamines (Baade et al., 1978). Multifactorial analyses of
heart infarctions identify serum cholesterol, blood pressure,
cigarette smoking, diabetes and angina pectoris as risk factors
(Goldbourt, Medalie and Neufeld, 1975). Serum cholesterol and blood
pressure are obviously related to catecholamines. Cigarette
smoking was higher in the Type A persons in the original reports on
the relationship between Type A personality and heart infarctions
(Friedman and Rosenman, 1959). Psychological traits seem to be
important links between environment and cardiovascular health, and
further research should exploit this possibility of more specific
psychosomatic hypotheses.

CONCLUDING DISCUSSION

There are two previous well known psychosomatic theories, Selye's
stress maladaptation theory, and the psychodynamic theory of
Alexander and Dunbar. Neither of them are supported by data. The
substantial evidence against the Alexander/Dunbar position has been
referred to already. Selye's maladaptation theory is also without
empirical support. Collapse or decrement in suprarenal cortical
activity has not been described or identified as an underlying cause
for any of the experimental psychosomatic models (see Murison this
volume), or any of the accepted psychosomatic diseases (see Weiner,
1977, for review of pathogenesis). Both theories have outplayed
their role as explanatory concepts, and should not be used for this
purpose in our textbooks any longer.

Contemporary research in psychology and physiology, as well as
epidemiological research, offers an empirical basis for a new

psychosomatic theory. This psychosomatic theory has not been
worked out firmly or formally, but is already in its present available
form more specific and more supported by data than any of the previous
theories. It also suggests new research by generating testable
hypotheses.

The theory addresses itself to the general, standardized somatic
response to psychosocial events, just as Selye did with his "stress"
response. Profound changes take place, affecting all endocrine and
autonomic processes, brain function and muscle tension. This
response is a normal, healthy response which is referred to as
activation in this paper, in accordance with the use of the term
psychophysiology, physiological psychology and neurophysiology.

The activation process relates to pathology in two ways. Normal
shortlasting activation may be too great a load for a diseased organ.
The other aspect is that sustained, longlasting activation may
produce somatic changes. Interactions with other pathogenic agents
is an obvious further development of the theory, since it must be
incorporated into our general, contemporary view of diseases as
multicausal phenomenon (Wiener, 1977). However, this has not been
dealt with in this paper since we have no such data as yet.

The essential element in this new psychosomatic theory is that
it is possible to specify the psychological conditions which produce
sustained activation. Activation depends on the individual perception of the stimulus situation, the available responses, and previous
experience with stimuli and responses. Processes identified as
defense and coping in the present paper are of decisive importance
for the resulting activation, and hence the internal state of the
organism. Activation is a multivariate process and should be
studied as such. The individual variance is related to personality
traits affecting both defense and coping mechanisms. This makes it
possible to develop specific hypotheses in psychosomatic theory,
identifying risk groups based on personality, somatic responses, and
life situations.

The theory explains why life changes (Rahe and Arthur, 1978)
are related to somatic disease, but only with low correlations
(Rabkin and Struening, 1976). This is due to the coping potential
of man. When these are surpassed sustained activation occurs, which
may result in pathology. Selye and Theorell point to "distress";
it is only the degree of experienced unsolved conflict which is the
important element, since this is what produces sustained activation.

REFERENCES

Alexander, F., 1950, "Psychosomatic Medicine," Norton, New York.
Baade, E., Halse, K., Stenhammer, P. E., Ellertsen, B., Johnsen, T. B.,
    Vollmer, F., and Ursin, H., 1978, Psychological tests, in:
    "Psychobiology of Stress: A Study of Coping Men," H. Ursin,
    E. Baade, and S. Levine eds., Academic Press, New York.
Bassett, J. R., Cairncross, K. D., and King, M. G., 1973, Parameters
    of novelty, shock predictability and response contingency in
    corticosterone release in the rat, Physiol. Behav., 10:901.
Cannon, J., 1931, "The Wisdom of the Body," W. W. Norton, New York.
Carrol, B. J., Curtis, G. C., and Mendels, J., 1976, Neuroendocrine
    regulation in depression. I. Limbic system - adrenocortical
    dysfunction, Arch. Gen. Psychiat., 33:1039.
Coover, G., Ursin, H., and Levine, S., 1973, Corticosterone and
    avoidance in rats with basolateral amygdala lesions, J. Comp.
    Physiol. Psychol., 85:111.
Corley, K. C., Shiel, F. O'M., Mauck, H. P., Clark, L. A., and
    Barber, J. H., 1977, Myocardial degeneration and cardiac arrest
    in squirrel monkey: Physiological and psychological correlates,
    Psychophysiology, 14:322.
Duffy, E., 1972, Activation, in: "Handbook of Psychophysiology,"
    N. Greenfield and R. Sternback eds., Holt, Rinehart and Winston,
    New York.
Dunbar, F., 1954, "Emotions and Bodily Changes," 4th ed., Columbia
    University Press, New York.
Dykman, R. A., Reese, W. G., Galbrecht, C. R., and Thomasson, P. J.,
    1959, Psychophysiological reactions to novel stimuli: Measure-
    ment, adaptation and relationship of psychological and physio-
    logical variables in the normal human, N.Y. Acad. Sci. Ann.,
    79:43.
Ellertsen, B., Johnsen, T. B., and Ursin, H., 1978, Relationship
    between the hormonal responses to activation and coping, in:
    "Psychobiology of Stress: A Study of Coping Men," H. Ursin,
    E. Baade, and S. Levine eds., Academic Press, New York.
Folkow, B., 1975, Central neurohormonal mechanisms in spontaneously
    hypertensive rats compared with human essential hypertension,
    Clin. Sci. Molec. Med., 48:205.
Frankenhaeuser, M., and Rissler, A., 1970, Effects of punishment
    on catecholamine release and efficiency of performance,
    Psychopharmacologia, 17:378.
French, J. R. P., Jr., Rodgers, W., and Cobb, S., 1974, Adjustment
    as person-environment fit, in: "Coping and Adaptation,"
    G. V. Coelho, D. A. Hamburg, and J. E. Adams eds., Basic Books,
    New York.
Friedman, M., and Rosenman, R. H., 1959, Association of specific
    overt behavior pattern with blood and cardiovascular findings,
    J. Am. Med. Assoc., 169:1286.
Friedman, S. B., Mason, J. W., and Hamburg, D. A., 1963, Urinary
    17-hydroxycorticosteroid levels in parents of children with neo-
    plastic disease: a study of chronic psychological stress,
    Psychosom. Med., 25:364.

Gardell, B., 1977, Psychological and social problems of industrial work in affluent societies, Int. J. Psychol., 12:125.

Glass, D. C., 1977, Stress, behavior patterns, and coronary disease, Am. Sci., 65:177.

Gouldbourt, U., Medalie, J. H., and Neufeld, H. N., 1975, Clinical myocardial infarction over a five-year period. III. A multi-variate analysis of incidence, the Israel ischemic heart disease study, J. Chron. Dis., 28:217.

Haan, N., 1969, Tripartite model of ego functioning values and clinical and research applications, J. Nerv. Ment. Dis., 148:14.

Hebb, D. O., 1955, Drives and the CNS (Conceptual nervous system), Psychol. Rev., 62:243.

Henry, J. P., and Stephens, P. M., 1977, "Stress, Health, and the Social Environment. A Sociobiologic Approach to Medicine," Springer, New York.

Jenkins, C. D., 1976, Recent evidence supporting psychologic and social risk factors for coronary disease (second of two parts), N. Eng. J. Med., 294:1033.

Kandel, E. R., 1970, Nerve cells and behavior, Sci. Am., 223:57.

Kragh, U., 1960, The defense mechanism test: A new method for diagnosis and personnel selection, J. Appl. Psychol., 44:303.

Kragh, U., 1962, Predictions of success of Danish attack divers by the defense mechanism test (DMT). Psychol. Res. Bull., Lund University, Sweden.

Kroeber, T. C., 1963, The coping functions of the ego mechanisms, in: "The Study of Lives: Essays of Personality in Honor of Henry A. Murray," R. W. White ed., Atherton Press, New York.

Lacey, J. I., 1950, Individual differences in somatic response patterns, J. Comp. Physiol. Psychol., 43:338.

Lazarus, R. S., and Alfert, E., 1964, Short-circuiting of threat by experimentally altering cognitive appraisal, J. Abnorm. Soc. Psychol., 69:195.

Lazarus, R. S., and Averill, J. R., 1972, Emotion and cognition: With special reference to anxiety, in: "Anxiety: Current trends in theory and research," Vol. 2, C. D. Spielberger ed., Academic Press, New York.

Levine, S., Goldman, L., and Coover, G. D., 1972, Expectancy and the pituitary-adrenal system, in: "Physiology, Emotion, and Psychosomatic Illness," Ciba Foundation Symposium 8, Elsevier, Amsterdam.

Levine, S., Weinberg, J., and Ursin, H., 1978, Definition of the coping process and statement of the problem, in: "Psychobiology of Stress: A Study of Coping Men," H. Ursin, E. Baade, and S. Levine eds., Academic Press, New York.

Lindsley, D. B., 1951, Emotion, in: "Handbook of Experimental Psychology," S. Stevens, ed., John Wiley, New York.

Lundberg, U., and Theorell, T., 1976, Scaling of life changes: Differences between three diagnostic groups and between recently experienced and non-experienced events, J. Hum. Stress, 2:7.

Mason, J. W., 1971, A re-evaluation of the concept of "non-specifi-
    city" in stress toeory, J. Psychiat. Res., 8:323.
Mason, J. W., Maher, J. T., Hartley, L. H., Mougey, E. H., Perlow,
    M. J., and Jones, L. G., 1976, Selectivity of corticosteroid
    and catecholamine responses to various natural stimuli, in:
    "Psychopathology of Human Adaptation," G. Serban ed., Plenum
    Press, New York.
Miller, G. A., Galanter, E., and Pribram, K. H., 1960, "Plans and
    the Structure of Behavior," Holt, Rinehart, Winston, New York.
Norum, K., and Ursin, H., 1978, Fatty acid mobilization, in: "Psy-
    chobiology of Stress: A Study of Coping Men," H. Ursin,
    E. Baade, and S. Levine eds., Academic Press, New York.
Persky, H., Zuckerman, M., and Curtis, G. C., 1968, Endocrine
    function in emotionally disturbed and normal men, J. Nerv.
    Ment. Dis., 146:488.
Price, D. B., Thaler, M., and Mason, J. W., 1957, Preoperative
    emotional states and adrenal cortical activity, Arch. Neurol.
    Psychiat., 77:646.
Rabkin, J. G., and Struening, E. L., 1976, Life events, stress and
    illness, Science, 194:1013.
Rahe, R. H., and Arthur, R. J., 1978, Life change and illness studies:
    Past history and future directions, J. Hum. Stress., 4:3.
Rescorla, R. A., and Solomon, R. L., 1967, Two process learning
    theory: Relationships between Pavlovian conditioning and
    instrumental learning, Psychol. Rev., 74:151.
Roessler, R., 1973, Personality, psychophysiology, and performance,
    Psychophysiology, 10:315.
Rose, R. M., Poe, R. O., and Mason, J. W., 1967, Observations on
    the relationship between psychological state, 17-OHCS excretion,
    and epinephrine, norepinephrine, insulin, BEI, estrogen and
    androgen levels during basic training, Psychosom. Med., 29:544.
Ryman, D., and Ursin, H., 1979, Factor analyses of the physiological
    responses of company commanders to stress, in preparation.
Sacher, E. J., Hellman, L., Roffwarg, H., Halpern, F. S., Fukushima,
    D. K., and Gallagher, T. F., 1973, Disrupted 24-hour patterns
    of cortisol secretion in psychotic depression, Arch. Gen.
    Psychiat., 28:19.
Sales, S. M., and House, J., 1971, Job dissatisfaction as a possible
    risk factor in coronary heart disease, J. Chron. Dis., 23:861.
Selye, H., 1974, "Stress Without Distress," J. B. Lippincott,
    Philadelphia.
Sokolov, Y. N., 1963, "Perception and the Conditioned Reflex,"
    Pergamon, Oxford.
Theorell, T., 1976, Selected illnesses and somatic factors in
    relation to two psychosocial stress indices: A prospective
    study on middle-aged construction building workers, J. Psycho-
    som. Res., 20:7.
Theorell, T., and Floderus-Myrhed, B., 1977, "Workload" and risk of
    myocardial infarction: A prospective psychosocial analysis,
    Int. J. Epid., 6:17.

Thompson, R. F., and Spencer, W. A., 1966, Habituation: A model
    phenomenon for the study of neuronal substrates of behavior,
    Psychol. Rev., 73:16.
Ursin, H., 1978, Activation, coping and psychosomatics, in: "Psycho-
    biology of Stress: A Study of Coping Men," H. Ursin, E. Baade,
    and S. Levine eds., Academic Press, New York.
Ursin, H., Baade, E., and Levine, S. eds., "Psychobiology of Stress:
    A Study of Coping Men," Academic Press, New York.
Ursin, H., Coover, G. D., Køhler, C., DeRyck, M., Sagvolden, T.,
    and Levine, S., 1975, Limbic structures and behavior: Endocrine
    correlates, in: "Progress in Brain Research. Hormone, Homeo-
    stasis and the Brain," Vol. 42, W. H. Gispen, T. B. Wimersma
    van Greidanus, B. Bohus, and D. deWied eds., Elsevier, Amsterdam.
Vaernes, R., 1978, Hovedoppgave. Thesis, University of Oslo, Oslo.
Vickers, G., 1973, Motivation theory: A cybernetic contribution,
    Behav. Sci., 18:242.
Ward, H. W., Rahe, R. H., Vickers, R. R., Hervig, L. K., Conway, T.
    L., and Ryman, D. H., 1979, "Occupational Stress in Navy
    Company Commanders: A psychobiological Study," in preparation.
Weiner, H., 1977, "Psychobiology and Human Disease," Elsevier,
    New York.
Weinstein, J., Averill, J. R., Opton, E. M., Jr., and Lazarus, R. S.,
    1968, Defensive style and discrepancy between self-report and
    physiological indexes of stress, J. Pers. Soc. Psychol., 10:406.
Weiss, J. M., 1972, Influence of psychological variables on stress-
    induced pathology, in: "Physiology, Emotion and Psychosomatic
    Illness," Ciba Foundation Symposium 8, Elsevier, Amsterdam.

EXPERIMENTALLY INDUCED GASTRIC ULCERATION:

A MODEL DISORDER FOR PSYCHOSOMATIC RESEARCH

Robert Murison

Department of Physiological Psychology

University of Bergen

INTRODUCTION

Understanding of coping and health problems in man will be greatly advanced by the study of stress-related disorders in animals. Analysis of the etiology of animal disorders suggests which variables might also be important factors in human disease processes. Thus, an understanding of the psychological factors involved in stress-related disorders in animals is highly relevant to a complete understanding of human psychosomatic problems. In this chapter, I shall review our state of knowledge of the psychological factors which are associated with one stress disorder, gastric ulceration, in rats. Psychologists may use such a "model" disorder either to generate a general psychosomatic model relevant to animals and man, or to test theories of psychosomatics which have been derived from human clinical and experimental studies. Any such theory must be tested empirically, and this may only be done by using animals. Apart from ethical reasons, use of laboratory animals with known genetic and developmental background eliminates to some extent the problems of individual differences and past history which beset human work. In this way, we shall be able to elucidate the major psychological factors associated with the development of stress disorders.

Selye (1936) described a non-specific stress syndrome, which is the animal's characteristic response when presented with noxious stimuli over an extended period of time. The syndrome is character- ised by atrophy of the thymus, hypertrophy of the adrenal glands, and gastric ulceration. There are therefore good historical reasons for choosing gastric ulceration as a model stress disorder, although the symptoms observed in the rat are not necessarily synonymous

281

with the peptic ulcer found in man. In the rat, the ulceration appears in the form of reversible erosions of the gastric mucosa, usually associated with haemorrhage, and is easily diagnosed and measurable.

Ulceration may be induced in rats by a number of methods: physical restraint (Ader, 1971), free access to a running wheel (Manning, Wall, Montgomery, Simmons and Sessions, 1978; Paré, 1976), cooling (Boyd, Caul and Bowen, 1977), electric shock (Glavin and Mikhail, 1976), psychological conflict (Sawrey, Conger and Turrel, 1956; Sawrey and Weisz, 1956; Weisz, 1957), attack by conspecifics (Lore and Luciano, 1977), and "social stress" (Allen, 1972). Most methods involve severe food deprivation in addition to the stressor of interest to the experimenter. The presence of either nutritive or non-nutritive bulk in the stomach protects the mucosa from injury (Essman, 1966; Mikhail and Hirschberg, 1972). Some methods, running wheel activity for example, might also involve an element of sleep deprivation, which is not normally taken into account as an important variable.

With any given method of inducing gastric ulceration, there are a number of factors which affect the animals' susceptibility to the disorder. Susceptibility is not the same in different strains of laboratory rat, or even within the same strain acquired from different vendors (Paré, Glavin and Vincent, 1977). Age and weight of the animals is also important. Although Sawrey and Sawrey (1966) reported that age and weight were not significant variables in conflict-induced ulceration, Miller (this volume) reports that Weiss has found it difficult to induce ulcerations in animals weighing over 400 grams. Given that "social stress" in artificial colonies of wild rats results in ulceration (Allen, 1972), it is likely that susceptibility to the disorder is also affected by social factors in the rat litter, over which the experimenter has little control.

Psychologists have been interested most in the relationship between ulcerogenesis and controllable psychological variables, notably 'behavioural control' and psychological conflict. Studies in these areas have led to a robust animal model of ulceration (Weiss, 1971a, 1972) which we have found extremely useful. In view of Ursin's activation theory of psychosomatics (this volume), we are also interested in the relationship between neuroendocrine stress responses and gastric pathology. Equally important, but outside the scope of this paper, is an understanding of the local physio-logical mechanisms of ulceration. This area has been comprehensively reviewed by Weiner (1977).

ULCERATION AND BEHAVIOURAL CONTROL

The earliest key study of the effects of behavioural control over a stressful situation was carried out on monkeys, and led to

the surprising suggestion that control was harmful to the individual (Brady, Porter, Conrad and Mason, 1958). Pairs of monkeys were trained in a Sidman avoidance task. The animals received electric shock to the feet every 20 seconds unless they made the lever-press avoidance repsonse. Performance of the response resulted in post-ponement of the shock for a further 20 seconds. The shock was not preceded by any signal. This design of avoidance tasks character-istically leads to high response rates. Within each animal pair, the monkey which learned the task fastest was assigned to the "executive" condition. Its slower learning partner was assigned to a "shock-yoked" condition. The executive animal of the pair received six hour sessions of the avoidance procedure, followed by a six hour rest period, continuously for several weeks. The shock-yoked animal was unable to control the delivery of foot shock, but received shock whenever the executive failed to make the appropriate avoidance response. The number, intensity and distribution of shocks received by the two animals were therefore identical. However, whilst the executive monkey had potentially total control over shock presentation the yoked animal received shock independently of its own behaviour.

The executive monkeys died between 23 and 48 days of this treatment. Shock-yoked animals were killed at the time of death of their executive partners. Post mortem examinations showed that in all the executive animals, gastric ulceration was a prominent feature of the pathology, whilst none of the shock-yoked animals exhibited gastro-intestinal symptoms. Under these particular conditions, sustained performance of the avoidance response was detrimental to the health of the animal.

Despite the impetus that these results gave to further research in this area, the experimental design suffered serious criticism. First, the executive animals were allocated to that condition on the basis that they had learned the avoidance task faster. We know that rats which are fastest at learning avoidance tasks are also more susceptible to gastric ulceration (Sines, Cleeland and Adkins, 1963), and the same could be true of monkeys. Second, the Sidman avoidance design leads to extremely high rates of response (15 to 20 responses per minute in the Brady study). Since the shock-yoked animals do not need to make these repsonses, there is an extreme physiological difference between the animals. Weiss (1971a) reported that rats performing an unsignaled avoidance task developed less severe ulceration than shock-yoked partners, although the executives were responding at a high rate. This suggests that the pre-selection factor in the "executive monkey experiment" was most important in leading to data which suggested that behavioural control was maladaptive.

One uncommon feature of the Brady et al. design was that the animals had periods of rest. In most studies, animals are kept in the stressful situation for twenty hours or more without any break.

Desiderato, MacKinnon and Hissom (1974) found that rats did not
develop significant ulceration after a six hour stress session unless
the animals were given at least a two hour rest period between the
end of the session and sacrifice. They suggested that ulceration
was associated with a "rebound" of the parasympathetic nervous
system following high sympathetic activity during the stress session.
The importance of the relationship between stress and rest periods
was demonstrated by a follow up study to the executive monkey
experiment. The design was identical to that of the first experiment,
except that stress sessions lasted for eighteen hours and were
interspersed with six hour rest periods. Despite a longer overall
time in the stress situation, none of the animals developed gastric
ulceration, even after several weeks of this treatment (Brady, 1958).

    In contrast to the monkey data, rat experiments have demon-
strated that behavioural control in avoidance tasks protects the
animal from ulceration. Weiss (1968) reported that when rats were
assigned at random to executive and shock-yoked groups, and a signaled
avoidance task was used, the shock-yoked animals developed significantly more ulceration than did the executives. The rats were
placed in separate restraint apparatuses. For the executive animal,
the avoidance response was nose contact with a metal plate after
presentation of an auditory signal. The shock-yoked animals
received the same number of shocks as the executive, with equal
distribution and intensity. A non-shock group was left undisturbed,
and served as controls for food deprivation. The stress session
lasted for twenty-one hours, and the animals were left another
twelve hours before being killed. Examination of the stomachs
indicated that behavioural control in this situation protected the
executive animals from the ulcerogenic effects of shock. Put
another way, lack of control increased the ulcerogenic effects of
shock.

    Weiss has been able to consistently replicate this effect using
warning signals of different information value, as long as the
avoidance response requirements are simple (Weiss, 1971a; 1972).
The executive animals in his experiments, however, have generally
exhibited poor avoidance performance. The importance of response
requirements in determining the direction of pathology differences
between executive and shock-yoked animals is demonstrated by a study
carried out by Eva Isaksen and myself (in preparation).

    Rats were allocated at random to executive, shock-yoked and
non-shock groups. The animals were deprived of food for twenty-
four hours before the stress session. They were then placed in
separate shuttleboxes. For the executive animal, the task was
signaled two-way active avoidance. A ten second auditory signal
was followed by foot shock unless the rat crossed from one side of
the shuttlebox to the other. Foot shock and the signal were
continued until the animal crossed. On the following trial, the

animal was required to avoid shock by crossing back to the original
side of the box. We employed experimental parameters which we knew
would lead to good avoidance performance. By using a short inter-
trial interval (thirty seconds) and intermittent shock of medium
intensity (0.1 mA), we obtained fast learning. The inter-trial
interval was systematically increased up to five minutes. Over the
twenty hour stress session, executive animals exhibited on
average avoidance performance of eighty percent. Shock-yoked animals
received shock whenever the executive failed to avoid. Non-shock
control animals were left undisturbed throughout the session.

The animals were killed six hours after the end of the stress
session. Post mortem examination of the stomachs revealed that the
executive animals developed significantly more ulceration than did
the shock-yoked or non-shock animals. To understand why the use of
a two-way active avoidance design produced results contrary to the
Weiss data, we need first to consider studies of conflict-induced
ulceration, and the Weiss ulceration model.

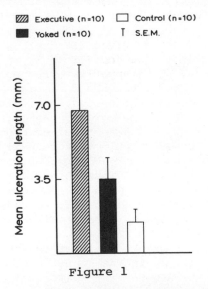

Figure 1

Mean ulceration length and standard error of the mean for
executive rats after 22 hours two-way active avoidance, and for
shock-yoked and non-shock animals (Murison and Isaksen, in
preparation).

ULCERATION AND PSYCHOLOGICAL CONFLICT

Early studies of gastric ulceration in rats employed experimental procedures which involved an approach/avoidance conflict. Sawrey and Weisz (1956) placed three food-deprived rats at a time in a large rectangular box with a grid floor. Food and water containers were placed at opposite ends of the box. To reach either food or water, the animals had to cross electrified areas of the grid floor. Only the central portion of the floor was safe. The shock was turned off in the end areas for one hour in every forty-eight, to allow free feeding and drinking. The animals remained in this conflict situation for thirty days. A non-shock control group of animals was placed on a forty-seven hour food and water deprivation schedule. Extensive gastric ulceration was found in the stomachs of the rats in the conflict situation, whilst none were found in the control group.

Using more adequate control groups, Sawrey, Conger and Turrel (1956) demonstrated that whilst hunger and shock were in themselves important variables in ulceration, conflict significantly increased the extent of the disorder. This was confirmed by Weisz (1957) who used several different approach/avoidance situations.

The important point in such conflict experiments is that the animals have control both over food and shock, but successful avoidance behaviour increases hunger and successful feeding necessitates shock. Moot, Cebula and Crabtree (1970) attempted to differentiate between the roles of psychological conflict and behavioural control. Food deprived rats were placed in separate Skinner boxes. Animals in the "conflict" group were able to obtain food by pressing a bar. This appetitive response also initiated foot shock. The duration of the shock was independent of the animal's behaviour, but equated over the stress session to that received by animals in the "conflict-escape" group. Animals in this group were also able to obtain food, and also received shock when they pressed the bar. They were, however, able to terminate shock by turning a wheel. Animals in a "food-shock-yoke" group received food and shock independently of their own behaviour whenever their partner in the "conflict" group responded. A group of "food-yoke" rats received food but no shock, yoked to the "conflict-escape" group. The animals were given three twenty hour sessions in these conditions.

Significantly fewer of the conflict-escape animals developed ulceration than did animals in the conflict group. Furthermore, the conflict-escape animals develop no more ulceration than did the food-yoked group. The data were interpreted as demonstrating that conflict is neither a necessary or sufficient condition for ulceration, and that the major factor in ulcerogenesis is lack of behavioural control.

Paré reached a similar conclusion (Paré, 1962). Food and water deprived animals were placed in shuttleboxes. Water containers at each end of the box delivered a small quantity of water whenever the rat approached. The grid in the central section of the box was electrified, so that to reach the other water source after exhausting the first, the animal had to cross over a dangerous area. Animals were placed in this conflict situation for eight hours a day for four weeks. Ulcerations in these animals were compared with injury in shock-yoked, water-yoked and home cage control animals. The conflict animals developed significantly less ulceration than did shock-yoked animals.

The conflict animals in Paré's experiment were in a completely different situation to the conflict animals in the earlier studies of Sawrey and Weisz (1956). In these experiments, animals which obtained food were shocked whilst making the consummatory response of feeding or drinking. In the Paré design, animals were shocked whilst approaching water, but were in a "safe" area whilst making the consummatory response of drinking. The same distinction occurs within the design used by Moot, Cebulla and Crabtree (1970). Animals in the conflict group were shocked whilst feeding, whilst those in the conflict-escape group were able to terminate shock and continue to feed. In both experiments, animals which were able to feed or drink after termination of shock developed less severe ulceration than shock-yoked animals. Perhaps the shock received by these animals during approach behaviour serves as a secondary cue that food and water is available. If this is so, the animals might not be in a serious conflict situation at all. Sawrey and Sawrey (1966) report that those animals which actually reached the food developed little ulceration, and suggest that these animals were not in a significant conflict situation.

The above conflict studies are made complicated by virtue of the involvement of two motivational systems, hunger and fear. Our own experiment using two-way active avoidance described in the previous section, involved conflict but only one motivation system, fear. In that situation, the ulcerogenic effects of conflict override the protective effects of behavioural control. The relationship between ulcerogenesis, control and conflict is simplified by making use of Weiss's ulceration model.

THE WEISS MODEL

Weiss (1971a, 1972) noted that ulceration increased as a function of the number of coping attempts made by shock-yoked animals. At the same time, the fact that executive animals developed less ulceration than the yoked partners indicated that ulceration decreases when the coping attempt is successful. Put more formally, the extent of ulceration suffered by an animal is a function of the number of coping attempts, and an inverse function

of the "relevant feedback" from those attempts. For Weiss, relevant feedback is the presentation of stimuli which are not associated with the stressor, or the removal of stimuli which are associated with the stressor. Thus animals performing an unsignaled avoidance task develop less severe ulceration than do animals performing a signaled avoidance task, where the avoidance response also terminates the signal (Weiss, 1971a).

Using these terms, conflict situations of the type used by Sawrey and Weisz (1956) involve low relevant feedback. Animals making coping attempts which result in the presentation of aversive stimuli will develop ulceration. Animals which attempt to "cope" with their hunger receive negative feedback in the form of shock. Animals which attempt to cope by avoiding shock receive negative feedback in the form of increased hunger. The contrary results of Paré (1962) and Moot, Cebulla and Crabtree (1970) may also be explained in terms of feedback. Paré's conflict animals obtained high feedback first from the alleviation of shock when they reached the water source, and second from the presentation of the water. The conflict-escape animals in the Moot et al. study in effect performed two responses, or coping attempts. First, they pressed a bar to obtain food. Second, they turned a wheel to terminate shock. Both these responses resulted in high relevant feedback. The ulceration would therefore be expected to be less in these animals than in shock-yoked animals, whose responses yielded no feedback.

Clearly it is more satisfactory to analyse the role of conflict and control in situations involving only one motivational system. Weiss (1971b) tested rats in a simple one-way signaled active avoidance task for twenty-four hours, with the usual shock-yoked and food-deprived control groups. After twenty-four hours, the conditions of the executive animals were changed such that, although an avoidance response was still necessary, the response also led to a train of shocks of fixed duration. These shocks were also given to the shock-yoked animals. After twenty-four hours of this treatment, extreme ulceration was found in the stomachs of the executive animals, compared to the shock-yoked rats. Each avoidance response made by the executive animal resulted in low feedback. Responses by yoked animals resulted in no feedback, but these animals made considerably fewer responses than the executives, and so developed less severe ulceration.

Although this experiment put the executive animal in a position of conflict, or low feedback after the avoidance response, it also involved loss of behavioural control. This might be an important variable in ulceration. The two-way active avoidance experiment described earlier (Murison and Isaksen, in preparation) put the executive animal in a conflict situation from the second trial onwards, but there was no loss of control. The two-way active

avoidance requires that on each trial the animal returns to a
location from which it has escaped on the previous trial. The
animal is therefore presented with stimuli which are associated
with the stressor, and so receives low relevant feedback from this
response. Although our animals exhibited excellent avoidance
performance, they developed more severe ulceration than did shock-
yoked animals. This confirms that conflict does play a part in
ulcerogenesis, and demonstrates the importance of response requirements and feedback in determining the extent of ulceration. The
concepts of behavioural control and psychological conflict per se
are of little use in predicting ulceration. Rather, each experimental situation must be considered in terms of whether or not
behavioural control results in high or low relevant feedback.

ACTIVATION, COPING AND ULCERATION

Above, I have discussed the relationship between ulceration
and behaviour. How does the central nervous system affect the
health of the target organ? An important part of the animal's
response to stressful situations is increased secretion of the
adrenal cortex (Selye, 1974). The level of circulating corticosterone in the blood has also been used as an index of activation,
or arousal (Hennessy and Levine, 1979). Treatment of humans or
animals with exogenous steroids results in ulceration (Robert and
Nezamis, 1964; Spiro and Milles, 1960). Is there any evidence for
a relationship between endogenous corticosterone levels and gastric
ulceration?

Brady, Porter, Conrad and Mason (1958), during their "executive
monkey experiment," measured 17-hydroxycorticosteroid levels from
executive and yoked animals every twenty-four or forty-eight hours.
Both groups of monkeys exhibited a slight increase in adrenocortical
secretion during the initial phases of avoidance conditioning, but
levels thereafter remained stable. No difference was reported
between the executive and yoked monkeys. Despite the severity of
ulceration later found in the executive animals., there was no
evidence that it was related to adrenocortical activity.

Weiss (1972) has reported that ulceration relates consistently
in some way with corticosterone levels at the end of stress sessions.
Under conflict conditions (Weiss, 1971b), post-session plasma
corticosterone levels of the executive animals were significantly
higher than those of the shock-yoked group. It will be remembered
that executive animals also developed greater ulceration than did
their shock-yoked partners. Under non-conflict conditions (Weiss,
1971a), group differences in adrenocortical activity were not found,
and there was considerable variance in corticosterone levels. There
was however a significant positive correlation between ulceration
and adrenocortical activity. The correlation was mainly

attributable to those animals with extreme corticosterone levels
(greater than 70 μg/100 ml), which invariably exhibited severe
ulceration.

We (Murison and Isaksen, in preparation) measured plasma
corticosterone levels at the end of the stress sessions in the two-
way active avoidance experiment described earlier. No differences
were found between executive, shock-yoked or non-shock control
groups, neither were we able to find any correlation between the
adrenocortical activity and gastric ulceration.

Generally, we have been unable to induce gastric ulceration
as severe as that reported by Weiss (1968, 1971a, 1971b, 1972), and
also have not observed animals with such high levels of corticosterone, although we know that our animals were not suffering from
adrenal exhaustion (Murison and Isaksen, in preparation). It is
possible that the high adrenocortical activity found in some of

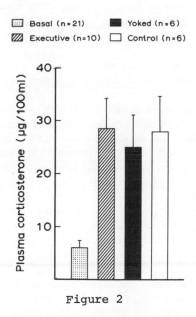

Figure 2

Mean and standard error of the mean levels of plasma
corticosterone under basal and post-session conditions in the two-
way active avoidance experiment (Murison and Isaksen, in preparation).

Weiss's rats reflected a stress response to the extreme discomfort suffered by the animals as a consequence of severe ulceration.

The data indicate that there is little evidence for any direct relationship between post-session levels of adrenocortical activity and ulceration. However, in his activation theory of psychosomatics, Ursin (see this volume) proposes that psychosomatic illness is a consequence of high sustained activation. "Coping" has also been defined in terms of activation. Levine, Weinberg and Ursin (1978) defined coping on the basis of the ultimate reduction of the physiological arousal produced as a consequence of any given stimulus complex's novelty or threat. The definition does not involve behavioural measures of what we might normally understand by coping. We know that after ten trials of a two-way active avoidance task, rats exhibit post test corticosterone levels in the order of 60 µg/100 ml (Coover, Ursin and Levine, 1973). Our own executive animals exhibited levels in the order of 30 µg/100 ml after twenty-two hours avoidance performance. Therefore, the animals were developing ulceration although there was evidence of physiological coping.

Unfortunately, there is no data on adrenocortical activity during stress session in the ulceration literature. The activation theory of Ursin depends on having available measures of activation whilst animals are subjected to stressors, and on finding some lawful relationship between the duration and peak values of activation and subsequent disease. Such parametric work, involving parallel measures of activation, behaviour and disease, even if it does not completely validate any one theory, will greatly help us to understand some of the mechanisms associated with stress-related disorders.

REFERENCES

Ader, R., 1971, Experimentally induced gastric lesions, Adv. Psychosom. Med., 6:1.

Allen, H. M., 1972, Gastrointestinal erosions in wild rats subjected to "social stress," Life Sci., 11:351.

Boyd, S. C., Caul, W. F., and Bowen, B. K., 1977, Use of cold-restraint to examine psychological factors in ulceration, Physiol. Behav., 18:865.

Brady, J. V., Porter, R. W., Conrad, D. G., and Mason, J. W., 1958, Avoidance behaviour and the development of gastroduodenal ulcers, J. Exp. Anal. Behav., 1:69.

Brady, J. V., 1958, Ulcers in "executive" monkeys, Sci. Am., 199:95.

Coover, G. D., Ursin, H., and Levine, S., 1973, Plasma corticosterone levels during active avoidance learning in rats, J. Comp. Physiol. Psychol., 82:170.

Desiderato, O., MacKinnon, J. R., and Hissom, H., 1974, Development
    of gastric ulcers in rats following stress termination, J. Comp.
    Physiol. Psychol., 87:208.
Essman, W. B., 1966, Gastric ulceration in differentially housed
    mice, Psychol. Rep., 19:173.
Glavin, G. B., and Mikhail, A. A., 1976, Stress and ulcer etiology
    in the rat, Physiol. Behav., 16:135.
Hennessy, J. W., and Levine, S., 1979, Stress arousal and the
    pituitary-adrenal system: a psychoendocrine hypothesis, in:
    "Progress in Psychobiology and Physiological Psychology, Vol.8,"
    J. M. Sprague and A. N. Epstein, eds., Academic Press, New York.
Lore, R., and Luciano, D., 1977, Attack stress induces gastrointes-
    tinal pathology in domesticated rats, Physiol. Behav., 18:743.
Levine, S., Weinberg, J., and Ursin, H., 1978, Definition of the
    coping process and statement of the problem, in: "Psychobiology
    of Stress: A Study of Coping Men," H. Ursin, E. Baade and
    S. Levine, eds., Academic Press, New York.
Manning, F. J., Wall, H. G., Montgomery, C. A., Simmons, C. J., and
    Sessions, G. R., 1978, Microscopic examination of the activity-
    stress ulcer in the rat, Physiol. Behav., 21:269.
Mikhail, A. A., and Hirschberg, J., 1972, Ulceration in the rat's
    forestomach: Its reduction by non-nutritive bulky substances,
    Physiol. Behav., 8:769.
Moot, S. A., Cebulla, R. P., and Crabtree, J. M., 1970, Instrumental
    control and ulceration in rats, J. Comp. Physiol. Psychol.,
    71:405.
Paré, W. P., 1962, The effects of conflict and shock stress on
    stomach ulceration in the rat, J. Psychosom. Res., 6:223.
Paré, W. P., 1976, Activity-stress ulcer in the rat: Frequency
    and chronicity, Physiol. Behav., 16:699.
Paré, W. P., Glavin, G. B., and Vincent, G. P., 1977, Vendor
    differences in starvation induced gastric ulceration, Physiol.
    Behav., 19:315.
Robert, A., and Nezamis, J., 1964, Histopathology of steroid-induced
    ulcers, Arch. Path., 77:407.
Sawrey, J. M., and Sawrey, W. L., 1966, Age, Weight and social effects
    of ulceration rate in rats, J. Comp. Physiol. Psychol., 61:464.
Sawrey, W. L., and Weisz, J. D., 1956, An experimental method of
    producing gastric ulcers, J. Comp. Physiol. Psychol., 49:269.
Sawrey, J. M., Conger, J. J., and Turrel, E. S., 1956, An experi-
    mental investigation of the role of psychological factors in
    the production of gastric ulcers in rats, J. Comp. Physiol.
    Psychol., 49:457.
Selye, H., 1936, A syndrome produced by diverse nocuous agents,
    Nature, 138:32.
Selye, H., 1974, "Stress without Distress," Hodder and Stoughton,
    London.
Sines, J. O., Cleeland, C., and Adkins, J., 1963, The behaviour of
    normal and stomach lesion susceptible rats in several learning
    situations, J. Genet. Psychol., 102:91.

Spiro, H. M., and Milles, S. S., 1960, Clinical and physiological
    implications of the steroid-induced peptic ulcer, N. E. J. Med.,
    26:286.
Weiner, H., 1977, "Psychobiology and Human Disease," Elsevier, N.Y.
    Oxford, Amsterdam.
Weiss, J. M., 1968, Effects of coping responses on stress, J. Comp.
    Physiol. Psychol., 65:251.
Weiss, J. M., 1971a, Effects of coping behaviour in different
    warning signal conditions on stress pathology in rats, J. Comp.
    Physiol. Psychol., 77:1.
Weiss, J. M., 1971b, Effects of punishing the coping response
    (conflict) on stress pathology in rats, J. Comp. Physiol.
    Psychol., 77:14.
Weiss, J. M., 1972, Influence of psychological variables on stress-
    induced pathology, in: "Physiology, Emotion and Psychosomatic
    Illness (CIBA Foundation Symposium 8)," R. Porter and J. Knight,
    eds., Elsevier, Amsterdam.
Weisz, J. D., 1957, The etiology of experimental gastric ulceration,
    Psychosom. Med., 19:61.

COPING AND HEALTH

A CLINICIAN'S PERSPECTIVE

John Cullen

Psychosomatic Unit, Irish Foundation

for Human Development, Garden Hill

Eastern Health Board, Dublin 8

Coping is a term which is unashamedly value laden. It implies competence in adaptive and interpersonal transactions and clearly has connotations of health and well-being. It is paradoxical, therefore, that the clinician will inevitably talk almost exclusively of ill-health or of disease when he addresses himself to the topic of this conference. The urgencies of his day to day experiences in the clinic determine his perceptions and interests in that direction. Nevertheless, the dilemmas of modern health-care delivery systems are constantly reminding him that the preservation of health is infinitely more important and economically more sustainable than the curing of disease. It is this departure from traditional "medical models" for professional practice which demands from him an understanding of the psychobiological processes which sustain coping. These are vital issues with an international relevance as witness the fact that the World Health Organisation confirmed as policy the document on "psychosocial factors and health" prepared for it by its Director General (W.H.O., 1975).

This widening of the remit of the health professional requires him to be able to incorporate psychosocial models of human behavior with the details of biological ones in an increasingly sophisticated way. Most are not prepared for this by traditional medical education and the reinforcers which sustain traditional medical practice are very powerful indeed. Nevertheless, the emergence in recent years of what is called "Behavioral Medicine" has challenged some of these traditions with new perspectives. These developments have yet to prove themselves efficacious in a way which will satisfy an apathetic, if not antipathetic, medical majority. Perhaps this is as it should

be, but there is a need to communicate findings and theories in
psychobiology in a manner which can be assimilated to those still
useful in the medical tradition.

Those of us from the clinical tradition who had the opportunity
to experience it will recall the excitement more than two decades
ago, in the 1950's, when the advent of a truly scientific psychopathology seemed imminent. Dollard and Miller (1950) had just made
an important contribution towards reconciling psychoanalytic ideas
with theories of learning. Maier, Massermann, Gantt, and Liddell
were seeking animal analogues for human behaviour disorders and even
for clinical syndromes. O. H. Mowrer (1950, 1953) had undertaken
similar applications of learning theory to psychopathology and
psychotherapy. Interest was mainly focussed on neurotic behaviours
although some aspects of psychosis, for example, catatonia, had
attracted attention. The insights deriving from ethology were also
in vogue at that time and one frequently heard reference to
"displacement activities" in the staff coffee room of the clinic.
The author was exposed at an impressionable age to these issues and
he was impressed enough to take time off from the clinical promotion
ladder to work for a number of years in a psychology laboratory. He
even made an assault, perhaps a minor sortie, against the disorders
of perception in psychosis and neurosis, (Davis and Cullen, 1958).
A little later, discontented with the almost exclusive sway held by
psychoanalytic theories, e.g., the Chicago School of Franz Alexander,
in the field of psychosomatic medicine he suggested (Cullen, 1960)
that learning in body organ systems might occur and even at
peripheral levels. After all cells had a life of their own as well
as what they shared in the body's community. (The callus on a work-
worn hand could be a kind of coping!) Of course, the work of Selye
was well known but "stress pathology" had attracted little interest
from behaviourists except from those working within the Pavlovian
paradigm.

There was, however, a much older tradition with a major impetus
from workers like W. B. Cannon who provide a historical identity for
what we would now call psychobiology. In the decades which have
passed from the 1950's to the 1970's psychobiology has been developing constructs of its own and has borrowed insights and theories
from many fields of experimental psychology, old and new. In this
it shares a common behaviour pattern with clinical medicine which
is a shameless parasite on almost all other sciences. An important
question then must be why medicine has not so avidly parasitised
psychobiology.

There are many possible reasons for this. Partly the answer
may lie in the politics of medicine where the presence of the
specialty of psychiatry may perpetuate a convenient dualism.
Psychiatry has not yet found a coherent psychopathology. It also,
by and large, in clinical practice perpetuates the image of itself

as competently responsive to all kinds of behaviour problems and
has probably faced, less honestly than other areas of medicine the
issue of sub-specialization. There are very few "clinical psycho-
biologists" and the "clinical psychobiopathologist" must be a rare
bird indeed. It seems to the author, however, that an even greater
impediment, for the medically trained clinician, must lie in the
sheer difficulty of following the nuances of behaviour theories and
the exquisite semantic issues with which it seems, to him, to be
pre-occupied.

Currently fashionable constructs such as coping and arousal
theories may provide a bridge because they seem more operational
and to have an easy fit to biological data. They are, however,
heavily dependent on a range of theories which they subsume and
which are not conveniently accessed or reconciled by the clinician.
He simply cannot understand the reification of theory endemic in
the behavioural sciences. Some of these theoretical substructures
of coping theory will receive cursory comment in the next section.
While these issues are, perhaps, tedious and a trifle old-fashioned,
they must still be faced even if only to express a hope that
ultimately a unified language will evolve and transcend "school"
and special interest boundaries.

Later sections of this paper will address the more vital areas
of disease models and the relevance of the new cognitive psychologies
for our understanding of coping in man.

THEORY AND THE CLINICIAN--SOME COMMENTS

Learning Theories

An attempt to provide a unifying guide through learning
theories and their supporting constructs would greatly help the
clinician. A contribution to this issue may be discerned in
Seligman's (1970) discussion of some fundamental issues in his paper
on "the generality of the laws of learning." He reviews a very wide
range of experiments conceived within what he calls the "assumption
of equivalence of associability," and more specifically identifies
the assumption that: "in classical conditioning, the choice of CS,
US, and response is a matter of relative indifference" and equally
in instrumental learning "the choice of response and reinforcer is
a matter of relative indifference." Amongst quotations he offers
in support, perhaps the one from Skinner (1938, pp. 45-46) is the
most pithy--"the general topography of operant behaviour is not
important because most, if not all, specific operants are conditioned.
I suggest that the dynamic properties of operant behaviour may be
studied with a single reflex." The gap between such parsimonious
formulae and the complexity of human psychosocial stimuli makes it
difficult for most clinicians to apply them in practice.

Seligman goes on to suggest that the arbitrariness of event relationships as opposed to "naturally-occurring events" has dominated the choice of experimental conditions over the past 60 years or so, and that this may have been driven by, and led to, the assumptions he outlines. "Inherent in emphasis on arbitrary events, however, he says, "is a danger that the laws so found will not be general, but peculiar to arbitrary events." This level of dissatisfaction led him to postulate a continuum of "preparedness" for learning in the organism, from "prepared" through "unprepared" to "contraprepared." Preparedness he saw as heavily phylogenetic in origin, even in man, and appears to give little scope for the idea of acquired preparedness. (Acquisition of preparedness may have a progenitor in the "priming" phenomenon reported in the ethological literature, e.g., Eiserer and Hoffman (1973)). Indeed, he goes on to strengthen this view by suggesting that preparedness, e.g., for associations between taste and nausea may be neurally prewired while unprepared and contraprepared associations may be mediated by more plastic structures and less resistant to extinction than the prepared ones. Presumably, this allows him to suggest for the human that we are prepared to associate a range of endeavors and objects (secondary motivators) with primary motivators. These acquired motivators (or secondary drives) may be extraordinarily resistant to extinction. This is not to be confused, he says, with the resistance to extinction of avoidance responses which he attributes conventionally to non-re-exposure. He extends this paradigm to phobias in a later paper (Seligman, 1971).

Now the notion of preparedness must have major implications for coping behaviour. The preparedness-persistence of response paradigm could represent one of the more dangerous shoals upon which coping may founder. Behavioural stereotyping and perseveration and the plateauing of physiological responses must surely comprise a syndrome for many pathological manifestations. There is, however, a growing view that neural tissue may regenerate, reinervate and reorganise. This retention of functional and structural neuro-plasticity has been described in the work of Azmitea (1978) for the 5-HT projections of the hippocampus. The "pre-wiring" hypothesis, then, must be reconsidered and this opens up the possibility of new receding horizons in developmental psychobiology.

Later and concurrent developments of Seligman's own thinking on helplessness, predictability and control seem to shift the specifying conditions for pathology firmly to the external stimulus situation. This dichotomy between preparedness factors and situational ones could be reconciled around a typology of responding organisms or the development of much more comprehensive models to include an ontogeny and learning theory of "preparedness." Physiological response typologies such as those which have grown up around Eysenck's introversion-extroversion scales (Gray, 1970, Passingham, 1970) with its distribution of conditionability may be appropos in

this regard.

Reinforcers and "Drives"

Hydrostatic models deriving from innate drive concepts have
been deeply engrained in the tradition of psychiatry. The force
of Freudian constructs in forming implicit models of this kind in
psychiatrists' heads has to be recognized and seen to be pervasive.

Recent work presented by Levine (1978) reports interesting
findings on the reduction of elevated cortisol levels in rats when
they are provided with access to "comsummatory responses." Now
the invoking of the consummatory response paradigm raises memories
and overtones of "drive psychologies" which are particularly
seductive for clinicians. The cognitive "set" of the clinician
prepares him for attempts at explanations within this sort of
reference frame. The difficulty, however, lies in the identification
of relevant "drives" which can explain the reinforcement patterns
with which he works. It is, perhaps, for this reason that the
Skinnerian operant paradigm has proved more congenial in the clinic.
This approach has been taken to its most austere refinement by
Premack (1965) in his Nebraska Symposium paper where, shorn of any
remaining overtones of "meaning" inferences, it is proposed that
the more probable of any pair of behaviours will reinforce the less
probable one. This suggests some kind of stochastic process to be
operating and it is not a congenial reference frame for the
clinician who deals, traditionally, in "meanings."

There are important potential applications of Levine's findings
on consummatory responses, however, to urgent clinical problems
like obesity, anorexia nervosa, and many others, but the clinician
observes a cascade of responses, each with its own reinforcer or
reinforcers. The consummatory response or consummatory stimulus
may determine symptom-formation but the coping trade-off has taken
place much earlier in the preparatory phases of the coping process.
Through these phases, stimulus situations, in anorexia nervosa for
example, may have included sexual identity problems, role-conformity,
conflicts, body-image distortions, and even "superstitious" events
related to clinical interventions.

These are extremely difficult to fit to a drive-reduction/
consummatory response model. This presents the clinician with
a series of dilemmas. It is all very well to define a coping
behaviour as one which leads to a reduction in arousal level or even
of some specific physiological parameter like cortisol, but the real
politik of patients and doctors, and clinics, moves in a different
milieu. Quite specifically, of course, a reduction of elevated
cortisol levels may accompany a whole cascade of coping behaviours
in a young anorexia nervosa patient who is coming to accept and
explore her sexual identity (Cullen, 1978) and this reduction may

be an index of progress clinically. It is this type of cascade of
coping responses which is the subject of the transaction between the
physician and his client. It is also these very same complexities
of psychosocial transactions which has led stress researchers into
a new rapprochment with old verities in cognitive and drive psychologies.

Activation and Arousal Theories

    Ursin has discussed these theories elsewhere in this symposium.
Activation and arousal theories could have an especial attraction
for the physician or biomedical scientist. They seem to address the
economics of homeostasis in a dynamic way with much relevance for
real-life transactions. Indeed, the present author tends to view
the modulation of arousal as a primary task of a living organism and
coping involves the core adaptive repertoire.

    Berlyne (1967, 1977) contributed a great deal to the extension
of arousal theory into the area of reinforcement. Initially, he
felt that arousal reduction was the main contributor to reinforcement and that while moderate increases in arousal may not be aversive
and may be succeeded by a reinforcing decrease at times, they may
in themselves be reinforcing. Recent work on the widespread distribution of the "reward-system" in the brain has intriguing relevance
in this area and the work of Meichenbaum on cognitive behaviour
"shaping" in therapy, quoted later in this paper, shows how high
arousal levels may be redeployed at the service of coping.

    Apart from these issues, there is the problem that arousal
theory seems to imply a unitary process for diverse physiological
systems which have many qualitative and quantative differences in
response patterns and mechanisms. For example, testosterone levels
may rise in acute stress and fall later (Davidson, Smith and Levine,
1978). Correlations amongst presumed arousal indices are expected
more often than they are found. We have, as yet, only a very
impoverished grasp of the appropriate orchestration of the different
physiological parameters in appropriate adaptive response to varying
environmental conditions.

    For all these reasons, the arousal constructs have suffered
much criticism. This will be a familiar problem to the clinician
who has similar nosological problems with the construct of anxiety.
Nevertheless, arousal, whether conceived of as a global biological
response or specified for a single system, for example, the pituitary-adrenal system, clearly contributes not only to performance
efficiency but also to efficacy dimensions of the coping process
in which S-R and arousal systems are integrated.

    We now understand a great deal about the interaction of S-R
and arousal systems. An excellent review by Hennessy and Levine

(1978) clarifies the salient achievements in our understanding of these matters. These systems may be mutually inhibitory or facilitatory in their effects. For example, frequency of stimulation may lead to habituation in S-R systems ("inhibition") or intensity of stimulation may lead to sensitization in arousal systems ("facilitation"). They may covary, but because they behave under the control of different parameters they may also dissociate. From these phenomena, clinically-relevant models for coping research might be made but a rapprochment with the clinical language of personality and trait variables is overdue. It is, however, highly unlikely that clinicians will adopt the language of the laboratory unless it can show applicability in the describing of "real-life" human situations.

A brief clinical anecdote from the author's experience may illustrate an example of the interaction of S-R and arousal systems. The patient, a man in middle-years and a graduate, working as an information scientist in a large research institute, had been seen for treatment of hypertension. He had a history of several years and had been on treatment with β-adrenergic blockade agents. These, he continued during treatment at the author's Psychosomatic Unit, in its early phases, at first with EMG biofeedback and later with pulse-pressure wave transit-time feedback. His blood pressure showed significant improvement over the course of several months and his G.P. had reduced his drug therapy by half. At this stage, at the patient's request and with his G.P.'s consent, the drugs were withheld and the patient took a week's leave from work to put in a more intensive daily series of practice sessions on biofeedback. During the week, his blood pressure showed marked fluctuations and there are clearly many explanations for this both psychological and pharmacological. However, subjective reports from the patient described a marked return of feelings of anger, anxiety and frustration while driving, especially when he perceived aberrant driving by fellow road-users. These feelings had not been present while he was taking the drug. The future course of the case has been favourable, but clearly the issue of generalization of coping behaviours learned at the clinic was at the time considerably confused by the situation where S-R, arousal and the coping skills were fragmented and at least some of this fragmentation seems to have been iatrogenically induced by the drug.

There are suggestions here for an approach to the pharmacology of coping. Jefferson's (1974) hope that βeta-blockers would be researched for their use in psychiatry has not been adequately fulfilled. Better models would contribute to a much better selectivity of pharmacological interventions at clinical level. (See Gray, this volume).

Coping

Despite the difficulty for the clinician in discerning from the literature of a coherent body of theory for coping which does

justice to the subtlety of the underlying mechanisms, the concept
does seem to connote, subsume or derive from many well-tilled
constructs. It has not yet succeeded in unifying these nor has it
faced the task of semantic "de-bugging" which is needed to help the
clinician to bring his "real-life" specimens of coping from the
clinic to the laboratory for analysis.

    The clinician might use a crude, outline, model of the coping
process which runs as follows:

        Stage I   Stress

        Stage II   Response or coping attempts:-

            (1)   Perceptual/Evaluative/Cognitive

            (2)   Operant/Conditioned

        Stage III   Stimulus alterations and/or physiological
                        change

        Stage IV   Reinforcement by stress/arousal reduction
                        (or elevation)

And, he would observe all this in human patients as being a very
rapid succession of transactions with all manner of self-referenc-
ing and validating feed-back processes going on. One general
approach which would help him is a phylogenetic approach which
would suggest that the neurological and neuroendocrine substrates
for all known types of behaviours and learning, in a hierarchy of
complexity, should be available in man for coping. Some may be
short-circuited by higher cognitive processes and some may decouple
and persist, autonomously, in pathological process with their own
reinforcers as for example in the phobias.

    Coping implies contingency management, dealing with danger
and risk-taking. Risk-taking may be an important facet of coping
behaviour and may relate to personality factors. Risk-taking enters
into many real-life situations, e.g., road-accidents and industrial
accidents which are a major health issue. Seligman (1975, pp. 37-38)
using the "learned helplessness" paradigm reported interesting
shifts towards increased "risk-taking" in the form of stereotyped
random responding or coping responding perceived as determined by
chance in subjects whose control over their arousal or task was
previously abolished or reduced in a different situation. Russell
Davis (1946; 1972, p. 21) made similar observations many years
earlier in his work on "Pilot Error." These studies with the
"Cambridge Cockpit," which permitted attenuation of the responsiveness of the controls, showed that subjects could react with control
attempts which were either wildly innappropriate or which settled

into irrelevant stereotyping or even total inactivity.

In human subjects, there are great inter-individual differences in arousal responses to a particular stimulus and in coping responses in different situations. Motivational factors, e.g., drive-reduction or consummatory behaviours, may be involved in the modulation of arousal and affect risk-taking. Reinforcement may be sought through the maintenance of reduced, optimal or heightened arousal levels, for instance, by novelty seeking. Rate of stimulus change may be important in arousal in, e.g., the pituitary-adrenal system, rapid onset or rapid change may constitute "novelty."

Taken together, these parameters may form an approach to the establishment of time-bases for change over time in risk-taking behaviour in, for example, the driving or other real-life situations and, perhaps, also the availability of various behaviours from the coping repertoire when the subject is faced with clinically significant life events. The degree of control over the arousing situation available to the individual may determine the degree of arousal or displacement types of activities, including some forms of aggression which may emerge, as well as stereotyped responses, and help to modulate arousal. Some of these stereotypic behaviours may involve fairly stable active-avoidance responding. Clinical raters would call these behaviour patterns personality factors if they are predictable and persistent behavioural traits. Clearly, all of these mechanisms are shaped over time and the modulation of arousal within the framework of the coping repertoire of the individual involves many factors antecedant to, or only inter- currently related to a specific experience, for example, motor- vehicle driving. They may be extremely important in determining patterns of risk-taking.

In the author's laboratory, research on drivers in a "real- life" task explored some of these issues. A study of professional heavy-good's vehicle drivers reported by Cullen, Fuller and Dolphin (1979) showed that in a task involving highway driving of a HGV for eleven hours, on each of four successive days, immediately preceded by a non-driving day (day 1), significant effects on hormones were found. Morning and evening shifts were studied.

Significant effects were:

(1) Cortisol levels in those with high initial levels on day (1) tended to show a drop in level over days while those with lower levels tended to show an increase.

(2) Time of day (i.e., shift) effects were noted especially for older drivers.

(3) High levels of cortisol in "pre-" and "post-" samples on the non-driving day immediately preceding the task and high levels for the pre-driving sample on driving days was significantly associated (r = -0.5) with low "safe-driving" ratings.

(4) Personality scores from the EPI also showed significant correlations with mean cortisol levels on non-driving days, but not on driving days.

(5) Extraversion correlated positively with cortisol whereas neuroticism correlated negatively. Testosterone levels also show some significant changes.

An interpretation for some of the findings suggested by Seymour Levine is that driving for some drivers could be a coping response rather than a stressful experience. A naive first hypothesis was that the task would be predominantly a stressful one.

THE DEVELOPMENT OF MODELS

There is a scarcity of comprehensive models of abnormal and coping behaviours in psychobiology. Indeed, these could be offered in combination, with great interest. From the clinician's viewpoint, however, explanatory or heuristic models may prove less than satisfactory when he tries to convince his non-behaviourally oriented colleagues of their usefullness and validity.

One difficulty, perhaps the most serious, which he will have will be the paucity of models which link stress, behavioural response, physiological change, pathophysiological change and the mechanisms of establishment of the morphological changes of disease. This incompleteness has been frequently stressed by Levi (1972) and Kagan (1974) in their well-known model for psychosocial factors and disease. Adaptive changes and the possible "precursors of disease" have fairly well established links especially viewed in the light of Selye's pathology but the link from precursors of disease to actual disease is not satisfactorily explained. For more general reasons, and in view of their special remit, Levi and Kagan are quite correct to pursue support from much needed epidemiological research on these matters. However, clinicians reared in the tradition of Ludwig Koch will seek more visible histopathology and its more sophisticated modern biochemical correlates.

Physical Illness

A valuable contribution from J. M. Weiss (1977) on gastro-intestinal lesions goes a long way as an example of what is required in a clinically-acceptable model. Perhaps, he was astute in

selecting an organ system which had been largely neglected in the laboratories of behavioural scientists, but has a tradition of regard from behaviourally-interested physicians like Harvey Cushing (1932), and Wolf and Wolff (1947) with their celebrated laboratory assistant with a gastric fistula. Weiss's careful elucidation of the pathology of the disease and his analysis of the relevant psychobiological processes is a significant contribution which merits a wide audience in clinical medicine and testing of his model in human clinical gastroenterology.

There are, however, still unexplained gaps in the account of the mechanisms leading to ulcer formation as a discrete morbid anatomical change in contrast with gastric erosion. Murison, elsewhere in this symposium, explores some of these issues further. It has been suggested that vascular phenomena such as arteriovenous shunting in the submucosa may lead to local necrotic areas. This has been said to have analogies with similar mechanisms in Raynaud's disease. The author's clinical experience has included cases of Raynaud's disease where decoupling of digital blood volume and skin temperature during biofeedback training may indicate vascular mechanisms of this kind.

The situation with organ systems more frequently studied by behavioural scientists is less favourable. For example, the cardio-vascular system, and especially heart-rate, has been the subject of a vast number of psychophysiological experiments. It is, indeed, well served with behavioural and psychophysiological models. Two notable contributions come immediately to mind. These are from Lacey (1967) and Lacey and Lacey (1970) and from Obrist (1976, 1977). Between them, these contributions may help greatly in providing us with a basis for a pathophysiology of hypertension and other cardio-vascular functional disorders. However, the links with lesions of the arterial system were not discernible and for many of us the conviction of the relevance of our story elicited in our cardiology colleagues was negligible. For this reason, some recently reported work by Oakes et al. (1978) shows great promise of making the necessary links between "precursors of disease" and disease, that is between pathophysiology and morphological change. In a series of studies, they have developed a methodology for studying morphological change in vascular tissue. Oakes and his colleagues have more recently (1979) shown that when they are subjected to continuous stretching, the smooth muscle cells of the vasculature synthesise large amounts of collagen, elastin and proteoglycan. Here, clearly, is a vital link in a model for the relationship between sustained pathophysiology, i.e., hypertension and morphological change, namely, arteriosclerosis.

Another recent work by Maseri et al. (1978) reports on a prospective study of a group of patients of high-risk for coronary artery disease before they had an attack. He and his colleagues

find that clotting in the coronary arteries is preceded by spasms in the arteries and that the clots form at the sites of earlier spasms. And, of course, catecholamines can modify serum lipids and platelet activity (Brit. Med. J., 1977). The work of Peter Frisch of the Karolinska Institute on the fibrin-fibrinolysin system, especially his elucidation of fibrinolysin-inhibiting factors--a very rapidly responding system, may contribute to our understanding of the mechanisms involved. Work on the continuous dynamic monitoring of coronary blood flow using ultrasound techniques and doppler analysis developed by a colleague working in the author's facility, D. E. Fitzgerald (Fitzgerald, Fortescue-Webb, Ekestrom, Liljeqvist, and Nordhus, 1977) promises to be a useful tool in elucidating some of these issues.

Unlike lesions in the gastrointestinal system which are usually acutely precipitated, lesions in the cardiovascular system are generally more slowly evolving. The conditions in coping failure which lead to sustained hypertension or coronary attacks are usually developed over time. This suggests a rationale for exploring variables like personality in these processes. The well-known work of Friedman and Rosenman (1974), on Type A personalities represented a start in this field. Work reported from the author's laboratory by Dolphin, Fitzgerald, Fischer, and Cullen, (1976) looked at personality factors and their physiological correlates in response to rapid forward tilting utilizing the tilt table and ultrasound monitoring of cardiovascular dynamics. Two clearly defined sub-groups of subjects tended to respond either with a heart-rate change or with a blood-pressure change. The heart-rate responders were characterised as anxious-extroverts on the Cattell 16PF scales and the blood-pressure responders as non-anxious extroverts. These subjects diverged from the typical response pattern to an ortho-static challenge, as described in the textbooks and as interpreted in terms of cardiovascular regulatory mechanisms.

Figure 1 shows the contrasting cardiovascular response patterns for the two groups of subjects. Confronted by interactions of this kind with personality variables the clinician immediately begins to think of "the history" and of childhood developmental experiences. These response patterns, if they are related to personality factors, must have origins in the early years. As a contribution to model building in this area of cardiovascular disease and coping, it is suggested as a hypothesis that the "stimulus intake" or "rejection" responses in heart rate, deceleration and acceleration respectively, described by Lacey and Lacey (1970) may be coping indicators. Further, as explored in various studies of children in the first year of life by developmental psychobiologists, these heart rate changes may provide the context in which either heart-rate coping response patterns or blood pressure ones are entrained in the course of early development.

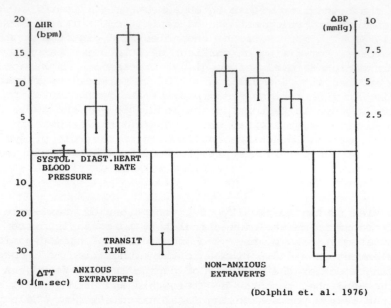

Figure 1

(Dolphin et. al. 1976)

An early study by Lipsit (1971) had found clear evidence of
cardiac deceleration in neonates as an attentional response. Around
the same time Campos and his colleagues had started an interesting
series of studies on the vicissitudes of the bidirectionality of
responses in heart rate in the evolution of coping in infants during
the first year of life. Summarizing this work, Campos (1976)
describes a series of studies with infants at various ages.
Within 55 days old (mean) infants placed on the deep side of the
visual cliff he elicited heart rate deceleration response indicating
a preponderance of attentional factors rather than ones of distress.
There was also less crying and motoric responding. Placement on
the shallow side did not evoke these patterns. Older children
placed on the deep side respond with distress and cardiac acceleration. He describes a further series of studies in 5- and 9-month
infants in response to strangers and/or separation from the mother.
Similar shifts from primarily attentional responses (HR decrease)
to distress ones (HR increase) were observed here. Campos finds
that the apparent conflict between the explanations for these
cardiac changes of Lacey and Lacey, described above, and those of
Obrist (op. cit.), who emphasises the role of motoric factors in
heart rate changes, are not irreconcilable. The author shares
this view.

Taken together all of these and related studies seem to
provide the boundaries within which an ontogeny of cardiovascular
responses in the development of the coping repertoire may be found.
Lacey (1967) with his theory of the effects of arotic and carotid
sinus baroreceptor firing on cortical de-activation takes these
issues into higher levels of cognitive processing. A recent study
by Donovan, Leavitt, and Balling (1978) on maternal heart rate
responding to infant signals may provide an intriguing approach
to monitoring dyadic factors in the modulation of arousal. The
recent experiments of Levine, which he reports elsewhere in this
conference, are an important contribution on the role of dyadic
modulation of arousal in the pituitary-adrenal system and are in
a valuable tradition from his earlier work in developmental
psychobiology.

In view of the complexity of interactions of heart-rate and
blood pressure in maintaining circulatory homeostasis, more
sophisticated studies of the psychophysiology of haemodynamics
in development should contribute to the elaboration of a more
satisfying model of the ontogeny of coping in this field. A
technique published recently by Fitzgerald and Drumm (1977) on an
ultrasound method for monitoring fetal circulation may help to
explore these issues in even earlier stages of development. The
possibility of accessing haemodynamics in the intrauterine dyadic
situation should help to elucidate baselines from which post-natal
arousal modulation takes off.

Mental Illness

Turning now to model-making for predominantly behavioural
illnesses, depressive disorders have recently attracted a great
deal of attention. The hare which Seligman (1975) released with
his learned helplessness model of depression is certainly a good
runner. The special issue of the Journal of Abnormal Psychology
(1978) devoted to "Learned Helplessness as a Model of Depression"
is perhaps the most significant indicator of the interest aroused
by the theory. However, several papers in the volume challenge
either the theoretical construct or fail to replicate some of the
findings upon which it was originally based. For example, Willis
and Blaney (1978) fail to find evidence to support "the claim that
the perception of non-contingency plays a role in depression"
in a series of studies on both depressed and non-depressed under-
graduates. McNitt and Thornton (1978) failed to differentiate
between depressed and non-depressed subjects on a skill task under
50% reinforcement and, contrary to prediction, the depressed group
showed larger expectancy shifts on a chance task under 75% reinforcement. The authors reject the model. Seligman himself in reply
to his critics, feels it necessary to reformulate the model and to
postulate a "sub-class of depression: helplessness depression,"
which he feels cuts across traditional partitions in the nosology

of depression. Buchwald, Coyne and Cole (1978) reject the Seligman model on several counts and conclude that there is little evidence linking learned helplessness to depression. They criticise Seligman's adoption of the common strategy of trying to equate laboratory variables to poorly-defined clinical phenomena. They suggest an alternative strategy of defining clinical manifestations precisely and then to test laboratory analogs. Huesmann (1978) in the concluding paper finds that the Seligman model fits only sub-populations in certain circumstances and proposes that more attention should be paid to the subjects cognitive processes and the heuristics he uses.

The unfolding story of the fate of Seligman's model of depression is likely to throw much light on the psychopathology of depression and other illnesses, e.g., schizophrenia. Already, new facets of behaviour change in depression are being explored and, hopefully, it will stimulate physicians to look at coping processes in their patients with greater care. As well, it may contribute to eroding the grip of conflicting assertions of continuity versus discontinuity theories of etiology in psychiatry. These are counterproductive and as Begelman (1971) has argued they are not at all necessarily incapable of being unified in behaviour theories. There are also endocrine findings in depression where psychobiological theories of coping may fit. For example, depressed patients have increased cortisol levels due to increased ACTH release and not due to increased adrenocortical responsiveness to ACTH. Furthermore, pituitary-adrenal activity is increased throughout the 24 hours in depressed patients. These hormonal changes may in themselves contribute to coping behaviour change, as deWied (1977) suggests, as well as representing a "cost" of chronic failure to cope. Sacher (1970) reviewed some of these phenomena in clinical material, tracing the alterations in pituitary adrenal hormones through the vicissitudes of ego-control in depressives and schizophrenics.

A very recent study by Brown and Harris (1978, p. 265) on the social origins of depression proposes a model which incorporates many interacting variables derived from both the clinical perspective and their own sociological one. It would be interesting but very challenging to attempt to fill out this model from the psychobiology of coping. In a study of women diagnosed as clinically depressed from the Camberwell district of London, they claim to identify:

I: "Vulnerability Factors":

   (a)   Lack of husband or boyfriend who "relates" to them.

   (b)   Early loss of mother (before 11 years).

   (c)   Three or more children under age of 14 years at home, and

   (d)   Lack of employment outside the home.

They also identify:
    II: "Provoking Agents":

       (a) Loss or threat of loss, and

       (b) Long-term difficulties.

Finally, they describe:
    III: "Cognitive Sets":

       (a) High self-esteem leading to mastery, or

       (b) Low self-esteem leading to failure to cope.

Brown and Harris relate some of their findings to the Seligman model which they partially accept although they "do not view learned helplessness essentially as depression." They go on to state: "We see it as a factor predisposing a person to a depression along the lines of vulnerability factors. But, like Seligman, we believe that this helpless predisposition, which is the obverse of Bowlby's concept of self-reliance, can be the result of trauma in early life."

Compared with our understanding of coping mechanisms in depression our understanding of these processes in schizophrenia is even less satisfactory. In the course of advancing a biological model of schizophrenia, Paul (1977) gives a cogent review of the issues. As he sees it, stress factors may be very important intervening factors in the process and progress of the disease without invoking aetiological significance for them. However, other theories like the well-known "double-bind" theory of Gregory Bateson may be susceptible to further scrutiny within the "learned helplessness" paradigm and there are certainly disruptions of control, expectancy and predictability contingencies in the psycho-social context of the "double-bind."

All of the foregoing model-making endeavors fail to incorporate, in a scientific manner, the complexity and richness of human cognitive processes which are at the service of coping. This arena must be entered if satisfying and clinically applicable coping theories are to be developed for human persons in health and sickness.

COGNITIVE PROCESSES, COPING AND REINFORCEMENT IN MAN

The coping perspective on the analysis of behaviour has exercised a powerful charm on an extraordinary range of workers in the field. Clinicians rub shoulders comfortably with animal psycho-biologists and share a feeling of common purpose. Apart from the everyday flavour of the world, it also has an ambience of parsimony which belies many hidden issues and a complexity of mechanisms which has driven theorists and explainers of data, alike, back to areas in psychology which have long been unfashionable, like cognitive psychology.

These considerations give added interest to the work of Martin and Levey (1978). In an extensive review of the theoretical and experimental literature, they attempt to reconcile classical conditioning to other behaviour theories and, especially, to cognitively oriented models. To this end, they suggest "an alternative formulation which retains the parsimony and generality of the classical conditioning model, while accommodating subjective responses in a central role" (p. 62). This formulation they call "evaluative conditioning."

Reviewing classical conditioning experiments, including a short series of their own, in which the dependent variables are "subjective responses, typically involving the evaluation of stimulus material" they postulate that an evaluative response is the core mechanism in conditioning. This response they see as a CR, on a "like" - "dislike" dichotomy, and assert that conditioning only occurs "if an evaluative response is first elicited, and that what is conditioned is the evaluative response itself." No mediating cognitive processes are required, they say, but the evaluative response is "'truly' subjective in the sense that it is unique to the individual organism." Nevertheless, they see it as prior to the perceptual analysis of stimuli or the attribution of "meaning" to them and thus feel they depart from the general ascription of the theories of Arnold (1970) and of Lazarus (1966) as "cognitive" and whom they rather selectively quote in their favour. A major scientific advantage they offer for their theory is their claim that it can provide for finer-grain analysis of behaviour mechanisms in adaptive processes or coping, for the clinician, than either cognitive theories or information processing theories. They even offer a model for the vicissitudes of evaluative responses in manic-depressive illness.

Throughout, they emphasise the biological significance of the evaluative response as being at the service of adaptive behaviour and coping and they offer this development of the classical conditioning paradigm as a way out of the dangers of much of the modern proliferation of cognitive mediators such as imagery, internal dialogue, etc., in the cognitive behaviour modification literature.

It could be said that their approach may offer considerable advantages if the "evaluative response" could become a reinforcer for other behaviours attainable by operant means. It is from this point of departure that the cognitive behaviour modification procedures seem to take off in the sense that the evaluative response may be a word, symbol or image. Many new approaches to our better understanding of human coping may thus be initiated. There are two sources of recent work which will undoubtedly contribute greatly to our understanding of human coping in health and sickness. The first of these derives from the rapidly-growing body of work is the "new psychology" of consciousness and the second is arising from the field of cognitive behaviour therapies.

A recent symposium volume edited by Pope and Singer (1978)
opens many new vistas in the psychology of consciousness. Rychlak
(1978), in a contribution which has surely some facets comparable
with the ideas of Martin and Levey (1978) cited earlier, proposes
an alternative to S-R behaviour theories when analysing human
behaviour. He calls it "logical learning theory." He argues
(p. 106-7), inter alia, that: "Human behaviour is not only responsive,
but also telesponsive. By restricting human actions to the concept
of 'response(s)', psychology has prejudiced the case in favour of
efficient causation. The stimulus-response theoretical construct,
including such variations as input-output or antecedent-consequent,
is the sine qua non of efficient causality. As an antidote to this
prejudicial terminology, which is so frequently confounded with the
language of method (refer above), logical learning theory proposes
the construct of telesponsivity in human affairs. A telesponse is
the person's taking on (i.e., premising, predication) a meaningful
item (image, word(s), judgemental comparison, etc.) relating to a
referent acting as a purpose for the sake of which behaviour is
then intended (Rychlak, 1977, p. 283)". Later he extends this
perspective in viewing reinforcement as occurring "when the learner's
predicated affirmations are successfully extended. Positive reinforcements further meanings that are rooted in positive premises,
the negative reinforcements further meanings that are rooted in
negative premises." This is, perhaps, a "cognitive" way of talking
about expectancy and predictability and, perhaps, one could also
say, within this paradigm that coping and the perception of coping
are the best reinforcers of coping.

The implication of images, words, judgemental comparisons, etc.,
in these processes finds an intriguing context in studies reported
by Singer (1978) later in the same volume. He describes experimental
studies of day-dreaming and the stream of thought (or, as he calls
it, "stimulus independent mentation"). He postulates a coping
function for these processes (p. 205): "Indeed, it seems likely
that one overriding purpose of the nature of ongoing thought may be
that it involves an adaptive preparation for future action, drawing
upon what Klinger has termed the many "current concerns," or the
many bits of "unfinished business" or "intentions" to use the
terminology of Kurt Lewin." Reading the neo-cognitive literature,
one is sharply reminded how impoverished is one's listening to
patients, how poor the fit of simple coping models to their reality
which is their evolving schema of the world, their experience and
the subtlety of their task in modulating their arousal.

Starker (1978) takes some of these phenomena into the area of
arousal and anxiety. He reports three studies which he claims
"indicate that level of anxiety, like affective polarity, is a
general parameter of fantasy life that transcends state of arousal.
When present to sufficient degree in dreams, it leads to abrupt
awakening and experience of "nightmare." When present in waking,
it may prevent entry into the vivid hypnagogic reveries that

facilitate the onset of sleep through its arousing qualities and its disruption of mental imagery." Later he writes: "Bearing all of these findings in mind, one possibility that emerges is that some people can more completely block incoming sensory stimuli than others, and this permits them more readily to escape the structuring effects of stimulus inputs and results in more bizarre fantasy productions. Such differences in stimulus blocking could reflect primarily physiological variations or the differential learning of cognitive controls, or both," Stimulus blocking by the firing of the baroreceptor cells in the aorta is hypothesised by Lacey (1967). Some relevance of these phenomena may be found for the establishment of types of cardiovascular responders and may also relate to Eysenck's and other personality typologies. Suzanne Miller's "blunters," described elsewhere in this symposium, may represent a group who cope through such mediating mechanisms.

Processes like those described must play a prominent part in determining individual differences in human coping repertoires, even in the preliminary phases of "rehearsal" for coping. A study by Kripke and Sonnenschein (1978) in the same symposium even suggests a biological rhythm in waking fantasy episodes.

Turning to the second source for new insights into the cognitive aspects of coping in man, the rapidly-developing area of cognitive behaviour modification suggests approaches to teaching coping behaviours. Goldfried and Merbaum (1973) edit an anthology which clearly shows that changing behaviour through self-control has a long tradition in modern psychology even within the behaviourist tradition. The "self-contracting" behaviour described by Bandura (1969, p. 255) and his other explorations of self-control variables in the reinforcement of desirable behaviours is well known. His participant modelling technique in cognitive "set" re-shaping (Bandura, 1974) is a further contribution to intervention in the coping processes. Masters and Mokros (1974) extended some of these concepts to work with children.

More recently, Meichenbaum (1977) discusses the nature of "internal dialogue" and its relationship to cognitive factors in stress, to physiological effects and to coping (pp. 203-211). "In our own research," he says, "the clients, following cognitive-behaviour modification treatment, came to label their physiological arousal as facilitative rather than debilitative. Sweaty palms, increased heart and respiratory rates, muscular tension now became "allies," cues to use the coping techniques for which they have been trained. The physiological arousal that the client had previously labelled as totally debilitating anxiety and fear, the harbinger of further behaviour deterioration leading to feelings of helplessness, was now relabelled as eagerness to demonstrate competence, as a desire to get on with a task and as a sign to cope. In other words, the client learned to respond to the same physio-

logical cues when they do arise with different cognition. Originally,
he entertained cognitions that mediated further autonomic arousal
(e.g., "I'm really nervous; I'm sweating, others will see it; I
can't handle this") after treatment, his cognitions had a coping
orientation and moved the focus away from his arousal towards
response alternatives. This shift in itself may mediate a shift
in autonomic functioning. The present theory postulates that it
is not the physiological arousal per se that is debilitating but
rather what the client says to himself about that arousal that
determines his eventual reactions."

     A clinical anecdote from the author's Psychosomatic Clinic
may show how subtle human cognitive reshaping can influence arousal
mechanisms. A fifteen year old girl was referred for treatment
of severe, excessive axillary sweating which was socially
incapacitating. She had initially been offered surgical sympathec-
tomy which her parents rejected. Treatment with GSR biofeedback
had shown very good results in the clinic and during a school
vacation the girl ventured out to a disco one evening. Soon, she
noticed the axillary sweating beginning and had momentary panic.
However, almost at once, she realized that the sweating was
confined to the opposite side to the arm used in bio-feedback
training at the clinic. She then surmised that this association
was not an appropriate one and the sweating came under her control.
She had no further trouble and enjoyed her evening out immensely.

     These sorts of processes involve control over attentional
processes. Csikazentmihalyi (1978) describes some of these
attention factors in optimal functioning. The clinician shapes the
attentional focus of his patients in exploring coping options with
him. In this process, he must try to communicate a real and "real-
life" awareness of adaptive processes and of coping to his patient
so that in the most productive situations the therapeutic relationship becomes one of colleagueship (cf. also Singer, 1974).

Some Practical Issues

     Further aspects of stress and coping merit study for a
comprehensive perspective on health issues. One of these relates
to the time factors involved in the achievement of coping in
everyday life. The bereavement syndrome is an obvious case in
point. What are the temporal constraints in the mechanisms of
coping strategy reshaping that determine how long it will take to
"get over" these and similar loss experiences? Another example
might be the adaptation processes and emergence of adequate coping
in people subject to housing relocation. A study by Lee (1971)
throws some light on this particular phenomenon. Using various
measures of social integration, he reckons periods of as long as
five years for achievement of social integration. An anthropological
study by George Gmelch, in the author's facility, on migration and
return-migration between Ireland and the United States suggests

similar patterns of adaptation time scales. The interest of WHO
in psychosocial factors in health (WHO 1975) could be facilitated
by an intensive review of such factors in the light of careful
hypotheses based on the postulates of coping theories.

Coping also need a taxonomy. The experimental literature is
heavily weighted towards acute coping phenomena. Habitual coping
patterns, personal coping-styles and life-style as coping behaviour
could all be considered in constructing such a taxonomy. So also,
the triad of predictability, control and feedback could be re-
scrutinised and extended. For example, excessive predictability
(monotony) could be seen as disruptive of both the availability and
quality of adequate coping behaviours in the work place.

Even if we merely distribute human subjects on the basic
biological parameter of gender, there are clearly socially
determined differences in the available repertoires of coping
behaviours. Control, predictability and perceived control factors
will not necessarily be the same for both sexes, and it has been
suggested by Bem (1975) that the androgynous personalities will be
better copers. This area has hardly been touched upon in psychobiological research in persons. Sex differences and similarities
research will surely be most important in future work in the coping
field. The author's laboratory is currently engaged in a programme
of research, led by Anna-Lisa Myrsten, in this field, in collabora-
tion with Frankenhaeuser's laboratory in Stockholm, where earlier
work in this field has been reported. A feature of the research
is an attempt to distribute both men and women on a continuum of
personality traits and cognitive sets which derive from the
traditional masculinity and femininity dichotomy. Already, data
obtained shows a wide scatter of these traits across gender
boundaries with some surprising constellations of factors. Now,
if cognitive sets can diverge from such fundamental biological
bases, the whole issue of primary and secondary "drives" and
reinforcers in man must be especially poignant.

In humans, coping must imply some kind of personally initiated
responding or "self-management" whatever the source of the challenges
to the response repertoire. Perhaps, one of the more poignant
syndromes in the clinic is that referred to by Nemiah, Freyberger,
and Sifneos (1976) as alexithymia. The inarticulate suffering of
meaningless arousal manifestations suggests that education, at all
levels, about psychobiology and about coping may provide a major
contribution to health as well as being culturally important. The
development of curricula, training programmes and other approaches
to prevention in this field has hardly even begun. The ability
to manipulate large models of complex contingencies in consciousness
may be learned. In therapy, the role of biofeedback as a servant of
self-management and coping carries questions of cognitive shaping

and re-shaping which are barely beginning to be articulated let alone to meet answers either at empirical or philosophical levels of discourse.

ENVOI - SOME PRACTICAL AND PHILOSOPHICAL MATTERS

The physician rarely has the opportunity to observe or intervene in isolated acute coping situations. What he usually sees are prolonged coping attempts or long-established, even lifelong, inadequate coping patterns. Now, it seems, that most laboratory studies of coping involve acute, or near acute, coping episodes. This presents a mismatch both in expectancies and in control of the variables between the laboratory worker and the health professional. It is as if, for the clinician, he was watching a movie with the timing of the exposure of the frames running far too slow. He is trying to pin down and isolate bits of behaviour which he can fit to the laboratory paradigms.

What we badly need are process models which can accommodate the shaping of coping repertoires over long periods of time and, perhaps, the laboratory worker could extend his experimental paradigms to allow, for example, of successive studies under different conditions but with the same subjects.

On the theoretical side, Gary Schwartz (1977) has made a useful contribution in this area with his "psychobiological model of disregulation."
"The basic model is as follows: When the environment places inappropriate demands on a person, his brain performs the regulations necessary to meet the specific demands. Depending on the nature of the environmental demands or stress, certain bodily systems will be activated while others may be simultaneously inhibited. However, if this process is sustained to the point where tissue suffers deterioration or injury, the negative feedback loops of the homeostatic mechanism will normally come into play, forcing the brain to modify its directives to aid the afflicted organ. Often this negative feedback loop causes the experience of pain." (pp. 279-80)

He postulates four process areas, where, in successive stages disregulation proceeds.

Stage I   Environmental Demands. which when they become overwhelming distract the subject and lead his attention away from negative feedback from the threatened organ(s).

Stage II   Information Processing of the CNS. The brain may select, for genetic or other reasons, to ignore the protective negative feedback from a body-organ or to divert it in inappropriate ways which may be damaging.

Stage III Peripheral Organ. The organ itself may be impaired and fail, for example, to respond to control impulses from the brain.

Stage IV Negative Feedback. The negative feedback from the organ may be inappropriate, less effective or even become inactivated.

There are ambiguities in Schwartz's descriptions of these factors but they may be helpful for indicating an approach to more chronic processes. His application of this kind of analysis to certain clinical syndromes or to treatment procedures, such as biofeedback is more successful.

The present author prefers to seek a more detailed profile of the decompensated individual which would enable us to identify the stress-prone subject or the person who has a failure of coping mechanisms. The profile would have to include the following dimensions:

(1)   Change to an inappropriate level in an inappropriate direction for thresholds for arousal.

(2)   A shift to faster or slower rise-times.

(3)   A change in maximum or minimum levels of response.

(4)   Sustained plateaux, their duration, onset and level.

(5)   Slower or faster decay-times after arousal. (e.g., Margaret Christie's "recovery from stress").

If we are to attain this level of sophistication in pathophysiology, we will have to develop a new "calculus of coping" which will replace the various ones available from learning theories. These systems are extremely complex and may require application of selected mathematical models. Even Thom's "Catastrophe Theory" or the engineers "Reliability Theory" may be helpful. The author, with Dr. Noel Murphy of the Chemical Engineering Department in University College, Dublin, offered a "first attempt" in this direction at the European Conference for Psychosomatic Research at Heidelberg in 1976 (Murphy and Cullen, 1976). We called it "A Systems Model of Man." There were no heavenly choirs. In retrospect it seems far too mechanistic and requires development into the sort of approach being explored by Francisco Varela (1976) in his descriptions of self-referential systems:

"So if you're interested in ecology, a certain kind of ecology, you split up the world in a certain way. If you're interested in economy, you split up the world in a different way. But given a criteria (sic) of

distinction, you always come up with systems that have
some sort of closure of their organization. And if you
are a biologist, that's pretty clear, right? In the
subject matter of the biologists, every one of the
interactions of an organism interacts with every other
interaction in a very closed fashion, a network of interactions."

"The fact that wholes have this closed organization implies
that in order to describe them, we have to deal with self-
referential description. You wind up with functions that
are functions of themselves, or interactions that interact
with themselves, and so on. This has a weird flavor for
most people, because the tradition in the scientific
discourse has been that this is not something we can
consider. The main trend has been to put it completely
aside; anything that is self-referential is a 'vicious
circle.' It has even been called a vicious circle by
St. Thomas Aquinas." (pp. 26-27).

Coping processes represent a self-referential cognitive system
which is the core of life. Perhaps, the way to teach people how
to cope is to teach them how to manage large systems in their heads.
O. H. Mowrer (1954) expressed the same idea more graphically in a
book I reopened recently after more than twenty years:

"Living organisms swim forward in a sea of time, and
those with the best "distance receptors," i.e., with the
best symbolic skills, will almost certainly have an edge
in the struggle for existence. "Use your head" (or head
end) is good advice both in the sense of using the special
senses and in the sense of moving back and forth through
time in the way that symbols make dramatically possible."

REFERENCES

Arnold, M. B., 1970, Perennial problems in the field of emotion, in:
      "Feelings and Emotions," M. B. Arnold ed., Loyola Symposium,
      Academic Press, New York.
Azmitia, E., 1978, Reorganization of the 5-HT projections to the
      hippocampus, Trends in Neuro-Sciences, 1, 45:8.
Bandura, A., 1969, "Principles of Behaviour Modification," Holt,
      Rinehart and Winston, New York.
Bandura, A., 1974, Behavioural engineering-reconstruction of responses:
      The process and practice of participant modelling treatment, in:
      "Experimental Behaviour-a Basis for the Study of Mental Disturb-
      ance," J. Cullen ed., Halstead Press, John Wiley, New York.

Begelman, D. A., 1971, Continuity vs. discontinuity theories of eti-
    ology in behaviourism, Behav. Ther., 2:560.
Bem, S. L., 1975, Sex role adaptability: One consequence of psycho-
    logical adrogyny, J. Person. Soc. Psychol., 31:634.
Berlyne, D. E., 1967, Arousal and reinforcement, Nebraska Symposium
    on Motivation, 1:110.
Berlyne, D., 1977, The affective significance of uncertainty, in:
    "Psychopathology of Human Adaptation," G. Serban ed., Plenum
    Press, New York.
Brit. Med. J., 1977, Stress, coronary disease and platelet behaviour,
    (Editorial) 12 Feb., 408.
Brown, G. W., and Harris, T., 1978, "Social Origins of Depression-
    A Study of Psychiatric Disorder in Women," Tavistock Publications,
    London.
Buchwald, A. M., Coyne, J. C., and Cole, C. S., 1978, A critical
    evaluation of the learned helplessness model of depression,
    J. Abn. Psychol., 87:180.
Campos, J. J., 1976, Heart rate: A sensitive tool for the study of
    emotional development in the infant, in: "Developmental Psycho-
    biology," L. P. Lipsitt ed., Halstead Press, John Wiley, New York.
Csikszenthmihalyi, M., 1978, Attention and the holistic approach to
    behaviour, in: "The Stream of Consciousness," K. S. Pope and
    J. L. Singer eds., John Wiley, New York.
Cullen, J., 1960, Psychological mechanisms in the psychosomatic
    skin affections, in: "Progress in the Biological Sciences in
    Relation to Dermatology," A. Rook ed., Cambridge University
    Press, Cambridge, England.
Cullen, J., 1978, Cyclical hormonal activity, in: "Society, Stress
    and Disease, Vol. 3, The Productive and Reproductive Age, Male
    Female Roles and Relationships," Oxford University Press,
    Oxford, England.
Cullen, J., Fuller, R., and Dolphin, C., 1979, Endocrine stress
    responses of drivers in a "real-life" heavy-goods vehicle
    driving task, Psychoneuroendocrinology, in press.
Cushing, H., 1932, Peptic ulcers and the interbrain, Surg. Gyn. Obs.,
    55:1.
Davidson, J. M., Smith, E. R., and Levine, S., 1978, Testosterone,
    in: "Psychobiology of Stress: A Study of Coping Men," Academic
    Press, New York.
Davis, D. R., 1946, Neurotic predisposition and the disorganisation
    observed in experiments with the Cambridge Cockpit, J. Neurol.
    Psychiat., 9:119.
Davis, D. R. and Cullen, J. H., 1958, Disorganization of perception
    in neurosis and psychosis, Amer. J. Psychol., 71:229.
Davis, D. R., 1972, "An Introduction to Psychopathology," Oxford
    University Press, London.
Dollard, J., and Miller, N. E., 1950, "Personality and Psychotherapy,"
    McGraw-Hill, New York.

Dolphin, C., Fitzgerald, D. E., Fischer, I., and Cullen, J. H., 1976, Physiological and psychological correlates of reaction to rapid forward tilting, Paper read to Eleventh European Psychosomatic Conference, Heidelberg.

Donovan, W. L., Leavitt, L. A., and Balling, J. D., 1978, Maternal physiological response to infant signals, Psychophysiology, 15:68.

Eiserer, L. A., and Hoffman, H. S., 1973, Priming of ducklings' responses by presenting an imprinted stimulus, J. Comp. Physiol. Psychol., 82:345.

Fitzgerald, D. E., and Drumm, J. E., 1977, Non-invasive measurement of human fetal circulation using ultrasound: A new method, Brit. Med. J., 2:1450.

Fitzgerald, D. E., Fortescue-Webb, C. M., Ekestrom, S., Liljeqvist, L., and Nordhus, O., 1977, Monitoring coronary artery blood-flow by doppler-shift ultra-sound, Scand. J. Thor. Cardiovas. Surg., 11:119.

Friedman, M., and Rosenman, R. H., 1974, "Type A Behaviour and Your Heart," Wildwood House, Ltd., London.

Goldfried, M. R., and Merbaum, M., 1973, "Behaviour Change Through Self-Control," Holt, Rinehart, and Winston, New York.

Gray, J. A., 1970, The psychophysiological basis of introversion-extraversion, Behav. Res. Ther., 8:249.

Hennessy, J. W., and Levine, S., 1978, Stress, arousal, and the pituitary-adrenal system-A psychoendocrine model, in: "Progress in Psychobiology and Physiological Psychology," Vol. 8, Academic Press, New York.

Huesmann, L. R., 1978, Cognitive processes and models of depression, J. Abnorm. Psychol., 87:194.

Jefferson, J. W., 1974, β-adrenergic receptor blocking drugs in psychiatry, Arch. Gen. Psychiat., 31:681.

Kagan, A., 1974, Need for experimental evaluation of the role of psychosocial stimuli in disease as a guide to rational health action, in: "Experimental Behaviour-A Basis for the Study of Mental Disturbance," Halstead Press, John Wiley, New York.

Kripke, D. F., and Sonneschein, D., 1978, A biologic rhythm in waking fantasy, in: "The Stream of Consciousness," K. S. Pope and J. L. Singer eds., John Wiley, New York.

Lacey, J. I., 1967, Somatic response patterning and stress: Some revisions of activation theory, in: "Psychological Stress: Issues in Research," M. H. Appley and R. Trumbull eds., Appleton, New York.

Lacey, J. I., and Lacey, B. C., 1970, Some autonomic-central nervous system interrelationships, in: "Physiological Correlates of Emotion," P. Black ed., Academic Press, New York.

Lazarus, R. S., 1966, "Psychological Stress and the Coping Process," McGraw-Hill, New York.

Lee, T., 1971, Psychology and architectural determinism, Part 2, The Architects J., 154:475.

Levi, L., editor, 1972, "Stress and Distress in Response to Psycho-social Stimuli," Pergamon Press, Oxford.

Levine, S., 1978, Comsummatory behaviour and the pituitary-adrenal system, Paper read to the ninth Congress of the Int. Soc. of Psychoneuroendocrinology, Dublin.

Lipsitt, L. P., and Jacklin, C. N., 1971, Cardiac deceleration and its stability in human newborns, Devel. Psychol., 5:535.

Martin, I., and Levey, A. B., 1978, Evaluative Conditioning, Adv. Behav. Res. Ther., 1:57.

Maseri, A., and l'Abbete, A., 1978, Coronary vaso-spasms as a possible cause of myocardial infarction-A conclusion derived from a study of 'pre-infarction angina.' NE J. Med., 299:1271.

Masters, J. C., and Mokros, J. R., 1974, Self-reinforcement processes in children, in: "Advances in Child Development and Behaviour," Vol. 9, Academic Press, New York.

McNitt, P. C., and Thornton, D. W., 1978, Depression and perceived reinforcement - a reconsideration, J. Abnorm. Psychol., 87:137.

Meichenbaum, D., 1977, "Cognitive-Behaviour Modification: An Integrative Approach," Plenum Press, New York.

Mowrer, O. H., 1950, "Learning Theory and Personality Dyanmics," Ronald Press, New York.

Mowrer, O. H., 1953, "Psychotherapy - Theory and Research," Ronald Press, New York.

Mowrer, O. H., 1954, Ego psychology, cybernetics and learning theory, in: "Learning Theory, Personality Theory and Clinical Research, The Kentucky Symposium," John Wiley, New York.

Murphy, N., and Cullen, J., 1976, An application of systems theory to the simulation of man, Paper read to the eleventh European Psychosomatic Conference, Heidelberg.

Nemiah, J. C., Freyberger, H., and Sifneos, P. E., 1976, Alexithymia A view of the psychosomatic process, in: "Modern Trends in Psychosomatic Medicine," O. Hil ed., Butterworths, London.

Oakes, B. W., Batley, A. C., and Handley, C. H., 1978, Biochemical and ultrastructural studies of the synthesis of elastin, proteoglycans and collagen by neonatal rat aortic smooth muscle cells in tissue culture, J. Anat., 126:631.

Oakes, B. W., 1979, Diseases linked by stretched cells, New Scientist, 81:93.

Obrist, P. A., 1976, Presidential Address, 1975-The Cardiovascular Behavioural Interaction-As it appears today, Psychophysiology, 13:95.

Obrist, P. A., 1977, Behavioural-cardiac interactions. The psycho-somatic hypothesis, Paper read to 21st Annual Conf., Soc. for Psychosomatic Res., London.

Passingham, R. E., 1970, The neurological basis of introversion-extraversion-Gray's theory, Behav. Res. Ther., 8:353.

Paul, S. M., 1977, Movement and madness. Towards a biological model of schizophrenia, in: "Psychopathology-Experimental Models," J. D. Maser and M. E. P. Seligman eds., W. H. Freeman, San Francisco.

Pope, K. S., and Singer, J. L., 1978, "The Stream of Consciousness-Scientific Investigations into the Flow of Human Experience," John Wiley, New York.

Premack, D., 1965, Reinforcement theory, in: "Nebraska Symposium on
     Motivation: 1965," D. Levine, ed., "Nebraska Symposium on
     Motivation, 1965," University of Nebraska Press, Lincoln.
Rychlak, J. F., 1977, "The Psychology of Rigorous Humanism,"
     Wiley-Interscience, New York.
Rychlak, J. F., 1978, The stream of consciousness-Implications for
     a humanistic psychological theory, in: The Stream of Conscious-
     ness," K. S. Pope and J. L. Singer eds., John Wiley, New York.
Sacher, E. J., 1970, Psychological factors relating to activation and
     inhibition of the adrenocortical stress response in man-A review,
     in: "Progress in Brain Research: Pituitary, Adrenal and the
     Brain," Vol. 32, D. deWied and J. A. W. Weijsen eds., American
     Elsevier, New York.
Schwartz, G. E., 1977, Psychosomatic disorders and biofeedback: A
     psychobiological model of disregulation, in: "Psychopathology-
     Experimental Models," J. D. Maser and M. E. P. Seligman eds.,
     W. H. Freeman, San, Francisco.
Seligman, M. E. P., 1970, On the generality of the laws of learning,
     Psychol. Rev., 77:406.
Seligman, M. E. P., 1971, Phobias and preparedness, Behav. Ther.,
     2:307.
Seligman, M. E. P., 1975, "Helplessness-On Depression, Development
     and Death," W. H. Freeman, San Francisco.
Singer, J. L., 1978, Experimental studies of daydreaming and the
     stream of thought, in: "The Stream of Consciousness," K. S.
     Pope, and J. L. Singer eds., John Wiley, New York.
Singer, M. T., 1974, Presidential address Engagement-involvement:
     A central phenomenon in psychophysiological research, Psychosom.
     Med., 36:1.
Skinner, B. F., 1938, "The Behaviour of Organisms," Appleton Century
     Crofts, New York.
Starker, S., 1978, Dreams and waking fantasy, in: "The Stream of
     Consciousness," K. S. Pope and J. L. Singer eds., John Wiley,
     New York.
Varela, F., 1976, On observing natural systems, The Co-Evolution
     Quart., Summer.
Weiss, J., 1977, Ulcers, in: "Psychopathology-Experimental Models,"
     J. D. Maser and M. E. P. Seligman eds., W. H. Freeman, New York.
     J. D. Maser and M. E. P. Seligman eds., W. H. Freeman, S
     J. D. Maser and M. E. P. Seligman eds., W. H. Freeman, San
     San Francisco.
deWied, D., 1977, Pituitary adrenal system hormones and behaviour,
     A. Endocrin. Supp., 214.
Willis, M. H., and Blaney, P. H., 1978, Three tests of the learned
     helplessness model of depression, J. Abnorm. Psychol., 87:131.
Wolf, S., and Wolff, H. G., 1947, "Human Gastric Function," Oxford
     University Press, New York.
W. H. O., 1975, Psychosocial factors and health: Report of the
     Director General, World Health Organization, Geneva (EB 57/22:
     20 Nov 75).

A PERSPECTIVE ON THE EFFECTS OF

STRESS AND COPING ON DISEASE AND HEALTH

Neal E. Miller

Department of Psychology

The Rockefeller University

The purpose of this paper is to provide a perspective for our discussions of the effects on health of coping with stress. I shall also cover briefly some topics, such as neurophysiological mechanisms, epidemiological evidence, and the effects of stress on the cardiovascular and immune systems, not strongly represented in other papers, pose some key issues for theoretical clarification, and suggest some urgent problems for further research. Although I shall discuss possible neurophysiological mechanisms first, the historical sequence often has been from clinical observations, to experimental models, and then to neurophysiological mechanisms.

The topic of this symposium is one aspect of a larger area, Behavioral Medicine, that recently has been rapidly developing. Behavioral medicine has been defined as "the (interdisciplinary) field concerned with the development of behavioral science knowledge and techniques relevant to the understanding of physical health and illness and the application of this knowledge and techniques to prevention, diagnosis, treatment, and rehabilitation. Psychosis, neurosis, and substance abuse are included only insofar as they contribute to physical disorders as an end point" (Schwartz and Weiss, 1978). Its development is represented by the recent formation of a Journal of Behavioral Medicine, an Academy of Behavioral Medicine Research, a Society for Behavioral Medicine, and a Division of Health Psychology in the American Psychological Association.

As the killer bacterial and viral plagues are being conquered, there is a growing recognition that some of the important next opportunities in medicine lie in preventive measures that have strong behavioral components; for example, avoiding excessive

exposure to stress, correcting noncompliance with medical regimes, and substituting healthier life styles for the cigarette smoking, the excessive use of alcohol, and the underexercise and overeating that produce obesity (Daedalus, 1977). The medical community's interest in the foregoing problems opens up challenging opportunities to the behavioral scientists. But it also confronts us with dangers. The problems of smoking, obesity, alcoholism, and stress are extremely difficult. Some over-optimistic behavioral scientists may propose extensive corrective programs in these areas that will fail because of our inadequate scientific base of knowledge and of insufficient pilot testing on progressively larger groups under conditions resembling those of large-scale application. If premature hopes are raised, the disillusionment--"oh yes, we tried behavioral approaches and they were worthless"--could set Behavioral Medicine back for another generation.

THE BRAIN AND THE NEUROHUMORAL MECHANISMS IT CONTROLS

The effects of stress and of coping with it, on the health of the body, are based on the intimate interrelations among the manifold functions of the brain. It is involved in perception and the highest processes of reasoning, in emotions and drives, and in the control of vital functions such as breathing, heart rate, blood pressure, and a variety of metabolic processes. All these functions of the brain are intimately interrelated. Thus, perception and reasoning leading to the conclusion that "my child may have cancer" arouses strong fear that causes one's face to pale, blood pressure to increase, digestion to cease, and interferes with mental work on other problems. We are beginning to understand some of the physiological mechanisms involved in certain types of stress, notably the flight-fight reaction. Some of these mechanisms can provide a possible logical basis for some of the empirically observed somatic effects of psychological stress to be described later; they can provide a useful guide to the types of research that will lead to a better understanding of these effects (Miller, 1979a).

Among the best-studied sets of mechanisms are those involving the pituitary-adrenal axis. Neurons in the median eminence of the brain release CRF, which causes the pituitary gland to release ACTH, which causes the cortex of the adrenal gland to release glucocorticoids, also called corticosteroids, into the blood. These in turn complete a negative feedback control loop by inhibiting the release of CRF from the median eminence. Under certain types of stress, for example, fear, the negative feedback control is overridden, presumably by neuromechanisms, so that much larger amounts of ACTH and corticosteroids are released.

The corticosteroids play an important role in the adaptation of the body to physical stress. They have anti-inflammatory

effects that, for example, are useful in the treatment of arthritis. They help to stabilize the membranes of lyosomes within cells to prevent, during injury, the diffusion of destructive hydrolytic enzymes. If a patient who is extremely deficient in corticosteroids is subjected to the physical stress of surgery or of a severe accident, he will die in acute vascular collapse. This fatal collapse can be prevented by the administration of corticosteroids.

Selye (1956) has shown that one of the first reactions to physical stressors, such as surgical injury, cold, sub-lethal injections of formaldehyde, is activation of the pituitary-adrenal axis, a phase that he calls "alarm." With continued exposure, the corticosteroid levels and the physical symptoms may be reduced during a phase described as adaptation but, with too great exposure, physical symptoms may reappear and terminate in death. The mechanisms involved in prolonged stress have not been as thoroughly studied as those involved in shorter periods of stress; they need to be more thoroughly studied.

When corticosteroids are given to patients for their anti-inflammatory effects, they can have a variety of side effects. They can interfere with the action of insulin and thus precipitate or exacerbate diabetes, contribute to peptic ulcers, cause loss of calcium from the bones, suppress growth, cause menstrual irregularities, and induce hypertension. But in some of these cases, the effects of corticosteroids may be confounded with those of the condition, for example, extremely painful arthritis, that these compounds are being used to ameliorate.

One especially important effect of the corticosteroids is on the immune mechanism. They cause the involution of lymphoid tissue, suppress gamma-globulin formation, reduce the eosinophil count (which used to be used as an indirect measure of stress), and interfere with the action of white blood cells. The immuno-suppressive effects of corticosteroids are clinically useful in reducing the body's tendency to reject organ transplants, but they greatly increase susceptibility to infection.

While the foregoing effects of corticosteroids usually are observed from pharmacological doses, the fact that similar effects are observed as a result of stress makes it plausible to investigate the possible role of endogenous corticosteroids in producing such effects.

Finally, corticosteroids are involved in mobilizing fatty acids from adipose tissue and in other aspects of energy metabolism.

Fear and the acute flight-fight response studied by Cannon (1953) involves strong activation of the sympathetic nervous system. During such arousal, the sympathetic nerve endings release norepin-

ephrine and the adrenal medulla pours epinephrine into the bloodstream.
These catecholamines cooperate with the corticosteroids in the
mobilization of fat stores. This can produce an increase in lipids
in the blood. It is believed that if these free fatty acids are not
burned up by muscular activity, they may lead to an increase in the
synthesis of very low-density lipoproteins in the liver, which may
contribute to the proliferation of vascular smooth muscle cells and
the development of atherosclerosis (Herd, 1978).

The catecholamines also increase the tendency of the blood to
coagulate, an effect that is useful in preventing bleeding during
injury but could also contribute to the formation of blood clots
blocking arteries. In high doses, the catecholamines cause platelet
aggregation that blocks arterioles. In rats stressed by repeated
electric shocks to the feet, similar platelet aggregations have
been observed (Haft and Fani, 1973).

High levels of sympathetic arousal also increase stroke volume,
heart rate and, hence, cardiac output. This produces an elevation
in blood pressure which is further aggravated by an increase in
peripheral resistance that is likely to occur, especially if no
activity of the large skeletal muscles is occurring to reduce their
resistance.

Under stress, yet other effects occur: thyroxin secretion is
increased, prolactin secretion is inhibited, resulting in interference with milk let-down; also testosterone and estrogen levels
can be reduced.

The flight-fight reaction is characterized by a state of
emotional arousal, increased skeletal-muscle activity, and an
increased cardiac output shunted away from the skin and viscera to
the skeletal muscles where vasodilatation reduces their peripheral
resistance. Williams (1975) has called attention to the existence
of a different pattern--a state of vigilance during which motor
activity and heart rate decrease and there is an active vaso-
constriction, increasing peripheral resistance, in skeletal muscle
as well as in skin and viscera. He believes that this second
pattern also could result in cardiovascular damage, but such
possibilities have scarcely been studied. Other relatively neglected
areas are the physiological mechanisms involved in chronic psychological stress and in the rebound from stress.

Most neurophysiological functions are under not only excitatory
but also inhibitory control. Although many of the actions of the
parasympathetic nervous system are opposite to those of the
sympathetic one, the relationship is far from one of simple reciprocal
inhibition. Stress may simultaneously activate components of both
the parasympathetic and sympathetic nervous systems: it may tip the
balance first one way and then the other, as when fear causes the

heart to beat wildly from inhibition of the vagus or causes the
heart to skip a beat from stimulation of the vagus. We shall
encounter many other examples in which stress can produce effects
in opposite directions. Such paradoxical opposite effects indicate
the need for studies, such as those of dose repsonse, time response,
and interactions with other variables, to define more exactly the
conditions under which the effects may be in one direction or in the
opposite one. They also indicate caution in generalizing conclusions
from one situation to another possibly different one.

Recently, pain-inhibiting tracts in the brain have been
discovered (Liebeskind and Paul, 1977). In these tracts, receptors
that bind to morphine have been found as well as morphine-like sub-
stances that presumably serve as neurotransmitters (Snyder, 1979).
Since morphine inhibits fear as well as pain, there is an excellent
possibility that this pathway has an inhibitory effect on fear and
perhaps on stress from other sources. Furthermore, the action of
anti-anxiety drugs suggests that the brain may contain distinctive
receptors and pathways more specifically involved in the inhibition
of fear.

While the neurophysiological mechanisms that have been discussed
appear to be available for potentially producing a variety of somatic
effects of stress, in most cases the exact mechanisms that actually
are involved in specific effects of specific stressors or specific
coping responses have not been determined. Such determination should
be a profitable type of investigation.

The foregoing mechanisms and a few additional, related ones will
be referred to again in connection with specific types of effects of
stress and with certain theoretical problems.

EPIDEMIOLOGICAL AND CLINICAL EVIDENCE FOR EFFECTS OF
STRESS ON HEALTH

Epidemiological studies show that situations that appear to
increase stress are associated with a variety of medically adverse
consequences. Some of these situations are bombing raids, immigration to a radically different social or physical environment, rapid
social changes in the same environment, social disorganization,
loss of social supports, and membership in groups with conflicting
mores or markedly different social status (Stewart and Winsor, 1942;
Cassel, 1973; Levi and Anderson, 1975; Wolf and Goodell, 1976;
Jenkins, 1977). Furthermore, studies of life changes indicate that
the greater the number and the more drastic the changes (e.g., losing
a spouse) that have occurred during the last two years, the greater
the risk is for a variety of physical disorders (Kraus and Lilienfeld,
1959; Jacobs, Spilken, and Norman, 1969; Rahe, 1972; Wolf and
Goodell, 1976; Klerman and Izen, 1977). Some of the consequences of
stress suggested by the clinical, epidemiological, and life-change

studies are an increased risk of mental disorders, ulcers, hypertension, stroke, myocardial infarction, sudden cardiac death,
tuberculosis, influenza, pneumonia, diabetes, cancer, and multiple
sclerosis.

The foregoing studies find large individual differences in the
reactions of people to similar stressors. In some cases, these
differences appear to involve organic factors (Weiner, Thaler,
Reiser, and Mirsky, 1957) and in others the availability of social
support and the effectiveness of coping mechanisms. In fact, a
common element of these stressful situations appears to be a
removal of social support and changes that cause old coping responses
to become inadequate or impossible. These studies find an increased
risk of a wide variety of medically adverse consequences rather than
any single peculiarly psychosomatic effect to be predicted from any
particular kind of stress. An apparent exception to this conclusion
is a particular behavior constellation--hard-driving, striving
intensely for achievement, competitive, easily provoked impatient,
driven by deadlines, abrupt in gestures and speech--that has been
called Type A. A large number of studies have shown that such
people are approximately twice as likely to have heart attacks as
those who show the opposite pattern (Dembroski, 1978; Rosenman,
Brand, Sholtz, and Friedman, 1976). But, until the susceptibility
of Type A people to other medical adversities has been studied more
carefully, one cannot be certain how specific the risk is to coronary
disease.

The foregoing studies have shown significant effects. But it
is difficult to prove that the effects were due to stress. Even
though ingenious controls are used, it is difficult to be certain
that confounding factors, such as increased amounts of saturated
fats in the diet or of exposure to pollution, have been completely
ruled out (Kasl, 1977; Ostfeld and D'Atri, 1977).

EXPERIMENTAL EVIDENCE FOR EFFECTS OF STRESS ON HEALTH

The foregoing, less well controlled, epidemiological and
clinical evidence is strongly supported by the results of a number
of experimental studies in which it was possible to control for
confounding variables. By necessity, most of these studies have
been performed on animals; together with the epidemiological and
clinical evidence on people, they make a strong case for a variety
of harmful effects of psychological stress on the body.

Effects on Immune System

A number of studies from different laboratories show that
stress produced in a variety of ways can affect the immune system
(Stein, Schiavi, and Camerino, 1976). Mice having to perform a
shuttle-avoidance response once every five minutes were found to

have involution of the thymus and spleen, reduction in the number of lymphocytes, a delay in the rejection of skin grafts, a decrease in susceptibility to acute anaphylaxis induced by the intravenous administration of antigen-antibody complexes, and a reduced level of interferon, which is believed to be important in the defense against viral infections. The same conditions that produced these reduced activities of the immune system increased the susceptibility of the mice to a variety of experimental infections: herpex simplex, polio-myelitis, Coxsackie B, and polyoma virus; they also increased the number of tumors produced by the polyoma infections. On the other hand, there was a slight but definite decrease in the progression of Rauscher leukemia. This reduction was not seen in adrenalecto-mized mice and probably is due to the fact that the Rauscher-virus-transformed cells are cells of the lymphatic system, the growth of which is inhibited by the corticosteroids released under stress by the adrenals (Rasmussen, 1969).

That not all of the effects of stress are mediated by the immuno-suppressant effects of the corticosteroids, however, is suggested by the fact that the increased susceptibility of stressed animals to an injection of vesicular stomatovirus can be seen even in adrenalectomized animals (Yamada, Jensen, and Rasmussen, 1964).

While there do seem to be clear effects of experimentally induced stress on certain measures of the immune system and on resistance to certain experimentally induced infections and tumors, there are a number of cases in which such effects have not been secured (Rasmussen, 1969; Stein et al., 1976). Some studies have even produced opposite effects. For example, Palmblad, Cantell, Strander, Pröberg, Karlsson, Levi, Granström, and Unger, 1976) subjected eight healthy human volunteers to a 3-day vigil without sleep or rest, during which they were exposed to loud noises. They found that interferon production was elevated during the stress and still higher five days afterward. At the same time, the ability of white blood cells to ingest heat-killed bacteria was lower during the stress period, but, after a 5-day rest period, was higher than that preceding the stress. The foregoing results indicate that it may be important to investigate the time course of stress on the immune response.

The fact that Jensen (1969) found that low doses of adrenalin caused an increase in the interferon response whereas high doses produced a decrease suggests that we need also to study the effect of the dose of stress on the response of the immune system. Finally, we need more studies of the mechanisms involved; for example, a study of the effects of stress on a "corticosteroid-clamp" prepara-tion of adrenalectomized animals maintained at a normal level by a subcutaneous pellet from which corticosterone slowly diffuses at a constant rate so that the results are not confounded by the debili-tating effects of a deficiency of corticosterone. The foregoing

studies should make use of the availability of improved techniques
for producing psychological stress and for measuring its effects
on the different components of the immune system. Such studies
should be especially worthwhile in the light of the fact that any
effects of stress on the immune system are likely to have a wide
range of significant medical consequences.

Cardiovascular Effects

Clinical evidence indicates that when a patient's heart is
damaged, emotional stress can cause arrhythmias that can lead to
fibrillation and sudden death. For example, Järvinen (1955) found
that patients with myocardial infarction were five times as likely
to experience sudden death when unfamiliar staff were making ward
rounds than would be expected in any other comparable time.

In an experimental study verifying such observations, Lown and
Wolf (1971) produced experimental infarcts in hearts of dogs by
tying off a branch of the coronary artery. In such dogs they found
that stimulating the stellate ganglion of the sympathetic nervous
system caused the damaged hearts to fibrillate so that the dogs would
have suddenly died if the investigators had not used equipment to
defibrillate the heart immediately so that it could beat normally
again.

In another experiment, Lown, Verrier, and Corbalan (1973) used
electrical stimulation via a chronic electrode in the ventricle of
the heart to produce a preventricular contraction (PVC) like the
arrhythmia that frequently occurs in a damaged heart. Gradually
increasing the strength of stimulation, they found that the stage
just short of the fatal fibrillation was one in which a single
stimulation elicited a series of PVCs. They used this stage to
spare the dogs the trauma of fibrillation and defibrillation.
Sometimes the dogs were tested in a room where they previously had
received electric shocks and at other times in a room where they
previously had been petted, fed, and never shocked. The threshold
for repeated PVCs was considerably lower in the shock- than in the
food-room. Since no physical stimulus of electric shock was given
during the test, the difference must have been produced by the
purely psychological stress of having learned to fear the room where
they had received shock.

In similar experiments, Skinner, Lie and, Entman (1975) produced
coronary occlusions in the hearts of pigs. If a pig was kept in a
laboratory and attended by staff with whom he was thoroughly familiar,
the occlusion did not result in fibrillation. But when pigs were
not adapted to the laboratory or were otherwise stressed, a lethal
arrhythmia was always produced. Johansson, Jonsson, Lannek, Blomgren,
Lindberg, and Pough (1974) found that in the pig immobilization plus
electric shocks to the skin were sufficient to produce cardiac

arrhythmias, permanent myocardial damage, and ventricular fibrillation. Similarly, Corley, Shiel, Path, Mauck, and Greenhoot (1973)
showed that exposing squirrel monkeys to restraint plus 8-hours-on
and 8-hours-off shock avoidance testing each day for approximately
a week produced cardiac arrhythmias and extensive myocardial fibrosis.

Finally, Corely, Mauck, and Shiel (1975) found two different
patterns of cardiovascular response to stress. Pairs of monkeys were
confined to chairs for 8 hours a day and exposed to exactly the same
electric shocks. The ones that had to turn off a light once a minute
to avoid tail shock showed evidence of strong sympathetic arousal,
indicated by hypertension, and eventually developed myocardial
fibrosis and degeneration. Their yoked partners, who received
exactly the same shocks via electrodes wired in series but had no
response available to control the shocks, showed bradycardia (slow
heart rate) and died earlier, usually in asystole. The particular
conditions determining which of these two opposite effects will occur
in a variety of situations have not been investigated.

Effects on Gastrointestinal System

In his classic studies of the flight-fight response, Cannon (1953)
showed that the effect of certain stresses was to shunt blood away
from the gastrointestinal system, to inhibit the secretion of
digestive juices, and to decrease stomach motility. These experimental observations were in line with clinical ones that emotional
stress can interfere with digestion.

Although it was generally recognised that emotional factors
seemed to play a role in ulcers of the stomach and duodenum, the fact
that the hydrochloride acid secreted as a digestive juice by the
stomach seemed to exacerbate ulcers and that anti-acid measures
seemed to ameliorate them, along with Cannon's observation that acute
fear inhibited gastric secretion posed a dilemma. In an attempt to
solve this dilemma, psychoanalysts such as Alexander (1950) proposed
a complex mechanism in which emotional blocks caused a patient to
regress to an oral stage in which intense craving for food caused
the stomach to start digesting itself.

Clinical evidence indicated that bombing raids (Stewart and
Winsor, 1942) caused an increase in the incidence of ulcers. This
led Mahl (1949) to advance the hypothesis that chronic fear might
have an effect opposite to that of the acute fear described by Cannon
and thus increase the secretion of stomach acid which, in turn, could
cause ulcers. In experiments on dogs and monkeys receiving electric
shocks, and observations on medical students about to take their
National Boards, Mahl (1949, 1950, 1952) secured impressive evidence
that fear can indeed increase the secretion of hydrochloric acid by
the stomach. He was unsuccessful, however, in producing stomach
lesions, perhaps because his major experiments were on dogs, animals

not naturally subject to ulcers. Since then, various investigators have produced stomach lesions in rats and monkeys by procedures involving extreme restraint (Selye, 1936; Brodie and Hanson, 1960), by approach-avoidance conflict (Sawrey, Conger, and Turrell, 1956), and by controllable electric shocks (Brady, 1958). A variety of procedures to be described in the next section have isolated psychological factors as antecedents of the stress and stomach lesions (Weiss, 1977). As the last-cited article points out, the lesions in all of the rat studies have an uncertain relationship to human ulcers; they appear to resemble pitting, a possible stage in the formation of ulcers. In any event, they do represent physical damage to the stomach. Incidentally, Weiss has found it considerably easier to produce stomach lesions in 150-250 gram rats than in those weighing over 400 grams.

In the experiments by Weiss (1977) and his colleagues, the procedures that produced the greatest increases in stomach lesions produced the greatest increases in the levels of plasma corticosterone. Furthermore, within each group given the same treatment, those animals that had larger amounts of stomach lesions also tended to have higher levels of plasma corticosterone. Taken together with the tendency for medical treatments by corticosterone to be associated with ulcers, these results suggest a role for corticosteroids in the production of stress-induced stomach lesions. On the other hand, it is possible that the increased corticosterone and the stomach lesions are linked together as parallel effects of stress rather than in a casual sequence. Experiments on animals in the previously suggested "corticosterone clamp" should be able to clarify this question.

Clinical observations that fear and other emotional stresses can lead to diarrhea are confirmed by the experimental observation that rats placed in an apparatus where they previously have received electric shocks will promptly defecate (Miller, 1948). There is clinical evidence that fear can lead to the opposite effect of constipation; Arlo Myers and I have informally observed that rats subjected to prolonged periods of continuous avoidance performance still have their stomachs full of rough particles of undigested food that have abraded large portions of their linings. The particular conditions determining which of these two opposite effects will occur have not been investigated.

Clinical evidence suggests also that a stress, such as fear (or anxiety as it is called when its source is vague or ubiquitous), can have the opposite effects of producing a loss of appetite or of motivating compulsive binges of over-eating (Stunkard, 1976). Many experimenters have observed that animals will stop eating or working for food in the presence of a stimulus that has been associated with electric shock (Estes, 1944), but we have observed that the after-effects of an electric shock can cause satiated animals to resume eating a considerable amount of food. Other investigators have demonstrated that a device that exerts the stress of a continual pinch

on a satiated rat's tail can induce appreicable eating (Rowland and
Antelman, 1976). Again, the precise conditions responsible for
these two opposite effects have not been determined.

SOME PSYCHOLOGICAL FACTORS AFFECTING STRESS AND ITS
SOMATIC CONSEQUENCES

We have shown that something loosely called "stress" can have
important medical consequences. Next we shall summarize evidence
that certain purely psychological factors can affect stress and its
somatic consequences.

Pain   → negative Reinforcer.

Many of the experiments that I have summarized have used pain as
a stressor. Experiments by Pavlov (1927, p. 30) on counterconditioning have shown that a variety of the reactions to pain can be
inhibited by making it the signal for a positively rewarding stimulus
such as the presentation of food to a hungry animal. To quote him:

"Subjected to the very closest scrutiny, not even the
tiniest and most subtle objective phenomenon usually
exhibited by animals under the influence of strong
injurious stimuli can be observed in these dogs. No
appreciable changes in the pulse or in the respiration
occur in these animals, whereas such changes are always
most prominent when the nocuous stimulus has not been
converted into an alimentary-conditioned stimulus."

In my laboratory we have verified this observation. By using,
first, a weak and then progressively stronger electric shocks as a
signal for the delivery of food to a hungry dog, we were gradually
able to work up to the point where the dog would eagerly jump into
the apparatus and wag its tail while receiving shocks of a strength
that otherwise would have elicited howling and struggling.
Unfortunately, an unexpected pregnancy of the dog and also other
urgent research distracted us from following through to measure
effects on the physiological responses of the animal. With modern
great improvements in physiological and hormonal techniques, it is
surprising that no one has studied counterconditioning more carefully.

Ball (1967) has observed that stimulating rewarding areas of the
rat brain will inhibit evoked potentials in the trigeminal nucleus
to presumably painful stimulation of the face.

Clinical observations from combat fit in with the foregoing
experimental evidence. Soldiers for whom severe wounds mean the end
of any further exposure to harrowing deadly combat may show
astoundingly little sign of distress and make no request for pain-
relieving morphine. The meaning of the "good wound" as a ticket for

going home and survival apparently counteracts what would otherwise
be excrutiating pain (Beecher, 1956). The soldiers have also been
indoctrinated in having pride in being tough.

The mechanism for the foregoing effects on pain could be the
already mentioned pathways in the brain that inhibit pain and
involve opiate receptors. But further research is needed to test
this plausible idea. There is also evidence that baroreceptor
stimulation produced by increased blood pressure may reduce the
reactivity to aversive stimulation (Dworkin, Filewich, Miller,
Craigmyle, and Pickering, 1979).

Fear

The experiment by Lown et al. (1973) on the response just short
of fatal fibrillation did not involve any exposure to the physical
stimulus of pain during the test trials but only exposure to a room
that the dogs had previously learned to associate with pain. Thus,
this experiment involved the purely psychological stress of a
learned emotional response, presumably fear.

Most experimental studies have used pain as the unconditioned
stimulus to induce fear. Fuller (1967), however, found that if
puppies reared in a barren isolation chamber were suddenly plunged
into the normal complex environment, they exhibited extreme fear
which produced a long-lasting inhibition of normal canine behavior.
Apparently, a sudden exposure to a complex, unfamiliar environment
can act as a traumatic fear-inducing event, perhaps by producing
a severe informational overload, by the complete removal of
familiar stimuli for security, and/or by exposing the animal to a
situation in which he has no adequate coping responses. The
previously mentioned immigration to a new environment or sudden
changes in the same one may be analogous to the experience of Fuller's
puppies. Clinical evidence indicates many other sources of fear,
such as sudden intense and unexpected stimuli, weird situations, and
threats of aggression, of social disapproval, of loss of love, of
loss of money, of injury, of illness, of loneliness, of helplessness,
or of death. Some objects may have a latent innate tendency to
elicit fear (Miller, 1951); experiments have shown that it is much
easier to condition and harder to extinguish fear to pictures of
potentially phobic objects such as snakes than to pictures of a
neutral object such as a house (Öhman, 1978; Öhman, Eriksson, and
Olofsson, 1975).

It is also possible to countercondition fear. In a classic
experiment, Jones (1924) eliminated an infant's persistent fear of
furry animals by associating gradually nearer exposures to a rabbit
with the presentation of food to the infant. Wolpe (1958) has used
similar procedures to countercondition fear in cats and somewhat
analogous ones in the treatment of patients.

Both monkey and human infants are less afraid in the presence
of their mother, especially when clinging to her (Miller, 1951,
1979a). Harlow and Zimmerman's (1959) experiments on artificial
mother-surrogates indicate that such an effect is innate rather than
completely dependent on the nutritive characteristics of the mother.
Gunnar will describe similar effects of separation from the mother
in increasing corticosteroid levels and other indices of fear and
closeness to the mother in reducing them. It is easy to see how
such an innate tendency could be selected for its survival value.
Under stress or dangerous circumstances, a reduction in the strength
of fear would reinforce approach to the mother; infants exhibiting
such approach would be more likely to survive. Perhaps a similar
selective tendency has operated to provide an innate basis for a
fear-reducing tendency from approaching and receiving support from
a social group. The importance of such support is indicated by the
epidemiological studies that I have cited; its effectiveness in
reducing the incidence of cardiovascular disease is strongly suggested
by studies such as those of Bruhn, Philips, and Wolf (1972) and
Lynch (1977). Dollard and Miller (1950) have also pointed out that
patients tend to imitate the calm behavior of a psychotherapist.
Bandura (1969) has renamed this process "modelling" and secured
additional evidence for it.

Discrimination: Safety Signals

Observations in psychotherapy and in combat emphasize the value
in reducing chronic exposure to fear of learning a discrimination
between what is dangerous and what is safe (Dollard and Miller, 1950).
Arlo Myers (1956) has demonstrated this effect using a tendency of
fear to inhibit drinking by thirsty rats as an index. Rescorla and
Lorlordo (1965) have demonstrated that, as would be expected from
the inhibitory effect of the negative stimulus in a discrimination
(Pavlov, 1927), the stimulus that signals that shock will not occur
functions as a safety signal; if the non-shock stimulus from one
situation is presented in a different situation involving a different fear-motivated response, it can reduce the rate of performing
that response.

The foregoing studies used behavioral indices of fear. In
additional work in my laboratory, Weiss (1970) found that in a semi-
restrained situation rats that receive a signal immediately before an
occasionally occurring brief shock, and hence can learn a discrimination between when it is dangerous and when it is safe, have
lower levels of plasma corticosterone. They also have only one-
sixth as extensive stomach lesions as rats in the same type of
situation but with the signal uncorrelated with the shocks so that
they cannot learn a discrimination. Since pairs of animals in
both groups received identically the same physical strength of
electric shocks via fixed electrodes on their tails, the difference
must have been produced by the purely psychological factor of being

able to learn a discrimination.

In Weiss's experiment, the discrimination was a simple one
involving the distinctive stimulus of a tone against a background of
silence. Pavlov (1927), however, has shown that if a dog is first
trained on a simple discrimination between two distinctive cues that
then are gradually made progressively more similar so that discrimination eventually becomes impossible, some dogs show obvious signs
of a severe emotional disturbance which he has called an experimental
neurosis. This can occur in the absence of any innately noxious
stimulation when one cue signals food and the other signals non-
feeding. Gantt (1944) has shown that prolonged exposure to such a
situation for a susceptible dog can lead to long-lasting cardiovascular and sexual disturbances. Since the animals do not show
emotional disturbance during the easy phase of the discrimination,
the emotional effects cannot be attributed to the frustration of
the negative cue signaling that food will not be delivered. If the
animals are presented with an impossible discrimination from the
beginning, the situation will be one of partial reinforcement which
does not produce such disturbances. Therefore a crucial feature in
producing the emotional disturbance must be learning to solve a
problem that gradually becomes impossibly difficult.

The foregoing results suggest that an easy discrimination may
reduce stress but a difficult one increase it, but the conditions
under which a discrimination may produce one effect or the opposite
one need further investigation. The effects of discrimination
obviously are closely related to those of predictability, which
will be discussed in later chapters.

A Successful Avoidance Response: Coping or Control

Observations in psychotherapy and in combat indicate that one
of the ways of reducing fear is to learn to perform a response that
reduces the danger (Miller, 1951). Such responses are sometimes
called coping responses. The epidemiological and life-change studies
suggest that changes that reduce the availability or effectiveness
of previously learned coping responses can increase stress and its
medically adverse consequences. Experimental studies confirm these
observations. Miller (1948, 1951) trained rats to learn to rotate
a small squirrel-cage wheel that caused a door to drop that allowed
them to escape from a compartment in which they previously had
received electric shocks into one in which they had escaped from
the shocks. He observed that as the rats became more skillful in
performing the avoidance response, the originally present signs of
fear--such as agitation, squealing, urination, and defecation--
dropped out till the animals eventually were performing in an utterly
casual manner with little sign of any motivation. It was as if the
cues produced by performing the avoidance response, since they always
were followed by the safe compartment and never by electric shock,

had become the negative cues (safety signals) in a thoroughly learned discrimination. That the fear of the starting compartment had been inhibited rather than completely eliminated, however, was demonstrated by the fact that if the performance of the avoidance response was interrupted, for example by disconnecting the wheel so that it no longer caused the door to drop, the signs of fear--urination, defecation, and agitated behavior--abruptly reappeared in spite of the fact that the shock remained turned off.

During prolonged avoidance training, Coover, Ursin, and Levine (1973) found that plasma corticosterone levels follow the same general course as the behavioral indices described above: a sharp increase during early stages of learning and mastery, followed by a gradual decrease during continued successful performance and a second marked increase if the avoidance response is thwarted. The changes after the initial stages of learning cannot be explained by changes in shock or response frequency. Similar results have been secured in other experiments summarized by Hennessy and Levine (1979).

Weiss (1971a) has isolated the factor of being able to perform the coping response by using pairs of animals each of which had fixed electrodes on its tail and with these electrodes wired in series so that each member of a pair received identical shocks. One member of each pair was able to rotate a little squirrel-cage wheel in order to escape the shock, or to avoid it if he performed promptly; the yoked animal had the same kind of wheel available but it was not connected to the shock-control apparatus. In a series of experiments of this type, Weiss found that the animals that could perform the simple avoidance response showed less fear in a behavioral test, had lower levels of plasma corticosterone, less depletion of brain norepinephrine, and only approximately one-third as many stomach lesions as their yoked partners who had no control over the shocks. Since both animals received identically strong electric shocks, the behavioral factor of being able to control the shock must have been responsible for the difference.

Miller and Weiss (1969) have speculated that the learned inhibitory, or, in other words safety-signal, value of the cues produced as feedback by complete, or even anticipatory, performance of the successful avoidance response was responsible for the reduced fear and less severe somatic effects in rats that had an avoidance response available.

Weiss (1971b) secured evidence supporting this hypothesis. He showed that giving the avoidance-coping rats a feedback signal that clearly informed them when they had performed a correct response caused them to have fewer stomach lesions than avoidance-coping rats without such a signal.

When rats receive electric shocks, they have a strong tendency

to attack each other. Conner, Vernikos-Dannellis, and Levine (1971)
have shown that rats shocked in pairs so that they can attack each
other have less ACTH secretion than those shocked individually
without any possibility to attack. Using fixed electrodes on the
tail for better control of strength of shock, Weiss, Pohorecky,
Salman, and Gruenthal (1976) have shown that being able to attack
another rat in this situation reduces the amount of stomach lesions.
These results show that performing a suitable innate response can
have the same effect as learning a response to control the shock.
Hennessy and Levine (1979) summarize data indicating that performing
consummatory responses can reduce the level of plasma corticosterone.

Conflict

    I have already mentioned that Sawrey et al. (1956) found that
an approach-avoidance conflict situation could induce stomach lesions
in rats. In order to determine whether the conflict had any effects
in addition to the electric shocks and the food deprivation that were
also involved, they ran, in a similar alley, rats that had not been
trained to receive food at a goal and that received exactly the same
shocks as their partner because the grids that were the floors of
the two alleys were wired in series. These animals did not show as
many stomach lesions. However, as I have pointed out (Miller, 1963a),
these results are not conclusive because it is quite possible that
the animals running to food received the electric current through
their front paws, which are much more sensitive, while those that
were not in conflict might have learned to sit on their tougher hind
paws. I made a similar criticism (Miller, 1951) of an earlier
experiment on helplessness by Mowrer and Viek (1948). Without fixed
electrodes it is possible that the behavior of the animal may be
determining whether the electric shock is administered in a way that
is less painful. Incidentally, a similar criticism applies to some
of the more recent experiments on helplessness, some of which will
be discussed later by Overmier. Under conditions approximating a
constant-current shock, if animals move on the grid they will at
times receive all the current through only a small area where its
high density will make it considerably more painful. Therefore,
they will be rewarded for grasping the grid firmly and remaining
motionless with the current distributed less densely over a larger
area.

    An experiment by Weiss (1971c) used fixed electrodes that
controlled for behavior that affects the painfulness of the shock.
In this experiment, turning the wheel that the animals had learned
to rotate in order to turn off the shock gave the avoidance animals
and their partners one additional shock via the tail. Thus, the
avoidance animals had to take a shock in order to escape or avoid
a longer train of shocks. They were in an avoidance-avoidance
conflict. Under these circumstances, instead of having far fewer
lesions than their yoked partners, the avoidance rats had many more;

the effect of having control was reversed. In this experiment, it is possible that the shock administered for rotating the wheel greatly reduced the fear-reducing effect of the feedback cues from performing this response. Perhaps a similar effect is involved in all conflict. In any event, since the strength of shock administered to the two groups was identical, this experiment further emphasizes the important role that purely psychological factors can have.

In another experiment, Tsuda and Hirai (1975) found that when pressing a bar one time was sufficient to turn off an electric shock, the animals that learned to perform this simple avoidance response had fewer lesions than their yoked partners. But if the avoidance response was made much more difficult by requiring the rats to press the bar 10 times to turn off the shock, the results were reversed: the avoidance animals had more stomach lesions than their yoked controls. This experiment, and the previous one by Weiss, show that when avoidance responses involve enough conflict or difficulty, performing them may shift from being an advantage to being a disadvantage. Weiss (1971a) has devised a model that predicts such effects.

Placebo Effects

It is well known that a variety of procedures, such as taking fancy-colored sugar pills reputed to be powerful drugs, receiving irrelevant surgery, and getting other types of treatment known to have no specific physical effect on the illness, can cause patients to experience relief and even reduce physically measured symptoms such as hypertension (Beecher, 1961; Miller 1979b; Shapiro, 1960, 1971). In fact, for thousands of years, during which most medical treatments were worthless or even harmful, the powerful placebo effect is believed to have played a major role in maintaining the prestige of physicians. The placebo effect is another example of the power of a purely psychological factor. To date, most of the attention of biomedical research has been directed toward ruling it out in the process of evaluating various forms of therapy. It deserves far more study than it has recieved. It seems likely to me that it may be related to the fear-reducing effects of clinging to the mother, of support from the social group, and of successful performance of a simple avoidance response that we have been reviewing. There is some evidence that placebo effects are stronger with anxious patients (Shapiro, 1960, 1971).

Effects of Piror Exposure

Zigmond and Harvey (1970) showed that prior exposure of rats to the stress of strong electric shocks could increase their resistance to central norepinephrine depletion during a subsequent exposure and decrease the number of rats killed by that exposure.

Extending these findings, Weiss, Glazer, Pohorecky, Brick, and Miller (1975) showed that a series of prior exposures of rats to strong, unpredictable, inescapable electric shocks increased the activity of tyrosine hydroxylase, the enzyme that synthesizes norepinephrine in the brain, and decreased the norepinephrine-depleting effects of a subsequent exposure. The prior exposures also increased the effectiveness of norepinephrine in the synapses by decreasing its rate of reabsorption into the presynaptic terminals, an effect similar to that of a tricyclic antidepressant. The prior exposures also decreased the level of plasma corticosterone elicited by the subsequent one. Finally, the behavioral depression occurring as an after-effect of the subsequent exposure was greatly reduced. These effects of prior exposure to stress from electric shocks transferred to have a protective effect on a subsequent exposure to stress from swimming in cold water. Conversely, toughening by swimming in cold water transferred to helping the rats to withstand the after-effects of traumatic electric shocks. That these results were an adjustment to the depleting effects of the prior exposure on norepinephrine (and possibly also other brain amines) or, in other words, were the result of a presumably unlearned physiological process, enzyme induction, was shown by the fact that similar protective effects could be produced by a series of prior exposures to a drug, tetrabenazine, that depletes norepinephrine and other brain amines (Glazer, Weiss, Pohorecky, and Miller, 1975).

As might be expected, the effects of prior exposure to a stress depend on the spacing of the stressors. Studying the effects of extreme restraint on stomach lesions in rats, Guth and Mendick (1964) found that periods of 4 hours of restraint and 20 hours of rest produced a decrease, while Brodie and Hanson (1960) found that periods of 18 hours of restraint and 6 hours of rest produced an increase.

Exposures to stress during certain critical periods of infancy may have especially significant effects. Thus, Levine (1962) showed that early exposures of infant rats to stress had a variety of effects: increasing their growth and, when adult, affecting the production of corticosterone during stress and improving their avoidance learning. As another effect of early experience, Ackerman, Hofer, and Weiner (1975) found that rats separated from their mothers 15 days after birth were more susceptible to restraint lesions of the stomach as adults than those separated 25 days after birth. We shall hear more about the important problem of developmental effects from Gunnar.

In yet another approach, Miller (1960) and Feirstein and Miller (1963) have shown that rats can be trained to resist the behavioral effects of pain and fear. But it has not been determined whether or not this behavioral effect is at the cost of greater stress as indicated by measures such as plasma levels of corticosterone, norepinephrine, and epinephrine. In one of the

chapters in this book, Overmier will discuss other proactive effects.
He is to be congratulated for using this term that is laden with much
less surplus meaning than the more striking learned helplessness.

SOME KEY PROBLEMS

The foregoing summary has established the importance of a
general problem area. Now let us briefly consider some key issues.

What is Stress? Is it a Unitary Phenomenon?

Following Selye (1976), stress can be considered to be a
response of the organism to some experimental treatment of environmental feature that can be called a stressor. Stress has been
defined as any deviation from homeostasis or, in other words, from
the normal level of internal conditions that the organism tends to
maintain. Many, but not all, such deviations produce drives
(Miller, 1959). But is fear a deviation from homeostasis? Ursin
(1978) has defined stress as a physiological activation based on
the arousing effects of the reticular formation and indicated by
desynchronized, low-voltage, high-frequency activity in the
cortical electroencephalogram and also by a variety of physiological
measures. He will discuss this further in his chapter.

An important question is the degree to which various phenomena
that are loosely described under the category of stress behave in
a unitary way. Ursin (1978) points out that with more knowledge
about the reticular formation, it looks less like a simple,
undifferentiated system for producing a single type of general
arousal. In fact, Ursin, Baade, and Levine (1978) state: "Our
general conclusion is that activation is a multi-dimensional and
complex phenomenon for hormones also." But it is barely conceivable
that there is some point in the brain where the level of activation
is summed. Vertes and Miller (1976) have found giant cells in the
poitine region of the reticular formation that fire to a conditioned
stimulus signaling an electric shock but not to one signaling the
delivery of water to a thirsty animal. It would be interesting to
see whether these cells fire in a variety of other situations, such
as active and passive avoidance and approach-avoidance conflict,
that have been assumed to involve fear. If so, would they fire also
to frustration?

Miller (1951) has pointed out that there are two quite different
patterns of behavioral response to a threatening situation, one
involving remaining motionless and mute as if to avoid attracting
attention, and the other involving intense activity and vocalization.
Sometimes the behavior may shift rapidly from one to the other as
when a frightened animal first freezes and then suddenly scurries
to shelter. Also, a CS signaling pain sometimes produces a reduced
heart rate and in other situations an increased one. Are these

opposite types of reaction related to William's (1975) distinction between a vigilance pattern and a flight-fight one? Do they contain enough of a central mechanism in common to be usefully described as reactions to fear?

Selye (1976) believes he has found that stress involves a unitary phenomenon; he defines stress as the nonspecific effects that widely different types of stressors all have in common and believes that the pituitary-adrenocortical system plays a key role in such effects. In addition to this general factor, there are specific effects due to the different characteristics of different stressors. On the other hand, Mason, Maher, Hartley, Mougey, Perlow, and Jones (1976) have secured evidence that food deprivation, severe exercise, heat, and avoidance learning involve different patterns of endocrine response and that the pituitary-adrenocortical system does not respond to all types of strong demands on the organism irrespective of the nature of the evocative stimulus. Since this system responds to emotion-inducing stimuli, unless one is careful the emotional by-products of various stressors can arouse the pituitary-adrenocortical system and cause one to over-estimate the ubiquity of its response. If Mason et al. (1976) are right, it could be that psychological stress fits Selye's definition better than do physical stresses. But at present, it probably is prudent to consider stress as a general area of research rather than as a unitary variable and to concentrate work on investigating specific relationships among variables and specific mechanisms.

As I have pointed out elsewhere (Miller, 1959, 1967), in order to determine whether or not it is useful to think of a unitary intervening variable, it is necessary to investigate the effects of a number of different treatments on a number of different measures. This is the design of Mason et al.'s (1976) experiments; it should be used more extensively in research on stress. A good many people have studied the effect of a number of different conditions on a single symptom, such as ulcers or hypertension; a few people have studied the effect of a single condition on a variety of symptoms, but there have been almost no studies of the effects of a variety of different stressors on each one of a variety of different symptoms. Thus, we do not know whether one type of stressor can predispose a subject to ulcers while another can predispose to cardiac infarct. But this is an important problem (Miller, 1972). In experimental studies on this problem, we need to separate the differential effects that may be due to the strength and duration of the stressor from those that may be due to qualitative differences between stressors.

Is All Arousal Equally Stressful?

Another question is whether only aversive situations serve as

stressors or whether purely pleasant ones also can serve as stressors.
Some of the life-change studies cited suggest that rewarding changes
can increase the incidence of medically adverse consequences. But a
generally rewarding life-change, such as promotion, may involve a
number of aversive consequences, such as losing associations with
one's old friends. Goldman, Coover, and Levine (1973) have found
that opposite shifts in schedules of reinforcement can change levels
of plasma corticosterone in opposite directions: shifts to schedules
of reinforcement that deliver fewer or no rewards produce elevations
of plasma corticosteroids while shifts to markedly improved schedules
of reinforcement produce reductions in the level of plasma corticosteroids. Frankenhaeuser (1976) has found that an exciting Bingo
game in which everyone is winning can cause as great an elevation in
urine metabolites of epinephrine and norepinephrine as can some of
the aversive situations that she studied earlier. She will present
data suggesting that epinephrine and norepinephrine indicate levels
of arousal while the corticosteroids are more specific to distress.
The foregoing data are tantalizing; we need more studies in which
the effects of high levels of happy arousal are studied on a variety
of endocrine and other functions.

What is Coping

When we try to define coping, we run into all of the same kinds
of problems that we do when we try to define stress, plus some
additional ones. Ursin (1978) defines a coping response as one that
reduces physiological activation, which of course involves the
question of whether there is one summing point where activations
from various sources add up to some unitary quantity. Ursin's
reduction in activation is somewhat similar to the notion of drive-
reduction, which makes a coping response rather similar to an
instrumental (or operant) response and raises some of the questions
involved in the drive-reduction hypothesis of reinforcement (Miller,
1959, 1963b). Another question is whether one should consider all
cases of habituation or experimental extinction that reduce activation to be examples of coping and, if not, how one can determine
whether reduced activity is produced by habituation, extinction,
or coping. Ursin will discuss such issues.

Another problem is raised when Beatrix Hamburg (this volume)
refers to the high incidence of adolescent drug abuse, suicide,
pregnancy, school failure, and violance as indices of adolescent
lack of coping. Of course, we know what she means. But certainly,
taking barbiturates reduces the level of physiological activation
and, in situations of high activation, is reinforced by producing
such a reduction (Davis and Miller, 1963). Thus Ursin would
describe taking such a drug as a coping response and I would call it
an instrumental response. Here the basic problem is that an
immediate small reduction of drive produces a stronger reinforcing
effect that overrides the effect of a large delayed punishment.

In many cases, the long-term stress-inducing consequences of a given response may be the result of the conditions of a particular social environment.

If one defines a coping response as one that reduces activation (or stress), perhaps one can avoid a confusion by not talking about a coping response but about the "coping effect" of a response. But in that case, why not merely say "the stress-reducing effect"? Then one would not say that a simple coping response reduces stomach lesions but a more difficult one increases them. In any event, the problem is to determine more precisely and to describe more parsimoniously the situations under which one gets the beneficial and those under which one gets the detrimental effects. One should also determine whether or not a given coping response can have beneficial effects on certain aspects of health and detrimental ones on other aspects--for example, reduce the probability of a stroke but increase that of an ulcer or a viral infection.

Control

Control emerges as an important variable in the studies of Frankenhaeuser, Gunnar, and Rodin that will be discussed in this symposium. The factor of control obviously is linked to instrumental responses because it is by these responses that we control our environment. In addition to the obvious practical advantages that control brings to us, it seems possible that there are some added psychological advantages. Some of these may come from the ability to produce safety signals that was discussed in connection with the experiments by Weiss. Some may come from past experience in which control has produced desirable effects and lack of control undesirable ones. As one watches the delight of an infant when he finds that pushing a button causes a bell to ring or that kicking his cradle causes a mobile to move, one can imagine that the survival value of learning what causes something to happen and testing it until one has mastered control may have selected an innate mechanism responsible for the rewarding effect of such activity.

But the problem of control is complex. Remember the results of Weiss's rats performing conflict-inducing avoidance responses and Tsuda and Hirai's rats on a high fixed-ratio schedule of avoidance responses. Having the responsibility for control may sometimes have adverse consequences.

Internal Responses that are Instrumental in Controlling Emotions

Both everyday observation and laboratory experiments have shown that learning can condition emotional responses to the cues produced by saying words or by thinking thoughts (e.g., see Figure 8 in Miller, 1951). Thus, the response of stopping thinking thoughts that evoke strong fear can have a fear-reducing effect which can

reward the response of stopping (Dollard and Miller, 1950). This process is called suppression when it is voluntary and repression when it is so strong that it is involuntary. It is one type of defense. But repression can be inefficient in the long run because it can interfere with the use of higher mental (cognitive) processes that could produce a better solution to the problem (Dollard and Miller, 1950; Miller, 1979b).

Closely related to suppression or repression is denial. Other defenses described by Hamburg, Hamburg, and deGoza (1953) in a study of the mechanisms that severely burned patients use to protect themselves from the emotional impact of their situation are depression, delusion, hallucination, regression, reworking, withdrawal, religion, and rationalization. David Hamburg will deal in more detail with the specific sequence of defenses that typically are involved in successfully coping with a severe calamity.

In addition to the traditional defenses, there is accumulating evidence that some of the phenomena of stress can be modified by learning responses such as muscular relaxation, meditation, and a prompt, quieting reflex (Benson, 1975; Stroebel, 1979). Visceral learning may be important in maintaining homeostasis in spite of stress (Miller and Dworkin, 1979b). Learning may also be involved in the acquisition of psychosomatic symptoms that are rewarded by escape from stress. Such learning may exert its effects indirectly via a skeletal response, such as hyperventilation, that has a visceral effect, such as tachycardia. It is also conceivable that either symptomatic or therapeutic visceral responses can be learned more directly (Miller, 1978).

Testing Theories by the Effectiveness of Practical Application

Hackett and Cassem (1972) present evidence suggesting that heart-attack patients who use denial have a better chance for survival than those who do not. But in this example, it is difficult to be sure whether the patients are more likely to survive because denial reduces their anxiety or whether the patients whose attacks seem milder to them in ways that their physician cannot measure are more able to deny the seriousness of their condition. If an appropriately controlled experimental trial showed that encouraging patients to use denial increased the rate of survival, we would have a test of the causal relationship. In situations where there is no clear-cut evidence that one approach is better than another, instead of having different types of treatment admin-istered in a haphazard manner, a suitably controlled experiment can improve our theoretical understanding as well as our practical procedures (Miller, 1972).

A study by Cromwell, Butterfield, Brayfield, and Curry (1977) illustrates the type of work that needs to be done. In an

experiment on the effects of different types of care after myocardial
infarction, they used a 2 X 2 X 2 design with high versus low levels
of three variables: medical information, diversion, and active
participation in treatment. One of their chief findings was that
giving the patient much information improved his recovery when
combined with a high level of participation in his therapy.
Apparently, this was because he was given an opportunity to do
something about the information. But, under the condition of minimal
participation, a high level of information had the opposite effect
of impairing the recovery. A somewhat similar type of interaction
was found with anxiety: high information appeared to improve the
recovery of anxious patients but to have the opposite effect on
non-anxious ones. This study illustrates the complexity of the
problem of designing optimal psychological conditions for recovery
and the need for detailed experimental analysis of the effects of
such conditions.

Studies such as those to be reported by Rodin in this volume
will further illustrate the possibilities of testing the effectiveness of specific interventions in practical situations.

Opportunities and Dangers

The increasing interest in Behavioral Medicine, including the
effects of stress and preventive measures to avoid stress, presents
us with new opportunities for research and applications. But in a
field that is complex, we must be cautious. You will have noticed
that in a considerable number of the examples I have summarized
relatively similar procedures can produce opposite effects; there
are a number of non-monotonic relationships and interactions. When
the phenomena are this complex, we have to be especially sure of our
scientific base before we make any firm recommendations for practical
applications, and we have to test these applications with adequate
pilot studies before we rush into a large-scale project that may
fail and thus completely destroy the weak faith that the biomedical
community is beginning to acquire in the value of behavioral science.

Ursin (1978) has pointed out another danger. If a population
is led to believe that there is a particular relationship between
a certain state of affairs and health, this may become true, not
because it was true originally but because the population is led to
expect either health or disease from that particular condition. An
expectation that a set of conditions will be stressful and lead to
medically adverse effects may cause people to worry and thus have
the effect of a self-fulfilling prophecy.

We must realize that the way a person perceives a situation
has a strong effect--the "good wound" is a striking example. But
we must not commit the fallacy of implying that because of the strong
cognitive effects the environmental stressors are relatively

unimportant. It is possible to determine the degree to which certain situations tend to serve as stressors; for example, war, glaring social inequalities, unrealistic expectations, responsibility without authority or the means to carry it out, overstimulation, understimulation, and certain instances of lack of control. It is not unreasonable to suppose that understanding more about the effects of such stressors can contribute significantly to both contentment and health.

Finally, the cumulative advances in science and mathematics that are now taught in our school systems enable many pupils to solve physical and engineering problems that baffled the brightest minds of the ancients. If we can acquire a sound enough scientific base, we may be able to teach our children better ways of coping with social and emotional problems.

At present, the problem of stress seems to be extremely complex; perhaps some of the complexities are not inherent in nature but instead in our clumsy way of conceptualizing it. The Ptolemaic system of cycles and epicycles to explain the motion of the planets and stars with earth as the center of the universe was complex. Changing to the sun as a point of reference produced one great simplification and Newton's laws of motion and gravity produced another one. Some of the chapters in this book will describe steps toward achieving simplification and clarification of our understanding of the effects of stress and coping on disease and health.

REFERENCES

Ackerman, S. H., Hofer, M. A., and Weiner, H., 1975, Age at maternal separation and gastric erosion susceptibility in the rat, Psychosom. Med., 37:180.

Alexander, F., 1950, "Psychosomatic Medicine: Its Principles and Applications," W. W. Norton, New York.

Ball, G. G., 1967, Electrical self-stimulation of the brain and sensory inhibition, Psychonom. Sci., 8:489.

Bandura, A., 1969, "Principles of Behavior Modification," Holt, Rinehart and Winston, New York.

Beecher, H. K., 1956, Relationship of significance of wound to pain experienced, J. Am. Med. Assoc., 161:1609.

Beecher, H. K., 1961, Surgery as Placebo, J. Am. Med. Assoc., 176: 1102.

Benson, H., 1975, "Relaxation Response," Wm. Morrow and Company, New York.

Brady, J. V., 1958, Ulcers in "executive" monkeys, Sci. Am., 199:95.

Brodie, D. A., and Hanson, H. M., 1960, A study of the factors involved in the production of gastric ulcers by the restraint technique, Gastroenterology, 38:353.

Bruhn, J. G., Philips, B. U., and Wolf, S., 1972, Social readjustment
    and illness patterns: Comparison between first, second, and
    third generation Italian-Americans living in the same community,
    J. Psychosom. Res., 16:387.
Cannon, W. B., 1953, "Bodily Changes in Pain, Hunger, Fear and Rage,"
    2nd ed., Branford, Boston.

Cassel, J., 1973, The relation of the urban environment to health:
    Implications for prevention, Mt. Sinai J. Med., 40:539.
Conner, R. L., Vernikos-Danellis, J., and Levine, S., 1971, Stress,
    fighting and neuroendocrine function, Nature, 234:564.
Coover, G. D., Ursin, H., and Levine, S., 1973, Plasma corticosterone
    levels during active-avoidance learning in rats, J. Comp.
    Physiol. Psychol., 82:170.
Corley, K. C., Shiel, F. O'M., Rath, M. R. C., Mauck, H. P., and
    Greenhoot, J., 1973, Electrocardiographic and cardiac morpho-
    logical changes associated with environmental stress in
    squirrel monkeys, Psychosom. Med., 35:361.
Corley, K. C., Mauck, H. P., and Shiel, F. O"M., 1975, Cardiac
    responses associated with "yoked-chair" shock avoidance in
    squirrel monkeys., Psychophysiology, 12:439.
Cromwell, R. L., Butterfield, E. C., Brayfield, F. M., and Curry,
    J. C., 1977, "Acute Myocardial Infarction: Reaction and Recovery,"
    C. V. Mosby, St. Louis.
Daedalus, 1977, Doing better and feeling worse: Health in the United
    States, Daedalus, 106:1 (1).
Davis, J. D., and Miller, N. E., 1963, Fear and pain: Their effect on
    self-injection of amobarbital sodium by rats, Science, 141:1286.
Dembroski, T. M., ed., 1978, Proceedings of the formun on coronary-
    prone behavior, DHEW Publication No. (NIH) 78-1451, Washington,
    D. C.
Dollard, J., and Miller, N. E., 1950, "Personality and Psychotherapy,"
    McGraw Hill, New York.
Dworkin, B. R., Filewich, R. J., Miller, N. E., Craigmyle, N., and
    Pickering, T. G., 1979, in press, Baroreceptor activation reduces
    reactivity to noxious stimulation: Implications for hypertension,
    Science.
Estes, W. K., 1944, An experimental study of punishment, Psychol.
    Mon., 57, No. 263.
Feirstein, A. R., and Miller, N. E., 1963, Learning to resist pain
    and fear: Effects of electric shock before versus after
    reaching goal, J. Comp Physiol. Psychol., 56:797.
Frankenhaeuser, M., 1976, The role of peripheral catecholamines in
    adaptation to understimulation and overstimulation, in: "Psycho-
    pathology of Human Adaptation," G. Serban, ed., Plenum Press,
    New York.
Fuller, J. L., 1967, Experimental deprivation and later behavior,
    Science, 158:1645.
Gantt, W. H., 1944, "Experimental Basis for Neurotic Behavior,"
    Hoeber, New York.

Glazer, H. I., Weiss, J. M., Pohorecky, L. A., and Miller, N. E.,
    Monamines as mediators of avoidance-escape behavior, Psychosom.
    Med., 37:535.

Goldman, L., Coover, G. D., and Levine, S., 1973, Bidirectional
    effects of reinforcement shifts on pituitary-adrenal activity,
    Physiol. Behav., 10:209.

Guth, P. H., and Mendick, R., 1964, The effect of chronic restraint
    stress on gastric ulceration in the rat, Gastroenterology, 46:285.

Hackett, T. P., and Cassem, N. H., 1972, Psychological effects of
    acute coronary care, in: "Textbook of Coronary Care," L. E.
    Meltzer and A. J. Dunning, eds., Excerpta Medica, Amsterdam.

Haft, J. I., and Fani, K., 1973, Stress and the induction of intra-
    vascular platelet aggregation in the heart, Circulation, 48:164.

Hamburg, D. A., Hamburg, B., and deGoza, S., 1953, Adaptive problems
    and mechanisms in severely burned patients, Psychiatry, 16:1.

Harlow, H. F., and Zimmerman, R. R., 1959, Affectional responses in
    the infant monkey, Science, 130:421.

Hennessy, J. W., and Levine, S., 1979, Stress, arousal, and the
    pituitary-adrenal system: A psychoendocrine hypothesis, Prog.
    Psychobiol. Physiol. Psychol., 8:133.

Herd, J. A., 1978, Physiological correlates of coronary-prone behav-
    ior, in: "Proceedings of the Forum on Coronary-Prone Behavior,"
    DHEW Publication No. (NIH)78-1451, Washington, D. C.

Jacobs, M. A., Spilken, A., and Norman, M., 1969, Relationship of
    life change, maladaptive aggression, and upper respiratory
    infection in male college students, Psychosom. Med., 31:31.

Järvinin, K. A. J., 1955, Can ward rounds be a danger to patients
    with myocardial infarction?, Brit. Med. J., 1:318.

Jenkins, C. D., 1977, Epidemiological studies of the psychosomatic
    aspects of coronary heart disease, Adv. Psychosom. Med., 9:1.

Jensen, M. M., 1969, The influence of vasoactive amines on interferon
    production in mice, Proc. Soc. Exp. Biol. Med., 130:34.

Johansson, G., Jonsson, L., Lannek, N., Blomgren, L., Lindberg, P.,
    and Pough, O., 1974, Severe stress-cardiopathy in pigs, Am.
    Heart J., 87:451.

Jones, M. C., 1924, Elimination of children's fears, J. Exp. Psychol.,
    7:382.

Kasl, S. V., 1977, Contributions of social epidemiology to studies
    in psychosomatic medicine, Adv. Psychosom. Med., 9:160.

Klerman, G. L., Izen, J. E., 1977, The effects of bereavement and
    grief on physical health and general well-being, Adv. Psychosom.
    Med., 9:63.

Kraus, A. S., and Lilienfeld, A. M., 1959, Some epidemiologic aspects
    of the high mortality rate in the young widowed group, J. Chron.
    Dis., 10:207.

Levi, L., and Andersson, L., 1975, "Psychosocial Stress--Population,
    Environment, and Quality of Life," Spectrum, New York.

Levine, S., 1962, Psychophysiological effects of infant stimulation,
    in: "Roots of Behavior," E. L. Bliss, ed., Hoeber, New York.

Liebeskind, J. C., and Paul, L. A., 1977, Psychological and physiological mechanisms of pain, Ann. Rev. Psychol., 28:41.

Lown, B., and Wolf, M., 1971, Approaches to sudden death from
coronary heart disease, Circulation, 44:130.

Lown, B., Verrier, R., and Corbalan, R., 1973, Psychologic stress
and threshold for repetitive ventricular response, Science,
182:834.

Lynch, J. J., 1977, "The Broken Heart: The Medical Consequences of
Loneliness," Basic Books, New York.

Mahl, G. F., 1949, Effect of chronic fear on the gastric secretion
of HCl in dogs, Psychosom. Med., 11:30.

Mahl, G. F., 1950, Anxiety, HCl secretion and peptic ulcer etiology,
Psychosom. Med., 12:140.

Mahl, G. F., 1952, Relationship between acute and chronic fear and
the gastric acidity and blood-sugar levels in Macaca mulatta
monkeys, Psychosom. Med., 14:182.

Mason, J. W., Maher, J. T., Hartley, L. H., Mougey, E. H., Perlow,
M. J., and Jones, L. G., 1976, Selectivity of corticosteroid
and catecholamine responses to various natural stimuli, in:
"Psychopathology of Human Adaptation," G. Serban, ed., Plenum
Press, New York.

Miller, N. E., 1948, Studies of fear as an acquirable drive: I.
Fear as motivation and fear reduction as reinforcement in the
learning of new responses, J. Exp. Psychol., 38:89.

Miller, N. E., 1951, Learnable drives and rewards, in: "Handbook
of Experimental Psychology," S. S. Stevens, ed., Wiley and Sons,
New York.

Miller, N. E., 1959, Liberalization of basic S-R concepts: Extensions
to conflict behavior, motivation and social learning, in:
"Psychology: A Study of a Science," Study 1, Vol. 2, S. Koch ed.,
McGraw-Hill, New York.

Miller, N. E., 1960, Learning resistance to pain and fear: Effects
of overlearning, exposure, and rewarded exposure in context,
J. Exp. Psychol, 60:137.

Miller, N. E., 1963a, Animal experiments on emotionally-induced
ulcers, "Proceedings of the World Congress of Psychiatry,
Montreal, 1961," Vol. 3, University of Toronto Press, Toronto.

Miller, N. E., 1963b, Some reflections on the law of effect produce
a new alternative to drive reduction, in: "Nebraska Symposium
on Motivation," M. R. Jones, ed., University of Nebraska Press,
Lincoln.

Miller, N. E., 1967, Behavioral and physiological techniques:
Rationale and experimental designs for combining their use,
in: "Handbook of Physiology," Sec. 6, Vol . 1, C. F. Code and
W. Heidel, eds, American Physiological Society, Washington, D. C.

Miller, N. E., 1972, A psychologist's perspective on neural and
psychological mechanisms in cardiovascular disease, in: "Neural
and Psychological Mechanisms in Cardiovascular Disease,"
A. Zanchetti, ed., Casa Editrice "Il Ponte", Milano.

Miller, N. E., 1978, Biofeedback and visceral learning, Ann. Rev. Psychol., 29:373.

Miller, N. E., 1979a, in press, Effects of learning on physical symptoms produced by psychological stress, in: "Guide to Stress Research," H. Selye, ed., Van Nostrand Reinhold, New York.

Miller, N. E., 1979b, in press, Applications of learning and biofeedback to psychiatry and medicine, in: "Comprehensive Textbook of Psychiatry," H. I. Kaplan, A. M. Freedman, and B. J. Sadock, eds., Williams & Wilkins, Baltimore.

Miller, N. E., and Dworkin, B. R., 1979b, in press, Homeostasis as goal-directed learned behavior, in: "Neurophysiological Mechanisms of Goal-Directed Behavior and Learning," R. F. Thompson, ed., Academic Press, New York.

Miller, N. E., and Weiss, J. M., 1969, Effects of the somatic or visceral responses to punishment, in: "Punishment and Aversive Behavior," B. A. Campbell and R. M. Church, eds., Appleton-Century-Crofts, New York.

Mowrer, O. H., and Viek, P., 1948, An experimental analogue of fear from a sense of helplessness, J. Abnorm. Soc. Psychol., 43:193.

Myers, A. K., 1956, The effects of predictable vs. unpredictable punishment in the albino rat, Doctoral Dissertation, Yale University, New Haven.

Ohman, A., 1978, Fear relevance, autonomic conditioning, and phobias: A laboratory model, in: "Trends in Behavior Therapy," S. Bates, W. S. Dockens, K. -G. Götestam, L. Melin, and P. -O. Sjöden, eds., Academic Press, New York.

Ohman, A., Eriksson, A., and Olofsson, C., One-trial learning and superior resistance to extinction of autonomic responses conditioned to potentially phobic stimuli, J. Comp. Physiol. Psychol., 88:619.

Ostfeld, A. M., and D'Atri, D. A., Rapid sociocultural change and high blood pressure, Adv. Psychosom. Med., 9:20.

Palmblad, J., Cantell, K., Strander, H., Fröberg, J., Karlsson, C. -G., Levi, L., Granström, M., and Unger, P., Stressor exposure and immunological response in man: Interferon-producing capacity and phagocytosis, J. Psychosom. Res., 20:193.

Pavlov, I. P., 1927, (Reprinted 1960, Dover, New York) "Conditioned Reflexes," G. V. Anrep, translator, Oxford University Press, London.

Rahe, R. H., 1972, Subjects' recent life changes and their near-future illness susceptibility, Adv. Psychosom. Med., 8:2.

Rasmussen, A. F., Jr., 1969, Emotions and immunity, Ann. N. Y. Acad. Sci., 164:458.

Rescorla, R. A., and Lolordo, V. M., 1965, Inhibition of avoidance behavior, J. Comp. Physiol. Psychol., 59:406.

Rosenman, R. H., Brand, R. J., Sholtz, R. I., and Friedman, M., 1976, Multivariate prediction of coronary heart disease during 8.5 year follow-up in the Western Collaborative Group Study, Am. J. Card., 37:902.

Rowland, N. E., and Antelman, S. M., 1976, Stress-induced hyperphagia and obesity in rats: A possible model for understanding human obesity, Science, 191:310.

Sawrey, W. L., Conger, J. J., and Turrell, E. S., 1956, An experimental investigation of the role of psychological factors in the production of gastric ulcers in rats., J. Comp. Physiol. Psychol., 49:457.

Schwartz, G. E., and Weiss, S. M., 1978, Yale conference on behavioral medicine: A proposed definition and statement of goals, J. Behav. Med., 1:3.

Selye, H., 1936, A syndrome produced by diverse nocuous agents, Nature, 138:32.

Selye, H., 1956, "Stress and Disease," McGraw-Hill, New York.

Selye, H., 1976, "The Stress of Life," 2nd ed., McGraw-Hill, New York.

Shapiro, A. K., 1960, A contribution to a history of the placebo effect, Behav. Sci., 5:109.

Shapiro, A. K., 1971, Placebo effects in medicine, psychotherapy, and psychoanalysis, in: "Handbook of Psychotherapy and Empirical Analysis," A. E. Bergin and S. L. Garfield, eds., Wiley and Sons, New York.

Skinner, J. E., Lie, J. T., and Entman, M. L., 1975, Modification of ventricular fibrillation latency following coronary artery occlusion in the conscious pig: The effects of psychologic stress and beta-adrenergic blockade, Circulation, 51:656.

Snyder, S. H., 1979, Opoid peptides in the brain, in: "The Neurosciences: Fourth Study Program," F. O. Schmitt and F. G. Worden, eds., MIT Press, Cambridge.

Stein, M., Schiavi, R. C., and Camerino, M., 1976, Influence of brain and behavior on the immune system, Science, 191:435.

Stewart, D. N., and Winsor, D. M. DeR., Incidence of perforated peptic ulcer: Effect of heavy air-raids, Lancet, 1:259.

Stroebel, C., 1979, in press, "The Quieting Reflex," Guilford Publishers, New York.

Stunkard, A. J., 1976, "The Pain of Obesity," Bull Publishing, Palo Alto.

Tsuda, A., and Hirai, H., 1975, Effects of the amount of required coping response tasks in gastrointestinal lesions in rats, Jap. Psychol. Res., 17:119.

Ursin, H., 1978, Activation, coping, and psychosomatics, in: "Psychobiology of Stress: A Study of Coping Men," H. Ursin, E. Baade, and S. Levine, eds., Academic Press, New York.

Ursin, H., Baade, E., and Levine, S., eds., 1978, "Psychobiology of Stress: A Study of Coping Men," Academic Press, New York.

Vertes, R. P., and Miller, N. E., 1976, Brain stem neurons that fire selectively to a conditioned stimulus for shock, Brain Res., 103:229.

Weiner, H., Thaler, M., Reiser, M. F., and Mirsky, I. A., 1957, Etiology of duodenal ulcer. I. Relation of specific psychological characteristics to rate of gastric secretion (serum Pepsinogen)., Psychosom. Med., 19:1.

Weiss, J. M., 1970, Somatic effects of predictable and unpredictable shock, Psychosom. Med., 32:397.

Weiss, J. M., 1971a, Effects of coping behavior in different warning signal conditions on stress pathology in rats, J. Comp. Physiol. Psychol., 77:1.

Weiss, J. M., 1971b, Effects of coping behavior with and without a feedback signal on stress pathology in rats, J. Comp. Physiol. Psychol., 77:22.

Weiss, J. M., 1971c, Effects of punishing the coping response (conflict) on stress pathology in rats, J. Comp. Physiol. Psychol., 77:14.

Weiss, J. M. 1977, Psychological and behavioral influences on gastro-intestinal lesions in animal models, in: "Psychopathology: Experimental Models," J. D. Maser and M. E. P. Seligman, eds., W. H. Freeman, San Francisco.

Weiss, J. M., Glazer, H. I., Pohorecky, L. A., Brick, J., and Miller, N. E., 1975, Effects of chronic exposure to stressors on avoidance-escape behavior and on brain norepinephrine., Psychosom. Med., 37:522.

Weiss, J. M., Pohorecky, L. A., Salman, S., and Gruenthal, M., 1976, Attenuation of gastric lesions by psychological aspects of aggression in rats., J. Comp. Physiol. Psychol., 90:252.

Williams, R. B., 1975, Physiologic mechanisms underlying the association between psychosocial factors and coronary heart disease, in: "Psychosocial Aspects of Myocardial Infarction and Coronary Care," W. D. Gentry and R. B. Williams, eds., C. V. Mosby, St. Louis.

Wolf, S. G., and Goodell, H., 1976, "Behavioral Science in Clinical Medicine," Charles C. Thomas, Springfield.

Wolpe, E., 1958, "Psychotherapy by Reciprocal Inhibition," Stanford University Press, Stanford.

Yamada, A., Jensen, M., and Rasmussen, A. R., Jr., 1964, Stress and susceptibility to viral infections, III. Antibody response and viral retention during avoidance learning stress, Proc. Soc. Exp. Biol. Med., 116:677.

Zigmond, M., and Harvey, J., 1970, Resistance to central norepin-ephrine depletion and decreased mortality in rats chronically exposed to electric foot shock, J. Neu-Visc. Rel., 31:373.

CONTRIBUTORS

John H. Cullen
    Psychosomatic Unit
    Irish Foundation for Human Development
    Eastern Health Board, Box 41-A
    Dublin 8, Ireland

Nicola Davis
    Department of Experimental Psychology
    University College
    South Parks Road
    Oxford, England OXI 4BH

Joram Feldon
    Department of Experimental Psychology
    University College
    South Parks Road
    Oxford, England OXI 4BH

Marianne Frankenhaeuser
    Department of Psychology
    University of Stockholm
    Box 6801
    S-113 86 Stockholm, Sweden

Jeffrey A. Gray
    Department of Experimental Psychology
    University College
    South Parks Road
    Oxford, England OXI 4BH

Megan R. Gunnar
    Department of Psychiatry
    and Behavioral Sciences
    Stanford University School of Medicine
    Stanford, California 94305

Beatrix A. Hamburg
        Department of Health, Education and Welfare
        Public Health Service
        Alcohol, Drug Abuse
        and Mental Health Administration
        5600 Fishers Lane
        Rockville, Maryland 20852

Seymour Levine
        Department of Psychiatry
        and Behavioral Sciences
        Stanford University School of Medicine
        Stanford, California 94305

Neal E. Miller
        Department of Psychology
        The Rockefeller University
        1230 York Avenue
        New York, New York 10021

Suzanne M. Miller
        Department of Psychiatry
        University of Pennsylvania
        Philadelphia, Pennsylvania 19104

G. Mulder
        Department of Experimental Psychology
        University of Groningen
        Kerklaan 30
        9751, NN Haren (Gn)
        The Netherlands

L. J. M. Mulder
        Department of Experimental Psychology
        University of Groningen
        Kerklaan 30
        9751, NN Haren (Gn)
        The Netherlands

Robert Murison
        Department of Psychology
        University of Bergen
        Arstadveien 21
        5000 Bergen, Norway

J. Bruce Overmier
        Department of Psychology
        University of Minnesota
        Minneapolis, Minnesota 55455

Susan Owen
Department of Experimental Psychology
University College
South Parks Road
Oxford, England OXI 4BH

Jeff Patterson
Department of Psychology
University of Minnesota
Minneapolis, Minnesota 55455

Judith Rodin
Department of Psychology
Yale University
Box 11A Yale Station
New Haven, Connecticut 06510

Holger Ursin
Department of Psychology
University of Bergen
Arstadveien 21
5000 Bergen, Norway

Joan Vernikos-Danellis
Biomedical Research Division
Ames Research Center, NASA
Moffett Field, California 94035

Joanne Weinberg
Department of Psychiatry
and Behavioral Sciences
Stanford University School of Medicine
Stanford, California 94305

Richard M. Wielkiewicz
Department of Psychology
University of Minnesota
Minneapolis, Minnesota 55455

Abnormality, 2,101,123,157,249
Achievement, 128,131,204,205,207,
     209,218,270,328
Activation, 175,184,185,190-193,
     204,205,209,236,239,240,
     243,259-275,282,289,291,
     300,325,341,343,344
Adolescence, 121-140
Adrenocortical system, 39,42,195,
     203,225,267,269,289-291,
     309,342
Adrenocorticotrophic hormone,
     40,85,309,324,338
After-effect, 9,62-69,72-76,84,
     85,210,213,332,340
     (see also Memory)
Aging, 171-199,249
Agitation, 88-90,94,95,336,337
Alertness, 171,175-177
Anticipation, 42,43,54,61-63,76,
     107,124,152-155,157,160,
     337
Anxiety, 20,66,129,135,138,145,
     157,159,161,164,186,234,
     262,267,269,300,301,306,
     307,312,313,332,339,345,
     346
Appraisal, 139,187,263
Arousal, 7,40,46,50,52,90-96,112,
     113,147-158,160,162,164-
     166,204,205,212,214,215,
     239,269,289,291,297,299,
     300,302,303,308,312-317,
     325,326,341-343
Arrhythmia, 241,242,249,250,330,
     331

Arteriosclerosis, 274,305,326
Associative mechanisms, 61-77,
     83-85
Attachment, 88,92-95,97,107,108
Attention, 21,96,105,149,151,164,
     165,189-194,197,205,215,
     233-238,244,246-248,256,
     307,314,316
Attributional processes, 182-185,
     187,199
Aunting, 89,90
Aversive stimuli, 6,8,11-14,18,
     20,23,26,40-48,53-57,63-
     66,101,106-108,112,145-
     157,163-166,196,208,241,
     281,288,300,334,336,342,
     343
Avoidance, 7,9,10,14-18,21,23,
     25-27,30,46-51,56,63,84,
     107,151-153,265,283-291,
     298,328,331,332,336-341,
     344

Baroreceptor, 240,241,243,249,
     308,313,334
Behavioral medicine, 295,323,324,
     346
β-adrenergic, 241,249,255,301
Biological rhythm, 84,206,225-
     231,272,313
Blood glucose, 263,267
Blood pressure,123,209,239-243,
     249,250,263,268,270,274,
     301,306-308,324,326,334
Blunting, 145-166,263,313
Body image, 125,126,133,299

Body temperature, 41,95,229
Brain, 15,62,66,70-74,77,240,
        260,269,275,298,300,316,
        317,324,327,333,334,340,
        341 (see also Hippo-
        campus, Hypothalamus,
        Septal area, Theta
        rhythm)
    lesions, 68-72
Buffer, 90,128,131,138

Cardiovascular system, 209,215,
        234,239-246,249,250,255,
        256,305-308,313,323,326,
        330,336 (see also
        Arrhythmia, Arterio-
        sclerosis, Blood
        pressure, Heart)
Caretaker, 93,106-108
Change, 20,26,61,84,121-134,138,
        150,171-174,177-184,189-
        191,194,196-199,212,231,
        236-239,261,270,271,275,
        302-305,309,327,336,343
Choice, 1,5,21,22,27,41,44,47,54,
        55,146,148-150,152,165,
        172,175,187,189,205,207,
        208,210,213,235
Cognitive functioning, 14,20-23,
        101,102,107-109,114,115,
        129,130,132-134,147,148,
        165,186,187,192,203,205,
        209,218,234-256,300,302,
        308-315,318,344-346
Competence, 137,140,171,207,273,
        313 (see also Efficacy)
Confinement, 226,227,331
Conflict, 1,46,85,204,213,218,219,
        271,272,274,275,282,285-
        289,299,327,332,338,339,
        341,344
Consummatory response, 287,299,
        303,338
Contact, 87,88,91-93,96,107,108,
        134
Contingency, 1,92-94,96,97,101-
        104,106,196,198,302,308,
        310,315

Contingent stimulation, 6,13,14,
        96,97,101-116,331,332,
        338
Corticosteroids, 25,26,41-46,49-
        53,88-91,94,113,183,195-
        199,205,206,208,211,212,
        225-231,263,266-270,273,
        289-291,299,303,304,309,
        324-326,329,332,335-340,
        343
Counterconditioning, 61,63-65,
        68,75-77,333,334
Cross-tolerance, 64,65,75

Danger, 146,147,155,273,287,302,
        324,335,336
Death, 3,42,122,123,171,174,177,
        179,180,183,195,219,261,
        283,325,328,330,331,334,
        339
Decision-making, 131,133,135,140,
        173-175,185,193,212,233,
        234,236,244,245,248
Defense
    mechanisms, 147,150,207,259,
        262,269,270,273,275,345
        (see also Blunting)
    responses, 18,262,264-266,269,
        273,275,344,345
Deficit, 21,22,29,30,186,234,237,
        247
Dependency, 1,65,66,83,84,96,128,
        138,181
Depression, 20,88,95,96,105,122,
        159-161,163,164,186,196,
        267,269,273,308,310,340,
        345
Deprivation, 46,84,94,103,106,
        108,212,226,261,272,282,
        284,286-288,338,342
Detachment, 147
Development, 101-116,121,122,
        125-130,133,138-140,263,
        267
Discrimination, 335-337
Dissociation effect, 22,23,30,
        204,301
Distraction, 146-157,163-166

Distress, 87,88,105-113,122,129,
    130,134,135,140,157,158,
    160-164,204,206-208,211,
    261,272,273,275,291,307,
    333,343
Dogs, 7-11,14,21,27,61,96,330,
    331,333,334,336
Dominance, 113,226,227
Driving, 255,256,301-304
Drugs, 14,65-70,72-74,76,78,327,
    340

Efficacy, 171,172,174,186,192,
    195,199,205,207,213,274,
    300 (see also Competence)
Effort, 5,172,204-208,210-213,
    233,235,236,239
Emotion, 23,40,42,62,66,84,102,
    105-108,126,129,130,140,
    149,163,165,185,187,203,
    206,216,234,249,260,269,
    272,324,326,330-336,342-
    347
Endocrine system, 88,89,126,127,
    196,205,206,219,259,260,
    263,265-270,272,275,281,
    289,290,300,303,304,309,
    324,326,329,341,343
    (see also Adrenocortical
    system, Corticosteroids,
    Neuroendocrine response,
    Pituitary-adrenal system)
Entrainment, 122,225,229,244-246,
    306
Epinephrine, 204-208,211-218,263,
    266,267,326,329,340,343
Escape, 7,9-12,14-23,26,27,30,41,
    45,47-50,52,63,107,151,
    286,288,289,336-338,345
Expectancy, 20,107,108,112-114,
    124,129,173,187,260,308,
    310,312
Exploratory behavior, 41,102,105,
    107,108,110,112-114,116
Extinction, 46,62-69,71-77,83,85,
    105,106,266,298,334,343

Fantasy, 312,313
Fatigue, 214,265
Fatty acids, 263,267,269,270,
    274,325,326
Fear, 6,18,44,54,61,64,94,106-
    108,111-114,131,135,147,
    148,154,155,207,209,262,
    267,269,287,313,324-327,
    330-344
Feedback, 24,40,48-57,92,93,104-
    106,114,116,124,139,186,
    196-199,260,288,289,301,
    302,314-318,324,337,338
Fight-flight response, 18,324,
    326,331,342
Frustration, 25,62-65,69,72,75,
    76,130,134,193,301,336,
    341

Group
  formation, 227,231
  interaction, 87-97,138,175,
    181,226,227,229,231
Growth (see Development)
Gynecologic patients, 146,157-
    165,173

Habituation, 7,8,109,112,153,
    154,196,265,266,301,343
Health, 122-124,133,134,137,140,
    171-175,179-184,190-199,
    211,212,216,234,259,272,
    274,281,283,289,295-318,
    323-347
  surveys, 123,125,136,177,179,
    180,212,215
Heart
  attack, 270-274,306,328,330,
    342,345,346
  disease, 122,209,211,212,249,
    250,328,330,335
  rate, 7,95,158,159,204,205,208,
    211,214,229,239-253,263,
    274,305-308,313,324,326,
    331,333,341 (see also
    Arrhythmia)

Helplessness, 20-30,63,101,102,
        108,126,138,172-174,181,
        187,189,207,269,298,302,
        308-310,313,334,338,341
Hippocampus, 66,68,71,298
Hypertension, 123,249,250,271,
        274,301,305,306,325,328,
        331,339,342
Hypothalamus, 71,240,249,250

Illness, 23,46,123,126,171,174,
        175,189,193,195,199,212,
        215,216,219,231,249,259,
        262,265,268-275,281-291,
        295,297,304,305,308,310,
        311,323,327-329,334,339,
        344-347 (see also
        Gynecologic patients,
        Pathology)
Immune system, 195,270,273,323,
        324,328-330
Impact, 122,124,137,147,148,154,
        157,160,163,165,185,203,
        215,262,263,345
Individual differences, 145,146,
        155,157,281,303,313
Infants, 87-97,101-116,307,308,
        334,335,340,344 (see
        also Mother-infant
        relationship)
Information, 40,42,48-57,124,126,
        131,132,135,138,139,145-
        166,183,187,190,198,205,
        209,212,226,233-256,284,
        311,334,346
Institutionalization, 157-165,
        174-186,189,193,196-199
Instrumental response, 64,96,
        102,108,181,297,299,343,
        344
Intelligence, 132,148,205,218
Interaction effect, 3,11-14,23,
        24,29,45,126,127,183,
        209,219,260,261,275,300,
        306,308,309,318,327,346
Interference, 7-30,104,105,108,
        164,165,187,204,205,273,
        325,331,341,345

Internal-External Locus of
        Control Scale, 208
Intervention, 173,175-185,190-
        196,301,313,342,346
Isolation, 134,262

Jenkins' Activity Survey, 209
Junior high school, 124,127,
        130-136,140

Kragh Defense Mechanism Test,
        262,269,270 (see also
        Defense mechanisms)

Learning, 1,9,10,12,18-21,30,49,
        50,63,83,85,92,96,102-
        105,108,109,112-115,132,
        135,138,186,187,239,256,
        265,266,272,283,285,296-
        298,302,312-315,317,334,
        337,339,344,345
Leisure, 134,212,213,215
Light, 225,226,229,231
Loss, 88,94,174,182,183,309,310,
        314,327,334

Maladaptive patterns, 2,129,135,
        212,283,304
Mammals, 330,334 (see also Dogs,
        Monkeys, Rats, Rodents)
Maturation (see Development)
Memory, 83,84,102,184,187,190,
        191,233,236-238,245,246
        (see also After-effect)
Miller Behavioral Style Scale,
        155,156
Monitoring, 145-166,233,236
Monkeys, 25,26,45,87-96,107,113,
        225,227,282-284,289,331,
        332,335
Monotony, 213,215-217,270,315
Mother-infant relationship, 87-
        97,101,107-114 (see also
        Infants)

Neuroendocrine response, 203,204,
        206,207,209,212,213,215,
        217-219,282,302

Neurosis, 296,299,302,304,308,
    311,323,336 (see also
    Anxiety, Depression)
Neurotoxin, 70-73
Neurotransmitters, 70-72,74,327
Noise, 25,45,105,205,208,212,329
Norepinephrine, 12,15-17,25,70-
    72,74,77,85,205-208,211,
    215-217,240,263,267,270,
    325,326,337,339,340,343

Observer ratings, 158,161,162,
    164,176-181,190,191,226,
    303

Pain, 61,145,149,150,158-164,
    173,316,327,333,334,338,
    340,341
Parachutists, 206,262,263,267,
    269,270,273
Parasympathetic nervous system,
    239,241,249,250,255,256,
    260,284,326,327
Parents, 124,131,136,138,139
Pathology, 1,2,30,101,256,260,
    264,265,272-275,282-284,
    296,298,302,304,305,308,
    316,317
Peers, 129,130,133-140
Performance, 21,49,52,64,74,84,
    85,130-134,204,205,207,
    210,218,236-238,241,242,
    245,246,252,262,269,273,
    274,283-285,288-291,300,
    328,335-337,339
Personality, 61,128,130,148,155,
    184,185,259,262,272-275,
    298,301-306,313,315
Pituitary-adrenal system, 40,42-
    44,47,53,84,85,90,91,94,
    195,196,199,203-207,210,
    267,269,300,303,308,309,
    324,325,342
Placebo, 67,339
Play, 89,105,106,219

Predictability, 1,23-30,40-57,
    103,124,125,145-157,165,
    166,173,207,231,238,248,
    252,255,298,310,312,315,
    336,340
Preparation, 42,44,54,145,157,
    158,162-165,173,207,235,
    299
Preparedness, 44,45,206,298
Problem-solving, 132,187,193,196,
    233,236,260,262
Protest, 88,89
Proximity, 87,88,91,92,95,96,
    107,113
Psychosis, 296,323 (see also
    Schizophrenia)
Psychosocial milieu, 122,129,134-
    137,203,275,295,300,304,
    310,315
Psychosomatic medicine, 259,274,
    275,281,282,291,295,314,
    317
Punishment, 62,64-67,70-74,76,77,
    84,85,343

Rats, 3-6,12-26,39-57,62,63,68,
    70,84,225,250,271,272,
    274,281-291,299,326,332-
    340,344
Relocation, 174,314,327,334
Repression, 156,262,345
Resistance, 62,64-66,68,72,74,75,
    77,83,140,239,249,261,
    298,326
Respiration, 241,243,333
Responsibility, 171,174-180,189-
    194,197,213
Retirement, 174
Retrieval, 87,89,92,93
Reunion, 89-91 (see also
    Separation)
Rodents, 40,91,92,195,225,274,
    328,329
Roles, 121,124,128,130,135,136,
    139,140,171,186,215,218,
    219,270,299,315

Safety, 50,54-57,107,108,146-148,
        151,173,182,287,335,336
Schizophrenia, 309,310
Self-esteem, 129,134,135,139,148,
        171,270,273,274,310
Self-management, 3,4,186-197,313,
        315
Self-ratings, 123,128,157-160,
        164,176,186-188,190,204,
        207,209,212,216,226,262,
        301
Selye, H., 39,265,274,275,281,
        295,304,324,341,342
Sensitization, 156,301
Separation, 88-91,94-96,113,307,
        335 (see also Reunion)
Septal area, 66,68-70,77
Setpoint, 240,249
Sex differences, 125,127,205,
        209,218,315
Signaling, 87-93,109-112,114,308
Signals
    danger, 146-152,155,164-166
    safety, 53-56,146,165,335,337,
        344
    warning, 41,42,45,48,54-56,152,
        153,156,284
Smoking, 122,140,274,324
Sociability, 106,175,177,178,
        182,183,185
Specificity, 95,96,203,259,269,
        272
Stroke, 239,326,328,344
Stroop test, 204
Support, 124,131,135,138-140,155,
        184,185,327,328,335,339
Suppression, 41,43,104,198,199,
        207,208,241,242,250,255,
        256,325,345
Surgery, 126,149,150,157,164,173,
        273,314,325,339
Surrogates, 89,93-96,139
Sympathetic nervous system, 203-
        207,210,212,218,239,249,
        250,256,260,284,325,326,
        330,331

Theta rhythm, 66,68-70,74,77
Threat, 131,145,146,149-152,156,
        157,163,165,173,185,209,
        211,234,235,240,249,255,
        262,264,266,270,272,273,
        291,334,341
Toughening, 63,72,74,77,84,85,
        340
Training, 49,62-77,84,104,106,
        136,164,186,189,193,198,
        248,261,263,267,282,315,
        336,337,340
Type A, 209-212,270,273,274,317,
        328
Type B, 209-211

Ulcers, 12,23-26,39-45,48,49,52,
        123,271-273,281-291,304-
        306,325,328,331,332,335,
        337-340,342,344
Uncontrollability, 4-8, 10,11,
        13,15,18-30,44,101-108,
        113,146,150-152,155,171,
        172,182,186,187,195,204,
        271,284,288,337,344,347

Vigilance, 209,212,326,342
Vocalization, 7,88-90,93-95,104-
        106,112,161,341

Withdrawal, 88,148,149,174,269,
        345
Work, 134,138,155,204-219,233-
        256,261,268,271,272,274,
        315
    absenteeism, 215,216
    hazardous, 215-217
    mechanization, 215-217
    overtime, 213-215,218
    repetitious (see Monotony)

Yoked experiments, 3,23,25,26,
        41,45,48,49,52,53,208,
        283-290,331,337-339